Article. VI.

Debts contracted and Engagements entered into, before the Adoption of this Constitution, shall be as va...

...as under the Confederation.

...and the Laws of the United States which shall be made in Pursuance thereof; and al...

...State to the Contrary notwithstanding.

...and Representatives before mentioned, and the Members of the several State Legislatur...

...Office or public Trust under the United States.

...to support this Constitution...

the Judges in every State sha...

Article. VII.

the Conventions of nine States, shall be sufficient for the Establish...

done in Convention by the Unani...

Day of September in the Year of our Lord...

of the Independance of the United S...

We have hereunto subscribed our...

Delaware

We the People

of the United States, in Order to form...

...domestic Tranquility, provide for the common defence, promote the general Welfare, and secu...

...our Posterity, do ordain and establish this Constitution for the United States of America.

Article. I.

Section. 1. All legislative Powers herein granted shall be vested in a Congress of the United States...

...Representatives.

Section. 2. The House of Representatives shall be composed of Members chosen every second...

...shall have the Qualifications requisite for Electors of the most numerous Branch of the...

...on shall be a Representative who shall not have attained to the Age of...

...when elected, be an Inhabitant of that State in which he shall be cho...

...and direct Taxes shall be apportioned among the several Sta...

...united States of America...

...people of these Colonies, solemnly publish and declare, That these United Colonies are, and of Right...

...the British Crown, and that all political connection between them and the State of Great Britain, is and...

...have full Power to levy War, conclude Peace, contract Alliances, establish Commerce, and to do all other Acts and Th...

...support of this Declaration, with a firm reliance on the Protection of divine Providence, we mutually pledge to each...

Wm. Hooper
Joseph Hewes,
John Penn

Edward Rutledge.

Thos. Heyward Junr.
Thomas Lynch Junr.
...ddleton

John Hancock

Samuel Chase
Wm. Paca
Thos. Stone
Charles Carroll of Carrollton

George Wythe
Richard Henry Lee
Th Jefferson
Benja. Harrison
...Nelson jr.

Robt Morris
Benjamin Rush
Benj. Franklin
John Morton
Geo Clymer
Jas. Smith
Geo. Taylor
James Wilson
Geo. Ross
Caesar Rodney
Geo. Read
Thos. M:Kean

Wm. Floyd
Phil. Livingston
Fran. Lewis
Lewis Morris

Richd. Stockton
Jno. Witherspoon
Fras. Hopkinson
John Hart
Abra. Clark

Josiah...
Wm. Whipp...
Saml. Adam...
John Adams
Robt Treat P...
Elbridge Ger...
Step...
William...
Roger S...
Sam...
Wm...

Colonial Williamsburg

George Washington at the Battle of Princeton
by Charles Willson Peale

Broad Street showing Federal Hall, New York, 1797

FOUNDERS OF FREEDOM

IN AMERICA

FOUNDERS OF FREEDOM
IN
AMERICA

Lives Of The Men Who

Signed The Declaration of Independence

And So Helped To Establish

The

UNITED STATES OF AMERICA

By

DAVID C. WHITNEY

Encyclopedia Editor and Historian

Coordinating Editor

THOMAS C. JONES

Editor of Prints and Photographs

KATHRINE B. SANBORN

Published By

J. G. FERGUSON PUBLISHING COMPANY

Chicago, Illinois

BOUND IN HANDCRAFTED MISSION LEATHER
BY BROWN AND BIGELOW, ST. PAUL, MINNESOTA
A DIVISION OF STANDARD PACKAGING CORPORATION

ACKNOWLEDGMENTS...

Two hundred years ago, the first feeble cries for separation from the burdens of colonial status signalled the birth of American liberty. After ten years of agitation and repeated frustrations, delegates to the Continental Congress, meeting in Philadelphia, voted the Declaration of Independence, on July 4, 1776. The biographies of the fifty-six Signers, and James Otis, and Patrick Henry, are largely the chronicle of that period. Separate volumes, in varying lengths, have been written by historians about many of the Signers. Few of even the larger libraries have information in detail about all these patriots.

The purpose of this volume is to provide a single illustrated reference, written for the student of history, who wishes to familiarize himself with the men and ideas of the Revolutionary period. The adult voter, who wishes information on the origins of American political thinking, will find this to be a useful source.

David Whitney has helped to revitalize this period of history, with vivid, human accounts of the lives of the Signers, which should interest teachers and students of American history, in elementary and high schools. Certainly, these very readable biographies show personal qualities and attainments, worthy of emulation by the young citizens of tomorrow. They are liberally flavored with quotations from letters, speeches, opinions, and statements of that period, which are inspirational reminders of what is collectively referred to as Americanism. The ideals of these men, and their thoughts, are largely the fundamentals of today's political traditions. Although their problems differed from those of the present day, their basic philosophies govern, or influence, politics, today. Knowledge of the lives of these men should reinforce the natural pride and appreciation of heritage that every citizen of the United States inherits.

All of these patriots suffered greatly in physical hardships, loss of loved ones, great financial losses, damage to, and in some instances, complete destruction of their dwellings, and exposure and imprisonment of themselves and members of their families. McKean described his hardships in a letter to John Adams, as follows:

> "I have had my full share of the anxieties, cares, and troubles of the present war. For some time, I was obliged to act as president of the Delaware state and as chief justice of this; General Howe had just landed at the head of the Elk river when I undertook to discharge these two important trusts. The consequence was to be hunted like a fox by the enemy, and envied by those who ought to have been my friends. I was compelled to remove my family five times in a few months and at last, find them in a little log house on the banks of the Susquehanna, more than a hundred miles from this place; but safety was not to be found there, for they were soon obliged to remove again, on account of the incursions of the Indians."

Robert Morris, at the beginning of the war, was one of the wealthiest men in the country. His credit was largely instrumental in financing Washington's army during the dark days when it appeared all was lost, and Morris's credit was more respected than that of the United States treasury. Ironically, he spent his declining years in bankruptcy that was largely attributable to the war and the events that followed.

John Hancock put up one-quarter million dollars to help finance the war. About one-third of the Signers were wiped out financially.

Certain statistics concerning these men are interesting. All but eight of the Signers were native-born. Of those born in America, their origin was about equally distributed between the settled portions of the country. Sixteen were from the northeastern colonies, fourteen from the middle Atlantic colonies, and eighteen came from the southern colonies. Of the foreign-born, two were from England, one from Wales, two from Scotland, and three from Ireland. The table that appears elsewhere in this volume gives other interesting statistics concerning this distinguished group.

It is particularly interesting that the engrossed document, which is the Declaration of Independence, was actually signed by fifty of the delegates, on August 2, 1776. George Wythe signed August 27. Richard Henry Lee, Elbridge Gerry, and Oliver Wolcott signed September 4, Matthew Thornton on November 19, and Thomas McKean, who was with Washington's army, did not sign until 1781.

In the category of personal interest, it is noted that they were prolific producers of children, averaging six per father. Only two were bachelors. They lived to an average age of sixty-six years. Twenty-four lived to the age of seventy, or more, and ten lived into their eighties. Three lived into their nineties.

Wherever possible, the illustrations used herein are contemporary to the days of the revolution. We are indebted to Kathrine B. Sanborn, for her indefatigible efforts to locate, and obtain permission to reproduce, many of the portraits and color scenes of this work. The quality of reproduction in all cases is governed by the condition of the original art. We are grateful to the Library of Congress, and the New York Public Library, for their prompt and gracious cooperation in this project. In addition, there are many societies, museums, and photographers, whose cooperation has made this work possible. Finally, but by no means least, we are grateful to our printer, Photopress, Inc., for patient, efficient, skillful service.

The following list is intended to be all-inclusive in terms of persons and organizations, to whom we are indebted for their cooperation in making this book possible: Kathrine B. Sanborn; Herbert J. Sanborn; Library of Congress; Metropolitan Museum of Art; The New York Historical Society; Mrs. Norma G. Rehder; The Corcoran Gallery of Art; The National Gallery of Art, Washington, D.C., Mellon Collection; The National Archives; U. S. Naval Academy Museum; J. William Middendorf II; Library of the Boston Athenaeum; Museum of Fine Arts, Boston; New York Public Library; The I. N. Phelps Stokes Collection, and Emmett Collection; Yale University Art Gallery; Baltimore Museum of Art, Bequest of Ellen H. Bayard; Fogg Art Museum, Harvard University; Mariners Museum, Newport News, Virginia; Suzanne Cooper; Wilmington Blue Print; Princeton University Portrait Collection; Independence National Historical Park Collection; Museum of the City of New York; New Hampshire Historical Society; Connecticut State Library and the Historical Society of Connecticut; Morris Shapiro; Fort Ticonderoga Museum; New York State Historical Association; Henry Francis DuPont Winterthur Museum; Frick Art Reference Library; Mt. Vernon Ladies' Association, Mt. Vernon, Virginia; Fackenthal Library, Franklin & Marshall College; Columbia University; Eastern National Park & Monument Association; Bishop Meade's "Old Churches, Ministers, and Families of Virginia, 1854"; Peter Dechert, PDA; Essex Institute, Salem, Massachusetts; Smithsonian Institute, National Collection of Fine Arts; Pennsylvania Academy of Fine Arts; The Old Print Shop; American Philosophical Society; Mrs. Jacob H. Whitebook, owner, Thos. Heyward, Jr.; Will Bond; Society for Preservation of New England Antiquities, Boston; Bob Wyer; Minor Congressional Commission; Virginia State Library; Don Swann; Taconic State Park Commission, Staatsburg, New York; Robert E. Lee Memorial Foundation, Inc., Stratford, Virginia; Society of the Lees; Gregory Stapko; The R. W. Norton Art Gallery, Shreveport, Louisiana; Menasco Studio, Shreveport, Louisiana; The Historical Society of Pennsylvania; Princeton University Library; "Life In America," by Davidson; Rodney McCay Morgan; National Historical Park; Grace Jameson; Arthur E. Scott; "Book Of Signers," by Wm. Brotherhead, Virginia State Library; "Homes Of America," and "Magazine Of American History," Library of Congress; Thomas J. Waterman, restoration drawing of Menokin; G. M. Cushing, home of John Adams; "Mansions Of Virginia," by Waterman, Library of Congress; Mrs. John T. Nichols, Wm. Floyd, by R. Earl; Hirst Milhollen; Pennsylvania Historical and Museum Commission; Colonial Williamsburg; The Beck Engraving Company, Incorporated; Historical Society of Delaware, Mrs. Harman Rumpelly Reed Collection; Lowdermilk Book Store; Goodspeed Bookstore; Library of Congress Photoduplication Service; The Catholic University of America; Free Public Library, Paterson, New Jersey; University of North Carolina Press; Georgia Department of Archives and History; Orlando Ridout, Annapolis, Maryland; A-1 Composition Company; G. R. Grubb & Company; and A. C. Engdahl & Company.

THOMAS C. JONES *For the Publisher*

TABLE OF CONTENTS

A LIST OF BLACK AND WHITE ILLUSTRATIONS

8

LIST OF COLOR ILLUSTRATIONS

EXPRESSIONS OF AMERICAN PRINCIPLES

by THE FOUNDERS

The Sum of Good Government

In his inaugural address, on March 4, 1801, Jefferson called for a healing of the political antagonism engendered by the election. "Every difference of opinion," he said, "is not a difference of principle. We have called by different names brethren of the same principle. We are all Republicans — we are all Federalists. If there be any among us who would wish to dissolve this Union, or to change its republican form, let them stand undisturbed as monuments of the safety with which error of opinion may be tolerated where reason is left free to combat it." Jefferson also stated his concept of the best government as that which governs least:

"A wise and frugal government, which shall restrain men from injuring one another, which shall leave them otherwise free to regulate their own pursuits of industry and improvement, and shall not take from the mouth of labor the bread it has earned. This is the sum of good government, and this is necessary to close the circle of our felicities."

Thomas Jefferson

Composing the Declaration

The thirty-three-year-old Jefferson did most of the writing of the Declaration of Independence on a portable writing desk that he had invented. He composed it while sitting in the parlor of the apartment he had rented on the second floor of a brick house at Market and Seventh Streets (Philadelphia). Of his composition, Jefferson later said:

"I turned to neither book nor pamphlet while writing it. I did not consider it as any part of my charge to invent new ideas altogether and to offer no sentiment which had ever been expressed before."

Thomas Jefferson

"Our Cause is Just"

"If this be our language, it is so, indeed. If we wear long faces, they will become fashionable. The people take their tone from ours, and if we despair, can it be expected that they will continue their efforts in what we conceive to be a hopeless cause? Let us banish such feelings, and show a spirit that will keep alive the confidence of the people, rather than damp their courage. Better tidings will soon arrive. Our cause is just and righteous, and we shall never be abandoned by Heaven while we show ourselves worthy of its aid and protection."

Samuel Adams

'Thrice is he armed, who hath his quarrel just'...

"Admitting the probable calculations to be against us, we are assured in holy writ, that the race is not to the swift, nor the battle to the strong; and if the language of genius may be added to that of inspiration, I will say with our immortal bard:

" 'Thrice is he armed, who hath his quarrel just,
  And he but naked, tho' locked up in steel
  Whose conscience with injustice is oppressed.' "

Richard Henry Lee

The Public Good

"Burn Boston, and make John Hancock a beggar, if the public good requires it."

John Hancock

"We must be unanimous..."

Franklin voted for the Declaration of Independence on July 4, 1776, and signed it with the other delegates on August 2. The story is told that at the signing ceremony, John Hancock, the president of the Continental Congress, remarked: "We must be unanimous; there must be no pulling different ways; we must all hang together." To this, Franklin is said to have quipped: "Yes, we must indeed all hang together, or most assuredly we shall all hang separately."

Benjamin Franklin

Do not insult us

"I trust I have long since made my peace with the King of Kings. No personal consideration shall induce me to abandon the righteous cause of my counrty. Tell Governor Gage, it is the advice of Samuel Adams to him, no longer to insult the feelings of an exasperated people."

Samuel Adams

"All men are born free"...

"Under the law of nature all men are born free, every one comes into the world with a right to his own person which includes the liberty of moving and using it at his own will. This is what is called personal liberty, and is given him by the author of nature, because necessary for his own sustenance . . ."

Thomas Jefferson

Deciding the greatest question

In a letter to his wife, July 2, 1776, John Adams said, "Yesterday the greatest question was decided, that was ever debated in America; and greater, perhaps, never was or will be decided among men. A resolution was passed, without one dissenting colony, 'that these united colonies are, and of right ought to be, free and independent states.' The day is passed. The second day of July, 1776, will be the most memorable epocha in the history of America. I am apt to believe that it will be celebrated by succeeding generations as the great Anniversary Festival. It ought to be commemorated, as the day of deliverance, by solemn acts of devotion to God Almighty. It ought to be solemnized with pomp and parade, with shows, games, sports, guns, bells, bonfires and illuminations, from one end of this continent to the other, from this time forward, forevermore. You will think me transported with enthusiasm, but I am not. I am well aware of the toil, and blood, and treasure, that it will cost to maintain this declaration, and support and defend these states; yet, through all the gloom, I can see the rays of light and glory. I can see that the end is worth more than all the means; and that posterity will triumph, although you and I may rue, which I hope we shall not."

John Adams

(The decisive vote was taken July 4, 1776)

Principles of right and wrong are legible to every reader

"Open your breast, sire, to liberal and expanded thought. It behooves you to think and act for your people. The great principles of right and wrong are legible to every reader; to peruse them, requires not the aid of many counsellors. The whole art of government consists in the art of being honest."

Thomas Jefferson

Fifty Years Without Fee or Reward

"Without the character of Samuel Adams, the true history of the American Revolution can never be written. For fifty years his pen, his tongue, his activity, were constantly exerted for his country without fee or reward."

John Adams

"I will do my duty . . ."

"God forbid that my countrymen should ever be guilty of so daring an outrage; but, sire, with the blessing of God, I will do my duty, — they may destroy my property, they may pull down my house over my head, yea, they may make a widow of my wife, and my children fatherless,— the life of one man is of little consequence compared to the prostration of the laws of the land — with the blessing of God, I will do my duty, be the consequences what they may."

Samuel Chase

Think for and not with

As a member of the first United States House of Representatives that convened in 1789, (George) Clymer followed an independent course, saying, "A representative of the people is appointed to think *for* and not *with* his constituents." He particularly rebelled at a proposal that the Constitution should be amended to give the people "the unalienable right of instructing their representatives." Clymer spoke out sharply: "Do gentlemen foresee the extent of these words? If they have a constitutional right to instruct us, it infers that we are bound by those instructions, and as we ought not to decide constitutional questions by implication, I presume that we shall be called upon to go further, and expressly declare the members of the legislature to be bound by the instructions of their constituents. This is a most dangerous principle, utterly destructive of all ideas of an independent and deliberative body, which are essential requisites in the legislatures of free governments: They prevent men of abilities and experience from rendering those services to the community that are in their power, destroying the object contemplated by establishing an efficient general government, and rendering Congress a mere passive machine."

George Clymer

A proper regard of justice and humanity

"I have seen it observed by a great writer, that Christianity, by introducing into Europe the truest principles of humanity, universal benevolence, and brotherly love, had happily abolished civil slaves. Let us, who profess the same religion, practice its precepts, and by agreeing to this duty, convince the world that we know and practice our true interests, and that we pay a proper regard to the dictates of justice and humanity."

Richard Henry Lee

Men shall be free to maintain their religious opinions

Among the various laws that Jefferson wrote for Virginia, the one he asked most to be remembered by was the statute for religious freedom. Here are words from it that reflect the same ability that he displayed in writing the Declaration of Independence:

"Well aware that the opinions and beliefs of men depend not on their own will, but follow involuntarily the evidence proposed to their minds; that Almighty God hath created the mind free, and manifested his will that free it shall remain by making it altogether insusceptible of restraint;

"—that our civil rights have no dependence on our religious opinions any more than our opinions in physics or geometry; that therefore the proscribing any citizen as unworthy of the public confidence by laying upon him an incapacity of being called to offices of trust and emolument unless he profess or renounce this or that religious opinion is depriving him injuriously of those privileges and advantages to which, in common with his fellow-citizens, he has a natural right;

"—that the opinions of men are not the subject of civil government nor under its jurisdiction;

"—and finally that truth is great and will prevail if she is left to herself; that she is the proper and sufficient antagonist to error, and has nothing to fear from the conflict unless by human interposition disarmed of her natural weapons, free argument and debate; errors ceasing to be dangerous when it is permitted freely to contradict them.

"We, the General Assembly, do enact, That no man shall be compelled to frequent or support any religious worship, place or ministry whatsoever, nor shall be enforced, restrained, molested or burdened in his body or goods, nor shall otherwise suffer, on account of his religious opinions or beliefs; but that all men shall be free to profess and by argument to maintain their opinions in matters of religion, and that the same shall in no wise diminish, enlarge or affect their civil capacities."

Thomas Jefferson

Legislature can exceed its bounds

"Nay, more, if the whole legislature, an event to be deprecated, should attempt to overleap the bounds prescribed to them by the people, I, in administering the public justice of the country, will meet the united powers, at my seat in this tribunal; and, pointing to the constitution, will say to them here is the limit of your authority; and hither shall you go, but no further."

George Wythe

First use of Americanism

"I understand an use of phrases or terms, or construction of sentences, even among people of rank and education, different from the use of the same terms or phrases, or the construction of similar sentences in Great Britain. It does not follow, from a man's using these, that he is ignorant, or his discourse upon the whole inelegant; nay, it does not follow in every case that the terms or phrases used are worse in themselves, but merely that they are of American and not of English growth. The word *Americanism,* which I have coined for the purpose, is exactly similar in its formation and significance to the word Scotticism."

John Witherspoon

THE ROAD TO REVOLUTION

by David C. Whitney

The men and women who settled the British colonies in North America crossed the Atlantic Ocean for a variety of reasons. Some escaped religious persecution. Others escaped their debtors. Some fled political injustice. Others fled unhappy homelife. Some sought adventure. Others sought riches. Some were idealists. Others were criminals. But no matter what their particular reason was, all colonists had one thing in common—they believed they would have more freedom and opportunity to do what they wanted to do in America.

As the clouds of revolution gathered in the middle 1700's, this belief in America as the land of freedom and opportunity was fresh in the minds of the colonists. All around them were the rich lands and plentiful resources of the New World; and, even more important, all around them was an atmosphere of freedom. When a bumbling British parliament began to threaten their opportunities and freedoms, and when a British king turned a deaf ear to their pleas, the colonists discovered that they were ready to fight for their rights. But this realization came slowly because the colonists believed in law and order, and to them that meant respect for the laws of England and loyalty to the British king.

Washington was trained by the British

The immediate events that led to the Revolutionary War in America had their roots in the French and Indian War from 1754 to 1763. In this war, the French and the British struggled for control of North America. The British finally won. During the war, the legislatures of the American colonies took on a greater degree of self-government than ever before as they argued with royal governors about imposing taxes and raising troops to aid the British in winning the war. Many of the Founding Fathers served in these colonial legislatures and became experienced in the art of government. In the fighting on the frontiers, American militiamen became battle-tested. American officers, such as George Washington, learned firsthand the contempt that British officers had for their American comrades-in-arms. They also learned that British generals could be defeated because they refused to adapt their European military tactics to meet the frontier methods of Indian fighting. In short, the American colonists were slowly coming to a realization that they were Americans, and that Americans were different from their British cousins.

The British had for many years tried to discourage the development of manufacturing industries in the American colonies by forbidding the importation of various raw materials, such as molasses, used in making rum. Americans had generally ignored these laws, known as the Navigation Acts. But, in 1760, British agents began an effort to enforce these laws strictly by hunting for contraband goods smuggled into the colonies. The British agents used search warrants called writs of assistance, to pry into the warehouses and shops of Boston merchants. The tempers of the colonists rose at what they regarded as an invasion of their private business. A popular Boston lawyer, James Otis, became one of the first leaders of the patriotic movement as he argued successfully against the issuance of the writs of assistance. John Adams, who at that time was a struggling young lawyer, was inspired to describe Otis as a "flame of fire."

London (Circa 1760)

Adams later wrote that with Otis, "American independence was then and there born; the seeds of patriots and heroes were then and there sown. . . . Every man of a crowded audience appeared to me to go away, as I did, ready to take arms against writs of assistance." Unfortunately for the patriotic cause, Otis was struck in the head by a British tax commissioner in 1769, and his brain was so badly damaged that he became permanently mentally deranged.

At the end of the French and Indian War, the British government decided to maintain a standing army in the American colonies and to tax the colonies to support the soldiers. The unswerving determination of the British parliament to stick to these policies led directly to every subsequent step along the colonists' road to revolution. The British added more fuel to the fire in 1763 with a proclamation recognizing the rights of Indians to lands they held, and for-bidding the American colonists to settle any lands west of the Appalachian Mountains. With this last measure, the British hoped to prevent the growth of manufacturing industries in the colonies that would be needed to supply west-ern settlers. At the same time they hoped to win the friendship of the Indians.

British policy prevented growth of industry and westward expansion

To implement their policies, the British parliament in 1765, under prod-ding by British Prime Minister George Grenville, passed two legislative acts—the Quartering Act and the Stamp Act. The Quartering Act required the colo-nists to provide housing, food, and transportation for any British troops sta-tioned in the colonies. The Stamp Act required the colonists to buy stamps and affix them to newspapers, legal documents, and various other printed materials.

In Virginia, Patrick Henry rose in the Virginia legislature to denounce the British acts. He proposed strong resolutions declaring that only the legislature had the right to tax the people of the colony and that the British parliament was usurping American freedom. The legislature passed the resolutions by a split vote, and the next day, when Henry had left the assembly, the most strongly-worded resolutions were rescinded. Nevertheless, word of Patrick Henry's stand swept like a whirlwind through the colonies.

Similarly, in Massachusetts, James Otis and Samuel Adams took leading roles in getting that colony's legislature to record its opposition to the Stamp Act. Secret patriotic societies called the Sons of Liberty sprang into existence in Massachusetts, New York, and Connecticut. These organizations led mob actions in Boston, New York City, and other places. Angry citizens hanged in effigy British officials and destroyed bundles of tax stamps. Throughout the colonies British stamp tax collectors resigned their jobs in fear.

Opposition to the Stamp Act

At the urging of the Massachusetts legislature, delegates from nine colonies met in New York City in October, 1765, in what became known as the Stamp Act Congress. The colonies sending representatives were Connecticut, Delaware, Maryland, Massachusetts, New Jersey, New York, Pennsylvania, Rhode Island, and South Carolina. This was the first time that delegates from so many colonies had ever come together to discuss a mutual problem. The delegates approved a Declaration of Rights and sent petitions to the king and to the British parliament protesting the stamp tax.

In the face of such strong opposition in the colonies, the British parliament in 1766 repealed the Stamp Act. At the same time, however, the parliament passed the Declaratory Act which maintained that parliament had full rights to pass any laws it pleased concerning the colonies.

Still in need of additional revenues to support the British troops in North America, and believing that the colonists would not so severely oppose taxes on goods not produced in the colonies, the British parliament passed the Townshend Acts in 1767. These new laws, prepared by British Chancellor of the Exchequer Charles Townshend, taxed various products being imported by the colonies, including tea, paper, and paint. Reaction from the colonies came swiftly. The Massachusetts legislature sent to the other colonies a circular letter prepared by Samuel Adams urging joint action against the new taxes. In Virginia, the legislature passed resolutions against the taxes and as a result was dissolved by the royal governor. Not to be thwarted, the Virginians moved their meeting to a nearby tavern where they adopted a non-importation, non-exportation agreement to boycott British goods—this resolution being proposed by George Washington. The boycott spread throughout the colonies, and in 1770 the British parliament again bowed to the pressure by repealing all the Townshend taxes except that on tea.

A proposal by George Washington

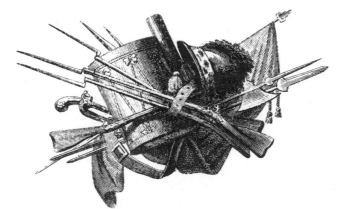

A View of New York, from the North West. (c. 1793)

The Boston Massacre incited further resistance

In Boston, anger against the stationing of British troops in Massachusetts touched off the Boston Massacre of March 5, 1770. On that day a mob of Bostonians attacked a squad of British soldiers led by a Captain Preston. The soldiers fired into the crowd. Three persons were killed outright and eight were wounded, two dying later of their wounds. The ensuing murder trial of the soldiers brought about an unusual confrontation between two patriotic leaders who were six years later to sign the Declaration of Independence—Robert Treat Paine and John Adams. Paine, then Boston's leading lawyer, was the prosecuting attorney for the trial. Adams, risking his own popularity because he did not believe in the use of violence against the British soldiers, accepted a position as one of the defense attorneys. Adams demonstrated his legal abilities by obtaining the release of Captain Preston and six of his soldiers, while Paine won the conviction of only two of the redcoats on the lesser charge of manslaughter.

By the early 1770's, Samuel Adams had become the leading agitator in the American cause. At his suggestion, a town meeting in Boston in 1772 established a Committee of Correspondence to send letters to leaders in other colonies to keep patriots informed of all oppressive acts by the British. A similar Committee of Correspondence was formed by patriotic leaders in Virginia.

The British parliament on May 10, 1773, proceeded to commit a new act of folly by passing the Tea Act. This act enabled the British East India Company to sell its surplus tea in the colonies at lower prices than other shippers. This action called new attention to the last of the Townshend taxes, the one remaining on tea, and again focused attention on British efforts to tax the colonies against their will.

15

Instigated by Samuel Adams, a crowd of several thousand persons gathered on the Boston waterfront on December 16, 1773, to protest the unloading of three British tea ships. Under the urging of various patriotic leaders the crowd became angrier and angrier. Finally, a band of forty to fifty patriots disguised as Indians boarded the ships and dumped the tea into the water.

This Boston Tea Party brought quick retaliation by the British parliament. Early in 1774, parliament passed the Intolerable Acts. These Acts closed Boston harbor to any trade and ordered the reorganization of the government of the Massachusetts colony to reduce its powers of self-government. Lt. Gen. Thomas Gage, commander-in-chief of British military forces in North America, was named governor of the Massachusetts colony.

Realizing that what was happening in Boston could happen to any of the colonies, Virginia sent out a call to all the colonies to bring together representatives in a congress that could decide on a united course of action. As a result, the first Continental Congress convened in Philadelphia on September 5, 1774. Delegates were sent by the legislatures of all the British colonies in North America except Canada and Georgia.

The first meetings of the Founding Fathers

The first Continental Congress brought about face-to-face meetings for the first time of many of the men who became the Founding Fathers of the United States. Samuel Adams and John Adams from Massachusetts met Patrick Henry, George Washington, and Richard Henry Lee of Virginia. "Every man is a great man," John Adams wrote, "an orator, a critic, a statesman; and therefore every man, upon every question, must show his oratory, his criticism, and his political abilities." The delegates from Massachusetts were careful not to bring up the idea of "independence" in order not to scare off the more conservative delegates from such colonies as Pennsylvania and New Jersey. After much oratory, the Congress decided to send resolutions to the king, the parliament, and to the British people asking that their rights be respected. Most of the delegates were confident that this united appeal would again bring about a repeal of the repressive measures that had been directed against Massachusetts. The Congress also set up a Continental Association to enforce a boycott of British goods. The Congress adjourned on October 26, 1774, after agreeing to meet again the following spring.

Patrick Henry rallied the Virginians

A rallying cry for patriots was sounded by Patrick Henry of Virginia in March, 1775. Because the royal governor of Virginia continued to forbid a meeting of the Virginia legislature, the delegates from Virginia counties were meeting at Old Saint John's Church in Richmond. Henry crystallized the issue that the colonists must take up arms or submit to tyranny with these words: "I know not what course others may take, but as for me, give me liberty, or give me death!" These straightforward words, repeated from colony to colony, brought home to every patriot the sacrifices he had to face to preserve the opportunities and freedom that America meant.

On the other hand, the British government in London was equally bent on enforcing its will on the colonies. The British cabinet sent word to General Gage in Boston on April 14, 1775, that Massachusetts, Connecticut, and Rhode Island were considered to be in a state of rebellion and that Gage should use force to put down the patriotic movement. Gage acted promptly. He sent a force of about 700 redcoats to confiscate military supplies that the patriots had gathered at Concord. Paul Revere and William Dawes set out to spread the alarm. American minutemen met the redcoats with musket fire at Lexington and Concord on April 19, 1775. The Revolutionary War in America had begun.

16

BATTLE OF LEXINGTON.

Drawn by Earl & engraved by A.Doolittle in 1775

Re-Engraved by A.Doolittle and J.W.Barber in 1832

1. Major Pitcairn at the head of the Regular Grenadiers.—2. The Party who first fired on the Provincials at Lexington
3. Part of the Provincial Company of Lexington.—4. Regular Companies on the road to Concord.—5. The Meeting house.
at Lexington.—6. The Public Inn.

Declaration of Independence
by John Trumbull

Diagram identifying the delegates in the color reproduction
of the Signers of the Declaration of Independence.

KEY TO DECLARATION OF INDEPENDENCE
BY JOHN TRUMBULL

1. George Wythe.
2. William Whipple.
3. Joseph Bartlett.
4. Thomas Lynch.
5. Benjamin Harrison.
6. Richard Henry Lee.
7. Samuel Adams.
8. George Clinton.
9. William Paca.
10. Samuel Chase.
11. Richard Stockton.
12. Lewis Morris.

13. William Floyd.
14. Arthur Middleton.
15. Thomas Heyward, Jr.
16. Charles Carroll.
17. Robert Morris.
18. Thomas Willing.
19. Benjamin Rush.
20. Elbridge Gerry.
21. Robert Treat Paine.
22. William Hooper.
23. Stephen Hopkins.
24. William Ellery.

25. George Clymer.
26. Joseph Hewes.
27. George Walton.
28. James Wilson.
29. Abraham Clark.
30. Francis Hopkinson.
31. John Adams.
32. Roger Sherman.
33. Robert R. Livingston.
34. Thomas Jefferson.
35. Benjamin Franklin.
36. Thomas Nelson, Jr.

37. Francis Lewis.
38. John Witherspoon.
39. Samuel Huntington.
40. William Williams.
41. Oliver Wolcott.
42. Charles Thomson.
43. John Hancock.
44. George Read.
45. John Dickinson.
46. Edward Rutledge.
47. Thomas McKean.
48. Philip Livingston.

GALLERY OF FINE ARTS · YALE UNIVERSITY

ADOPTING THE DECLARATION
OF INDEPENDENCE

by DAVID C. WHITNEY

A distinguished group of men

The fifty-six men who signed their names to the Declaration of Independence did not come easily to their decision. Most of them were not rebels by nature. They included large landowners, wealthy merchants, and successful lawyers. Most were well educated—more than half were graduates of colleges or had been educated in Europe. They were mature in their thinking—their average age was over forty. Most of them had been brought up with a deep sense of loyalty to the British king—all were born either in the American colonies or in the British isles. The generally conservative background of these men who made up the second Continental Congress helps account for the fact that more than a year went by after fighting began in Massachusetts until the Declaration of Independence was written and approved.

The delegates to the second Continental Congress convened in Philadelphia on May 10, 1775, with news of the fighting at Lexington and Concord ringing in their ears. In an open act of defiance, the delegates elected John Hancock of Massachusetts as President of the Congress—he, along with Samuel Adams, had been declared a rebel by the British government. The main concern of the delegates was to find practical ways to help the people of Massachusetts in their troubles with the British. For several weeks the representatives argued among themselves. Then on June 14, 1775, they agreed to establish a Continental Army and to ask Maryland, Pennsylvania, and Virginia to send militia troops to aid Boston. That same day, John Adams nominated Colonel George Washington as commander in chief of the Army. Samuel Adams seconded the nomination. After thinking about it overnight, the delegates approved Washington's appointment on June 15. Washington set out at once for Boston, arriving after the Battle of Bunker Hill had been fought. The Continental Army settled down to a long siege of Boston that lasted until British forces withdrew by sea in March 1776.

"Common Sense" by Thomas Paine minced no words

By the spring of 1776, a majority of the delegates of the Continental Congress had come round to the opinion that complete independence from Great Britain was their only course of action. They had been urged into this state of mind partly as a result of the pamphlet *Common Sense* written by Thomas Paine. This pamphlet minced no words in its attack on the tyranny of the British monarchy and called clearly for "a government of our own." The delegates also had learned that the British government was contracting with various German princes to hire mercenaries to fight in America—news that indicated the British had no intention of trying to conciliate the problems with the colonies.

Early in May John Adams, who was growing more and more impatient because the Congress would not declare itself in favor of independence, offered resolutions calling for the colonies to form separate governments of their own, independent of Britain. Congress adopted Adams' proposals. By the end of May, Congress had received resolutions from the legislatures of North Carolina and Virginia calling for complete independence.

Then, on June 7, 1776, Richard Henry Lee of Virginia presented the resolution that finally led to the Declaration of Independence. Lee's resolution, seconded by John Adams, read as follows:

"Resolved

"That these United Colonies are, and of right ought to be, free and independent States, that they are absolved from all allegiance to the British Crown, and that all political connection between them and the state of Great Britain is, and ought to be, totally dissolved.

"That it is expedient forthwith to take the most effectual measures for forming foreign Alliances.

"That a plan of confederation be prepared and transmitted to the respective Colonies for their consideration and approbation."

In the arguments that followed, some of the more conservative delegates, such as Robert R. Livingston of New York and John Dickinson of Pennsylvania, suggested that the time was not yet ripe to declare for independence. Thomas Jefferson wrote, "it appearing in the course of these debates that the colonies of New York, New Jersey, Pennsylvania, Delaware, Maryland, and South Carolina were not yet matured for falling from the parent stem, but that they were fast advancing to that state, it was thought most prudent to wait a while for them and to postpone the final decision to July 1."

Great events affecting lives of present and future generations

At this time, John Adams wrote: "Objects of the most stupendous magnitude, and measures in which the lives and liberties of millions yet unborn are intimately interested, are now before us. We are in the midst of a revolution, the most complete, unexpected and remarkable, of any in the history of nations."

Meanwhile, because it was apparent that Lee's resolution ultimately would be adopted, a committee was appointed by the Congress to prepare the Declaration of Independence. This committee included Thomas Jefferson of Virginia, John Adams of Massachusetts, Benjamin Franklin of Pennsylvania, Roger Sherman of Connecticut, and Robert R. Livingston of New York.

Independence Hall, Philadelphia where the Declaration of Independence was signed.

Why was the 33-year-old Jefferson named first on this committee? "There were more reasons than one," John Adams later wrote, "Mr. Jefferson came into Congress in June, 1775, and brought with him a reputation for literature, science, and a happy talent of composition. Writings of his were handed about remarkable for the peculiar felicity of expression. Though a silent member in Congress, he was so prompt, frank, explicit and decisive upon committees and in conversation . . . that he soon seized upon my heart, and upon this occasion I gave him my vote and did all in my power to procure the votes of others. I think he had one more vote than any other, and that placed him at the head of the Committee. I had the next highest number and that placed me second."

"Jefferson had a happy talent for composition."

Many years later Adams and Jefferson disagreed in their writings as to how Jefferson came to be chosen as the person to write the first draft of the Declaration. Jefferson said the whole committee chose him. Adams said the committee appointed himself and Jefferson to a subcommittee to prepare the draft, and that Jefferson urged him to write the draft. "This I declined," Adams wrote in his *Autobiography*, "and gave several reasons for declining (1) that he was a Virginian and I a Massachusettensian. (2) that he was a Southern Man and I a northern one. (3) that I had been so obnoxious for my early and constant Zeal in promoting the Measure, that any draught of mine, would undergo a more severe Scrutiny and Criticism in Congress, than one of his composition. 4thly and lastly, and that would be reason enough if there were no other. I had a great opinion of the Elegance of his pen, and none at all of my own. I therefore insisted that no hesitation should be made on his part."

Jefferson wrote the Declaration sitting at a portable writing desk of his own design that he had brought with him. He did his work in the upstairs parlor of the house of a German bricklayer where he was lodging. Jefferson apparently wrote and rewrote the document a good many times. He showed it to Adams and Franklin and incorporated various changes that they suggested. Finally, on June 28, the committee submitted the Declaration to Congress where it was tabled awaiting action on Lee's earlier resolution.

On July 1, the delegates, sitting as the committee of the whole, resumed their discussion of the Lee resolution. A new delegation had arrived from New Jersey and they wanted a thorough airing of the matter. John Dickinson of Pennsylvania spoke against the resolution, again pointing out that he did not feel the time was right for such a strong measure. Adams, called "the Atlas of American independence," by Richard Stockton of New Jersey, outlined the reasons why independence should be declared. Jefferson wrote later in describing Adams' presentation that he "was not graceful nor eloquent, nor remarkably fluent, but he came out occasionally with a power of thought and expression that moved us from our seats." At the end of the first day's debate, only nine of the colonies were ready to approve the resolution. New York abstained, awaiting instructions from home. Delaware's delegation was split. Pennsylvania and South Carolina opposed the resolution, but the South Carolinians indicated they would switch their vote to achieve unanimity.

John Adams was the Atlas of American Independence

The next day, July 2, Delaware could now report that it would vote for independence because a delayed delegate, Caesar Rodney, had ridden eighty miles night-and-day through heavy rain to break the tie in favor of liberty.

Two Pennsylvania delegates who opposed the resolution, John Dickinson and Robert Morris, stayed away from the meeting, and, thus, of the remaining five Pennsylvania delegates, three were in favor—Benjamin Franklin, John Morton, and James Wilson—and two were opposed. So Pennsylvania was able to vote for independence. South Carolina decided to go along with the majority. New York abstained.

With the approval of Lee's resolution, all ties were broken with Great Britain. The excited and pleased John Adams wrote to his wife: "The second day of July, 1776, will be the most memorable epocha in the history of America. I am apt to believe that it will be celebrated by succeeding generations as the great anniversary Festival. It ought to be commemorated, as the day of deliverance, by solemn acts of devotion to God Almighty. It ought to be solemnized with pomp and parade, with shows, games, sports, guns, bells, bonfires, and illuminations, from one end of this continent to the other, from this time forward, forevermore."

Jefferson's composition was carefully edited, but unchanged in the essentials

For the rest of July 2 and for two days thereafter, Congress turned its attention to Jefferson's Declaration of Independence—the official statement that was to be Congress' announcement to the world of its action. In these three days, the delegates acted as a board of editors. Jefferson sat silently by, no doubt biting his underlip as he watched the delegates add a word here, delete a word there, and even cut out whole paragraphs. Scholars have counted thirty-nine changes that were made in the document by the congressional delegates. On the whole, the changes improved the Declaration. Surprisingly, the congressional editors deleted more words than they added, so that the document ended up even more concisely stated than when Jefferson submitted it; but the greatest phrases and the timeless philosophy that had come from Jefferson's pen remained unscathed.

FANUEIL HALL, BOSTON.

21

Although celebration followed in city after city, the adoption of the Declaration of Independence did not mean that everyone in the thirteen colonies agreed with it. Even many members of Congress did not favor a complete break with Great Britain; and throughout the country there were many Loyalists, or Tories, who ardently supported the British side of the dispute. In general, however, the Declaration of Independence was greeted with popular enthusiasm.

A convention in New York on July 9 approved independence, and word of this action was received by Congress on July 15. Now the wording on the heading of the Declaration could be changed from "A Declaration by the Representatives of the United States of America, in General Congress Assembled" to the now familiar "The unanimous Declaration of the thirteen united States of America."

Fifty members of Congress signed a parchment copy of the Declaration of Independence on August 2, 1776. These signers included some representatives who had not been present when the Declaration was adopted. Other delegates who had been present at the adoption had meanwhile left Philadelphia. George Wythe of Virginia signed on August 27. On September 4, the Declaration was signed by Richard Henry Lee of Virginia, Elbridge Gerry of Massachusetts, and Oliver Wolcott of Connecticut. On November 19, it was signed by Matthew Thornton of New Hampshire. The last to sign was Thomas McKean of Delaware, who is believed to have signed it sometime in 1781. The name of Charles Thomson, secretary to the Congress, also is signed to the document, but, because he was not a delegate, he generally is not counted among the fifty-six signers of the Declaration.

It was evening on July 4 when the delegates finally approved the Declaration of Independence. John Hancock, the President of the Congress, signed it with such a flourish that his name later became a synonym for the word *signature*. An old bellman, who is said to have waited all day in the tower of Independence Hall, received a signal that the Declaration had been signed, and he rang out the Liberty Bell for all the people of Philadelphia to hear that a new nation had been born.

On the night of July 4, printer John Dunlap set the document in type and printed it. Copies immediately were dispatched throughout the colonies. The Declaration was read to the public in Philadelphia for the first time on July 8 —it had taken that long to arrange a suitable celebration. In New York City, which was momentarily awaiting attack from a British fleet anchored in the harbor, George Washington assembled his troops on July 9 and had the Declaration read to them. That night the Sons of Liberty pulled down New York City's lead statue of King George III. A copy of the Declaration did not reach Georgia until August—its delay a reminder of the difficulty of transportation and communication in those days.

Table of post offices in the United States, with the distance from Philadelphia to every other post office here listed.

		Miles.
Abbeville c. h.	S. C.	782
Abbotstown	P.	103
Abingdon	Va.	511
Accomac c. h.	Va.	199
Albany	N. Y.	265
Alexandria	Va.	156
Allensfresh	Md.	203
Amboy	N. J.	74
Amherst	[illegible]	384
Andover	Ms.	372
Annapolis	Md.	132
Anson c. h.	N. C.	583
Averysborough	N. C.	482
Augusta	G.	763
Baltimore	Md.	102
Bairdstown	K.	875
Barnstable	Ms.	423
Bath	Me.	512
e Bath	N. Y.	248
Bath c. h.	Va.	337
Beaufort	S. C.	836
Bedford	P.	204
Belfast	Me.	590
Bel Air	Md.	86
Benedict	Md.	191
Bennington	Vt.	302
Bermuda Hundred	Va.	502
Berwick	Me.	432
Bethania	N. C.	538
Bethlehem	P.	58
Beverly	Ms.	367
Biddeford	Me.	451
Blackhorse	Md.	101
Bladensburg	Md.	140
Bluehill	Me.	623
Booneton	N. J.	116
Boston	Ms.	347
Bourbontown	[illegible]	749
Bowling Green	Va.	230
Brattleborough	Vt.	311
Brewers or Schoodick	Me.	745
Bridgehampton	N. Y.	196
Bridgetown East	N. J.	74
Bridgetown West	N. J.	57
Bristol	R. I.	306
Bristol	P.	20
Brookfield	Ms.	278
Brookhaven	N. Y.	161
Brownsville	P.	341
Brunswick	Me.	500
Brunswick (New)	N. J.	60
Burlington	Vt.	429
Butternutts	N. Y.	375
Cabbin Point	Va.	329
Cabellsburg	Va.	352
Cambridge	S. C.	762
Camden	Me.	571
Camden	S. C.	643
Canaan	Me.	577
Canaan	C.	257
Cantwell's Bridge	D.	52
Carlisle	P.	125
Cartersville	Va.	323
Centreville	Md.	98
Centreharbour	N. H.	486
e Catskill	N. Y.	233
Castine	Me.	610
Chambersburg	P.	157
Chandler's River	Me.	697
Chapel Hill	N. C.	472
Chaptico	Md.	215
Charlestown	N. H.	341
Charlestown	Md.	59
Charleston	S. C.	763
Charlotte c. h.	Va.	379
Charlotte c. h.	N. C.	617
Charlottesville	Va.	303
Chatham c. h.	N. C.	584
e Chenango	N. Y.	375
Cheraw c. h.	S. C.	591
Cherryvalley	N. Y.	336
Chester	N. H.	396
Chester	P.	15
Chester c. h.	S. C.	736
Chestertown	Md.	81
Christiana	D.	37
Cincinnati	N. T.	779
Claverack	N. Y.	231
Clermont	N. Y.	212
Clowes	D.	108

		Miles.
Colchester	Va.	172
Columbia	Me.	688
Columbia	Va.	328
Columbia	S. C.	678
Conajohary	N. Y.	318
Concord	N. H	420
Concord	Ms.	368
Cooperstown	N. Y.	348
Coosawatchy	S. C.	833
Culpeper	Va.	253
Cumberland	Md.	227
Cumberland c. h.	Va.	330
Dagsborough	D.	127
Danbury	C.	171
Danville	K.	830
Dedham	Ms.	321
Dighton	Ms.	314
Dover	N. H.	426
Dover	D.	76
Downingtown	P.	33
Duck Creek	D.	64
Duck trap	Me.	578
Dumfries	Va.	182
Duplin c. h.	N. C.	566
Durham	N. H.	426
Dresden	Me.	540
Doutysfalls	Me.	439
East Greenwich	R. I.	306
Easton	P.	70
Easton	Md.	118
Edenton	N. C.	440
Edgartown	Ms.	446
Edgefield c. h.	S. C.	738
Elberton	G.	859
Elizabethtown	N. J.	80
Elizabethtown	N. C.	547
Elkton	Md.	49
Ephrata	P.	74
Exeter	N. H.	402
Fairfield	Me.	563
Fairfield	C.	161
Falmouth	Ms.	429
Falmouth	Va.	207
Fayetteville	N. C.	507
Fincastle	Va	358
Fishkill	N. Y.	165
Flemington	N. J.	53
Frankfort	K.	790
Franklin c. h.	G.	834
Frederica	D.	88
Fredericksburg	Va.	208
Fredericktown	Md.	148
Freeport	Me.	493
Gallipolis	N. T.	559
Geneva	N. Y.	457
Georgetown, Cr. R.	Md.	65
Georgetown, Ptk.	Md.	148
Georgetown	S. C.	681
Georgetown	G.	873
Germanton	N. C.	528
Gettisburg	P.	119
Gloucester	Ms.	384
Gloucester c. h.	Va.	321
Goldson's	Va.	355
Goochland c. h.	Va.	308
Gouldsborough	Me.	657
Goshen	N. Y.	146
Gray	Me.	489
Greene	Me.	514
Greenfield	Ms.	291
Greenbrier c. h.	Va.	410
Greensborough	G.	841
Greensburg	P.	272
Greensville	T.	577
Greenville	N. C.	445
Greenville c. h.	S. C.	781
Guilford	C.	201
Hackettstown	N. J.	130
Hagerstown	Md.	149
Halifax	N. C.	384
Halifax c. h.	Va.	414
Hallowell c. h.	Me.	539
Hallowellhook	Me.	542
Hamburg	N. J.	121
Hampton	Va.	371
Hancock	Md.	179
Hanover	N. H.	377
Hanover	Ms.	375

		Miles.
Hanover	P.	106
Hanover c. h.	Va.	255
Hanovertown	Va.	300
Harford	Md.	77
e Harpersfield	N. Y.	289
Harrisburg	P.	107
Harris's	V.	336
Harrodsburg	K	820
Hartford	C.	222
Haverhill	N. H.	412
Haverhill	Ms.	382
Havre-de-Grace	Md	65
Hertford	N. C.	458
Hicks's Ford	Va.	356
Hillsborough	N C.	456
Hingham	Ms.	369
Hogtown	N. C.	419
Holmes's-Hole	Ms.	438
Horntown	Va.	174
Hudson	N. Y.	227
Huntington	Md.	171
Huntsville	N. C.	553
Indiantown	N. C.	492
Ipswich.	Ms	377
Iredell c. h.	N. C.	592
Johnsonburg	N. J.	98
Johnston	N. Y.	307
Jonesborough	T.	551
Kanandaigua	N. Y.	473
Keen	N. H.	344
Killingworth	C.	210
Kinderhook	N. Y.	244
Kingston (Esopus)	N. Y.	192
Kinsale	Va.	305
Kinston	N. C.	522
Knoxville	T.	652
Lancaster	Ms.	385
Lancaster	P.	66
Lancaster c. h.	Va.	335
Lansingburg	N. Y.	274
Laurens c. h.	S. C.	755
Laytons	Va.	245
Lebanon	P.	82
Leesburg	Va	173
Leesburg	N. C.	510
Leominster	Ms.	390
Leonardtown	Md.	227
Lewisburg	Pa.	132
Lexington	Va.	322
Lexington	K.	769
Liberty	Va.	393
Lincolnton	N. C.	652
Litchfield	C.	207
Little Germ. Flats	N. Y.	348
Londonderry	N. H.	403
Louisburg	N. C.	415
Louisville	K.	913
Louisville	G.	825
Lumberton	N. C.	539
Lower Marlboro'	Md.	162
Lynchburg	Va.	381
Lynn	Ms.	361
Machias	Me.	705
Manchester	Vt.	324
Marblehead	Ms.	372
Marietta	N. T.	456
Martinsburg	Va.	168
Marlborough	N. H	350
Martinsville	Va.	478
Martinville	N. C.	504
Mecklenburg	Va.	395
Mendon	Ms	295
Middlebury	Vt.	392
Middletown	C.	208
Middletown	D.	49
Middletownpoint	N. J.	95
Milford	C.	173
Milford	D.	96
Millerstown	P.	134
Monmouth	Me.	524
Monmouth c. h.	N. J.	64
Montgomery c. h.	Md.	158
Montgomery c. h.	Va.	408
Montgomery c. h.	N. C.	607
Moore c. h.	N. C.	547
Moorefields	Va.	267
Morgantown	Va.	303
Morganton	N. C.	651

		Miles.
Morristown	N. J.	108
Morrisville	P.	29
Mount Tirzah	N. C.	480
Murfreesborough	N. C.	422
Nantucket	Ms.	382
Narraguagus	Me.	673
Nash c. h.	N. C.	443
Nashville	T.	1015
Newark	N. J.	86
New Bedford	Ms	322
Newbern	N. C.	501
Newburg	N. Y.	170
Newbury	Vt.	417
New Brunswick	N. J.	60
Newbury c. h.	S. C.	723
Newburyport	Ms.	389
Newcastle	Me.	535
Newcastle	D.	33
New Germantown	N. J.	73
New Gloucester	Me.	499
New Hartford	C.	242
New Haven	C.	183
New Kent c. h.	Va.	308
New Lebanon	N. Y.	293
New London	C.	237
New London	Va.	393
New Market	Va.	242
New Milford	C.	187
New Milford	Me.	538
Newport	R. I.	292
Newport	D.	51
Newportbridge	G.	959
e Newtown	N. Y.	250
New-York city	N. Y.	95
Nixonton	N. C.	468
Norfolk	Va.	389
Northampton	Ms.	270
Northampton c. h.	Va.	239
Norridgeworth	Me.	587
Northumberland	P.	124
Northumberland c. h.	Va	317
North Yarmouth	Me.	483
Norwalk	C.	149
Norwick	C.	251
Nottingham	N. H.	437
Nottingham	Md.	265
Old Fort Schuyler	N. Y.	364
Oldtown	Md.	213
Onondaigua	N. Y.	422
Orangeburg	S. C.	721
Orange c. h.	Va.	273
Orford	N. H.	395
e Ouliout	N. Y.	325
e Owego	N. Y.	284
Oxford Ac.	N. Y.	395
Painted Post	N. Y.	230
Passamaquoddy	Me.	728
Peekskill	N. Y.	145
Pendleton c. h.	S. C.	801
(Penobscot or Castine	Me.)	606
Peterborough	N. H.	366
Petersburg	P.	113
Petersburg	Va	303
Petersburg	G.	836
Philadelphia	P.	—
Pinkneyville	S. C.	716
Piscataway	Md.	178
Pittsburg	P.	303
Pittsfield	Ms.	299
Pittsylvania c. h.	Va.	448
Pittston	Me.	547
Pittston	N. J.	58
Plumstead	P.	36
Plymouth	N. H.	445
Plymouth	Ms	393
Plymouth	N. C.	463
Pomfret	C.	264
Portland	Me.	469
Portroyal	Va	230
Portsmouth	N. H.	411
Portsmouth	Va.	390
Port Tobacco	Md.	194
Pottsgrove	P.	37
Poughkeepsie	N. Y.	180
Powhatan c. h.	Va.	310
Prince Edward c. h.	Va.	358
Princess-Ann	Md.	178
Princeton	N. J.	42

		Miles.
Princeton	N. C.	419
Prospect	Me.	602
Providence	R. I.	29[illegible]
Queen Anns	Md.	141
Quincy	Ms.	360
Raleigh	N. C.	448
Randolph c. h.	N. C.	585
Reading	P.	54
Redhook	N. Y.	206
Rhinebeck	N. Y.	198
Richland	N. C.	551
Richmond	Va.	278
Richmond c. h.	Va.	273
Richmond c. h.	N. C.	563
Ridgefield	C.	161
Rockaway	N. J.	123
Rockford	N. C.	573
Rockingham c. h.	Va.	262
Rockingham c. h.	N. C.	535
Rocky Mount	Va.	433
Rome	N. Y.	376
Rutland	Vt.	359
Romney	Va.	242
Saggharbour	N. Y.	202
St. Leonards	Md.	186
St. Mary's	G.	1054
St. Tammanys	Va.	380
Salem	Ms.	365
Salem	N. J.	37
Salem	N. C.	531
Salisbury	Md.	163
Salisbury	N. C.	567
Sampson c. h.	N. C.	543
Sandwich	Ms.	411
Sanford	Me.	447
Savannah	G.	92
Sawyersferry	N. C.	482
Saybrook	C.	219
Scotland Neck	N. C.	396
Schenectady	N. Y.	281
Scipio	N. Y.	461
Sharpsburg	Md.	181
Sheffield	Ms.	257
Shepherdstown	Va.	178
Shippensburg	P.	146
Shrewsbury	N. J.	79
Smithfield	Va.	364
Smithfield	N. C.	473
Smithtown	N. Y.	147
Snowhill	Md.	158
Somerset	Ms.	311
Southampton c. h.	Va.	399
Sparta	N. J.	117
Spartan c. h.	S. C.	746
Springfield	Ms.	250
Springfield	K.	729
Stamford	C.	139
Statesburg	S. C.	663
Staunton	Va.	287
Stevensburg	Va.	200
Stockbridge	Ms.	249
Stonington	C.	251
Strasburg	Va.	210
Stratford	C.	169
Suffield	C.	232
Suffolk	Va.	386
Sullivan	Me.	645
Sumner	S. C.	
Suffex c. h.	N. J.	108
Sunbury	P.	122
Sunbury	G.	974
Swedesborough	N. J.	20
Sweet-Springs	Va.	380
Taneytown	Md.	121
Tappahannock	Va.	263
Tarborough	N. C.	420
Taunton	Ms.	312
Thomaston	Me.	564
Todds	Va.	283
Towerhill	R. I.	282
Trenton	Me.	633
Trenton	N. J.	30
Trenton	N. C.	521
Troy	N. Y.	271
Uniontown	P.	327
Union	N. Y.	340
Upper Marlboro'	Md.	162
Urbanna	Va.	291

		Miles.
Vassalborough	Me.	551
Vergennes	Vt.	407
Vienna	Md.	150
Waldoborough	Me.	545
Wallingford	C.	195
Walpole	N. H.	230
Wardsbridge	N. Y.	156
Warminster	Va.	332
Warren	Me.	557
Warren	R. I.	302
Warren	Va.	326
Warrenton	N. C.	390
Warwick	Md.	57
WASHINGTON, City		144
Washington	P.	325
Washington	K.	709
Washington	N. C.	460
Washington	G.	813
Waterbury	Me.	466
Waynesborough	N. C.	498
Waynesborough	G.	800
Wells	Me.	441
Westerly	R. I.	256
Westfield	Ms.	260
West Liberty	Va.	348
Westminster	Vt.	329
Westmoreland c. h.	Va.	28[illegible]
Wethersfield	C.	218
Wheeling	Va.	363
Whitestown	N. Y.	368
Wilkes	N. C.	611
Wilkesbarre	P.	118
Williamsboro'	N. C.	407
e Williamsburg	N. Y.	288
Williamsburg	Va.	338
Williamsport	Md.	155
Williamston	N. C.	444
Wilmington	D.	28
Wilmington	N. C.	600
Winchendon	Ms.	370
Winchester	Va.	192
Windham	C.	253
Windsor	Vt.	255
Windsor	N. C.	481
Winnsborough	S. C.	708
Winslow	Me.	559
Winthrop	Me.	529
Winton	N. C.	434
Wiscasset	Me.	525
Woodbridge	N. J.	70
Woodbury	N. J.	9
Woodstock	Va.	222
Woodstown	N. J.	26
Worcester	Ms.	299
Worthington	Ms.	289
Wythe c. h.	Va.	454
Yarmouth	Ms.	427
Yonkers	N. Y.	114
York	Me.	421
Yorktown	Va.	350
York	P.	88

EXPLANATION.

Me. for	Maine
N. H.	New Hampshire
Vt.	Vermont
Ms.	Massachusetts
R. I.	Rhode Island
C.	Connecticut
N. Y.	New York
N. J.	New Jersey
P.	Pennsylvania
N. T.	North Western Territory
D.	Delaware
Md.	Maryland
Va.	Virginia
K.	Kentucky
N. C.	North Carolina
T.	Tennassee
S. C.	South Carolina
G.	Georgia

e Offices on Extended Post-Roads under the second Section of the Law.
Ptk. Potowmack
C. R. Cross Road
c. h. Courthouse.

Library of Congress

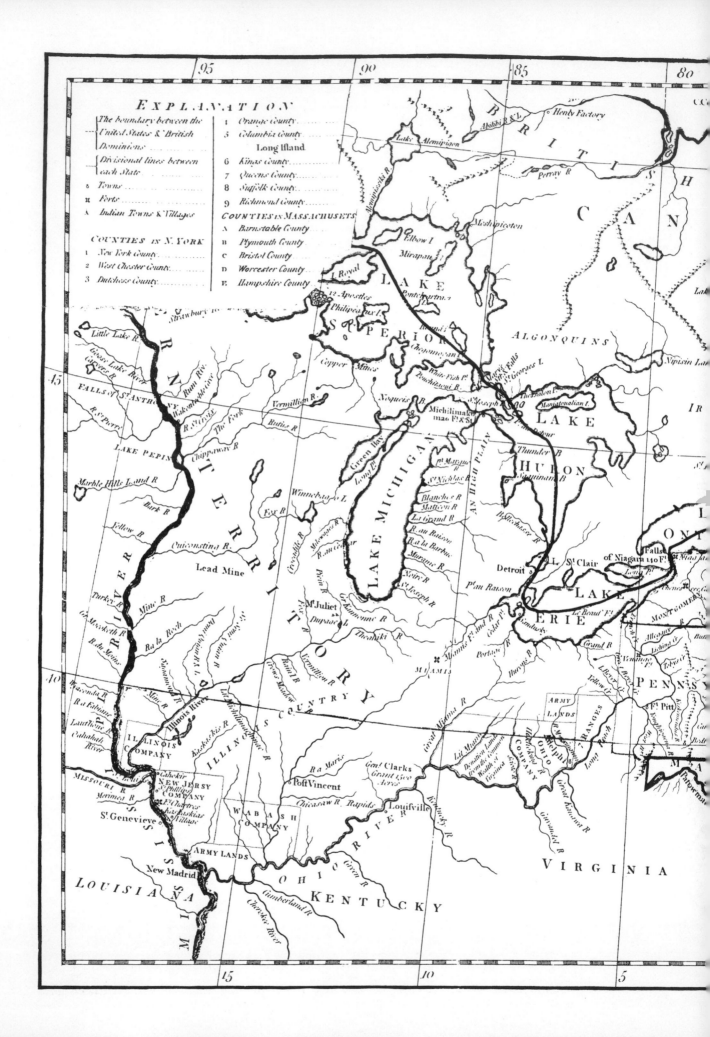

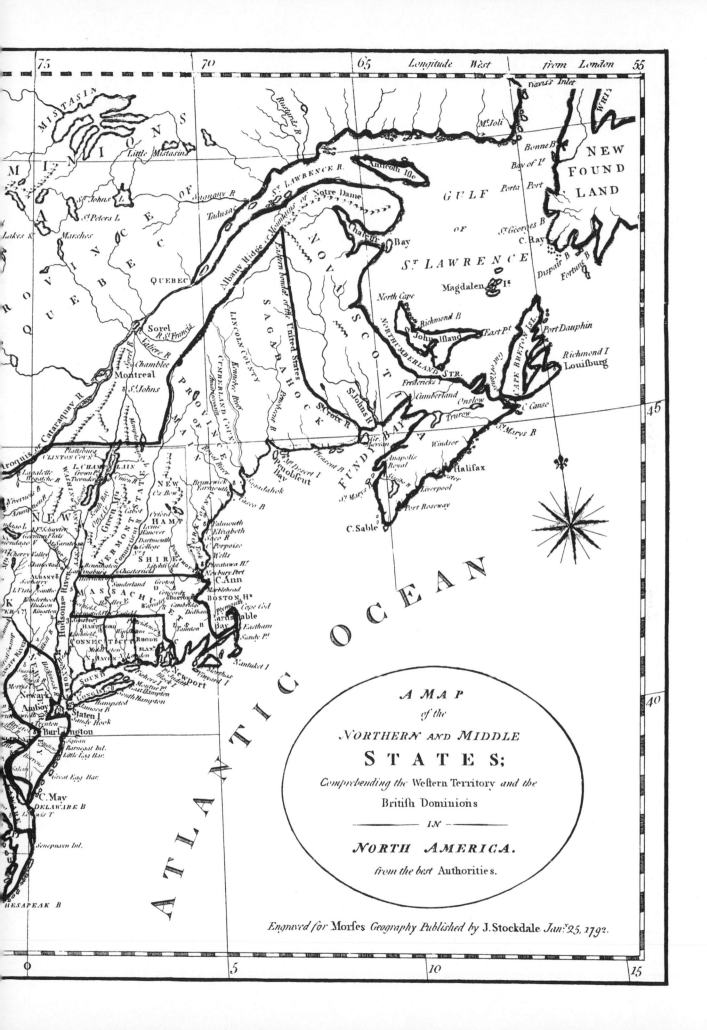

A MAP

of the

NORTHERN AND MIDDLE

STATES;

Comprehending the Western Territory *and the*

British Dominions

— IN —

NORTH AMERICA.

from the best Authorities.

Engraved for Morses *Geography Published by* J. Stockdale *Jan:* 25, 1792.

Vital Facts About the Signers of..

Name	Born	Died	Birthplace	Age at Adoption of Declaration
John Adams	October 30, 1735	July 4, 1826	Braintree (now Quincy), Mass.	40
Samuel Adams	September 27, 1722	October 2, 1803	Boston, Mass.	53
Josiah Bartlett	November 21, 1729	May 19, 1795	Amesbury, Mass.	46
Carter Braxton	September 10, 1736	October 10, 1797	Newington, Va.	39
Charles Carroll	September 20, 1737	November 14, 1832	Annapolis, Md.	38
Samuel Chase	April 17, 1741	June 19, 1811	Somerset County, Md.	35
Abraham Clark	February 15, 1726	September 15, 1794	Elizabethtown, N.J.	50
George Clymer	March 16, 1739	January 23, 1813	Philadelphia, Pa.	37
William Ellery	December 22, 1727	February 15, 1820	Newport, R.I.	48
William Floyd	December 17, 1734	August 4, 1821	Suffolk County, N.Y.	41
Benjamin Franklin	January 17, 1706	April 17, 1790	Boston, Mass.	70
Elbridge Gerry	July 17, 1744	November 23, 1814	Marblehead, Mass.	31
Button Gwinnett	1735 (?)	May 27, 1777	Gloucestershire, England	41
Lyman Hall	April 12, 1724	October 19, 1790	Wallingford, Conn.	52
John Hancock	January 23, 1737	October 8, 1793	Braintree (now Quincy), Mass.	39
Benjamin Harrison	1726 (?)	April 24, 1791	Charles City County, Va.	50
John Hart	1711 (?)	May 11, 1779	Stonington, Conn.	65
Joseph Hewes	January 23, 1730	November 10, 1779	Kingston, N.J.	46
Thomas Heyward, Jr.	July 28, 1746	March 4, 1809	(now) Saint Luke's Parish, S.C.	29
William Hooper	June 17, 1742	October 14, 1790	Boston, Mass.	34
Stephen Hopkins	March 7, 1707	July 13, 1785	Cranston, R.I.	69
Francis Hopkinson	October 2, 1737	May 9, 1791	Philadelphia, Pa.	38
Samuel Huntington	July 3, 1731	January 5, 1796	Windham, Conn.	45
Thomas Jefferson	April 13, 1743	July 4, 1826	Albemarle County, Va.	33
Francis Lightfoot Lee	October 14, 1734	January 11, 1797	Westmoreland County, Va.	41
Richard Henry Lee	January 20, 1732	June 19, 1794	Westmoreland County, Va.	44
Francis Lewis	March 21, 1713	December 31, 1802	Llandaff, Wales	63
Philip Livingston	January 15, 1716	June 12, 1778	Albany, N.Y.	60

Colony represented	University or College	Profession	Later Achievements	Age at Death
Massachusetts	Harvard	Lawyer	Vice-president of U.S. 1789-1797; President of U.S. 1797-1801	90
Massachusetts	Harvard	Businessman	Governor of Massachusetts 1794-1797	81
New Hampshire		Physician	Governor of New Hampshire 1793-1794	65
Virginia	William and Mary	Planter	Member of Virginia Council of State 1786-1791, 1794-1797	61
Maryland	Educated in France and England	Lawyer-Planter	U. S. Senator from Maryland 1789-1792	95
Maryland		Lawyer	Associate Justice, Supreme Court of U. S. 1796-1811	70
New Jersey		Politician	U. S. Rep. from New Jersey 1791-1794	68
Pennsylvania	Philadelphia (U. of Pa.)	Banker	Signed U. S. Constitution; U. S. Rep. from Pennsylvania 1789-1791	73
Rhode Island	Harvard	Lawyer	Collector of Customs, Newport, R. I. 1790-1820	92
New York		Farmer	U. S. Rep. from New York 1789-1791	86
Pennsylvania		Publisher	Signed U. S. Constitution	84
Massachusetts	Harvard	Merchant	Vice-president of U. S. 1813-1814	70
Georgia		Merchant	Acting President of Georgia 1777	42
Georgia	Yale	Physician	Governor of Georgia 1783	66
Massachusetts	Harvard	Merchant	Governor of Massachusetts 1780-1785, 1787-1793	56
Virginia	William and Mary	Planter	Governor of Virginia 1781-1784	65
New Jersey		Farmer	Died before Independence was won	68
North Carolina		Merchant	First executive head of American navy	49
South Carolina	Educated in England	Lawyer	Artillery officer during Revolutionary War, captured and imprisoned by British	62
North Carolina	Harvard	Lawyer	North Carolina State legislator 1777-1782	48
Rhode Island		Merchant	Delegate to the Continental Congress 1778	78
New Jersey	Philadelphia (U. of Pa.)	Lawyer	Said to have designed U. S. Flag 1777, U. S. District Court judge 1789-1791	53
Connecticut		Lawyer	President of Continental Congress 1779-1781 Governor of Connecticut 1786-1796	64
Virginia	William and Mary	Planter-Lawyer	U. S. Secretary of State 1789-1793, Vice-president of U. S. 1797-1801, President of U. S. 1801-1809	83
Virginia		Planter	Delegate to Continental Congress 1775-1779	62
Virginia	Educated in England	Planter	President of Continental Congress 1784, U. S. Senator from Virginia 1789-1792	62
New York		Merchant	Retired	89
New York	Yale	Merchant	Died before Independence was won	62

Name	Born	Died	Birthplace	Age at Adoption of Declaration
Thomas Lynch, Jr.	August 5, 1749	1779	Prince George's Parish, S.C.	26
Thomas McKean	March 19, 1734	June 24, 1817	New London, Pa.	42
Arthur Middleton	June 26, 1742	January 1, 1787	near Charleston, S.C.	34
Lewis Morris	April 8, 1726	January 22, 1798	Morrisania, N.Y.	50
Robert Morris	January 31, 1734	May 8, 1806	Liverpool, England	42
John Morton	1724	April, 1777	Ridley, Pa.	52
Thomas Nelson	December 26, 1738	January 4, 1789	Yorktown, Va.	37
William Paca	October 31, 1740	October 13, 1799	near Abingdon, Md.	35
Robert Treat Paine	March 11, 1731	May 11, 1814	Boston, Mass.	45
John Penn	May 17, 1740	September, 1788	Caroline County, Va.	36
George Read	September 18, 1733	September 21, 1798	North East, Md.	42
Caesar Rodney	October 7, 1728	June 29, 1784	Dover, Del.	47
George Ross	May 10, 1730	July 14, 1779	New Castle, Del.	46
Benjamin Rush	December 24, 1745	April 19, 1813	Byberry, Pa.	30
Edward Rutledge	November 23, 1749	January 23, 1800	Charleston, S.C.	26
Roger Sherman	April 19, 1721	July 23, 1793	Newtown, Mass.	55
James Smith	1719 (?)	July 11, 1806	Ireland	57
Richard Stockton	October 1, 1730	February 28, 1781	Princeton, N.J.	45
Thomas Stone	1743	October 5, 1787	Charles County, Md.	33
George Taylor	1716	February 23, 1781	Ireland	60
Matthew Thornton	1714 (?)	June 24, 1803	Ireland	62
George Walton	1741	February 2, 1804	near Farmville, Va.	35
William Whipple	January 14, 1730	November 28, 1785	Kittery, Me.	46
William Williams	April 8, 1731	August 2, 1811	Lebanon, Conn.	45
James Wilson	September 14, 1742	August 21, 1798	St. Andrews, Scotland	33
John Witherspoon	February 5, 1723	November 15, 1794	Yester, Scotland	53
Oliver Wolcott	November 26, 1726	December 1, 1797	Windsor, Conn.	49
George Wythe	1726	June 8, 1806	Back River, Va.	50

Colony Represented	University or College	Profession	Later Achievements	Age at Death
South Carolina	Educated in England	Planter-Lawyer	Died before Independence was won	30
Delaware		Lawyer	Governor of Pennsylvania 1799-1808	83
South Carolina	Educated in England	Lawyer-Planter	Militia officer during Revolutionary War, captured and imprisoned by British	44
New York	Yale	Landowner	Major general in state militia during Revolutionary War	71
Pennsylvania		Financier	Signed U. S. Constitution, U. S. Senator from Pennsylvania 1789-1795	72
Pennsylvania		Farmer	Died before Independence was won	53
Virginia	Educated in England	Planter-merchant	Commander-in-chief of state militia in Revolutionary War, Governor of Virginia 1781	50
Maryland	Philadelphia (U. of Pa.)	Lawyer	Governor of Maryland 1782-1785, U. S. District Court judge 1789-1799	58
Massachusetts	Harvard	Lawyer	Massachusetts Supreme Court justice 1790-1804	83
North Carolina		Lawyer	Retired by ill health	47
Delaware		Lawyer	Signed U.S. Constitution, U.S. Senator 1789-1793; Chief justice of Delaware 1793-1798	65
Delaware		Planter	Commanded state militia in Revolutionary War, President of Delaware 1778-1781	55
Pennsylvania		Lawyer	Admiralty judge of Pennsylvania 1779	49
Pennsylvania	Col. of New Jersey (now Princeton) and U. of Edinburgh	Physician	Treasurer of U. S. Mint 1797-1813	67
South Carolina	Educated in England	Planter-Lawyer	Governor of South Carolina 1798-1800	50
Connecticut		Merchant-Lawyer	Signed U. S. Constitution, U. S. Senator from Connecticut 1791-1793	72
Pennsylvania		Lawyer	Pennsylvania Court of Appeals judge 1781	87
New Jersey	Col. of New Jersey (now Princeton)	Lawyer	Imprisoned by British during Revolutionary War	50
Maryland		Lawyer	Helped frame Articles of Confederation	44
Pennsylvania		Iron-maker	Retired by ill health	65
New Hampshire		Physician	Associate justice of New Hampshire Superior Court	89
Georgia		Lawyer	U. S. Senator from Georgia 1795-1796	63
New Hampshire		Merchant	Brigadier general during Revolutionary War	55
Connecticut	Harvard	Merchant	Helped frame Articles of Confederation	80
Pennsylvania	U. of Edinburgh	Lawyer	Signed U. S. Constitution, Associate justice of Supreme Court of U. S. 1789-1798	55
New Jersey	U. of Edinburgh	Clergyman	President, College of New Jersey (now Princeton)	71
Connecticut	Yale	Politician-Soldier	Governor of Connecticut 1796-1797	71
Virginia	William and Mary	Lawyer	First professor of law in America, Chancellor of Virginia 1786-1806	80

The Declaration

In Congress, July 4, 1776. The unanimous Declaration of the thirteen united States of America.

When in the Course of human events, it becomes necessary for one people to dissolve the political bands which have connected them with another, and to assume among the powers of the earth, the separate and equal station to which the Laws of Nature and of Nature's God entitle them, a decent respect to the opinions of mankind requires that they should declare the causes which impel them to the separation.—

We hold these truths to be self-evident, that all men are created equal, that they are endowed by their Creator with certain unalienable Rights, that among these are Life, Liberty and the pursuit of Happiness.—

That to secure these rights, Governments are instituted among Men, deriving their just powers from the consent of the governed,—

That whenever any Form of Government becomes destructive of these ends, it is the Right of the People to alter or to abolish it, and to institute new Government, laying its foundation on such principles and organizing its powers in such form, as to them shall seem most likely to effect their Safety and Happiness. Prudence, indeed, will dictate that Governments long established should not be changed for light and transient causes; and accordingly all experience hath shown, that mankind are more disposed to suffer, while evils are sufferable, than to right themselves by abolishing the forms to which they are accustomed. But when a long train of abuses and usurpations, pursuing invariably the same Object evinces a design to reduce them under absolute Despotism, it is their right, it is their duty, to throw off such Government, and to provide new Guards for their future security.—

Such has been the patient sufferance of these Colonies; and such is now the necessity which constrains them to alter their former Systems of Government. The history of the present King of Great Britain is a history of repeated injuries and usurpations, all having in direct object the establishment of an absolute Tyranny over these States.

To prove this, let Facts be submitted to a candid world.—

He has refused his Assent to Laws, the most wholesome and necessary for the public good.—

He has forbidden his Governors to pass Laws of immediate and pressing importance, unless suspended in their operation till his Assent should be obtained; and when so suspended, he has utterly neglected to attend to them.—

He has refused to pass other Laws for the accommodation of large districts of people, unless those people would relinquish the right of Representation in the Legislature, a right inestimable to them and formidable to tyrants only.—

He has called together legislative bodies at places unusual, uncomfortable, and distant from the depository of their public Records, for the sole purpose of fatiguing them into compliance with his measures.—

He has dissolved Representative Houses repeatedly, for opposing with manly firmness his invasions on the rights of the people.—

He has refused for a long time, after such dissolutions, to cause others to be elected; whereby the Legislative powers, incapable of Annihilation, have returned to the People at large for their exercise; the State remaining in the mean time exposed to all the dangers of invasion from without, and convulsions within.—

He has endeavoured to prevent the population of these States; for that purpose obstructing the Laws for Naturalization of Foreigners; refusing to pass others to encourage their migrations hither, and raising the conditions of new Appropriations of Lands.—

He has obstructed the Administration of Justice, by refusing his Assent to Laws for establishing Judiciary powers.—

He has made Judges dependent on his Will alone, for the tenure of their offices, and the amount and payment of their salaries.—

He has erected a multitude of New Offices, and sent hither swarms of Officers to harrass our people, and eat out their substance.—

He has kept among us in times of peace, Standing Armies without the Consent of our legislatures.—

of Independence

He has affected to render the Military independent of and superior to the Civil power.—

He has combined with others to subject us to a jurisdiction foreign to our constitution, and unacknowledged by our laws; giving his Assent to their Acts of pretended Legislation:—

For quartering large bodies of armed troops among us:—

For protecting them, by a mock Trial, from punishment for any Murders which they should commit on the Inhabitants of these States:—

For cutting off our Trade with all parts of the world:—

For imposing Taxes on us without our Consent:—

For depriving us in many cases, of the benefits of Trial by Jury:—

For transporting us beyond Seas to be tried for pretended offences:—

For abolishing the free System of English Laws in a neighbouring Province, establishing therein an Arbitrary government, and enlarging its Boundaries so as to render it at once an example and fit instrument for introducing the same absolute rule in these Colonies:—

For taking away our Charters, abolishing our most valuable Laws, and altering fundamentally the Forms of our Governments:—

For suspending our own Legislatures, and declaring themselves invested with power to legislate for us in all cases whatsoever.—

He has abdicated Government here, by declaring us out of his Protection and waging War against us.—

He has plundered our seas, ravaged our Coasts, burnt our towns, and destroyed the lives of our people.—

He is at this time transporting large Armies of foreign Mercenaries to compleat the works of death, desolation and tyranny, already begun with circumstances of Cruelty & perfidy scarcely paralleled in the most barbarous ages, and totally unworthy the Head of a civilized nation.—

He has constrained our fellow Citizens taken Captive on the high Seas to bear Arms against their Country, to become the executioners of their friends and Brethren, or to fall themselves by their Hands.—

He has excited domestic insurrections amongst us, and has endeavoured to bring on the inhabitants of our frontiers, the merciless Indian Savages, whose known rule of warfare, is an undistinguished destruction of all ages, sexes and conditions.

In every stage of these Oppressions We have Petitioned for Redress in the most humble terms: Our repeated Petitions have been answered only by repeated injury. A Prince, whose character is thus marked by every act which may define a Tyrant, is unfit to be the ruler of a free people.

Nor have We been wanting in attentions to our British brethren. We have warned them from time to time of attempts by their legislature to extend an unwarrantable jurisdiction over us. We have reminded them of the circumstances of our emigration and settlement here. We have appealed to their native justice and magnanimity, and we have conjured them by the ties of our common kindred to disavow these usurpations, which, would inevitably interrupt our connections and correspondence. They too have been deaf to the voice of justice and of consanguinity. We must, therefore, acquiesce in the necessity, which denounces our Separation, and hold them, as we hold the rest of mankind, Enemies in War, in Peace Friends.—

We, therefore, the Representatives of the united States of America, in General Congress, Assembled, appealing to the Supreme Judge of the world for the rectitude of our intentions, do, in the Name, and by Authority of the good People of these Colonies, solemnly publish and declare, That these United Colonies are, and of Right ought to be, Free and Independent States; that they are Absolved from all Allegiance to the British Crown, and that all political connection between them and the State of Great Britain, is and ought to be totally dissolved; and that as Free and Independent States, they have full Power to levy War, conclude Peace, contract Alliances, establish Commerce, and to do all other Acts and Things which Independent States may of right do.—

And for the support of this Declaration, with a firm reliance on the protection of divine Providence, we mutually pledge to each other our Lives, our Fortunes and our sacred Honor.

Fac-similes of the Signatures to the Declaration of Independence July 4 1776.

John Penn   **John Hancock**   John Hart

Wm Floyd   Wm Paca

Geo Read   Wm Hooper   Saml Adams

                Geo Clymer

Step Hopkins   Thos Nelson jr.

    Charles Carroll of Carrollton   Elbridge Gerry

Thos M. Kean   Roger Sherman   Saml Huntington

Wm Whipple   Thomas Lynch Junr.

Geo Taylor   Josiah Bartlett   Benj Franklin

Wm Williams   Rich Stockton

                         John Morton

Oliver Wolcott   Jno Witherspoon   **Geo Ross**

Thos Stone   Samuel Chase   Robt Treat Paine

George Wythe   Matthew Thornton

Frans Lewis   Th Jefferson   Benja Harrison

Lewis Morris   Abra Clark   Phil Livingston

                       Casar Rodney

Arthur Middleton   Fras Hopkinson

Geo Walton   Carter Braxton   James Wilson

Richard Henry Lee   Thos Heyward Jun

Benjamin Rush   John Adams   Robt Morris

Lyman Hall   Joseph Hewes   Button Gwinnett

Francis Lightfoot Lee

       Edward Rutledge   Jas Smith

William Ellery

"Department of State 19th April 1819. I Certify that this is a CORRECT Copy of the original Declaration of Independence deposited at this Department, and that I have compared all the signatures with those of the original and have found them EXACT IMITATIONS." John Quincy Adams

Prospect des Plazes vor dem Rath | Vüe de la Rue et de ta Maison
Haus zu Boston. | de Ville a Boston.

(Translation)

View of the Street and the City Hall in Boston.

John Adams in Court Dress

By J. S. Copley

JOHN ADAMS of MASSACHUSETTS

Along with George Washington, Thomas Jefferson, and James Madison, John Adams stands among the greatest of the Founding Fathers. Before the Revolutionary War, he inspired his fellow colonists in Massachusetts to stand up for their rights against British tyranny. At the beginning of the war, he nominated Washington as the general who could lead the combined troops of the colonies to victory. His powerful arguments helped his fellow members of the Continental Congress see the need for severing all ties with Great Britain; then he helped Jefferson write the Declaration of Independence and obtained its adoption. As a diplomat, he helped negotiate the peace treaty with Great Britain that recognized American independence, and then he served as the first U. S. minister in London. After the ratification of the United States Constitution, he was elected as the first Vice-President of the United States. In this office, he helped President Washington establish the traditions of the new government. When Washington retired, the nation that Adams had helped found honored him with election as the second President of the United States. He lived to the age of 90 and saw his son, John Quincy Adams, chosen as the sixth President of the United States.

Utterly incapable of dishonesty

One of the finest contemporary descriptions of Adams' character came from the pen of Thomas Jefferson, who said: "There is not upon this earth a more perfectly honest man than John Adams. Concealment is no part of his character; of that he is utterly incapable. It is not in his nature to meditate anything that he would not publish to the world. The measures of the general government are a fair subject for difference of opinion, but do not found your opinions on the notion that there is the smallest spice of dishonesty, moral or political, in the character of John Adams; for I know him well, and I repeat that a man more perfectly honest never issued from the hands of his Creator." Part of the value of this observation comes from the fact that it was made by Jefferson at the time he was running against Adams for the presidency in a particularly heated campaign, marked by much name-calling and mud-slinging.

"Never could keep his mouth shut"

Adams did not look the part of a great patriot. He was short and pudgy. His manners were as unbending as were his principles, and he neither sought nor won great popularity. He did not know how to conceal his feelings, even when it might have been prudent to do so. He was aware of his own ability to say the right thing at the wrong time, but made no effort to change his ways. The story is told that once while viewing portraits of himself and Washington—his own picture showing the lips slightly parted and that of Washington showing the lips firmly closed—Adams pointed to the portrait of himself and remarked, "That fellow never could keep his mouth shut."

John Adams was born in a plain frame house in Braintree (now Quincy), Mass., on October 30, 1735. His Puritan great-great-grandfather, Henry Adams, had sailed from England seeking religious freedom and had received a land grant at Braintree in 1640. The quaint inscription of Henry Adams' tomb states that he "Took his flight from the dragon Persecution in Devonshire, England, and

---

JOHN ADAMS

1735 (Oct. 30) Born in Braintree (now Quincy), Mass.

1755 Graduated from Harvard College.

1758 Began practicing law.

1764 (Oct. 25) Married Abigail Smith.

1774-1777 Delegate from Massachusetts to the Continental Congress; helped write and signed the Declaration of Independence.

1777-1779 Served as U.S. diplomat in France.

1779 Wrote new constitution for the state of Massachusetts.

1780-1785 Served in Europe as diplomatic representative for the Continental Congress and as a member of the commission that negotiated peace with Great Britain.

1785-1788 U.S. minister to Great Britain.

1789-1797 First Vice-President of the United States.

1797-1801 Second President of the United States.

1820 Helped write a new constitution for the state of Massachusetts; served as a presidential elector, voting for President Monroe.

1826 (July 4) Died in Quincy on the 50th anniversary of the adoption of the Declaration of Independence.

alighted with eight sons near Mount Wollaston." John Adams also counted among his ancestors John Alden of the Pilgrim band who landed at Plymouth Rock from the *Mayflower*.

John Adams' father, whose name also was John Adams, was a small farmer who supplemented his income by making shoes. His mother was Susanna Boylston Adams, daughter of a prominent Massachusetts family. The elder John Adams believed strongly in education, having himself been a graduate of Harvard College. Although not particularly well-to-do, he was determined that John, his eldest son, should have the best education possible, so when John was 16, he was enrolled at Harvard. Four years later he was graduated, ranking as one of the best students in his class of twenty-four.

An Understanding Teacher

Learning of his reputation as a scholar, the citizens of Worcester, Mass., invited the young college graduate to come to be their schoolmaster. When Adams indicated his willingness to serve, they sent him a horse for transportation. Adams is said to have ridden the sixty miles to Worcester in a single day - a long, hard ride. His students apparently found him to be a kind and understanding teacher, for he wrote this in his diary:

"I find by repeated observation and experiment in my school, that human nature is more easily wrought upon and governed by promises and encouragement and praise, than by punishment and threatening and blame."

Shortly before his twentieth birthday in 1755, Adams wrote a letter that showed his depth of understanding of political science and his belief in the future potential of America. In it he said in part:

Divide et impera

"Soon after the reformation, a few people came over into this new world for conscience sake. Perhaps this apparently trivial incident may transfer the great seat of empire into America. It looks likely to me if we can remove the turbulent Gallics, our people, according to the exactest computations, will in another century become more numerous than England herself. Should this be the case, since we have, I may say, all the naval stores of the nations in our hands, it will be easy to obtain the mastery of the seas; and then the united force of all England will not be able to subdue us. The only way to keep us from setting up for our-

selves, is to disunite us. *Divide et impera*. Keep us in distinct colonies, and then some great men in each colony desiring the monarchy of the whole, they will destroy each other's influence, and keep the country in equilibrio."

After teaching for about a year, Adams decided that to improve himself he should become a lawyer. He moved into the home of James Putnam, a Worcester attorney, and in the hours that he was free from teaching he began to read all the law books that were available. Finally, after about two years of study, he was admitted to the bar in October, 1758, and began practicing law in Braintree.

Marriage at twenty-nine

A few days before Adams' twenty-ninth birthday, in October, 1764, he married nineteen-year-old Abigail Smith, the daughter of a clergyman. She was a witty, well-read girl. Their marriage was an especially happy one that lasted fifty-four years, until her death in 1818. They had five children, including John Quincy Adams who became the sixth President of the United States.

In 1765, the British parliament passed the infamous Stamp Act that taxed the American colonies to support the British occupation army in Massachusetts. Like many other colonists, Adams was dismayed by the act of British tyranny. Soon, he published in the *Boston Gazette* several essays under the formidable title "A Dissertation on the Canon and the Feudal Law." In these essays, he appealed to the people to oppose the act of parliament because lack of action by the people "has always prompted the princes and nobles of the earth, by every species of fraud and violence, to shake off all the limitations of their power."

Defending British Soldiers

The next year Adams moved his law office to Boston where he became more active in colonial politics and won a steadily improving reputation as a lawyer. Although the Stamp Act had been repealed, the feelings of the people of Boston had been rising against the presence of the British soldiers stationed in their midst. On March 5, 1770, the Boston Massacre occurred when a mob attacked a squad of British soldiers. The soldiers fired into the crowd, killing three persons and founding eight others, two of whom died later. Angry citizens demanded that the commander of the soldiers, a Captain Preston, and his men be

THE BOSTON TEA PARTY
"BOSTON HARBOR A TEAPOT TO-NIGHT! HURRA FOR GRIFFIN'S WHARF!"

tried for murder. Adams, who felt that the real criminals were the higher British authorities who had ordered the stationing of troops in Boston, volunteered with his friend Josiah Quincy to act as defense attorneys for the soldiers. The lawyer for the prosecution was Robert Treat Paine, the most prominent attorney in Massachusetts and an ardent patriot. It is testimony to the eloquence and legal abilities of Adams and Quincy that they won the acquittal of Captain Preston and all but two of his soldiers—these two being convicted of the lesser charge of manslaughter and released with little more than a reprimand. The case did not hurt Adams' popularity, for shortly after he was elected to the Massachusetts General Court (legislature). Recognizing that his election was but the first step in what was to be a long career of public service devoted to his country, Adams said of it, "I consider the step as a devotion of my family to ruin and myself to death."

Back to Braintree

The legislature spent most of its time in bitter arguments with the acting British governor. When Adams became ill, he resigned his seat in the legislature and moved back to Braintree. He did not give up his interest in the patriotic cause, however, and lent his writing skill to the Committee of Correspondence that his cousin Sam Adams had been instrumental in setting up to keep the fire of patriotism glowing throughout the colonies.

The Boston Tea Party

In December, 1773, a band of patriots egged on by Sam Adams dumped tea from British ships into Boston Harbor in protest against a parliamentary tax on tea. A few months later the British retaliated by closing the port of Boston to shipping —an act that in effect signed a death warrant for the city. As word of the British action spread throughout the colonies, patriotic indignation rose to a fever pitch and a meeting of colonial delegates was called to convene in Philadelphia in September, 1774.

John Adams was elected by the Massachusetts legislature as one of the colony's delegates to the first Continental Congress. He and the other Massachusetts delegates, including Samuel Adams, Robert Treat Paine, and Thomas Cushing, traveled together in one coach through Connecticut, New York, and New Jersey on the way to Philadelphia. Along the way, Adams, who already favored immediately declaring independence from Great Britain, was advised to restrain himself from calling for such drastic measures that might frighten the delegates from other colonies.

35

First Meeting with Washington and Patrick Henry

At the Congress, Adams met for the first time most of the notable men of the colonies, including Washington and Patrick Henry. He cynically observed, however, that, "Every man is a great man, an orator, a critic, a statesman; and therefore every man, upon every question, must show his oratory, his criticism, and his political abilities." In his conferences with other delegates, Adams kept to himself his wishes for independence. When the Congress formed an association to boycott trade with Great Britain and wrote addresses to the British king and parliament appealing for a relaxation of controls on the colonies, Adams was sure that these mild measures would be ignored.

'After all, we must fight'

"When congress had finished their business, as they thought," Adams wrote years later, "in the autumn of 1774, I had with Mr. Henry, before we took leave of each other, some familiar conversation, in which I expressed a full conviction that our resolves, declaration of rights, enumeration of wrongs, petitions, remonstrances, and addresses, associations, and non-importation agreements, however they might be respected in America, and however necessary to cement the union of the colo-

nies, would be but waste water in England. Mr. Henry said, they might make some impression among the people of England, but agreed with me that they would be totally lost upon the government. I had but just received a short and hasty letter, written to me by Major Joseph Hawley of Northampton, containing 'a few broken hints,' as he called them, of what he thought was proper to be done, and concluding with these words, 'after all we must fight.' This letter I read to Mr. Henry, who listened with great attention; and as soon as I had pronounced the words, 'after all we must fight,' he raised his head, and with an energy and vehemence that I can never forget, broke out with, 'By G-d, I am of that man's mind.' I put the letter into his hand, and when he had read it he returned it to me, with an equally solemn asseveration that he agreed entirely in opinion with the writer.

'We shall carry all our points'

"The other delegates from Virginia returned to their state in full confidence, that all our grievances would be redressed. The last words that Mr. Richard Henry Lee said to me, when we parted, were, 'we shall infallibly carry all our points. You will be completely relieved; all the offensive acts will be repealed; the army and fleet will be re-

BOSTON COMMON AS A COW PASTURE, WITH THE GREAT ELM.

called, and Britain will give up her foolish project.'

"Washington only was in doubt. He never spoke in public. In private he joined with those who advocated a non-exportation, as well as a non-importation agreement. With both he thought we should prevail; without either he thought it doubtful. Henry was clear in one opinion, Richard Henry Lee in an opposite opinion, and Washington doubted between the two."

Returning home from the Congress in November, Adams again took up his pen in the cause of liberty. A series of articles had been appearing in the Boston newspapers signed "Massachusettensis" that argued for the supreme authority of the British parliament against the growing revolutionary movement. Adams retaliated in a series of essays signed with the name "Novanglus" that he later described as having "the effect of an antidote to the poison." The temper of the times, however, was demonstrated in the cautious tone of Adams' essays that avoided advocating outright independence while taking pains to remind the readers of the tragedy of the Boston Massacre and the necessity of the Boston Tea Party. These essays were interrupted by the clash of American minutemen and British redcoats at Lexington and Concord.

George Washington elected head of the army

The second Continental Congress gathered in a state of alarm in Philadelphia on May 10, 1775, and again Adams attended as a delegate from Massachusetts. For more than a month the delegates argued about what should be done. Finally, on June 14, the Congress decided to form a Continental Army and to ask Maryland, Pennsylvania, and Virginia to send soldiers to help the people of Massachusetts. That same day, John Adams proposed that to weld the forces of the colonies together a strong commander in chief was needed and that he felt that leader should be George Washington of Virginia. The nomination was seconded by Samuel Adams. The next day Congress unanimously elected Washington as head of the army.

In the ensuing months, Adams was active on many committees of the Congress. As he later wrote, "I was incessantly employed through the whole fall, winter, and spring of 1775 and 1776, in Congress during their sittings, and on committees in the mornings and evenings, and unquestionably did more business than any other member of the house." He also found time early in 1776 to publish his *Thoughts on Government* in which he outlined a model constitution for a state. In it he expressed the belief that the legislature should consist of two houses and that the chief executive should be a member of the legislature.

Adams promoted independence

All the while, Adams promoted the idea that it was necessary for the colonies to declare their complete independence from Great Britain. By the spring of 1776, a majority of members of the Congress were coming to the conclusion that it was unlikely that a reconciliation with Great Britain could be obtained. On May 6, 1776, Adams offered a resolution that each of the colonies should form its own independent government. Four days later the Congress passed a watered‚down version of the resolution. Then, on May 15, Adams proposed and won adoption of the strongest language yet used by Congress as a preamble to his previously passed resolution. The preamble said in part:

". . . it is necessary that the exercise of every kind of authority under the said crown should be totally surpressed, and all the powers of government exerted under the authority of the people of the colonies, for the preservation of internal peace, virtue and good order, as well as for the defense of their lives, liberties, and properties, against the hostile invasions and cruel depredations of their enemies."

Richard Henry Lee's resolution

Congress still was not ready to declare independence. The legislatures of Massachusetts and North Carolina already had declared their belief

Paul Revere

in independence, but the other colonies were slower to act. Then, on June 7, at the request of the Virginia assembly, Richard Henry Lee presented his famous resolution that said in part "That these United Colonies are, and of right ought to be, free and independent States . . ." Adams quickly seconded the resolution. The delegates from Pennsylvania, New York, and South Carolina, however, opposed the resolution because their colonial assemblies had not yet taken a stand for independence. So the Congress postponed further discussion until July 1.

By now it was evident that independence would be declared, so a committee was appointed to draft the announcement that eventually would be made public. Adams was appointed to this committee to draft the Declaration of Independence, but he deferred to his younger colleague Thomas Jefferson the actual task of writing the document. Adams lent his advice in making certain changes in the draft before it was presented to Congress, but his more important role was in exerting increasing pressure on some of the more reluctant delegates to accept the idea of independence.

Adams led the debate

When debate on Lee's resolution for independence was resumed on July 1, Adams took a leading part in the arguments. Thomas Jefferson described Adams' role as "our Colossus on the floor; not graceful, not elegant, not always fluent in his public addresses, he yet came out with a power both of thought and of expression that moved us from our seats." When Congress voted approval of Lee's resolution on July 2, Adams was overwhelmed with joy. He wrote to his wife:

"Yesterday the greatest question was decided, that was ever debated in America; and greater, perhaps, never was or will be decided among men. A resolution was passed, without one dissenting colony, 'that these united colonies are, and of right ought to be, free and independent states.' The day is passed. The second day of July, 1776, will be the most memorable epocha in the history of America. I am apt to believe that it will be celebrated by succeeding generations as the great Anniversary Festival. It ought to be commemorated, as the day of deliverance, by solemn acts of devotion to God Almighty. It ought to be solemnized with pomp and parade, with shows, games, sports, guns, bells, bonfires and illuminations, from one end of this continent to the other, from this time forward, forevermore. You will think me transported with enthusiasm, but I am not. I am well aware of the toil, and blood, and treasure, that it will cost to maintain this declaration, and support and defend these states; yet, through all the gloom, I can see the rays of light and glory. I can see that the end is worth more than all the means; and that posterity will triumph, although you and I may rue, which I hope we shall not."

The Fourth of July

The passage of the Declaration of Independence two days later on July 4, 1776, was anti-climactic to Adams. The important thing to him was the fact that independence had been declared without a single colony dissenting, although the New York delegates had abstained from the vote.

Shortly after the disastrous battle of Long Island had been lost by Washington's troops in August, 1776, the British commander, Lord Howe, sent word to Congress that he would like to discuss peace. Although Adams opposed any such discussion, the Congress appointed him, along with Benjamin Franklin and Edward Rutledge, as a committee of negotiators to visit Howe. They traveled to British headquarters on Staten Island, N.Y., and there Howe told them he was not authorized to negotiate with an official committee of Congress, but that he preferred to consider that they were private gentlemen who might use their influence to bring peace in the colonies. "You may view me in any light you please," answered the forthright Adams, "except in that of a British subject." As Adams had expected, Howe offered no concessions for peace and asked that the colonists reaffirm their allegiance to the British king and parliament.

For the remainder of 1776 and throughout 1777, Adams worked tirelessly on the affairs of Congress. He was a member of ninety different committees, and was chairman of twenty-five. His most important assignment was as chairman of the Board of War and Ordnance, a position relative to a modern-day Secretary of Defense. Adams' responsibilities became particularly arduous because as the war went on, fewer and fewer members of the Congress were willing to stay away from their homes. At times the number of delegates in session dropped to as few as twenty or twenty-one.

Establishing Old Glory

One of Adams' most lasting contributions in Congress came on June 14, 1777, when he intro-

In CONGRESS, July 4, 1776.

A DECLARATION

By the REPRESENTATIVES of the

UNITED STATES OF AMERICA,

In GENERAL CONGRESS ASSEMBLED.

WHEN in the Courfe of human Events, it becomes neceffary for one People to diffolve the Political Bands which have connected them with another, and to affume among the Powers of the Earth, the feparate and equal Station to which the Laws of Nature and of Nature's God entitle them, a decent Refpect to the Opinions of Mankind requires that they fhould declare the caufes which impel them to the Separation.

We hold thefe Truths to be felf-evident, that all Men are created equal, that they are endowed by their Creator with certain unalienable Rights, that among thefe are Life, Liberty, and the Purfuit of Happinefs—That to fecure thefe Rights, Governments are inftituted among Men, deriving their juft Powers from the Confent of the Governed, that whenever any Form of Government becomes deftructive of thefe Ends, it is the Right of the People to alter or to abolifh it, and to inftitute new Government, laying its Foundation on fuch Principles, and organizing its Powers in fuch Form, as to them fhall feem moft likely to effect their Safety and Happinefs. Prudence, indeed, will dictate that Governments long eftablifhed fhould not be changed for light and tranfient Caufes; and accordingly all Experience hath fhewn, that Mankind are more difpofed to fuffer, while Evils are fufferable, than to right themfelves by abolifhing the Forms to which they are accuftomed. But when a long Train of Abufes and Ufurpations, purfuing invariably the fame Object, evinces a Defign to reduce them under abfolute Defpotifm, it is their Right, it is their Duty, to throw off fuch Government, and to provide new Guards for their future Security. Such has been the patient Sufferance of thefe Colonies; and fuch is now the Neceffity which conftrains them to alter their former Syftems of Government. The Hiftory of the prefent King of Great-Britain is a Hiftory of repeated Injuries and Ufurpations, all having in direct Object the Eftablifhment of an abfolute Tyranny over thefe States. To prove this, let Facts be fubmitted to a candid World.

He has refufed his Affent to Laws, the moft wholefome and neceffary for the public Good.

He has forbidden his Governors to pafs Laws of immediate and preffing Importance, unlefs fufpended in their Operation till his Affent fhould be obtained; and when fo fufpended, he has utterly neglected to attend to them.

He has refufed to pafs other Laws for the Accommodation of large Diftricts of People, unlefs thofe People would relinquifh the Right of Reprefentation in the Legiflature, a Right ineftimable to them, and formidable to Tyrants only.

He has called together Legiflative Bodies at Places unufual, uncomfortable, and diftant from the Depofitory of their public Records, for the fole Purpofe of fatiguing them into Compliance with his Meafures.

He has diffolved Reprefentative Houfes repeatedly, for oppofing with manly Firmnefs his Invafions on the Rights of the People.

He has refufed for a long Time, after fuch Diffolutions, to caufe others to be elected; whereby the Legiflative Powers, incapable of Annihilation, have returned to the People at large for their exercife; the State remaining in the mean time expofed to all the Dangers of Invafion from without, and Convulfions within.

He has endeavoured to prevent the Population of thefe States; for that Purpofe obftructing the Laws for Naturalization of Foreigners; refufing to pafs others to encourage their Migrations hither, and raifing the Conditions of new Appropriations of Lands.

He has obftructed the Adminiftration of Juftice, by refufing his Affent to Laws for eftablifhing Judiciary Powers.

He has made Judges dependent on his Will alone, for the Tenure of their Offices, and the Amount and Payment of their Salaries.

He has erected a Multitude of new Offices, and fent hither Swarms of Officers to harrafs our People, and eat out their Subftance.

He has kept among us, in Times of Peace, Standing Armies, without the confent of our Legiflatures.

He has affected to render the Military independent of and fuperior to the Civil Power.

He has combined with others to fubject us to a Jurifdiction foreign to our Conftitution, and unacknowledged by our Laws; giving his Affent to their Acts of pretended Legiflation:

For quartering large Bodies of Armed Troops among us:

For protecting them, by a mock Trial, from Punifhment for any Murders which they fhould commit on the Inhabitants of thefe States:

For cutting off our Trade with all Parts of the World:

For impofing Taxes on us without our Confent:

For depriving us, in many Cafes, of the Benefits of Trial by Jury:

For transporting us beyond Seas to be tried for pretended Offences:

For abolifhing the free Syftem of Englifh Laws in a neighbouring Province, eftablifhing therein an arbitrary Government, and enlarging its Boundaries, fo as to render it at once an Example and fit Inftrument for introducing the fame abfolute Rule into thefe Colonies:

For taking away our Charters, abolifhing our moft valuable Laws, and altering fundamentally the Forms of our Governments:

For fufpending our own Legiflatures, and declaring themfelves invefted with Power to legiflate for us in all Cafes whatfoever.

He has abdicated Government here, by declaring us out of his Protection and waging War againft us.

He has plundered our Seas, ravaged our Coafts, burnt our Towns, and deftroyed the Lives of our People.

He is, at this Time, transporting large Armies of foreign Mercenaries to compleat the Works of Death, Defolation, and Tyranny, already begun with circumftances of Cruelty and Perfidy, fcarcely paralleled in the moft barbarous Ages, and totally unworthy the Head of a civilized Nation.

He has conftrained our fellow Citizens taken Captive on the high Seas to bear Arms againft their Country, to become the Executioners of their Friends and Brethren, or to fall themfelves by their Hands.

He has excited domeftic Infurrections amongft us, and has endeavoured to bring on the Inhabitants of our Frontiers, the mercilefs Indian Savages, whofe known Rule of Warfare, is an undiftinguifhed Deftruction, of all Ages, Sexes and Conditions.

In every ftage of thefe Oppreffions we have Petitioned for Redrefs in the moft humble Terms: Our repeated Petitions have been anfwered only by repeated Injury. A Prince, whofe Character is thus marked by every act which may define a Tyrant, is unfit to be the Ruler of a free People.

Nor have we been wanting in Attentions to our Britifh Brethren. We have warned them from Time to Time of Attempts by their Legiflature to extend an unwarrantable Jurifdiction over us. We have reminded them of the Circumftances of our Emigration and Settlement here. We have appealed to their native Juftice and Magnanimity, and we have conjured them by the Ties of our common Kindred to difavow thefe Ufurpations, which, would inevitably interrupt our Connections and Correfpondence. They too have been deaf to the Voice of Juftice and of Confanguinity. We muft, therefore, acquiefce in the Neceffity, which denounces our Separation, and hold them, as we hold the reft of Mankind, Enemies in War, in Peace, Friends.

We, therefore, the Reprefentatives of the UNITED STATES OF AMERICA, in GENERAL CONGRESS, Affembled, appealing to the Supreme Judge of the World for the Rectitude of our Intentions, do, in the Name, and by Authority of the good People of thefe Colonies, folemnly Publifh and Declare, That thefe United Colonies are, and of Right ought to be, FREE AND INDEPENDENT STATES; that they are abfolved from all Allegiance to the Britifh Crown, and that all political Connection between them and the State of Great-Britain, is and ought to be totally diffolved; and that as FREE AND INDEPENDENT STATES, they have full Power to levy War, conclude Peace, contract Alliances, eftablifh Commerce, and to do all other Acts and Things which INDEPENDENT STATES may of right do. And for the fupport of this Declaration, with a firm Reliance on the Protection of divine Providence, we mutually pledge to each other our Lives, our Fortunes, and our facred Honor.

Signed by ORDER and in BEHALF of the CONGRESS,

JOHN HANCOCK, PRESIDENT.

ATTEST.
CHARLES THOMSON, SECRETARY.

PHILADELPHIA: PRINTED BY JOHN DUNLAP.

The Manner in which the American Colonies Declared themselves Independent
of the King of England, throughout the different provinces, on July 4, 1776.
Library of Congress

cessful in negotiating a treaty of alliance and a treaty of friendship and trade. Soon friction began to develop among the three commissioners because of their overlapping responsibilities, so Adams recommended to Congress that some division of duties be established. Congress responded by appointing Franklin as minister to France and Lee as minister to Spain. Adams, left without an assignment, returned to the United States in August, 1779.

A delegate to the Massachusetts convention

Within a week after his return home, the citizens of Braintree elected Adams as their delegate to a Massachusetts state constitutional convention. Adams was appointed to the committee to prepare a draft of the constitution, and proceeded to do most of the work himself. Many of the features of the constitution he wrote, including its detailed bill of rights, were later adopted by other states.

Adams' work on the Massachusetts constitution was interrupted by a new appointment from Congress. Benjamin Franklin had sent word from Paris that he had been contacted by a member of the British government who indicated the British were ready to negotiate peace, so Congress appointed Adams as "minister plenipotentiary for negotiating a treaty of peace and a treaty of commerce with Great Britain." He set sail for France in October, taking with him his two oldest sons, John Quincy and Charles. Their ship sprang a leak and was forced to put into port in Spain. From there the Adamses had to travel across Europe by land, finally reaching Paris in February, 1780. Meanwhile, the British had lost interest in discussing peace, having become more confident they would finally beat Washington's army.

Negotiations with the Dutch

Adams did not remain idle. The British had captured an American envoy, Henry Laurens, who was enroute to negotiate a loan from the Netherlands, so Adams was appointed to carry out this mission. For nearly two years Adams carried on negotiations with the cautious people of the Netherlands. In order to win popular support, Adams wrote many articles about the American cause and had them published in the Dutch newspapers. At the height of the negotiations, in the summer of 1781, he became seriously ill with typhus fever. But he recovered and went on to conclude successfully the matter in October, 1782, by achieving

An American Rifleman

duced the following resolution that was passed unanimously:

"Resolved, that the flag of the thirteen United States shall be thirteen stripes, alternate red and white; that the union be thirteen stars, white on a blue field, representing a new constellation."

Late in 1777, Adams was appointed by Congress to join Benjamin Franklin and Arthur Lee in Paris to negotiate for aid from France. He set sail from Boston in February, 1778, taking with him his son, John Quincy Adams, then a boy of 10. When Adams arrived in France six weeks later, he discovered that Franklin already had been suc-

full recognition of the independence of the United States by the Netherlands. The Netherlands signed treaties of friendship and trade, and, even more important, agreed to loan the United States eight million guilders to help carry on the war with Britain.

Adams' successful discussions with the Dutch apparently quickened British interest in a peace treaty, for now the British government appointed agents to negotiate in earnest. Adams returned to Paris where he joined Jay, Franklin, and Laurens, all three of whom had been appointed with Adams as peace commissioners. The negotiations moved swiftly; and on November 30, 1782, a provisional peace treaty with the British was signed. However, nine more months went by before a final peace treaty was concluded on September 3, 1783. Throughout the efforts to negotiate a peace treaty with the British, Adams had difficulties with the French government, which repeatedly tried to manipulate the talks in such a way that the interests of France might best be served regardless of American interests. As a result, Adams formed a wariness of French diplomacy that surely colored his thinking almost twenty years later when as President he nearly led the United States into war with France.

George III recognizes American independence

A few days after signing the historic peace treaty with Great Britain, Adams again fell ill with fever. In an effort to regain his health, he visited England. There, while attending a meeting of parliament, he had the satisfaction of hearing King George III announce Britain's recognition of American independence.

Congress next asked Adams to return to the Netherlands to negotiate another loan, and followed that assignment by appointing him with Franklin and Thomas Jefferson to conclude trade treaties with other European powers. For the rest of 1784, Adams lived in Paris, where he was joined by Mrs. Adams.

In 1785, Congress appointed Adams as America's first minister to Great Britain — an office that was to keep him abroad for three more years during the critical period while the United States Constitution was being written and debated. Adams and his family took up residence in England in May, 1785. His report on his first reception by the British king illuminates his character and his abilities as a diplomat:

The manner in which the American Colonies declared themselves independent of the King of England, July 4, 1776.

Conversation with George III

"The king then asked me, whether I came last from France? and upon my answering in the affirmative, he put on an air of familiarity, and smiling, or rather laughing, said, 'there is an opinion among some people that you are not the most attached of all your countrymen to the manners of France.' I was surprised at this, because I thought it an indiscretion, and a descent from his dignity. I was a little embarrassed, but determined not to deny the truth on one hand, nor leave him to infer from it any attachment to England on the other, I threw off as much gravity as I could, and assumed an air of gaiety, and a tone of decision, as far as it was decent, and said, — 'that opinion sir is not mistaken; I must avow to your majesty I have no attachment but to my own country.' The king replied, as quick as lightning, ' an honest man will never have any other.' "

Although he was received in a friendly fashion in England, the British government was not interested in seriously discussing an American trade treaty with Adams. To keep himself busy, and to reply to criticisms of American government being made by French philosophers, Adams wrote a

41

three-volume work entitled *The Defence of the Constitutions of Government of the United States of America*. In it he upheld the American use of constitutional authority to establish a balance of power between the executive, legislative, and judicial branches of government. Tiring of his long stay in Europe, Adams asked Congress to relieve him of his diplomatic duties. He returned home in June, 1788, just as the ninth state ratified the United States Constitution, enabling it to become effective.

Vice-President by a narrow margin

Adams soon was swept up in discussions about the forthcoming selection for President and Vice-President of the United States. It was a foregone conclusion that George Washington should be elected President, but Adams' friends in New England were equally determined that Adams should be elected Vice-President. Washington let it be known that he was pleased with the suggestion of Adams for Vice-President. When the votes of the presidential electors were counted in February, 1789, Washington won the Presidency unanimously; but Adams won office as Vice-President with only 34 of the 69 votes that were cast, the other votes being split among several candidates.

Upon his election, Adams observed wryly, "My country has in its wisdom contrived for me the most insignificant office that ever the invention of man contrived or his imagination conceived."

As Vice-President, Adams presided over the Senate, casting his tie-breaking vote in support of Washington's policies. He gave his advice to Washington when it was asked, but he tried to stand apart from the controversies that were building up between Hamilton, the head of the Federalist party, and Jefferson, the head of the Anti-Federalists. In 1790, he published a series of articles called "Discourses on Davilia" in which he supported the principle of government with a single executive and a two-house legislature as opposed to a government with a plural executive and a single-house legislature. At that time, the French Revolution was underway and the Anti-Federalists, who strongly supported the French Revolution, interpreted Adams' articles as favoring the French monarchy against the French revolutionists.

Opposition by the Anti-Federalists

As the elections of 1792 approached, Washington seemed sure to win unanimous approval as

Market Square, Newburyport, Massachusetts, 1800.

Essex Institute Collection

President, so the contest between the Federalists and the Anti-Federalists was waged for the office of Vice-President. Adams was supported by the Federalists, and Governor George Clinton of New York was the choice of the Anti-Federalists. The pre-election campaigning gave some hint of future party politics in the United States as the Anti-Federalist newspapers ridiculed Adams for his "breadth of belly" and hinted that he favored setting up a monarchy in America. When the electoral votes were counted in February, 1793, Washington won unanimously, and Adams was re-elected with 77 votes to Clinton's 50.

During the second administration of Washington and Adams, rivalry continued to mount between Hamilton's Federalist party and Jefferson's Anti-Federalist Party. Adams, who tried to maintain neutrality between Secretary of the Treasury Hamilton and Secretary of State Jefferson, was described by Jefferson "as disinterested as the Being Who made him." Bickering within the cabinet subsided when both Hamilton and Jefferson resigned and returned to private life.

Adams versus Jefferson

When Washington indicated that he was through with public office by publishing his *Farewell Address* in September, 1796, an election campaign began in earnest. The Federalists decided to support Adams for President, and the Anti-Federalists chose Jefferson. The Anti-Federalist newspapers again attacked Adams as favoring monarchy. The Federalist newspapers labeled Jefferson as an atheist. The vote in the electoral college was very close. Adams received 71 electoral votes, only three more votes than Jefferson's 68. As a result, under the rules then in effect, Adams became President, and Jefferson became, Vice-President.

Jefferson had refused to take part in personal attacks on Adams during the campaign, and at the outset of the new administration he lauded Adams in an address to the Senate, saying that Adams was a man "whose talents and integrity have been known and revered by me through a long course of years; have been the foundation of a cordial and uninterrupted friendship between us; and I devoutly pray that he may be long preserved for the government, the happiness and prosperity of our country."

'Ay! I am fairly out and you fairly in.'

Adams described his own inauguration as President in a letter to his wife, who was unable to attend. "A solemn scene it was indeed," Adams wrote, "and it was made affecting to me by the presence of the General (Washington), whose countenance was as serene and unclouded as the day. He seemed to me to enjoy a triumph over me. Methought I heard him say, 'Ay! I am fairly out and you fairly in! See which of us will be the happiest!'"

Adams' administration was plunged into difficulties from the start. England was at war with France, and both nations wanted to draw the United States into war on their own side. Hamilton's Federalists were violently opposed to the leaders of France, who had overthrown the French king and established a revolutionary government. On the other hand, Jefferson's Anti-Federalists were sympathetic to the French cause, overlooking the bloody Reign of Terror imposed by the French revolutionists. Adams, caught in the middle, wanted to avoid war, and as a result pleased neither side.

Problems of the Presidency

James Madison wrote to Jefferson in 1799 a devastating comparison of Adams with Washington: "There never was perhaps a greater contrast between two characters than between those of the present President and his predecessor . . .The one cool, considerate and cautious, the other headlong and kindled into flame by every spark that lights on his passions; the one ever scrutinizing into the public opinion, and ready to follow where he could not lead it; the other insulting it by the most adverse sentiments and pursuits. Washington a hero in the field, yet overweighing every danger in the Cabinet—Adams with a single pretension to the character of a soldier, a perfect Quixotte as a statesman; the former Chief Magistrate pursuing peace everywhere with sincerity, though mistaking the means; the latter taking as much pains to get into wars, as the former took to keep out of it . . ."

It is particularly interesting to note that while Adams managed to avoid war, Madison as President thirteen years later did plunge the nation into the War of 1812.

Department of the Navy established

Adams advocated strong military preparedness. Under his urging, a Department of the Navy was established, and the construction of warships was begun-one of them being the famous *Constitution*

Abigail Adams *by* RALPH EARL

that became known as "Old Ironsides." Washington was asked to take command of the army and prepare it for war. Because French sympathizers continued to pile abuses on the President and the government, the Congress passed the Alien Act by which the President could deport or imprison any foreigner, and the Sedition Act under which it became a crime to criticize the President, the Congress, or the government. Several Anti-Federalist newspapermen were arrested and sent to jail under the Sedition Act. These acts increased Adams' unpopularity.

"From the day when he took his seat as President of the Senate," John Quincy Adams later wrote of his father, "until that when his administration expired, he was assailed with unappeasable virulence; nor did it even cease with his retirement to private life."

Defeat by Jefferson and Burr

In the election of 1800, the Federalists were split. Hamilton had urged Adams to go to war against France, and, when Adams refused, Hamilton withdrew his support for Adams' re-election.

When the electoral votes were counted, Adams had lost by eight votes. Jefferson and his running-mate Aaron Burr each received 73 electoral votes, while Adams received 65. Because Jefferson and Burr had tied, the election had to be decided in the House of Representatives, which awarded the office of President to Jefferson and that of Vice-President to Burr.

Adams was so disappointed at his defeat, and so bitter at Jefferson for the partisan attacks that had been made on him during the election campaign, that he refused to attend the inauguration of the new President on March 4, 1801. Instead, he hurried home to Quincy, Mass., where he spent most of the last twenty-five years of his life in quiet retirement. After Jefferson completed his administration as President, a mutual acquaintance healed the differences between the two old patriots, and in the last years of their lives they carried on a friendly correspondence.

A vote for James Monroe

With his increasing age, Adams' health declined, although he remained clear of mind. In 1818, his wife, Abigail died, ending a marriage of fifty-four years. Two years later, at the age of 85, Adams was honored by being chosen one of the presidential electors for the state of Massachusetts, and he cast his vote for President James Monroe, the last President to run for office without opposition. That same year Adams was unanimously elected president of a Massachusetts constitutional convention to revise the state constitution he had largely written forty years earlier. He declined the office because of his age, but attended the convention as a member and took some part in the debates. Five years later, in 1825, he was overjoyed to see his oldest son, John Quincy Adams, become the sixth President of the United States.

"Independence forever!"

A few days before Adams' death, the orator who was to speak at the Fourth of July banquet in Quincy asked him what toast should be proposed at the celebration, and Adams replied, "Independence forever!" On July 4, 1826, Adams, feeling himself slipping into death, spoke his last words, "Thomas Jefferson still survives." But, by a remarkable coincidence, Jefferson, too, died that day. Thus, the two patriots who were most responsible for the Declaration of Independence died on the fiftieth anniversary of its adoption.

Home of John Adams (1828)

New Bedford, Massachusetts

SAMUEL ADAMS of MASSACHUSETTS

More than any other of the Founding Fathers, Samuel Adams most deserves the title "Father of the Revolution." His agitation, his plots, and his patriotic speeches fanned the flame of liberty in Massachusetts in the 1770's. A leader of the revolutionary Sons of Liberty, his inflammatory oratory led to the Boston Massacre and the Boston Tea Party that brought on the Revolutionary War. British soldiers were hunting Adams and his fellow patriot John Hancock to arrest them for treason when the redcoats first clashed with American minutemen at Lexington and Concord on the fateful day of April 19, 1775—described by Adams as "a glorious day for America!"

A man of medium height, Sam Adams had the upbringing and deep religious convictions of a Puritan. He had steel-gray eyes, and in his portraits his face appears severe; but his friends regarded him as a genial companion. The evidence is indisputable that he knew how to get along with other people, and he perhaps can best be described as the popular "political boss" of Boston of his time. His forte was in moulding opinion in a backroom meeting or in haranguing a street mob.

A man of moderate means

Once the Revolutionary War had begun, Adams served as a delegate from Massachusetts in the Continental Congress until the fighting was nearly over. In Congress, he seconded the nomination of George Washington as commander in chief of the armies, and he signed the Declaration of Independence; but he was a local politician at heart and never became particularly effective on the national scene. A friend said of him: "Samuel Adams would have the state of Massachusetts govern the union, the town of Boston govern Massachusetts, and that he should govern the town of Boston, and then the whole would not be intentionally ill-governed." At the end of the war, Adams returned to Massachusetts politics. He served in succession as a state senator, lieutenant governor, and then as governor. Throughout his life, Adams did not seek nor did he win wealth, finally and, died in poverty at the age of 81.

Samuel Adams was born in Boston on September 27, 1722. His father, also named Samuel Adams, was a businessman who served for many years as a representative of the town of Boston in the colonial legislature. Young Sam received a classical education at Boston Latin school, and entered Harvard College at the age of fourteen. He received his bachelor's degree in 1740, and went on to acquire a master's degree in 1743. His father's participation in politics must have influenced him to an early interest in political science. He gave evidence of already leaning toward becoming a revolutionary by choosing as the topic for his master's thesis: "Whether it be lawful to resist the supreme magistrate, if the commonwealth cannot be otherwise preserved?" While he was a student, he also saved enough money from his allowance to pay for the publishing of a pamphlet he wrote called "Englishmen's Rights."

Introduction to politics

Adams had planned to become a minister but his father wanted him to be a lawyer, and his mother wanted him to go into business. His mother won out, so he was apprenticed as a clerk to Thomas Cushing, a prominent Boston merchant. Being more interested in politics than business, he formed a club of young men who wrote political essays for the Boston *Independent Advertiser* and he spent no more time than was necessary learning to be a clerk.

SAMUEL ADAMS

1722 (Sept. 27) Born in Boston.
1740 Graduated from Harvard College.
1743 Received Master's Degree from Harvard.
1756 Elected as a tax collector in Boston.
1765-1774 Member and clerk of the Massachusetts legislature.
1770 His patriotic agitation brought about the Boston Massacre.
1772 On his motion, the Boston town meeting established a Committee of Correspondence.
1773 Instigated the Boston Tea Party.
1774-1781 Member of the Continental Congress.
1779 Helped write the Massachusetts state constitution.
1781-1788 President of the Massachusetts senate.
1789-1793 Lieutenant governor of Massachusetts.
1794-1797 Governor of Massachusetts.
1803 (Oct. 2) Died in Boston.

THE EVACUATION OF BOSTON

An unsuccessful businessman

When Adams was twenty-five, his father died, leaving him to manage the family's money affairs. Through lack of interest and poor judgment in business matters, the money from his father's estate was used up within a few years. His father's friends then helped him earn a living by getting him various minor political jobs. About this time, he married Elizabeth Checkley, an understanding woman who managed to provide their son and daughter with necessities out of her husband's meager income. After her death, Adams married for a second time to Elizabeth Wells.

Picking the candidates

In 1756, Adams was elected to the thankless job of tax collector. In this new position he learned more of the ins-and-outs of politics and became a member of the powerful Caucus Club that ran Boston's government from behind the scenes. In 1763, John Adams, the future President of the United States, wrote this concerning his cousin Sam's membership in the Caucus Club: ". . . the whole club meets in one room. There they smoke tobacco till you cannot see from one end of the garret to the other. There they drink flip, I suppose, and there they choose a moderator, who puts questions to the vote regularly; and select-men, assessors, collectors, wardens, fire-wards and representatives, are regularly chosen before they are chosen in the town."

Samuel Adams first came into real prominence at the age of 41 when the Boston town meeting appointed him in May, 1764, to write instructions to their representatives in the legislature as to the position they should take in regard to the British Stamp Act. The document that Adams prepared is believed to be the first which questioned the right of the British parliament to tax the colonies without their consent. He also suggested the need for a meeting of representatives of all the colonies to decide on a united course of action—a suggestion that eventually resulted in the meeting of the Stamp Act Congress in New York in 1765.

Sons of Liberty

Adams became a leading spirit in the Sons of Liberty, a secret patriotic society that agitated against British oppression. This club was believed responsible for the hanging in effigy of the British stamp tax collector, and for encouraging a mob to storm the acting governor's home to destroy his books and papers.

In 1765, the people of Boston elected Adams as one of their representatives in the colonial legislature. Soon after, the representatives elected him clerk of the assembly, a position that gave him a hand in writing every report and a seat on every committee. He held this office until the beginning of the Revolutionary War, becoming the most influential man in Massachusetts politics.

The quartering of British troops in Boston as an army of occupation in the late 1760's was bitterly opposed by Adams. He helped rouse the people to such a fever pitch against the British troops that a mob attacked a squad of redcoats and precipitated the Boston Massacre of March 5, 1770.

47

The fable of the field-mouse

A story is told that illustrates Adams' means of inspiring a crowd. At a Boston meeting, Adams listened to speaker after speaker discuss the problems that were faced, with each speaker carefully avoiding any remark that might be considered treasonous. Finally, Adams in disgust rose and told this fable:

"A Grecian philosopher who was lying asleep on the grass was suddenly roused by the bite of some animal on the palm of his hand. He closed his hand suddenly as he awoke, and found that he had caught in it a small field-mouse. As he was examining the little animal which had dared to attack him, it bit him unexpectedly, a second time; he dropped it, and it made its escape. Now, fellow citizens, what think you was the reflection which this trifling circumstance gave birth to in the mind of the philosopher? It was this: that there is no animal, however weak and contemptible, which cannot defend its own liberty, if it will only fight for it."

After the bloodshed of the "Boston Massacre," Adams was elected by a town meeting to go to Acting-Governor Thomas Hutchinson and demand the withdrawal of British troops from Boston. In the meeting with Adams, Hutchinson at first denied that he had the authority to remove the troops, then, weakening a little, he agreed to remove one of the two regiments quartered in the town. Adams replied angrily that if Hutchinson had the power to remove one regiment then he obviously had the power to remove both, and that unless this were done immediately he alone "must be answerable for the fatal consequences that would ensue." At this, Hutchinson gave in to the demand, and ordered the two regiments withdrawn to a fort in the harbor. This act, of course, greatly boosted Adams' prestige and at the same time lowered that of the acting governor.

For several years Adams had advocated the need for establishing committees of correspondence in the various colonies to keep in touch with each other on patriotic affairs. Now, in 1772, he succeeded in having a motion passed by the Boston town meeting setting up such a committee. In rapid succession, similar committees were formed in other colonies, providing the communications network that was essential for united action in the revolutionary cause.

The "Boston Tea Party"

In 1773, the British granting of a monopoly on the sale of tea in the colonies to the British East India Company and their insistence on the payment by the colonists of a tax on tea, brought new outcries of rage from the Sons of Liberty. On the evening of December 16, 1773, Adams gathered a crowd on the Boston waterfront to protest the arrival of British tea ships. At Adams' urging, a band of patriots went aboard the ships and dumped several hundred chests of tea into the harbor.

When word of the "Boston Tea Party" reached England, the British parliament reacted angrily. The Coercive Acts passed by parliament early in 1774 ordered Boston harbor closed to shipping until the town paid damages for the tea that had been destroyed by the patriots. The colonial legislature also was ordered to meet in Salem, Mass., and Massachusetts' powers of self-government were reduced. Lt. Gen. Thomas Gage, commander-in-chief of British military forces in North America, was ordered to go to Boston as governor.

Elected as delegate to Continental Congress

At the urging of Samuel Adams, the Massachusetts legislature on June 17, 1774, took up the question of appointing delegates to attend a meeting in Philadelphia with representatives of other colonies. As a precaution against interference by the British, Adams locked the door to the assembly hall and kept the key in his pocket. Governor Gage, learning of what was going on in the legislature, sent his secretary with an order dissolving the assembly; but, finding the door locked, the governor's secretary was forced to read the order disbanding the legislature outside the locked door. Meanwhile, inside the hall, the representatives elected their delegates to the Continental Congress —one of whom was Samuel Adams. Then they obeyed the governor and dissolved.

Adams and the other Massachusetts delegates, including his cousin John Adams, were present when the Continental Congress began meeting in Philadelphia on September 5, 1774. Samuel Adams demonstrated his deep belief in tolerance on the second day of the meeting, when the delegates deadlocked over the question of which faith should provide religious guidance for the Congress. Although he was a Puritan, Adams rose, and, in the words of a contemporary account, said, "that he was no bigot, and could hear a prayer from a gentleman of piety and virtue who was, at

SAMUEL ADAMS
Painting by John Singleton Copley

Village of Salem

Showing town square with brick schoolhouse and whipping post

the same time, a friend to his country. He was a stranger in Philadelphia, but he had heard that Mr. Duché (Reverend Jacob Duché) deserved that character, and therefore he moved that Mr. Duché, an Episcopal clergyman, might be desired to read prayers to the Congress tomorrow morning." Adams's motion was accepted, and the next day the clergyman was present, reading the militant Thirty-fifth Psalm.

Patience and Unity

Although Adams was eager for prompt action by the colonies, he had also learned that patience was an important virtue. He demonstrated this in a letter he wrote after Congress had been in session for three weeks. In a letter to a Boston friend about the delegates, Adams said, "It becomes them to be deliberate. I have been assured, in private conversation with individuals, that, if you should be driven to the necessity of acting in the defence of your lives or liberty, you would be justified by their constituents, and openly supported by all the means in their power . . . It is of the greatest importance that the American opposition should be united, and that it should be conducted so as to concur with the opposition of our friends in England."

The Congress adjourned late in October after agreeing to set up a continental association to enforce a ban on imports, and to prepare to ban all exports, starting in September, 1775, if the British parliament refused to withdraw the Coercive Acts. Adams returned to Boston satisfied that the patriotic cause had been strengthened.

Governor Gage becomes desperate

As the situation worsened in Massachusetts, with the British confined to Boston as the patriots armed themselves, Governor Gage decided on a desperate move. Knowing the tremendous influence Adams had in the patriotic movement, but underestimating Adams's honesty and integrity, Gage sent a military aide, a Colonel Fenton, in an effort to bribe Adams to stop his patriotic agitation. Moreover, Fenton warned Adams that if he did not accept the offer, he could be arrested for treason and sent to England for trial. Adams listened with apparent interest, then made Fenton swear that he would deliver Adams' exact reply to Gage. Upon receiving this assurance, Adams is said to have answered Gage by saying:

"I trust I have long since made my peace with the King of Kings. No personal consideration shall induce me to abandon the righteous cause of my country. Tell Governor Gage, it is the advice of Samuel Adams to him, no longer to insult the feelings of an exasperated people."

Paul Revere's ride

Adams and John Hancock were at Lexington on the night of April 18, 1775, preparing to leave for the second meeting of the second Continental Congress. They were awakened about midnight by Paul Revere, who had ridden from Boston with word that British soldiers were on their way to arrest them both. Revere rode on, was captured by the British, escaped, and returned to join Adams and Hancock. Revere joined the two revolutionary leaders in a coach that carried them away from Lexington about dawn. Adams, knowing that the British were soon to be met by the fire of American minutemen, is said to have remarked, "This is a glorious day for America."

Adams worked diligently at the second session of the Continental Congress, that convened in Philadelphia in May, 1775. When John Adams nominated George Washington as commander-in-chief of an army for all the colonies, Samuel Adams seconded the nomination, which was approved unanimously the next day, June 15, 1775.

Congress had not yet received word of Gage's latest desperate move—one that insured Adams' fame throughout the world. Gage had issued a proclamation on June 12, 1775, acknowledging Adams's role of leadership in the revolution. It said in part:

"In this exigency of complicated calamities, I avail myself of the last efforts within the bounds of my duty to spare the further effusion of blood, to offer, and I do hereby in his majesty's name offer and promise, his most gracious pardon to all persons who shall forthwith lay down their arms, and return to the duties of peaceable subjects, excepting only from the benefit of such pardon, Samuel Adams and John Hancock, whose offences are of too flagitious a nature to admit of any other consideration than that of condign punishment."

Adams and Hancock led the cause

Looking back on this period some fifty years later, John Adams wrote of his cousin: "Mr. Adams was born and tempered a wedge of steel to split the knot of *lignum vitae* which tied North America to Great Britain. Blunderheaded as were the British ministry, they had sagacity enough to discriminate from all others, for inexorable venge-

Congress Voting Independence

ance, the two men most to be dreaded by them, Samuel Adams and John Hancock . . ."

In the months that followed, even the great patience of Adams began to wear thin as many of his fellow delegates continued to hope for a reconciliation with Great Britain and refused to recognize the need for declaring independence. In April, 1776, he wrote to a friend in Boston:

"I am perfectly satisfied of the necessity of a public and explicit declaration of independence. I cannot conceive what good reason can be assigned against it. Will it widen the breach? This would be a strange question after we have raised armies and fought battles with the British troops; set up an American navy, permitted the inhabitants of these colonies to fit out armed vessels to capture the ships, etc., belonging to any of the inhabitants of Great Britain; declaring them the enemies of the United Colonies, and torn into shivers their acts of trade, by allowing commerce, subject to regulations to be made by ourselves, with the people of all countries, except such as are subject to the British king. It cannot, surely, after all this, be imagined that we consider ourselves, or mean to be considered by others, in any other state than that of independence."

Months after the Declaration of Independence had been adopted and Adams had signed his name to it, he still expressed disappointment at the earlier procrastination of the members of Congress. He wrote on December 31, 1776:

"I assure you business has been done since we came to this place, more to my satisfaction than any or everything done before, excepting the 'Declaration of Independence,' which should have been made immediately after the 19th of April, 1775."

'Our cause is just and righteous'

In the autumn of 1777, when the fortunes of war were running at low ebb and the attendance at the Congress had fallen to fewer than thirty members, Adams's resolute courage helped hold the national government together. Hearing one of the other members of the Congress remark that the chances of success were "desperate," Adams is quoted as having said:

"If this be our language, it is so, indeed. If we wear long faces, they will become fashionable. The people take their tone from ours, and if we despair, can it be expected that they will continue their efforts in what we conceive to be a hopeless cause? Let us banish such feelings, and show a spirit that will keep alive the confidence of the people, rather than damp their courage. Better tidings will soon arrive. Our cause is just and righteous, and we shall never be abandoned by Heaven while we show ourselves worthy of its aid and protection."

With the firing of the first shots at Lexington and Concord, Samuel Adams had achieved the central purpose of his life. Although he continued in public office for many years, the rest of his life was an anticlimax. In 1779 he helped John Adams draw up a new constitution for the state of Massachusetts that served as a model for other states. Two years later, in 1781, he retired from Congress and became a member of the Massachusetts state senate, where he served as president of that body.

Demarking the Bill of Rights

Adams did not take part in the writing of the United States Constitution and led the opposition to its ratification in Massachusetts. He was elected as a member of the state ratification convention in 1787. Finally, when he obtained an agreement that the Constitution should be amended with the addition of a bill of rights, he accepted ratification, which was voted 187 to 168 by the convention.

Because of his Anti-Federalist views, Adams was defeated when he ran for election to the U.S. House of Representatives in 1788. The next year, and each year through 1793, Adams was elected lieutenant governor of Massachusetts. During this period he served under his old friend John Hancock, who annually was elected governor. With Hancock's death in 1793, Adams became acting governor. In the next year, 1794, he won election as governor and remained in that office through 1797, being elected each year. He continued to be a strong Anti-Federalist, supporting Thomas Jefferson against his cousin John Adams. In the presidential election of 1796, Virginia honored Sam Adams by casting its 15 electoral votes for him as Vice-President.

Adams retired from public life at the age of 76 and spent his last few years in ill-health and poverty. John Adams wrote of him in this period as "Sam Adams, a grief and distress to his family, a weeping, helpless object of compassion for years." After Samuel Adams' death on October 2, 1803, John Adams penned this eulogy:

"Without the character of Samuel Adams, the true history of the American Revolution can never be written. For fifty years his pen, his tongue, his activity, were constantly exerted for his country without fee or reward."

JOSIAH BARTLETT of NEW HAMPSHIRE

Josiah Bartlett, the first delegate to vote for adoption of the Declaration of Independence, successfully combined three careers—physician, judge, and statesman. A tall, handsome man with curly reddish-brown hair, Bartlett won the highest honors that New Hampshire could bestow in return for his selfless devotion to public service.

Born in Amesbury, Mass., on November 21, 1729, Bartlett received his early education from private tutors. Having mastered Greek and Latin by the time he was sixteen, he then began the study of medicine.

Bartlett began to practice medicine at the age of twenty-one when he moved to Kingston, N.H. As a physician, he experimented with new ideas, constantly seeking better ways to treat his patients. His lack of reliance on some of the non-scientific medical beliefs of his day stemmed from a personal experience that occurred shortly after his arrival in Kingston. The story is told that Bartlett became seriously ill with a high fever. The physician who treated him insisted that the windows to his room be tightly closed and that he should receive no liquids. The fever continued to rise, and the doctor diagnosed Bartlett's condition as hopeless. Finally, rallying slightly, Bartlett prevailed upon friends to bring him a jug of cider which he drank in small quantities throughout the night. In the morning, the cider he had drunk enabled him to perspire heavily; the fever broke; and his life was saved. Later, one of his most important discoveries as a physician was the use of Peruvian bark, or cinchona, to relieve cases of severe sore throat. This was long before the drug quinine had been extracted from cinchona.

Married to a cousin

Bartlett married a cousin, Mary Barton of Newton, Mass. During their long marriage, they had twelve children. Three of their sons became physicians, as did seven of their grandsons. Mrs. Bartlett died in 1789, six years before the death of her husband.

Bartlett's devotion to his profession, his friendliness, and his intelligence, soon won him a wide medical practice and many friends. Although he had no formal training in the law, he was elected

JOSIAH BARTLETT
by TRUMBULL, 1790
New Hampshire Historical Society

JOSIAH BARTLETT

1729 (Nov. 21) Born in Amesbury, Mass.

1750 Began practicing medicine in Kingston, N. H.

1765-1775 Delegate of New Hampshire legislature.

1775-1776 Delegate of New Hampshire in Continental Congress; first delegate to vote approval of the Declaration of Independence.

1778 Delegate of New Hampshire to the Continental Congress; first delegate to sign the Articles of Confederation.

1779-1782 Chief justice of New Hampshire court of common pleas.

1782-1788 Associate justice of New Hampshire Supreme Court

1788 Member of state ratification convention of U.S. Constitution.

1788-1790 Chief justice of New Hampshire Supreme Court.

1790-1793 President of state of New Hampshire.

1791 First president of the New Hampshire Medical Society.

1793-1794 First governor of the state of New Hampshire.

1795 (May 19) Died in Kingston, N. H.

as a local justice of the peace because the community knew it could rely on his impartiality. His rising community leadership also led to his appointment by the royal governor as a commander of militia troops.

For ten years, from 1765 to 1775, Bartlett served as Kingston's representative in the colonial legislature of New Hampshire. In his office, Bartlett learned at first hand the inequities being forced upon the colonies by the British government. In the developing controversy with Great Britain, Bartlett became an active member of the patriotic cause.

In trouble with the royal governor

In response to requests from the legislatures of other colonies, the New Hampshire house of representatives in 1774 created a Committee of Correspondence as part of the patriotic communication network. Bartlett's role in this patriotic activity was recognized by the royal governor, who ordered him removed from his office as justice of the peace and dismissed him from his command in the militia.

As Bartlett and others in the legislature became more independent in their actions, the royal governor repeatedly ordered the dissolution of the legislature. The legislators would dutifully dissolve, then continue meeting elsewhere. Bartlett and other members of the legislature formed a Committee of Safety which soon became the executive government of New Hampshire when the governor fled to the safety of British troops in September, 1775.

First to vote independence

Bartlett was elected as a delegate to the second Continental Congress where he served in 1775 and 1776. He vigorously supported independence from Great Britain, and, because New Hampshire was the most northerly colony, he had the honor of being the first delegate to vote in favor of adopting the Declaration of Independence on July 4, 1776.

During the year 1777, Bartlett remained in New Hampshire. He occupied himself mainly in recruiting soldiers to serve in the state's regiments in the Continental Army. He also aided in the administration of the government of the state.

Bartlett returned to Congress in May, 1778, while it was meeting at York, Pa. When the British evacuated Philadelphia, Congress adjourned to

New Hampshire Historical Society
Josiah Bartlett House

that city in July. In a letter written shortly after his arrival in Philadelphia, Bartlett described changes made in the city by the British occupation:

"The Congress meets in the college hall, as the state house was left by the enemy in a most filthy and sordid situation, as were many of the public and private buildings in the city; some of the genteel houses were used for stables, and holes cut in the parlour floors, and their dung shovelled into the cellars. The country northward of the city for several miles is one common waste; the houses burnt, the fruit trees and others cut down and carried off, fences carried away, gardens and orchards destroyed; Mr. (John) Dickinson's and Mr. (Robert) Morris's fine seats all demolished; in short, I could hardly find the great roads that used to pass that way: the enemy built a strong abbatis with the fruit and other trees, from the Delaware to the Schuylkill, and at about forty or fifty rods distance along the abbatis, a quadrangular fort for cannon, and a number of redoubts for small arms; the same on the several eminences along the Schuylkill, against the city."

A change in styles

The returning patriots also found that the British occupation had resulted in a change in clothing fashions. Tory ladies had adopted towering hair styles and were wearing bustles. The gentlemen of the city had abandoned wearing the customary small round hats of the pre-revolutionary period and instead were wearing three-cornered hats.

Congress resumed its business at Philadelphia on July 2, 1778. Bartlett had the honor on July 9 of being the first delegate to sign the Articles of Confederation, again because New Hampshire was the most northerly of the states. On October 31, Bartlett obtained a leave of absence to return home to attend to his medical practice and his family. He never again served in Congress, devoting the rest of his life to the affairs of his state.

For the next eleven years, Bartlett devoted much of his time to New Hampshire's judicial affairs. In 1779 he was appointed chief justice of the New Hampshire court of common pleas. After holding this office for three years, Bartlett was appointed associate justice of the Supreme Court of New Hampshire in 1782. Six years later, in 1788, he was appointed Chief Justice of the New Hampshire Supreme Court.

Declined appointment as senator

Bartlett actively supported the United States Constitution at the state ratification convenfion of which he was a member in 1788. He was especially gratified when by a vote of 55 to 47 New Hampshire on June 21, 1788, became the ninth state to ratify, placing the Constitution into effect. The legislature chose Bartlett to represent New Hampshire in the new Congress as a U. S. senator, but he declined the office on grounds of his advancing age.

After two years as the state's Chief Justice, Bartlett was elected President of New Hampshire, the state's highest office in June, 1790. He likewise was honored when a state medical society was formed in 1791 by being elected its president. When a new state constitution went into effect in 1793, he was elected as the state's first governor. Early in 1794, Bartlett decided to retire at the end of his term of office. In a letter to the legislature he said:

"Gentlemen of the legislature: After having served the public for a number of years, to the best of my abilities, in the various offices to which I have had the honour to be appointed, I think it proper, before your adjournment, to signify to you, and through you to my fellow citizens at large, that I now find myself so far advanced in age, that it will be expedient for me at the close of the session, to retire from the cares and fatigues of public business to the repose of a private life, with a grateful sense of the repeated marks of trust and confidence that my fellow citizens have reposed in me, and with my best wishes for the future peace and prosperity of the state."

The "cares and fatigues of public business" had already taken their toll on the health of Bartlett. Less than a year after retiring as governor, he died at the age of 65 in Kingston on May 19, 1795.

Essex Institute Collection

Portsmouth, New Hampshire
shortly before the Revolutionary War

54

CARTER BRAXTON of VIRGINIA

A wealthy Virginia tobacco planter, Carter Braxton was the least enthusiastic of the Virginia delegates in signing the Declaration of Independence. His marriage to the daughter of a British official made it difficult for him to accept the idea of a complete break with Great Britain despite his patriotism. A short pudgy man with elegant manners and rich tastes, he lost his fortune during the Revolutionary War by investing in trading ships that were captured by the British. Braxton was perhaps the most devoted family man among the Founding Fathers, marrying twice and having 18 children. For more than half his life he served Virginia—first as a delegate in the colonial house of burgesses, then as a representative in the state legislature.

Born in Newington, Va., on September 10, 1736, Carter Braxton was the son of George Braxton, a wealthy planter. In his early teens, the boy was sent to William and Mary College where he received a liberal education. He did not study for a profession because he was assured of a comfortable life as a country gentleman. While still in his teens, his father died, leaving him an estate that included five plantations and many slaves.

A widower at an early age

At the age of 19, Braxton married Judith Robinson, the beautiful daughter of a socially prominent Virginia family whose dowry added to his fortune. Less than two years later, his wife died while giving birth to their second child.

Grieving over the death of his young wife,

CARTER BRAXTON,
Signer of the Declaration of Independence.
(Never before published or engraved.)
From a miniature in the possession of his family.

Braxton sailed to England in 1758. He was introduced into British society, and enjoyed himself in London for nearly two years. Returning home to Virginia in 1760, he found that his brother, George Braxton Jr., had built him a beautiful brick Georgian-style mansion overlooking the Pamunkey River. He called the house "Elsing Green" and made it his home for the next twenty-five years.

On May 15, 1761, Braxton remarried. His second wife was Elizabeth Corbin, whose father, Colonel Richard Corbin, held the important position of receiver-general of customs for the king in Virginia. Braxton and his second wife had sixteen children.

Braxton has been described as an "affectionate and obliging" husband, father, friend, and neighbor. He enjoyed entertaining his friends, who included the wealthiest members of Virginia society. His home was noted for the richness and beauty of its furniture and silverware, and his wine cellar was filled with the best wines.

CARTER BRAXTON

1736 (Sept. 10) Born in Newington, Va.

1758-1760 Visited England.

1761-17771 Member of the Virginia house of burgesses.

1772-1773 Sheriff of King William County, Virginia.

1774-1775 Member of Virginia convention that chose delegates to the Continental Congress; member of the Virginia house of burgesses.

1775-1776 Delegate to Continental Congress; signed Declaration of Independence.

1776-1797 Member of Virginia state legislature.

1786-1791 and 1794-1797 Member of Virginia's executive council.

1797 (Oct. 10) Died in Richmond, Va.

A member of the house of burgesses

It is believed that Braxton was first elected to Virginia's colonial house of burgesses (legislature) in 1761. As a representative of King William County, he served in the house of burgesses throughout most of the pre-Revolutionary War period, associating with such patriots as George Washington, Thomas Jefferson, Richard Henry Lee, and Patrick Henry. Although Braxton was not so active a representative as those more famous leaders, his name was signed with the others to the famous Virginia non-importation agreement of May 18, 1769, which protested the British parliament's Townshend Act taxes on glass, paper, paint, and tea.

Braxton did not serve in the house of burgesses in 1772 and 1773, having been elected sheriff of King William County; but, when the colony's royal governor, the Earl of Dunmore, dissolved the legislature in 1774 and a convention of Virginia patriots was called to decide a course of action, Braxton was elected as a delegate from his county. The convention pledged itself to aid the people of Boston, whose harbor had been closed by the British as a penalty for the "Boston Tea Party," and it appointed delegates to the first Continental Congress.

Hopeful of peaceful solution

In the spring of 1775, Braxton, who was hopeful that some peaceful solution might be found to end the dispute with Britain, succeeded in preventing an early outbreak of fighting in Virginia. Governor Dunmore had seized all the colony's

gunpowder and had put it aboard a British warship. Angered at this action, Patrick Henry had called together the militia of Hanover County and started marching on Williamsburg, demanding either the return of the gunpowder or payment for it. The governor refused the demand and prepared to meet Henry's advance with a company of British marines. Volunteering his services as a mediator, Braxton met with Henry and counseled him to give up his hot-headed action. When Henry refused, Braxton went to his father-in-law, the receiver-general of customs, and persuaded him to pay Henry in order to avert bloodshed. Upon receipt of the money for the gunpowder, Henry disbanded his force.

Braxton served in the last session of the Virginia house of burgesses that convened on June 1, 1775, and met for two weeks. The representatives at this session were inflamed by the news of the fighting between the patriots and the British in Massachusetts, and quickly fell into serious arguments with Governor Dunmore. Fearing for his safety, Dunmore fled to a British warship on the night of June 7, and refused to return to Williamsburg.

With the royal governor gone, a convention was called at Richmond in July, 1775, to take over all functions of government for the colony. Braxton was elected as a delegate to this convention, and he took an active part on many of its committees. The patriots had to raise money, men, and arms for their defense, because Dunmore began marauding up and down the Virginia coast attacking towns and plantations from his warships.

A delegate to the Continental Congress

In December, 1775, the Virginia convention elected Braxton as a delegate to the Continental Congress to replace Peyton Randolph, a Virginia delegate who had died in Philadelphia in October while serving as President of the Continental Congress. At the Congress in Philadelphia, Braxton made no outstanding contribution to the debates preceding the adoption of the Declaration of Independence. Because of his hopes for a peaceful solution to the problems with Britain, he no doubt was one of the delegates described by John Adams as having "signed with regret" on August 2, 1776. Nine days later, on August 11, 1776, Braxton's term in the Congress ended, the Virginia legislature having decided to reduce the size of the state's delegation to Congress, and Braxton returned home.

William and Mary College, Williamsburg, Virginia, before the fire of 1859
from Bishop Mead's *Old Churches, Ministers, and Families of Virginia*

Colonial Williamsburg

When the first Virginia legislature under the state's new constitution met on October, 1776, Braxton represented King William County. His long experience in the house of burgesses won him the chairmanship of such important committees as those on religion and on propositions and grievances. He also was occasionally chairman of the committee of the whole. He was described by an acquaintance as "an agreeable, though not a remarkably forcible, public speaker. His eloquence was easy and gentlemanly; his language good; and his manner agreeable." For the rest of his life, Braxton served almost continuously as a delegate to the legislature.

Financial disaster

At the beginning of the Revolutionary War, as normal trade channels to Great Britain were cut off, Braxton thought he saw an opportunity to multiply his fortune. He began outfitting merchant ships to carry American cargoes to other countries. Unfortunately for his dreams of greater wealth, his plans met with disaster as one-by-one his ships were captured by the British. He went deeper and deeper into debt, selling his plantations, mortgaging his slaves and furniture, and borrowing from his relatives and friends. When the debts could not be paid, his creditors seized his estate. Finally, Braxton and his family were forced to move to Richmond in 1786, giving up the rich country life they were used to.

Recognizing Braxton's ability as a legislator, his new neighbors in Henrico County, where Richmond is located, elected him as one of their representatives in the legislature. From 1786 to 1791 and from 1793 until his death in 1797, Braxton served as a member of the state's executive council. At the age of 61, he died of a paralytic stroke on October 10, 1797.

CHARLES CARROLL of MARYLAND

The only Roman Catholic among the signers of the Declaration of Independence, Charles Carroll had strong motives in seeking freedom from the persecution suffered by the Catholic minority in Maryland under British rule. Carroll also was one of the three wealthiest men in America—the others being George Washington of Virginia and Henry Middleton of South Carolina. But the short, delicate-appearing Carroll gladly risked his life and his millions for the cause of liberty and religious freedom. He was the last signer of the Declaration to die, and the only one to live long enough to see a railroad train.

Charles Carroll was born in Annapolis, Md., on September 20, 1737. Both his father and grandfather also were named Charles Carroll. The Irish Carrolls traced their ancestry to the ancient kings of Ireland, and they lived in an aristocratic manner that befitted kings. The first Charles Carroll, a friend of Lord Baltimore, came to Maryland in 1688. He became the colony's attorney-general, register of land, and receiver-general of customs. He received large land grants that became the basis of the family fortune.

Educated in France

In 1745, eight-year-old Charles Carroll was taken to France by his father to receive a Catholic education, because the Catholics in Maryland were denied all political, religious, and educational freedom. His father also took the opportunity of the trip to try unsuccessfully to persuade the French government to give him a huge tract of land on the Arkansas River in the Louisiana Territory, where he proposed to resettle the Maryland Catholics. For six years young Charles attended a school run by English Jesuits at St. Omer. His two young second cousins, John and Daniel Carroll attended the same school. John Carroll later became the first Roman Catholic bishop in America and the founder of Georgetown College. Daniel Carroll became a signer of the United States Constitution and a representative from Maryland in the first United States Congress. After completing his early education at St. Omer, Charles Carroll then spent six more years in college-level studies at Rheims, Bourges, and Paris.

In 1757, he went to London where he studied law in the Temple for another six years.

Returned home at twenty-six

When Carroll returned to his home in Maryland in 1764 at the age of 26, he had more the manners of a European gentleman than those of an American. He spoke French fluently, he was an accomplished horseman, and he had the graces and manners of an aristocrat. His father gave him the Manor of Carrollton, a 10,000-acre estate in Frederick County, Maryland. From that time on he was known as *Charles Carroll of Carrollton* to distinguish him from his father, who was known as *Charles Carroll of Annapolis*. However, Carroll did not live at Carrollton, spending most of his time at his father's townhouse in Annapolis or on the family's country estate at Doughoregan, near Ellicott City, Md. At the age of 30, in June, 1768, Carroll married his cousin, Mary "Molly" Darnall. Their son was named *Charles Carroll of Homewood*.

After his return from Europe, Carroll soon became recognized as a leader of the patriotic movement in Maryland. He actively opposed the British Stamp Act of 1765. When the governor of Maryland proclaimed in 1771 that civil officers of the colony should collect specific fees that he enumerated, Carroll denounced the measure as taxation by proclamation. He wrote newspaper articles signed by the pseudonym "Second Citizen" argu-

---

CHARLES CARROLL

1737 (Sept. 20) Born in Annapolis, Md.

1745-1757 Educated in France.

1757-1764 Studied law at the Temple in London.

1775-1776 Delegate to Maryland's patriotic convention; helped write Maryland's state constitution.

1776 Appointed by Continental Congress to a commission to urge Canadians to support the United Colonies against Great Britain.

1776-1778 Delegate from Maryland to the Continental Congress; signed the Declaration of Independence.

1777-1804 State senator in Maryland legislature.

1789-1792 Represented Maryland as U.S. senator in Congress.

1832 (Nov. 14) Died in Baltimore, the last surviving signer of the Declaration of Independence.

Departure of Charles Carroll, Jr.
by R. E. PINE, *Coll. Philip Acosta Carroll*
Frick Art Reference Library

ing the legality of the proclamation being issued without the approval of the legislature. After the proclamation had been hanged on a gallows by the public hangman, the people of Annapolis came in a body to thank Carroll for defending their rights and to make him their "First Citizen."

Convinced that revolution was the solution

Carroll already had made up his mind that revolution was the only likely way by which the dispute with Britain could ultimately be settled. He is said to have disclosed this in the following conversation with Samuel Chase, who also later signed the Declaration of Independence:

Chase: "We have the better of our opponents; we have completely written them down."

Carroll: "And do you think that writing will settle the question between us?"

Chase: "To be sure, what else can we resort to?"

Carroll: "The bayonet! Our arguments will only raise the feeling of the people to that pitch, when

open war will be looked to as the arbiter of the dispute."

'We have no doubt of ultimate success.'

About this same time, a member of the British parliament had written to Carroll speaking scornfully of the idea of armed resistance by the colonies. He stated that 6,000 British soldiers could march from one end of the colonies to the other. Carroll wrote back the following reply:

"So they may, but they will be masters of the spot only on which they encamp. They will find nought but enemies before and around them. If we are beaten on the plains, we will retreat to our mountains and defy them. Our resources will increase with our difficulties. Necessity will force us to exertion; until, tired of combating, in vain, against a spirit which victory after victory cannot subdue, your armies will evacuate our soil, and your country retire, an immense loser, from the contest. — No, sire. — We have made up our minds

59

Mrs. Charles Carroll of Carrollton
by C. W. PEALE, 1771, MORRIS SHAPIRO, *owner*

to abide the issue of the approaching struggle, and though much blood may be spilt, we have no doubt of ultimate success."

The "Annapolis Tea Party"

In 1774, Carroll took an important role in Maryland's version of the "Boston Tea Party." As a protest against the British tax on tea, the patriots of the colony had forbidden any imports of tea. The brig *Peggy Stewart* had arrived in Annapolis loaded with tea, and an angry mob had gathered on the waterfront threatening violence to the owner and the crew. Friends of the owner, Anthony Stewart, called on Carroll, asking for his advice and protection. Carroll is said to have replied: "Whatever may be my personal esteem for Mr. Stewart, and my wish to prevent violence, it will not be in my power to protect him, unless he consents to pursue a decisive course of conduct. My advice is, that he set fire to the vessel, and burn her, together with the tea that she contains, to the water's edge." Within a few hours, the ship was burned, and mob violence was averted.

Because he was a Catholic, Carroll could not be elected to public office under the colonial law of Maryland; but, as the ferment of the approaching revolution rose to greater heights, he was chosen in January, 1775, as a member of the Maryland "Committee of Observation," a group that became a sort of unofficial executive government for the colony. Later that same year, he was elected to represent Anne Arundel County in Maryland's patriotic convention, the unofficial legislature.

Mission to Canada

In February, 1776, Carroll was appointed by the Continental Congress to a commission to go to Canada to try to persuade the Canadians to join the United Colonies in their struggle against Britain. The others who were asked to go on the journey were Benjamin Franklin, Samuel Chase, and Carroll's cousin, John Carroll, who had become a prominent Jesuit father. The Congress hoped that the Carrolls could influence the Roman Catholic French-Canadians to join in the rebellion. At this time, American forces had captured Montreal and had Quebec City under siege. The commissioners discovered that conditions were extremely bad with the American troops in Canada—that the soldiers were sick, poorly equipped, and badly led, and that the American invasion of Canada had destroyed any hope of winning support from the people. The commissioners returned to Philadelphia in June, 1776, and reported to the Continental Congress that "We cannot find words to describe our miserable situation . . ."

Successful persuasion

At Philadelphia, Carroll discovered that the Congress was in the midst of a debate as to whether or not the colonies should declare themselves free and independent from Great Britain, but that a decision was being delayed in part because the Maryland delegation had instructions from their convention to oppose independence. Having completed his report on the situation in Canada, Carroll hurried back to Annapolis where he again took his seat in the provincial convention. He demanded that the instructions to the Maryland delegates at the Continental Congress be changed "to concur with the other United Colonies, or a majority of them, in declaring the United Colonies free and independent states." Carroll was successful in his efforts, thus making it possible for the Maryland representatives in Congress to vote for independence on July 2 and to approve the Declaration of Independence on July 4.

A tardy delegate

In recognition of Carroll's zeal for independence, the state convention appointed him on July 4, 1776, as a representative to the Continental Congress. Of course, because of the poor communications of the times, they had no way of knowing that the Congress already had approved independence. Carroll presented his credentials to Congress on July 18 and took his seat as a delegate. On August 2, when the engrossed copy of the Declaration of Independence was laid before the Congress, President John Hancock asked Carroll if he cared to sign, even though he had not been present at its adoption. "Most willingly," Carroll is said to have replied. As he took up the pen to write his signature, one of the other delegates is reported to have said, "There goes a few millions!"—referring to the fortune Carroll risked losing by placing himself on record as a traitor in the eyes of the British.

Although Carroll continued to hold office as a member of Congress until 1778, he was more interested in developments in Maryland; so he retained his seat in the Maryland convention and helped in the drafting of the state constitution, making sure that it upheld freedom of religion.

In December, 1776, he was chosen as a state senator to serve in Maryland's first state legislature. For more than twenty-five years Carroll continued to be re-elected as a state senator, until 1804 when the Democratic-Republican party won control of the state government.

Refused appointment to Constitutional Convention

Carroll turned down an appointment as a delegate to the Constitutional Convention of 1787. But after the United States Constitution had been written, he became one of its strong supporters. The Maryland legislature chose Carroll as one of the state's first two U. S. senators in the first United States Congress that convened in 1789. Carroll took part in many important actions in the new Congress. He was a member of the joint Senate-House conference committee that decided the final wording of the Bill of Rights amendments to the United States Constitution. In 1790, he headed the senatorial committee that proposed that all trade should be cut off from Rhode Island, the only state that had refused to ratify the Constitution. The proposed action was effective, for Rhode Island's convention soon approved ratification. Carroll also strongly supported George Washing-

ton's desire to establish the permanent capital in the District of Columbia on the Potomac River.

Preferring his position as state senator in the Maryland legislature, Carroll generally attended sessions of Congress in New York only when the state legislature was not in session. Then, in 1792, Maryland adopted an amendment to the state constitution which forbade any member of Congress from simultaneously holding a state office. In order to continue his service in the Maryland state senate, Carroll resigned as a U. S. senator.

The last surviving signer

In 1804, after Carroll failed to be re-elected to the Maryland senate, he retired to private life at the age of 67. During his old age, Carroll lived a quiet life, enjoying his large estates, his family, and the freedoms that he had such an important part in winning. In 1828, he helped open a new era in transportation by laying the cornerstone for the Baltimore & Ohio Railroad, and he no doubt was present in 1830 at the famous race between Peter Cooper's *Tom Thumb* locomotive and a stage coach horse. The last surviving signer of the Declaration of Independence, Carroll died at the age of 95 in Baltimore on November 14, 1832.

Doughoregan Manor
Home of Charles Carroll of Carrollton

From an original etching by Don Swann

SAMUEL CHASE of MARYLAND

A tall, beefy, red-faced man, Samuel Chase received the nickname "Bacon face" as he played the role of patriotic agitator in Maryland before the Revolutionary War. The conservative mayor and alderman of Annapolis, Md., described him as a "busy, restless incendiary, a ringleader of mobs, a foul-mouthed and inflaming son of discord and faction, a common disturber of the public tranquility, and a promoter of the lawless excesses of the multitude." Like Samuel Adams in Massachusetts, Chase worked tirelessly for revolt against the British, and won his greatest triumph by voting for and signing the Declaration of Independence.

Barely escaped conviction

Becoming much more conservative in his later years, Chase infuriated Thomas Jefferson's Democratic-Republican party with his outspoken Federalist opinions in his position as an associate justice of the United States Supreme Court. He was impeached for improper conduct by the U. S. House of Representatives and narrowly escaped being convicted by the U. S. Senate.

Samuel Chase was born on April 17, 1741, in Somerset County, Maryland, the only son of Thomas Chase, an Episcopal clergyman. His

Essex Institute Collection
Chase House, 1770, Annapolis, Maryland

SAMUEL CHASE

1741 (April 17) Born in Somerset County, Maryland.

1761 Admitted to the bar in Annapolis, Md.

1764-1775 Member of the colonial general assembly of Maryland.

1774-1778 Represented Maryland in the Continental Congress; signed the Declaration of Independence.

1776-1784 Member of the Maryland state legislature.

1783-1784 Emmisary to London seeking to recover money for Bank of England stock owned by Maryland.

1788 Delegate to the Maryland convention that ratified the United States Constitution.

1788-1795 Judge of he criminal court of Baltimore County.

1791-1794 Chief justice of the general court of Maryland.

1796-1811 Associate justice of the Supreme Court of the United States.

1804 Impeached by the U.S. House of Representatives for malfeasance in office.

1805 Acquitted of charges of malfeasance by the U.S. Senate.

1811 (June 19) Died in Baltimore, Md.

mother, Matilda Walker Chase, the daughter of a Maryland farmer, died during his birth. The boy grew up in Baltimore, Md., where his father had become the rector of St. Paul's parish. At that time, Baltimore was a small village that offered little opportunity for formal education. However, the elder Chase had been a professor of Latin and Hebrew in England before coming to America, and he was able to tutor Samuel so that the boy received the equivalent of a college education in the classics. The fact that he was raised without a mother no doubt accounts for the many later descriptions of Samuel Chase as a man with uncouth and ungentlemanly manners.

When he was eighteen, Chase went to Annapolis, Md., where he studied law under John Hammond and John Hall. A quick-learner, he was admitted to the bar and began practicing law in Annapolis at the age of twenty. In 1762, he married 19-year-old Anne Baldwin of Annapolis. They had six children, four of whom survived infancy.

A man of the people

When he was 23, Chase was elected to the colonial legislature, and he continued to be re-elected

**MRS. SAMUEL CHASE (ANN BALDWIN)
AND DAUGHTERS**
by C. W. PEALE
*Maryland Historical Society Coll., Baltimore
Frick Art Reference Library*

openly disputed the parliamentary right to tax the colonies, while you skulked in your houses, some of you asserting the parliamentary right, and esteeming the stamp act as a beneficial law. Others of you meanly grumbled in your corners, not daring to speak out your sentiments."

As the tempo of events moved the colonies closer to revolution, Chase strengthened his leadership in the colonial legislature, speaking out against the tyrannical acts of the British government. He helped organize Maryland's Committee of Correspondence and took part in the rapidly forming unofficial patriotic government of the colony. He was sent as one of the Maryland delegates to the first Continental Congress in 1774, and he was disappointed at its efforts to find a peaceful solution to the dispute with Britain.

The Demosthenes of Maryland

In 1775, Chase again attended the Continental Congress, after the fighting had begun at Lexington and Concord. This session was much more to his liking as he supported the appointment of George Washington as commander-in-chief and voted for the organization of the Continental Army. Because of his florid oratory, Chase became known as the "Demosthenes of Maryland." Long before Congress was ready to declare the colonies independent, Chase made speeches in Congress in which he declared "by the God of heaven he owed no allegiance to the king of Great Britain"— shocking words to the more conservative delegates.

Chase discovered in the autumn of 1775 that one of the delegates from Georgia, a Presbyterian clergyman by the name of John Joachim Zubly, had been writing to the royal governor of Georgia disclosing that the Continental Congress was discussing the likelihood of declaring the colonies independent. Chase took the floor of Congress to denounce Zubly as a traitor; but before the Georgia delegate could be arrested for treason Zubly admitted his guilt by fleeing back to Georgia and the protection of the royal governor. There Zubly became an active Tory, siding with the British until his death late in the Revolutionary War. Chase won many friends and admirers for his fearless exposure of the traitor.

In the spring of 1776, Chase was appointed by the Continental Congress to go to Canada to try to encourage the people there to join in the rebellion against the British. He was accompanied by Benjamin Franklin, Charles Carroll, and John

for the next twenty years as the colony became a state. In the legislature, Chase became known as a man of the people who had little regard for the feelings of the royal governor and his followers. Although Chase was a member of the Episcopalian church, which at that time was the only faith allowed to worship in the colony, he helped pass regulations opposed by the royal governor that reduced the amount of payments to the church and cut in half the income of clergymen, including that of his own father.

The passage by the British parliament of the Stamp Act of 1765 caused a groundswell of indignation throughout the colonies. In Maryland, Chase instigated mob actions to show the displeasure of the people against "taxation without representation." Chase was proud of his accomplishments when the British repealed the stamp tax and wrote: "I admit, gentlemen, that I was one of those who committed to the flames, in effigy, the stamp distributor of this province, and who

Drawn by G. Beck, Philadelphia.

George Town, and FEDERAL CITY,

or CITY of Washington.

Published June 1 1801 by Atkins & Nightingale, No 143 Leadenhall Street, London & No 51 North Front Street, Philadelphia.

Engraved by T. Cartwright, London

Library of Congress

circa 1800

William Birch's view of the Capitol Wing (1800)

Carroll, who later became the first Roman Catholic bishop in the United States. The commissioners discovered that the armed intervention by American troops in Canada had been badly managed and that there was little that they could do to win the support of the Canadian people.

Persuading the villagers

Upon returning to Congress in June, 1776, Chase learned that the delegates were at last seriously considering declaring the colonies independent, but that one of the major obstacles lay in the instructions to the Maryland delegates which prevented them from voting for independence. Chase and Charles Carroll hurried back to Maryland, determined to change the instructions for their delegation in Congress. Chase made a whirlwind tour of Maryland, making stump speeches before hastily assembled groups of farmers and villagers. In his most forceful oratory, Chase urged the people to let the Maryland convention sitting in Annapolis know their sentiments. The tide of patriotism that Chase and others stirred, swayed the conservative members of the Maryland convention. On June 28, 1776, Chase wrote to John Adams in Philadelphia: "Friday evening, nine o'clock. I am just this moment from the house to procure an express to follow the post, with an unanimous vote of our convention for independence. See the glorious effect of county instructions. The people have fire, if it is not smothered."

Riding horseback, Chase hurried back to Philadelphia, arriving in time to vote with the rest of the Maryland delegation on July 2 in support of Richard Henry Lee's resolutions for independence, to approve the Declaration of Independence on July 4, and to sign it on August 2.

Chase continued to serve in Congress until 1778. One of the committees on which he was particularly active sought ways to restrict the activities of Tories and other enemies of the patriotic cause. The committee was responsible for the arrest and imprisonment of many Quakers in Pennsylvania and New Jersey who were accused of publishing articles opposing the Continental Congress and of communicating with the British forces. Chase suffered two blows in 1778 that brought his career in Congress to an end. It was disclosed that he had been using inside information gained in Congress in order to make a profit on the sale of flour to the army, and his wife died, leaving him to rear their children.

An act of kindness

Returning to Annapolis, Chase continued to serve in the state legislature, and strengthened his law practice. During this period, an incident took place that demonstrates a warmer side of Chase's personality. On a trip to Baltimore, he attended a meeting of a local debating society where the speaking ability of one of the young men, William Pinkney, particularly attracted his attention. He learned that Pinkney was apprenticed to a pharmacist and had no money to pay for law studies. So Chase invited Pinkney to come to Annapolis and study law at Chase's expense and under Chase's guidance. Pinkney accepted the invitation and proved the clarity of Chase's judgement by a distinguished career as a U. S. representative, diplomat, Attorney-General of the United States, and U. S. senator.

After the peace treaty with Great Britain had been signed in 1783, Chase was appointed by the governor of Maryland to go to London in an effort to collect about $800,000 owed to the state by the Bank of England. Although Chase was unsuccessful in the negotiations, his protege Pinkney finally collected the money thirteen years later while assigned as a U. S. commmissioner in England. While in London, Chase married Hannay Kitty Giles on March 3, 1784. Chase had two daughters by his second wife.

In 1786, Chase moved to Baltimore at the urging of John Eager Howard, a Revolutionary War hero and later governor of Maryland. Howard offered to give Chase a large tract of land in Baltimore if he would come live there and help build the future of the town. Chase accepted and made Baltimore his home for the rest of his life.

An Anti-Federalist

Chase declined an offer to serve as a delegate to the Constitutional Convention in 1787. He became an active Anti-Federalist during this period, and led the opposition in the Maryland convention that was called to consider ratification of the United States Constitution. However, Chase had lost much of his popularity, and the state convention voted overwhelmingly in 1788 to ratify the Constitution.

In 1788, Chase turned to a judicial career with his appointment as judge of the newly established criminal court of Baltimore County. He continued to practice law, however, until he received a fur-

The French squadron entering the Delaware River.
They are pursuing the frigate Mermaid.

ther appointment in 1791 as chief justice of the general court of Maryland.

An incident occurred in 1794 that showed Chase's unswerving belief in the supremacy of the law. A riot had taken place in which a mob had tarred and feathered some men who had spoken out against the ruling party in Baltimore. The two leaders of the mob had been arrested, and when they were brought to court many members of the mob appeared in their support. The prisoners refused to give bond for their further appearance in court, and the sheriff was afraid to take them to jail against the wishes of the mob. Chase then asked the sheriff to swear him in as an officer so that he personally could take the men to jail. On hearing this, a fellow-lawyer warned him that he would endanger his life and property by such an action. "God forbid," he replied, "that my countrymen should ever be guilty of so daring an outrage; but, sire, with the blessing of God, I will do my duty,—they may destroy my property, they may pull down my house over my head, yea, they may make a widow of my wife, and my children fatherless,—the life of one man is of little consequence compared to the prostration of the laws of the land—with the blessing of God, I will do my duty, be the consequences what they may." Chase carried his point, and bond was provided for the accused leaders of the mob.

Commissioned as U.S. Supreme Court judge

As a judge, Chase became an outspoken member of the Federalist party, reversing most of his previous statements and opinions as an Anti-Federalist. On January 27, 1796, he received from President George Washington his commission as an associate justice of the Supreme Court of the United States, a position that he held for the remainder of his life. Chase had long been noted for his forthright statements of opinion on any and all matters, and he did not change his mode of con-

SAMUEL CHASE
by C. W. PEALE
Maryland Historical Society Coll., Baltimore
Frick Art Reference Library

66

View from Bushongo Tavern, 5 miles from York Town on the Baltimore Road

duct when he assumed the judicial robes of the Supreme Court. The sedition laws that were in effect during the administration of President John Adams forbade any public expressions of opposition to the laws and government of the United States, and Chase's vigorous upholding of the sedition laws won him enemies among the Democratic-Republican party that opposed President Adams. In 1803, after the election of Thomas Jefferson as President, Chase brought down the wrath of the administration by addressing a speech to a grand jury in Baltimore in which he denounced changes in the Maryland state constitution that would reduce property qualifications for voting and enable a wider base of suffrage.

Impeachment proceedings

Because of his injudicious courtroom statements, Chase was impeached in 1804 by the Democratic-Republican-controlled U. S. House of Representatives on several charges of malfeasance. In February, 1805, Chase was brought to trial before the United States Senate with Vice-President Aaron Burr presiding. A majority of the senate voted to find him guilty on two of the charges; but, because a two-thirds plurality was necessary for conviction, Chase was acquitted of

all charges. If the action against Chase had been successful, it was believed that other justices appointed by Washington and Adams might have been removed by impeachment.

Associate Justice Joseph Story, who was appointed to the Supreme Court after Chase's death, described Chase in his last years: "His manners are coarse, and in appearance harsh; but in reality he abounds with good humor . . . In person, in manners, in unwieldly strength, in severity of reproof, in real tenderness of heart, and above all in intellect, he is the living, I had almost said the exact, image of Samuel Johnson." In his final years, Chase was severely afflicted with the gout. This prevented much activity on his part, and he became a less controversial figure. On June 19, 1811, at the age of 70, Chase died at his home in Baltimore.

More than twenty years later, Chief Justice John Marshall wrote of his former colleague: "He possessed a strong mind, great legal knowledge, and was a valuable judge, whose loss was seriously felt by his survivors. He was remarkable also for his vivacity and his companionable qualities. He said many things which were much admired at the time, but I have not treasured them in my memory so as to be able to communicate them."

67

ABRAHAM CLARK of NEW JERSEY

A short, slender man with heavy black eyebrows, Abraham Clark signed the Declaration of Independence and served throughout the Revolutionary War as a member of Congress. He was a watchdog for the rights of the common man, suspicious of General George Washington's power during the war, and unfriendly to President George Washington's administration of the government after the war.

Clark was born in Elizabethtown, N. J., on February 15, 1726, the only child of Thomas Clark, a farmer. He is said to have been too frail as a child to help with the farm chores, and consequently could devote more of his time to reading than could other farm boys. He became particularly fond of mathematics, and this led to his becoming a surveyor.

At the age of 22, Clark married Sarah Hetfield, of Elizabethtown. Altogether they had ten children. Two of his sons became officers during the Revolutionary War and were captured by the British; they were reported to have been treated worse than other prisoners because of their father's patriotic activities.

ABRAHAM CLARK

The "Poor Man's Counselor"

Because Clark's surveying jobs were often the result of disputes between neighbors over the ownership of land, he gradually became familiar with civil law. Whether or not he ever was admitted to the bar, he became known as "the Poor Man's Counselor" because of his freely given advice on legal matters.

Clark's popularity with the farmers won him election as sheriff of Essex County, New Jersey. He then went on to win a seat in the colonial legislature, where he held the important post of clerk.

As the revolution neared, Clark became an active member of New Jersey's patriotic movement. He served as a member of the Committee of Safety, and then as a delegate to the colony's patriotic convention that elected representatives to the Continental Congress. In June, 1776, the patriotic convention arrested and imprisoned the colony's royal governor, William Franklin, the son of Benjamin Franklin, who had remained a loyalist even though his famous father was a leading patriot. At the same time, the convention elected a new delegation to represent New Jersey in the Continental Congress, the earlier delegation having opposed the idea of independence from Britain. Clark was elected as one of the new representatives to the Continental Congress.

Clark and the other new delegates from New Jersey arrived in Philadelphia and took their seats on July 1, in time to hear the debate between John Dickinson of Pennsylvania and John Adams of Massachusetts on whether or not the colonies should declare themselves independent. On the following day, Clark cast his vote for independence. He voted for the adoption of the Declaration of Independence on July 4, and signed his name to the document with the other members of Congress on August 2.

ABRAHAM CLARK

1726 (Feb. 15) Born in Elizabethtown, N. J.

1776-1783 Represented New Jersey in the Continental Congress; signed the Declaration of Independence.

1784-1787 Member of the New Jersey state legislature.

1786 Delegate to the Annapolis Convention.

1789-1790 Commissioner to settle accounts of New Jersey with the federal government.

1791-1794 Representative from New Jersey in the U.S. House of Representatives.

1794 (Sept. 15) Died in Rahway, N. J.

Critical of Washington

Until the peace treaty was signed with Great Britain in 1783, Clark continued to represent New Jersey in Congress. In 1777, Clark stirred a storm in Congress by contending that George Washington had exceeded his authority as commander-in-chief by issuing a proclamation that offered amnesty to loyalists who would take an oath of allegiance to the United States. Clark declared that the proclamation would interfere with the "trial and punishment of traitors." He wrote to the New Jersey legislature urging it not to "tamely submit their authority to the control of a power unknown in our constitution." He further warned that "we are set out to oppose tyranny in all its strides." After a Congressional committee had considered the matter and tabled it, Clark angrily wrote to a friend: "In many instances the proclamation is exceptionable and very improper and I believe was the production, or at least set on foot, by some too much in the General's good grace; he is too much encumbered to attend to everything, and though I believe him honest, I think him fallible."

A watchdog of the treasury

Clark won a reputation for keeping a close eye on the way that money was spent by Congress, and in so doing he won many enemies, particularly among the army officers. During the war, the states had agreed that officers who were incapacitated or retired should receive half-pay for life; but, at the end of the war, the officers suggested that they would prefer instead to receive full pay for several years so that they could repay debts they had incurred and still have enough money to re-establish themselves in civilian life. Clark objected strongly to this proposal, not only on grounds that he felt it would cost too much money, but also because he and other civilians had made sacrifices in the war that would not be repaid by the federal treasury. He pointed out that the army officers should feel that the successful conclusion of the war was in itself adequate compensation for their sacrifices. For a time, an open rebellion was threatened by the army officers, and only the intervention of George Washington persuaded the officers from starting an open rebellion against Congress.

Clark was not returned to Congress in 1784, and instead he served in the state legislature from 1784 to 1787. Clark believed that the Articles of Confederation should be strengthened, and he was sent as a delegate to the Annapolis Convention in 1786 to discuss these plans. When the results of the Annapolis Convention brought about the calling of a Constitutional Convention, Clark was appointed as a member of the New Jersey delegation. However, sickness prevented him from attending the Constitutional Convention.

Opposed ratification

After the United States Constitution had been written, Clark opposed its ratification because it did not include a Bill of Rights. He became identified as an Anti-Federalist, and was defeated when he ran for the office of U. S. Representative in the first United States Congress. During the years 1789 and 1790, while he was out of elective office for the first time in many years, Clark was appointed as commissioner of the state of New Jersey to help settle its debts with the federal government.

Clark won election to the second United States Congress, and served in the House of Representatives for two terms from 1791 to 1794. In Congress he sided with Thomas Jefferson's Democratic-Republicans against Alexander Hamilton's Federalists. Clark achieved his greatest notoriety as a Congressman in the spring of 1794. At this time, President Washington's administration was trying to avoid being drawn into the fighting then going on between England and France. Clark and other Democratic-Republicans favored France, which was then in the throes of the French Revolution; so Clark introduced a resolution calling for all trade to be cut off with England until that country had paid damages for American ships seized in the blockade of France and until all British troops had been withdrawn from frontier forts in the United States, as had been agreed to in the peace treaty of 1783. Clarks' resolution was approved by the House of Representatives on April 25, 1794; but three days later a 13 to 13 tie vote in the Senate was broken by Federal Vice-President John Adams' "nay" that defeated the resolution and saved Washington's administration from having its hands tied in negotiations with the British.

Upon the adjournment of Congress in June, 1794, Clark retired to private life. However, he did not have long to enjoy it, for he died three months later on September 15, 1794, after suffering a sunstroke in Rahway, N. J. His body was buried there in the cemetery of the Presbyterian Church.

GEORGE CLYMER of PENNSYLVANIA

One of the six Founding Fathers who signed both the Declaration of Independence and the United States Constitution, George Clymer was a man of genius who combined such diverse talents as becoming a successful banker, enjoying writing humorous poetry, promoting the development of scientific agriculture, and admiring good music and fine paintings. Above everything else, Clymer was an ardent patriot who dedicated himself to more than twenty years of public service to aid in the establishment of the United States.

An extremely honest man, Clymer always spoke the truth and kept his word, even when it might have profited him not to do so. "He who justly estimates the value of a punctual promise," he said, "will not, without very good reason, disregard it, whether it be to sign a contract or walk with a friend; to pay a debt, or present a toy to a child."

Born in Philadelphia on March 16, 1739, Clymer became an orphan while he was still a small boy. An uncle, William Coleman who was a well-to-do Philadelphia merchant, became the boy's guardian. Clymer was educated at the College of Philadelphia (now the University of Pennsylvania), then entered his uncle's counting house as an apprentice clerk.

When Clymer was twenty-six years old, he married Elizabeth Meredith. His father-in-law, Reese Meredith, a prosperous merchant, took the young man into his firm as a partner, renaming it Meredith & Clymer. Clymer and his wife had nine children, four of whom died as infants.

A captain in the militia

As troubles mounted between Great Britain and the colonies, Clymer became a diligent worker in the patriotic cause. He attended meetings protesting the British taxation policies and spoke out for the rights of the American colonists. To help prepare for the defense of the colony, he became a captain in the militia. In 1773, he was appointed by a town meeting as chairman of a committee that persuaded Philadelphia merchants to refuse to handle tea that was taxed by the British. As the crisis worsened, Clymer's patriotic zeal won him a place on the Committee of Safety that became Pennsylvania's unofficial patriotic governing body.

Courtesy: The Pennsylvania Academy of the Fine Arts
© The Phillips Studio, Philadelphia, Penna.

George Clymer by CHARLES WILLSON PEALE

GEORGE CLYMER

1739 (March 16) Born in Philadelphia.

1775-1776 Served as one of first Continental treasurers for the United Colonies.

1776-1777 Delegate to the Continental Congress from Pennsylvania; signed the Declaration of Independence.

1777-1778 Served as special commissioner of Congress to investigate Indian massacres on Pennsylvania's western frontier.

1780-1782 Member of Congress of Confederation from Pennsylvania.

1784-1788 Representative in Pennsylvania state legislature.

1787 Delegate to Constitutional Convention; signed United States Constitution.

1789-1791 U. S. Representative from Pennsylvania in first United States Congress.

1791-1794 Chief U. S. collector in Pennsylvania for excise tax on alcoholic beverages during period of the Whiskey Rebellion.

1795-1796 Member of commission appointed by President Washington that negotiated a peace treaty with Creek Indians in Georgia.

1813 (Jan. 23) Died in Morrisville, Pa.

The Continental Congress appointed Clymer as one of its first treasurers on July 29, 1775. Clymer plunged with enthusiasm into the thankless work of raising money for the support of George Washington's army that was then besieging Boston. Clymer turned over all his own funds in exchange for Continental currency and persuaded many of his wealthy friends to do likewise.

Fulfillment of his "dearest wish"

The next year, after several of Pennsylvania's delegates to the Continental Congress refused to vote in favor of the Declaration of Independence, Clymer was among the members of a new delegation appointed to replace the less ardent patriots. Although Clymer's appointment to Congress came on July 20, 1776, after independence had been declared, he said it was his "dearest wish" to sign the Declaration of Independence, and he did so with the other delegates on August 2, 1776. Because his duties as a member of Congress took more and more of his time, Clymer resigned his position as one of the Continental treasurers.

As British troops marched into New Jersey and threatened Philadelphia in December, 1776, Congress decided to flee to Baltimore, leaving a committee composed of Clymer, Robert Morris, and George Walton with unusual powers to conduct much of the executive business of the government. During this period, Clymer, who also was a member of the important congressional boards of war and treasury, overworked himself endeavoring to raise men and money for the support of the Continental Army. The threat to Philadelphia was averted by Washington's victories in New Jersey, and Congress returned to Philadelphia in March, 1777. Two months later, in May, Clymer obtained a leave of absence to recover his health.

Clymer had sufficiently recovered by July, 1777, to accept an appointment to a congressional committee asked to investigate a report from General Washington that "this Army must be disbanded" unless better plans could be worked out to provide food for the soldiers. When Clymer and the other members of the committee visited Washington's headquarters at Morristown, N. J., they were told by the commander-in-chief that "our soldiers have scarcely tasted any kind of vegetables" since Congress had changed the regulations applying to the Army's commissary department. Clymer reported back to Congress the necessary steps that had to be taken to insure the delivery of more food to the hungry soldiers.

Victim of British troops

The British capture of Philadelphia in September, 1777, brought special hardship to Clymer. His home was in Chester County, outside Philadelphia, in the path of the British march. Although his family fled to safety, British-sympathizers pointed his house out to British troops who sacked it, destroying most of Clymer's possessions. This disaster may have caused Clymer to ask to be relieved of his duties so that he could care for his family; but, whatever the reason, the Pennsylvania legislature meeting later that month did not re-elect Clymer to Congress.

Clymer resumed his public service three months later, in December, 1777, when he accepted an appointment by Congress as one of three commissioners asked to investigate reports of Indian massacres in western Pennsylvania. After a hazardous roundtrip to Fort Pitt (now Pittsburgh), Clymer and the other commissioners reported back to Congress late in April, 1778, that the Indian uprisings were inspired and financed by the British. As a result, Congress sent the southern general Lachlan McIntosh and a force of 500 soldiers

Taken from Mr MOALE'S View of BALTIMORE in 1752.

Population about 300 Persons.

Tonnage 1 Brig 122 Tons burthen.

DESCRIPTION OF THE SITUATION, HARBOUR &c OF THE CITY AND PORT OF PHILADELPHIA.

To the Honourable Thomas Penn and Richard Penn, Tru and Counties of NEWCASTLE, KENT and SUSSEX on DELAWAR

with orders to march from Fort Pitt to the British stronghold at Detroit in order to end the Indian war. However, lack of supplies doomed the expedition to failure.

Chartering the Bank of America

In November, 1780, Clymer was elected to Congress for a two-year firm. The financial problems of carrying on the war absorbed much of Clymer's time. He worked closely with Robert Morris, the superintendent of finance, in chartering the Bank of North America, the first national bank, and actively promoted subscriptions to the bank. He also was sent by Congress on an extended tour of the southern states to obtain their aid in financing the war effort.

When Clymer's term in Congress ended in November, 1782, the war was nearly over, so he decided that it was now time to make up to his family for the neglect of them that his public duties had forced upon him. His sons were now of college age and he wanted them to attend the College of New Jersey at Princeton. So that the entire family could remain together, Clymer moved them all to Princeton.

In 1784, at the urging of his friend Robert Morris, Clymer returned to Philadelphia to oppose a group that had won control of the state govern-

ment and seemed determined to destroy the Bank of North America that Clymer and Morris had worked to establish. Clymer won election to the state legislature in 1784, but was unable to forestall the cancellation of the bank's charter in 1785. However, in the next session of the legislature, Clymer and Morris succeeded in renewing the bank's charter. While in the legislature, Clymer took an active part in revising the state's penal code to end harsh public punishment of criminals. He sponsored the establishment of penitentiaries, so that criminals could be imprisoned away from public view instead of being forced to work in chains on road gangs.

Delegate to the Constitutional Convention

Because of his distinguished record of public service, Clymer was chosen as one of Pennsylvania's delegates to attend the Constitutional Convention of 1787. He worked patiently with the other delegates to resolve the many different viewpoints held by the various states and aided substantially in the preparation of the United States Constitution. He particularly opposed a plan that was submitted by which the Senate would have been given the power to appoint all federal officials; and he joined Roger Sherman in holding out against the use of the word "slaves" in the Constitution, because he felt that the term was too degrading to use in a document intended to stand the test of time. When the Constitution finally was approved by the convention, Clymer signed it with the other delegates from Pennsylvania.

Still a member of Pennsylvania's legislature in 1788, Clymer was chairman of the committee that prepared for the state's first election under the new Constitution. A Federalist party convention in Lancaster, Pa., in November, 1788, nominated Clymer as one of eight candidates for the offices of U.S. Representatives. The Federalists were strongly opposed by a slate of Anti-Federalist candidates and by the German population of the state. However, Clymer and five other Federalist candidates won easily, and the only two Anti-Federalist candidates who won were supported by the German party.

Thinking for his constituents

As a member of the first United States House of Representatives that convened in 1789, Clymer followed an independent course, saying, "A representative of the people is appointed to think *for* and not *with* his constituents." He particularly rebelled at a proposal that the Constitution should be amended to give the people "the unalienable right of instructing their representatives." Clymer spoke out sharply:

"Do gentlemen forsee the extent of these words? If they have a constitutional right to instruct us, it infers that we are bound by those instructions, and as we ought not to decide constitutional questions by implication, I presume that we shall be called upon to go further, and expressly declare the members of the legislature to be bound by the instructions of their constituents. This is a most dangerous principle, utterly destructive of all ideas of an independent and deliberative body, which are essential requisites in the legislatures of free governments: They prevent men of abilities and experience from rendering those services to the community that are in their power, destroying the object contemplated by establishing an efficient general government, and rendering congress a mere passive machine."

When James Madison proposed in Congress that the Bill of Rights amendments should be interspersed throughout the Constitution, rather than merely being tagged on at the end, Clymer angrily attacked the idea. The *Congressional Journal* repoted him as saying: "The amendments ought not to be incorporated in the body of the work, which he hoped would remain a monument to justify those who made it; by a comparison, the world would discover the perfection of the original, and the superfluity of the amendments."

Family tragedy in the Whiskey Rebellion

Upon completion of his term in Congress in 1791, Clymer was appointed by President Washington as the chief collector in Pennsylvania for the excise tax levied by Congress on alcoholic beverages. The tax had been supported by Alexander Hamilton and the Federalist party as the best way of collecting enough money to pay the government's debts, but it was strongly opposed by Thomas Jefferson's Anti-Federalists as being an unfair tax akin to those levied by the British parliament that had led to the Revolutionary War. The Anti-Federalist farmers of western Pennsylvania soon were in open rebellion against Clymer's efforts to collect the tax. President Washington finally was forced to call up an army of 12,000 militia to put down the Whisky Rebellion in 1794. As well as suffering much abuse as the chief collector of the tax, Clymer received a further blow when one of his sons, who had joined the militia, was killed in a skirmish with the rebels.

In 1795, President Washington again called upon Clymer for assistance, appointing him with two other commissioners to go to Georgia to try to bring peace between the settlers and the Indians. In an effort to help overcome his wife's grief over the death of their son, Clymer took her with him

Fighting Fire
(circa 1800)

Library of Congress

73

on the sea voyage to Georgia. Clymer soon discovered that most of the trouble in Georgia was being caused by greedy settlers trying to drive the Indians of their lands without paying them for it. Clymer's sympathy for the Indians is evident in the report he wrote on June 30, 1796: "Our treaty was finished yesterday at noon, and the last signing is just published by our cannon. I am sure it is an honest treaty, for it was negotiated without artifice or threats; it is honest because it will greatly benefit each of the contracting parties; it is honest because it is protested against by the Georgia commissioners, who found all the customary avenues to the Indian lands barred by the principles we had laid down in conducting it."

For the last few years of his life, Clymer devoted himself to building his private fortune and enjoying the pursuit of knowledge. He was elected president of the Philadelphia Bank, president of the Academy of Fine Arts, and vice-president of the Philadelphia Agriculture Society. On January 23, 1813, Clymer died at the age of 73 at the home of a son in Morrisville, Pa. His body was buried in the Friends Graveyard at Trenton, N. J.

The BLOODY MASSACRE perpetrated in King—Street BOSTON on March 5th 1770 by a party of the 29th REGT.

Unhappy Boston! see thy Sons deplore,
Thy hallow'd Walks besmear'd with guiltless Gore.
While faithless P—n and his savage Bands,
With murd'rous Rancour stretch their bloody Hands;
Like fierce Barbarians grinning o'er their Prey,

If scalding drops from Rage from Anguish Wrung
If speechless Sorrows lab'ring for a Tongue,
Or if a weeping World can ought appease
The plaintive Ghosts of Victims such as these;
The Patriot's copious Tears for each are shed,

But know Fate summons to that awful Goal.
Where Justice strips the Murd'rer of his Soul:
Should venal C—ts the scandal of the Land.
Snatch the relentless Villain from her Hand,
Keen Execrations on this Plate inscrib'd.

74

WILLIAM ELLERY of RHODE ISLAND

As a representative of Rhode Island, the first colony to declare its independence from Great Britain, William Ellery ardently believed that no sacrifice was too great to make for the freedom of his country. While he was serving in Congress during the Revolutionary War, one of his children died; and, while confiding his grief in a letter to a friend, Ellery commented, "He that loveth father or mother, he that loveth son or daughter more than liberty, is not worthy of her." Believing in freedom for the individual as well as for his country, Ellery seconded and strongly supported legislation in 1785 in which the Congress of the Confederation forbade slavery in the states to be formed from the Northwest Territory.

A noted wit

A man of medium height with a head that seemed too large for his body, Ellery was noted among his fellow members of Congress for his ready wit and for his distaste for exercise. He is said to have been able to bring laughter from his colleagues with dry comments on almost any subject that came before them for discussion. Unfortunately, examples of his humor have not survived, no doubt largely because most such jokes of the moment are amusing only to those involved at the time. The fact that he always preferred to ride when he might have walked had no effect on Ellery's health, for he lived happily to the age of ninety-two.

William Ellery was born at Newport, R.I., on December 22, 1727. His father, whose name also was William Ellery, was a respected citizen of the colony who had held the offices of judge, senator, and lieutenant-governor. Most of young William's early education was received from his father; but, when he reached the age of fifteen, he was sent off to Cambridge, Mass., to attend Harvard College.

WILLIAM ELLERY

1727 (Dec. 22) Born at Newport, R. I.

1747 Graduated from Harvard College.

1776-1779, 1781-1785 Represented Rhode Island in Congress; signed the Declaration of Independence and the Articles of Confederation.

1790-1820 U. S. collector of customs at Newport.

1820 (Feb. 15) Died at Newport.

His favorite studies at Harvard were the Greek and Latin languages. He acquired a fondness for reading the classics in those languages that lasted until his death, which came while he was reading Cicero in bed.

After his graduation from Harvard in 1747, Ellery returned to Newport and took up the study of law. He became a successful attorney and built a large practice. He married twice. His first wife was Ann Remington of Cambridge, Mass. After she died, Ellery married Abigail Cary.

In the years leading up to the Revolutionary War, Ellery became an active figure in Rhode Island's patriotic movement, opposing the British taxation of the American colonies without their consent. After the fighting began in neighboring Massachusetts in 1775, the Rhode Island patriots became impatient with the failure of the Continental Congress to vote for independence from Great Britain. So the legislature of little Rhode Island declared itself completely free of British rule in May, 1776. That same month, Ellery was appointed as a delegate to go to Congress and forcefully urge the adoption of independence by all the colonies.

William Ellery *by* J. R. LAMBDIN

A view of the attack against Fort Washington and Rebel Redoubts, near New York, on the 16 of November, 1776, by the British and Hessian Brigades. Drawn on the spot by Tho. Davies, Capt. R.R. of Artillery.

'Undaunted resolution in every countenance'

Ellery took his seat in Congress in May 14, 1776, but six weeks went by before he had the pleasure of voting for the Declaration of Independence. The intensity of his interest in achieving liberty for his country is evidenced by his own description of the signing of the Declaration by the delegates in August, 1776: "I was determined to see how they all looked, as they signed what might be their death warrant. I placed myself beside the secretary, Charles Thomson, and eyed each closely as he affixed his name to the document. Undaunted resolution was displayed in every countenance."

During the next three years, Ellery worked diligently on many committees of Congress, while at the same time the war brought about the destruction of most of his private property and fortune. The British had invaded Rhode Island and occupied Newport from December, 1776, to October, 1779. During this occupation, the British burned

Ellery's home and wrecked other property that he owned as a reprisal for his patriotic activities. In 1778, Ellery voted for and signed the Articles of Confederation. After the British forces retired from Newport, Ellery left Congress to help reestablish his family and salvage what he could of his personal property.

Ellery returned to Congress in November, 1781, and continued to serve as a delegate from Rhode Island until 1785. During this entire period he served on dozens of committees that endeavored to carry out both the executive and legislative functions of the federal government. Near the end of his service in Congress, Ellery seconded the resolution offered by Rufus King and adopted by Congress that declared "their shall be neither slavery nor involuntary servitude in any of the states" that were to be formed in the Northwest Territory—Ohio, Indiana, Illinois, Michigan, Minnesota, and Wisconsin.

After retiring from Congress, Ellery held relatively minor government jobs the rest of his life because he did not want power and needed only enough income to live quietly in the enjoyment of books. He was appointed in 1786 as a commissioner of the continental loan office for Rhode Island. Shortly after this appointment, he was offered the office of chief justice of the superior court of Rhode Island, but he refused to serve. In 1790, President George Washington appointed Ellery as U. S. collector of customs for Newport —a position that he held for the next thirty years.

"I am going off the stage of life"

The story is told that on the day of his death, February 15, 1820, Ellery was sitting in a chair reading one of his favorite books in Latin when his doctor stopped by his home. Upon taking Ellery's pulse, the doctor exclaimed that he could feel none. Ellery then drank a glass of wine, and the physician upon checking his pulse again found that it had revived.

"Oh yes, doctor," Ellery is said to have replied. "I have a charming pulse. But it is idle to talk to me in this way. I am going off the stage of life, and it is a great blessing that I go free from sickness, pain, and sorrow."

Later that day the 92-year-old Ellery retired to his bedroom. Sometime after, his daughter looked into his room and discovered that he had died quietly sitting upright in bed, his chin resting on a copy of Cicero that he had been reading.

Ellery's famous descendants include a grandson, William Ellery Channing, the founder of Unitarianism, and a great-grandson, Richard Henry Dana, Jr., the author of *Two Years Before the Mast*.

Washington Resigning His Commission
at Annapolis, December 23, 1783.
(from an original picture by Trumbull)

WILLIAM FLOYD of NEW YORK

A landowner of Long Island, William Floyd at 41 was the youngest member of the New York delegation to sign the Declaration of Independence. He continued to serve in the Continental Congress throughout the Revolutionary War. Afterward, he was elected as U. S. Representative from New York to the 1st United States Congress. As a member of the post-war Democratic-Republican party, he was an ardent supporter of Thomas Jefferson and served several times as a presidential elector.

A man of medium height, he usually was known as "General" Floyd because he had held the rank of major general in the militia of Suffolk County before the Revolutionary War. Although he had little education, Floyd is said to have made up in practical logic and sincerity what he lacked in formal training. He seldom took part in congressional debates, but he consistently voted to support the patriotic cause. His continuing popularity was evidenced by his repeated re-election to public office for nearly fifty years.

Floyd was born on Dec. 17, 1734, at Brook-

William Floyd
by Ralph Earl,
with his home in the background.

Library of Congress

haven, his father's estate in Suffolk County on Long Island. As a boy, he received only the most basic kind of education. He preferred to spend his time riding, hunting, and taking part in rural social life. When Floyd was 18 his father died, and he took over the managemenet of the estate. He was married twice, to Isabella Jones of Southampton and later to Joanna Strong of Setauket. There is no record of children by either marriage.

A false invasion threat

Having become active in the patriotic movements of the 1760's and having risen to command of the Suffolk County militia, Floyd was a natural choice as a member of the New York delegation to the First Continental Congress in 1774. When he returned home from the Congress, he discovered that the British were threatening an invasion of Long Island with a naval force assembled in Gardiner's Bay. When the landing of the enemy had been reported to him, Floyd assembled the militia and marched to the beach. However, the landing report was false and no clash occurred.

In 1775, Floyd again was chosen as a member of the New York delegation to the Second Continental Congress. He served on many important committees, helping obtain supplies for the army and organizing the militia. Although he was present during the debate and adoption of the Declaration of Independence in 1776, he with other members of the New York delegation abstained from voting. When the Declaration had been approved in New York, he signed it with the other members of the Congress in August.

British seized his estate

While Floyd was attending the session of Congress, the British seized his estate. His family fled

---

WILLIAM FLOYD

1734 (Dec. 17) Born in Suffolk County, N. Y.

1774-1783 Member of New York delegation to Continental Congress.

1777-1788 State senator in New York assembly.

1789-1791 U.S. Representative from New York in 1st United States Congress.

1808 State senator in New York assembly.

1821 (Aug. 4) Died in Westernville, N.Y., at the age of 86.

Tontine Coffee House, New York, 1786
STOKES ICONOGRAPHY of Manhattan
Library of Congress

to Connecticut. Floyd was left with no means of income and no home for the rest of the Revolutionary War.

Although Floyd continued to serve in the Continental Congress until 1783, he took an important part in the affairs of the state of New York. On May 8, 1777, he was appointed a state senator under New York's new constitution. He continued to serve as a state senator until 1788. He became a leading member of the state senate, generally presiding when the lieutenant-general was absent.

Floyd was elected as U.S. representative from New York to the First United States Congress that began meeting in New York in 1789. At the end of his term in 1791, he declined re-election.

With the growth of the party system in the United States, Floyd became an active supporter of Thomas Jefferson's Democratic-Republican party.

In 1800, he was named as a presidential elector and helped elect Jefferson as the third President of the United States. In 1801, he was named a member of the convention to revise the New York state constitution.

To rebuild his fortune that was destroyed during the war, he moved to upper New York state in 1803. At the age of 68, he pioneered a vast tract of land near Oneida, N. Y. His new neighbors respected his career as one of the Founding Fathers and in 1808 he was once more elected as a state senator. However, his advancing age prevented him from taking a very active part in the New York assembly. By 1820, he was unable to leave his home, but he again was complimented by being named a presidential elector. On Aug. 4, 1821, Floyd died at the age of 86 in his home in Westernville, N. Y.

BENJAMIN FRANKLIN of PENNSYLVANIA

The elder statesman of the American Revolution, Benjamin Franklin was the oldest man to sign either the Declaration of Independence or the United States Constitution. Before some of the other signers of the Constitution had even been born, Franklin had promoted the joining of the American colonies with his Albany Plan of Union. Recognized both in America and Europe as a universal genius in the arts and sciences, Franklin repeatedly stepped into crisis after crisis during the Revolutionary period and lent the weight of his wisdom and diplomatic skill to tip the scales in favor of the American cause. He spent almost a third of his life representing America in the courts of Europe; there, he won France's crucial aid in the Revolutionary War with a treaty of alliance, and he negotiated the peace treaty that forced Great Britain to recognize American independence. Thomas Jefferson lauded him as "the greatest man and ornament of the age and country in which he lived."

One of seventeen children

Born in Boston, Mass., on January 17, 1706, Benjamin Franklin was the youngest son in a family of seventeen children. His father Josiah Franklin, who had come to America in 1683 seeking religious freedom, operated a small shop that made soap and candles. With so many mouths to feed, Franklin's father could only afford to send the boy to school long enough to learn to read and write. At the age of ten, Benjamin Franklin was taken out of school and put to work helping make soap and candles.

At the age of twelve, Benjamin Franklin was apprenticed to his brother James Franklin to learn the printing trade. While becoming an expert printer in the next several years, the youth also educated himself, reading every book that he could borrow or buy from his small wages. James Franklin founded one of the earliest newspapers in America, the *New England Courant*. Benjamin Franklin wrote essays for the newspaper signed by the name "Mrs. Silence Dogood," but he slipped them under the door of the print shop because he knew his older brother would not print them if he knew the real author. In 1722, James Franklin

was arrested because of criticisms of the Massachusetts authorities that had appeared in the paper, so for a time 16-year-old Benjamin carried on the newspaper as editor and publisher. James Franklin was a man of irritable temper, and when he and his younger brother quarreled he figured that he had the right to beat Benjamin as he did his other apprentices. Unwilling to put up with this treatment, Benjamin sold his small collection of books and used the money he received to buy passage on a ship to New York.

Off to New York and Philadelphia

Franklin could not find work in New York City, so he traveled on to Philadelphia, arriving there at the age of seventeen, in October, 1723. In his *Autobiography* written many years later, Franklin described how he walked across New Jersey to Philadelphia. He bought three loaves of bread for a Sunday morning breakfast, walked about town, met his future wife, Deborah Read, and eventually went to sleep in a Quaker meeting. He soon found work as a printer's helper, and moved into the house of his future wife as a boarder.

Sir William Keith, the governor of Pennsylva-

Benjamin Franklin
From a painting by DAVID MARTIN

The City & Port of PHILADELPHIA, on the River Delaware from Kensington.

CONGRESS HALL and NEW THEATRE, in Chesnut Street PHILADELPHIA

Drawn, Engraved & Published by W.Birch & Son. Neshaminy Bridge. 1800.

nia, became interested in the boy and encouraged him to set up his own print shop. Keith gave Franklin a letter to take to his father in Boston, suggesting that the elder Franklin give his son enough money to establish him in business as a printer in Philadelphia. Franklin went back to Boston, was unable to interest his father in the proposition, and returned to Philadelphia. Governor Keith now proposed that Franklin should go to London and buy printing equipment, and he promised the boy letters of credit to pay for the machinery and the assistance of friends in England; so, in 1724, Franklin kissed his sweetheart Deborah goodbye and sailed for England.

Journey to London

Arriving in England in 1725, the 19-year-old Franklin discovered that Governor Keith had not made good on his promises; there were no letters of credit; and Keith's friends were not interested in helping the young printer. Penniless, he went to work as a printer's helper. In the eighteen months he spent in London, Franklin lived a carefree Bohemian life in the company of an aspiring poet named James Ralph, but eventually the two fell out in a quarrel over a girl. Franklin attained some notoriety in literary circles by publishing a pamphlet called "A Dissertation on Liberty and Necessity, Pleasure and Pain" in which he set forth views that God had no control over the affairs of the world and that man had no moral responsibilities for his actions.

Franklin had become acquainted with a well-to-do Philadelphia merchant, Thomas Denham, who was in London on business; and Denham persuaded Franklin to return to America to go to work in his shipping business. Upon his return to Philadelphia in 1726, Franklin discovered that his "dear Debby" had married another man, having given Benjamin Franklin up because he had only written to her once during his absence. A few months later, Denham's death ended Franklin's plans to become a wealthy merchant.

Origin of the American Philosophical Society

Returning to his trade as a printer, Franklin began to save his money in order eventually to go into business for himself. In 1727, Franklin formed the Junto, or Leather Apron Club, a social and philosophical club for young craftsmen. This club later became part of the American Philosophical Society which Franklin founded in 1743.

The Junto club's library also became the basis for the Library Company of Philadelphia, the first subscription or circulating library, founded by Franklin in 1731. Franklin went into partnership with fellow-printer Hugh Meredith in 1728, and the next year they began publishing the newspaper *The Pennsylvania Gazette*, which gained a wide circulation under Franklin's editorial direction. Franklin obtained a lucrative printing contract to print Pennsylvania's paper money after he published a pamphlet in 1729 called a "Modest Enquiry Into the Nature and Necessity of Paper Currency" that called for the issuance of more paper money.

Deborah Read's husband having run away and left her, Franklin's interest in her "rekindled" and he took her as his common-law wife in September, 1730. They had two children, a son who died while still an infant, and a daughter who became Mrs. Richard Bache. Franklin also dallied with a number of other women; and by one of them he had a son in the winter of 1730-1731 that he and his wife took into their home and reared. This

Deborah Franklin
Attributed to Benjamin Wilson

American Philosophical Society

81

natural son was William Franklin who became the royal governor of New Jersey from 1763 to 1775, remained loyal to the British during the Revolutionary War, and lived the rest of his life in England. Deborah Read Franklin was a devoted wife,

but was no match for her husband in education or intellect. Franklin did not take her with him on his extended trips to Europe, and he had been absent from the country for ten years when she died in 1774.

BENJAMIN FRANKLIN

1706 (Jan. 17) Born in Boston.

1716-1718 Helped father make candles and soap.

1718-1723 Apprentice printer working for his brother James Franklin.

1723 Ran away to Philadelphia at the age of 17.

1724-1726 Worked as a printer in London, England.

1726 Returned to Philadelphia.

1729 Began publishing the newspaper the Pennsylvania Gazette.

1731 Founded the first subscription library, the Library Company of Philadelphia.

1733-1758 Published Poor Richard's Almanac.

1736-1751 Clerk of the Pennsylvania colonial legislature.

1737-1753 Deputy postmaster of Philadelphia.

1744-1754 Representative in the Pennsylvania colonial legislature.

1740 Invented the Franklin stove.

1747 Discovered positive and negative electricity.

1749 Invented the lightning rod.

1749 Helped found the Academy of Philadelphia that later became the University of Pennsylvania.

1752 Used a kite to prove that lightning is electricity.

1753-1774 Deputy postmaster general of the American colonies.

1753 Received honorary masters degrees from Harvard and Yale.

1754 Represented Pennsylvania in the Albany Congress; wrote the Albany Plan of Union for the colonies.

1757-1762 Represented the Pennsylvania colonial legislature in London.

1762 Awarded honorary degree of doctor of civil law by Oxford University.

1763 Made a 1,600-mile tour of the American colonies inspecting post offices.

1764-1775 Represented Pennsylvania, Georgia, New Jersey, and Massachusetts in London.

1775 Appointed postmaster general by the Continental Congress.

1775-1776 Member of the Pennsylvania Committee of Safety; delegate from Pennsylvania to the Continental Congress; signed the Declaration of Independence.

1776 President of the Pennsylvania state constitutional convention.

1776-1785 Represented the Continental Congress in Paris; negotiated and signed the treaty of alliance with France in 1778; negotiated and signed the treaty of peace with Great Britain in 1783.

1785-1788 President of the state of Pennsylvania.

1787 Delegate from Pennsylvania to the Constitutional Convention; signed the United States Constitution.

1788 Elected president of the first antislavery society in the United States.

1790 (April 17) Died in Philadelphia.

"Poor Richard's Almanac"

One of Franklin's most successful publishing ventures was "Poor Richard's Almanac" that was issued each year from 1733 to 1758. Edited by Franklin under the pseudonym "Richard Saunders," this book sold about 10,000 copies a year —a huge number of copies for the time. It contained all the regular features of an almanac, but won a wide audience largely because of its pokes, witty verses, and thoughtful proverbs. Franklin became known throughout the world for such sayings as: "God helps them that help themselves," "A penny saved is a penny earned," "He's a fool that makes a doctor his heir," and "Early to bed and early to rise, makes a man healthy, wealthy, and wise."

Franklin began his long career in public office at the age of thirty when he was chosen as clerk of the Pennsylvania legislature, an office that he held until 1751. He accepted a second public office in 1737, agreeing to become Philadelphia's deputy postmaster in order to improve the city's distribution of mail. He continued in this position for sixteen years. From 1744 to 1754, Franklin served as a representative in the Pennsylvania legislature.

Experiments in science

Becoming interested in science, he invented the Franklin stove in 1740, a device that conserved on fuel and improve the heating of homes. He saw some electrical experiments performed in Boston in 1746, and upon returning home he began working with electricity, making many new discoveries such as the positive and negative qualities of electricity, and developing such new words as "battery," "condenser," "conductor," and "armature."

Joseph Priestly, the English chemist who was the co-discoverer of oxygen and a close friend of Franklin, described some of the experiments as follows:

"Franklin, after having published his method of verifying his hypothesis concerning the sameness of electricity with the matter of lightning, was waiting for the erection of a spire in Philadelphia to carry his views into execution, not imagining that a pointed rod of a moderate height, could

A S.W. View of the STATE HOUSE in BOSTON.

answer the purpose; when it occurred to him, that by means of a common kite, he could have a readier and better access to the regions of thunder than by any spire whatever. Preparing, therefore, a large silk handkerchief, and two cross sticks, of a proper length, on which to extend it, he took the opportunity of the first approaching thunderstorm to take a walk into the field, in which there was a shed convenient for his purpose. But dreading the ridicule which too commonly attends unsuccessful attempts in science, he communicated his intended experiment to nobody but his son, who assisted him in raising the kite.

"The kite being raised, a considerable time elapsed before there was any appearance of its being electrified. One very promising cloud had passed over without any effect; when, at length, just as he was beginning to despair of his contrivance, he observed some loose threads of the hempen string to stand erect, and to avoid one another, just as if they had been suspended on a common conductor. Struck with this favourable appearance, he immediately presented his knuckle to the key,—and let the reader judge of the exquisite pleasure he must have felt at that moment,— the discovery was complete. He perceived a very evident electric spark. Others succeeded even before the string was wet, so as to put the matter past all dispute; and when the rain had wet the string, he collected electric fire very copiously. This happened in June, 1752, a month after the electricians in France had verified the same theory, but before he had heard of any thing they had done."

Franklin's inquiring mind led him to make countless other scientific discoveries in the course of his life. He discovered that ocean waves could be calmed by pouring oil on the water. He invented bifocal glasses for reading. Franklin did not patent any of his inventions or discoveries, feeling that his best reward would be their widespread use by mankind.

An early postmaster general

In 1753, Franklin was appointed as one of the deputy postmasters general for the American colonies. In this office that he held for twenty-one years, Franklin made many innovations to speed the delivery of mail between the colonies and to overseas countries. He ordered mail couriers to ride by night as well as by day and established mail service by messenger between Montreal and New York.

In 1754 the French and Indian Wars had broken out, and Franklin was elected as a delegate from Pennsylvania to attend a Congress called in Albany, N. Y., by the seven northern colonies to determine how they should defend themselves. After the conference opened on June 19, 1754, Franklin presented a Plan of Union to bring about a confederation of the colonies. His plan, as described by Franklin, provided that "the general government was to be administered by a president-general, appointed and supported by the Crown, and a grand council, to be chosen by the representatives of the people of the several colonies, met in their respective assemblies." The Albany Congress approved the Plan of Union; but the colonies failed to ratify it, and the British government looked upon the plan with disfavor. "Everyone cries a union is absolutely necessary," Franklin said, "but when it comes to the manner and form of the union, their weak noddles are perfectly distracted."

Because the American colonies could not agree to work together for mutual defense against the French and the Indians, the British sent General Edward Braddock and two British regiments to America. Franklin was given the task of aiding Braddock in obtaining horses, wagons, and supplies for a march on the French Fort Duquesne (now Pittsburgh). Franklin advanced a large part of his personal fortune to obtain the supplies. He warned Braddock that he must be wary of ambush attack by the French and Indians, a warning that was echoed by George Washington, then a young militia officer acting as an aide to Braddock. Braddock ignored the warnings, was ambushed, and fatally wounded. Franklin then set about organizing western defenses using colonial forces, and was himself elected colonel of a militia company.

Back to Europe

From 1757 to 1762 Franklin represented the Pennsylvania legislature in London. He was sent there in an effort to settle a tax dispute between the legislature and the proprietors of the colony. The proprietors, the descendants of William Penn, refused to let the legislature pass a tax for defense unless their own estates were allowed to remain untaxed. In 1759, Franklin published the "Historical Review of Pennsylvania" which reviewed the entire history of the proprietory government of the colony. This publication helped sway the opinion of the British parliament against the colony's proprietors, and Franklin achieved a compromise

whereby only the unsurveyed lands of the proprietors would remain untaxed.

By the early 1760's, France had lost the French and Indian War and offered Britain as a settlement either the province of Canada in North America or the island of Guadeloupe in the West Indies. Franklin published a pamphlet in London in 1760 entitled "The Interest of Great Britain Considered With Regard to Her Colonies, and the Acquisitions of Canada and Guadeloupe." In this publication, Franklin compared the size and importance of Canada with that of Guadeloupe, influencing British policy-makers to take Canada from the French.

Journeys in the colonies and back to England

Returning to Philadelphia in 1762, Franklin was greeted as a hero for his work in helping overcome the power of the proprietors. During the next year, he went on an extensive tour of about 1,600 miles throughout the American colonies inspecting post offices in his capacity of deputy postmaster

A colonial printing press and type case
(said to have been used by Franklin)

84

general. Upon his return from this trip, he was named commissioner to raise troops for the defense of western Pennsylvania against Indian attacks.

In 1764 the Pennsylvania legislature decided to petition the British government to abolish the powers of the proprietors and establish Pennsylvania as a crown colony, and the legislature asked Franklin to return to England to represent the colonial views. He arrived in London in time to testify unsuccessfully against the adoption by the British parliament of the Stamp Act of 1765. Misjudging what the reaction of the colonies would be to the Stamp tax, Franklin recommended one of his friends as tax collector for Philadelphia and ordered stamps delivered to his printing firm there. Soon he heard from his wife that the feeling against him in Philadelphia was so strong that she had obtained guns to defend their house, and he heard of the reaction of the Stamp Act Congress called in New York. Now, Franklin busied himself endeavoring to have the Stamp Act repealed, and on February 3, 1766, he subjected himself to hours of questioning before the British parliament in which he answered 174 questions, giving the British legislators a clear understanding of the feelings of America on the issue of taxation without representation. Franklin's reputation in America was restored when the parliament repealed the Stamp Act.

Failing in the mission

For the remainder of his stay in London until 1775, Franklin worked unsuccessfully to convince British government leaders of the folly of the policies they were pursuing in regard to the American colonies. As well as being the agent of Pennsylvania, Franklin also was employed as agent of Georgia, New Jersey, and Massachusetts. To successfully carry out his diplomacy he had to remain on good terms with the British leaders even though he recognized "that this course would render him suspected, in England of being too much an American, and in America, of being too much of an Englishman." Franklin published two satiric essays in 1773 portraying his views on the bumbling course of the British government, "Rules by Which a Great Empire May be Reduced to a Small One" and "An Edict by the King of Prussia." He also saw to it that some controversial letters by Thomas Hutchinson, governor of Massachusetts, were given wide circulation. To punish him, the British government in 1774 dismissed Franklin from his post

as deputy postmaster general of the American colonies. As the British government closed the port of Boston in retaliation for the "Boston Tea Party," Franklin offered to pay from his own pocket for the tea that had been destroyed if parliament would repeal the Tea Act. However, the British refused. Realizing that war was likely to break out, Franklin sailed for home on March 21, 1775.

Arriving in Philadelphia on May 5, 1775, Franklin was greeted by news of the battles at Lexington and Concord. He immediately was elected as one of Pennsylvania's delegates to the Continental Congress. He also became a member of the Pennsylvania Committee of Safety, the revolutionary government of the state. The Continental Congress appointed Franklin as its postmaster general, and he set about insuring an adequate communication system among the colonies. A Plan of Union submitted by Franklin to the Congress on July 21, 1775, later became the basis for the Articles of Confederation that were written by John Dickinson. Franklin served on many committees of the Congress, and was a member of the congressional commission that went to Canada in an unsuccessful effort to persuade the French Canadians to take part in the struggle against Great Britain. Franklin also served as the president of the Pennsylvania convention in 1776 that drew up a state constitution providing for a single house legislature and an executive council chaired by a president.

A lesson for Jefferson

The 70-year-old Franklin, the oldest delegate in the Continental Congress, believed strongly that independence from Great Britain should be declared by the colonies, and he served with Thomas Jefferson and John Adams on the committee that was assigned the task of drafting a Declaration of Independence in the spring of 1776. Although the main task of writing the historic document was delegated to Jefferson, various changes in Jefferson's original version have been attributed to Franklin. When the delegates took up the consideration of the Declaration of Independence on July 3 and began acting as a board of editors by cutting out passages and rewriting others, Franklin comforted Jefferson, whose pride of authorship was hurt, by telling him a characteristic story: This tale concerned a hat-maker who decided to put a sign in front of his shop that showed a picture of a hat and read "John Thompson, Hatter, makes

FRANKLIN'S BIRTHPLACE

interest that country in providing assistance to the American patriots in their war with Great Britain. Before setting sail in October, Franklin, as a demonstration of his loyalty, turned over his entire fortune of 3,000 to 4,000 pounds to the Congress for its use in fighting the war. Franklin arrived in Paris in December, where he was to remain for the next nine years. In a letter to a friend, Franklin described his appearance in Paris:

"Figure me in your mind as jolly as formerly, and as strong and hearty, only a few years older; very plainly dressed, wearing my thin grey straight hair, that peeps out under my only coeffure, a fine fur cap, which comes down my forehead almost to my spectacles. Think how this must appear among the powdered heads of Paris!"

For many months Franklin received a deaf ear from French officials to his appeals for help; but news of the American defeat of the British general

and sells hats for ready money." One friend said the word "Hatter" was not needed, another said that "makes and" was unnecessary, and a third friend said that the sign would be simpler if it just said, "John Thompson sells hats." Finally, a fourth friend reminded him that people seeing the picture of the hat on the sign would not expect him to give hats away, so that really all he needed on the sign was his name and the picture of the hat. No one recorded whether Jefferson laughed at this lesson in editing.

'All hang together'

Franklin voted for the Declaration of Independence on July 4, 1776, and signed it with the other delegates on August 2. The story is told that at the signing ceremony, John Hancock, the president of the Continental Congress, remarked: "We must be unanimous; there must be no pulling different ways; we must all hang together." To this, Franklin is said to have quipped: "Yes, we must indeed all hang together, or most assuredly we shall all hang separately."

Back to Paris

Late in 1776, the Continental Congress appointed Franklin to go to France in an effort to

GENERAL BURGOYNE.

John Burgoyne at Saratoga, N. Y., in October, 1777, created a sensation in Paris, and aided Franklin's negotiations. Finally, on February 6, 1778, Franklin signed a treaty of alliance with France.

No peace on those terms

The British, alarmed at the aid France was offering, endeavored to negotiate a peace treaty that did not include a guarantee of independence, and Franklin replied: "I never think of your ministry and their abettors, but with the image strongly painted in my view, of their hands red, and dripping with the blood of my countrymen, friends, and relations: *No peace can be signed with those hands.*"

In 1782, after George Washington's armies with the aid of the French fleet had defeated the British, Franklin, along with other American peace commissioners that included John Adams, John Jay, and Henry Laurens, agreed upon a preliminary peace treaty. This was finally concluded and signed by Franklin on September 3, 1783.

During the next two years he spent in Paris, Franklin enjoyed respect and admiration as the representative of the new American republic. "How happy should I be to see you in Europe," Franklin wrote to George Washington, "to accompany you, if my age and strength would permit, in visiting some of its ancient and famous kingdoms. You would on this side of the sea enjoy the great reputation you have acquired, free from those shades that the jealousy and envy of a man's countrymen and contemporaries are ever endeavouring to cast upon living merit. Here you would know and enjoy what posterity will say of Washington; for a thousand leagues have nearly the same effect as a thousand years. The feeble voice of those grovelling passions cannot extend so far in time or distance. At present I enjoy that pleasure for you, as I frequently hear the old generals of this martial country, who study the maps of America, and mark upon them all your operations, speak with sincere approbation and great applause of your conduct, and join in giving you the character of one of the greatest captains of your age."

When Thomas Jefferson arrived to relieve Franklin of his duties as American minister to France in 1785, Jefferson wrote: "There appeared to me more respect and veneration attached to the character of Dr. Franklin, in France, than to that of any other person in the same country, foreigner or native."

Home after twenty-four years

After stopping briefly in England on his homeward journey, Franklin arrived in Philadelphia on September 14, 1785, where he was wildly greeted by the ringing of bells, bonfires, and artillery salutes. Shortly after his arrival, Franklin was elected to succeed John Dickinson as president of the state of Pennsylvania, an office that he held until 1788. He now, for the first time in many years, enjoyed a life of peace in his native land. As he described it: "I am now in the bosom of my family, and find four new little prattlers, who cling about the knees of their grandpapa, and afford me great pleasure. I am surrounded by my friends, and have an affectionate, good daughter and son-in-law to take care of me. I have got into my *niche,* a very good house which I built twenty-four years ago, and out of which I have been ever since kept by foreign employments."

Franklin's attendance as a Pennsylvania delegate at the Constitutional Convention in 1787 was one of the major factors that led to the successful

Benjamin Franklin
From a portrait by M. Chamberlin, engraved by E. Fisher

drafting of the United States Constitution and its ratification by the states. As he had been the oldest man who signed the Declaration of Independence, now at the age of eighty-one Franklin was to become the oldest man to sign the Constitution. Franklin took an important part in the debates of the Constitutional Convention, constantly endeavoring to insure that the government it created would be as democratic as possible. He objected to many parts of the Constitution, favoring a single-house legislature and an executive council to share the power of the presidency; but on the final day of the convention he appealed to the delegates for unanimity in a speech read for him by his fellow-delegate from Pennsylvania, James Wilson:

An appeal for tolerance

"I confess that there are several parts of this Constitution which I do not at present approve, but I am not sure I shall never approve them. For having lived long, I have experienced many instances of being obliged by better information, or fuller consideration, to change opinions even on important subjects, which I once thought right, but found to be otherwise. It is therefore that, the older I grow, the more apt I am to doubt my own judgment, and to pay more respect to the judgment, of others. Most men, indeed, as well as most sects in religion, think themselves in possession of all truth, and that wherever others differ from them, it is so far error. Steele, a Protestant, in a dedication, tells the pope, that the only difference between our churches, in their opinions of the certainty of their doctrines, is, 'the Church of Rome is infallible, and the Church of England is never in the wrong.' But though many private persons think almost as highly of their own infallibility as of that of their sect, few express it so naturally as a certain French lady, who, in a dispute with her sister, said, 'I don't know how it happens, sister, but I meet with nobody but myself, that is always in the right—il n'y a que moi a toujours raison.'

I am not sure this is not the best

"In these sentiments sir, I agree to this Constitution, with all its faults, if they are such; because I think a General Government necessary for us, and there is no form of government, but what may be a blessing to the people if well administered for a course of years, and can only end in despotism, as other forms have done before it, when the people shall become so corrupted as to need despotic government, being incapable of any other. I doubt, too, whether any other Convention we can obtain may be able to make a better Constitution. For when you assemble a number of men to have the advantage of their joint wisdom, you inevitably assemble with those men all their prejudices, their passions, their errors of opinion, their local interests and their selfish views. From such an assembly can a perfect production be expected? It therefore astonishes me, sir, to find this system approaching so near to perfection as it does; and I think it will astonish our enemies, who are waiting with confidence to hear that our councils are confounded, like those of the builders of Babel; and that our States are on the point of separation, only to meet hereafter for the purpose of cutting one another's throats. Thus I consent, sir, to this Constitution, because I expect no better, and because I am not sure, that it is not the best. The opinions I have had of its errors I sacrifice to the public good. I have never whispered a syllable of them abroad. Within these walls they were born, and here they shall die. If every one of us, in returning to our constitutents, were to report the objections he has had to it, and endeavour to gain partisans in support of them, we might prevent its being generally received, and thereby lose all the salutary effects and great advantages resulting naturally in our favor among foreign nations as well as among ourselves, from our real or apparent unanimity. Much of the strength and efficiency of any government, in procuring and securing happiness to the people, depends on opinion—on the general opinion of the goodness of the government as well as of the wisdom and integrity of its governors. I hope, therefore, that for our own sakes, as a part of the people, and for the sake of posterity, we shall act heartily and unanimously in recommending this Constitution (if approved by Congress and confirmed by the Conventions) wherever our influence may extend, and turn our future thoughts and endeavours to the means of having it well administered.

'Each member put name to this'

"On the whole, sir, I cannot help expressing a wish that every member of the Convention who may still have objections to it, would with me, on this occasion, doubt a little of his own infallibility, and to make manifest our unanimity, put his name to this instrument."

Benjamin Franklin
Before the House of Lords in Council, London, 1774
Painted by SCHUISSELE. *Engraved by* ROBERT WHITECHURCH

Only three delegates to the Convention refused to sign the document after Franklin's stirring appeal — Edmund Randolph, George Mason, and Elbridge Gerry; and, as the other delegates scrawled their names to the United States Constitution on this 17th day of September in 1787, Benjamin Franklin dreamed of the future of his country, as described by James Madison:

"Whilst the last members were signing, Doctor Franklin looking towards the President's chair, at the back of which a rising sun happened to be painted, observed to a few members near him, that painters had found it difficult to distinguish in their art, a rising, from a setting, sun. 'I have,' said he, 'often and often, in the course of the session, and the vicissitudes of my hopes and fears as to its issue, looked at that behind the President, without being able to tell whether it was rising or setting; but now at length, I have the happiness to know, that it is a rising, and not a setting sun.'"

After his retirement from office as president of Pennsylvania, Franklin was largely confined to his home by gout and by a painful stone in his bladder; however, he continued to hold the office of president in various societies, most notably the Society for Promoting the Abolition of Slavery. Near the close of his life he told a friend: "Death is as necessary to the constitution as sleep; we shall rise refreshed in the morning. The course of nature must soon put a period to my present mode of existence. This I shall submit to with the less regret, as having seen, during a long life, a good deal of this world, I feel a growing curiosity to become acquainted with some other; and can cheerfully, with filial confidence, resign my spirit to the conduct of that great and good Parent of mankind, who created it, and who has so graciously protected and preserved me from my birth to the present hour." On April 17, 1790, at the age of eighty-four, Franklin died at his home in Philadelphia, and his body was buried with that of his wife in Christ Church cemetery.

89

ELBRIDGE GERRY of MASSACHUSETTS

One of the most controversial figures among the Founding Fathers, Elbridge Gerry signed the Declaration of Independence and the Articles of Confederation, but he refused to sign the United States Constitution because he felt that the government it created would be too democratic and at the same time would not protect the civil rights of the people. His name became part of the American language in the word "gerrymander" from an odd-shaped election district that he authorized while he was governor of Massachusetts. Serving as Vice-President of the United States when he died at the age of seventy, Gerry lived to the last his saying that "It is the duty of every citizen, though he may have but one day to live, to devote that day to the service of his country."

Gerry was such a slight, thin man that one of his fellow signers of the Declaration of Independence is said to have told him that if all the signers were hanged by the British he would be the unluckiest because he was so light that he would kick the longest. Gerry may not have appreciated the grim joke, because he was generally considered very intense and humourless. Throughout his long public career he sometimes switched from side to side on public controversies, but throughout it all he retained the close friendship of John Adams.

Born in Marblehead, Mass., on July 17, 1744, Gerry was the son of a merchant whose main business was shipping codfish. After his graduation from Harvard College in 1762, Gerry entered his father's business and soon became one of the leading merchants of Marblehead.

A busy patriot

At the age of twenty-eight Gerry entered public life, being elected to the general court (colonial legislature) of Massachusetts. Gerry was chosen as a member of the committee of correspondence to keep in touch with the other colonies in regard to the actions of the British administration. He became one of Samuel Adams' lieutenants in working toward the overthrow of British power. When the patriots came to an open break with the royal governor of Massachusetts and set up a provincial congress to replace the general court, Gerry was elected a member. He served on the two most important committees of the provincial congress—the committee of safety and the committee of supplies. On the night before the battles of Lexington and Concord, Gerry and other members of the committee of safety escaped in their nightshirts when a detachment of British soldiers attempted to capture them; then they helped spread the alarm that resulted in the resistance by the Minutemen on the next day.

The soldier's friend

In 1776 Gerry was elected by the provincial congress as a member of the Massachusetts delegation to the Continental Congress, an office that he held until 1785 with the exception of a few years toward the end of the Revolutionary War. Like other members of his state's delegation, he was an ardent supporter of independence; however, he was absent from Congress when most of the other delegates signed the Declaration of Independence, and he did not sign it until November 19, 1776. He took part in the debates concerning the Articles of Confederation, opposing a plan that was proposed that would have given small states fewer votes in the Congress than large states; and he signed the Articles as a member of the Massachusetts delegation. Throughout his many

---

ELBRIDGE GERRY

1744 (July 17) Born in Marblehead, Mass.
1762 Graduated from Harvard College.
1772-1773 Representative in the Massachusetts colonial legislature.
1774-1775 Member of the Massachusetts provincial congress.
1776-1780, 1783-1785 Delegate from Massachusetts to the national Congress; signed the Declaration of Independence and the Articles of Confederation.
1786 Member of the Massachusetts house of representatives.
1787 Delegate from Massachusetts to the Constitutional Convention; refused to sign the United States Constitution.
1789-1793 Represented Massachusetts in the U.S. House of Representatives.
1797-1798 U.S. diplomatic representative in France during the X Y Z affair.
1810-1812 Governor of Massachusetts.
1813-1814 Vice-President of the United States.
1814 (Nov. 23) Died in Washington, D.C.

Lent by Elbridge T. Gerry

Elbridge Gerry by John Ramage

years of service in the Congress, Gerry served on many committees, but he took a particular interest in those dealing with military affairs, winning the nickname of the "soldier's friend" because of his support for better pay and equipment for the troops.

At the age of forty-one, Gerry retired from Congress and made Cambridge, Mass., his home. In the next year, 1786, he was elected a member of the Massachusetts state legislature, and he was married to Ann Thompson of New York. Gerry and his wife had seven children. One of his great-grandsons later became a U. S. Senator from Rhode Island.

'People are the dupes of pretended patriots'

When a Constitutional Convention of the thirteen states was called in 1787, Gerry was elected as one of the Massachusetts delegates to the meeting in Philadelphia. The Convention was less than a week old when Gerry rose to make his first speech, one in which he bore strongly in mind the recently crushed rebellion of Daniel Shays in Massachusetts; as reported by James Madison, Gerry said: "The evils we experience flow from the excess of democracy. The people do not want virtue, but are the dupes of pretended patriots. In Massachusetts it had been fully confirmed by experience, that they are daily misled into the most baneful measures and opinions, by the false reports circulated by designing men, and which no one on the spot can refute. One principal evil arises from the

want of due provision for those employed in the administration of government. It would seem to be a maxim of democracy to starve the public servants. He mentioned the popular clamor in Massachusetts for the reduction of salaries, and the attack made on that of the Governor, though secured by the spirit of the Constitution itself. He had, he said, been too republican heretofore: he was still, however, republican; but had been taught by experience the danger of the leveling spirit."

Less than a week later Gerry spoke out again on the same subject in supporting the idea of having the state legislatures elect the members of the Senate instead of having them directly elected by the people. His remarks as reported by Madison were: "Much depends on the mode of election. In England the people will probably lose their liberty from the smallness of the proportion having a right of suffrage. Our danger arises from the opposite extreme. Hence in Massachusetts the worst men get into the Legislature. Several members of that body had lately been convicted of infamous crimes. Men of indigence, ignorance, and baseness, spare no pains, however dirty, to carry their point against men who are superior to the artifices practised. He was not disposed to run into extremes. He was as much principled as ever against aristocracy and monarchy. It was necessary, on the one hand, that the people should appoint one branch of the government, in order to inspire them with the necessary confidence; but he wished the election, on the other, to be so modified as to secure more effectually a just preference of merit. His idea was, that the people should nominate certain persons, in certain districts, out of whom the State Legislatures should make the appointment."

Gerry's objections to the Constitution

Throughout the hot summer of 1787, Gerry was one of the most vocal delegates on the floor of the Convention. He spoke out on almost every issue, and was described as "unable always to distinguish between what was essential and what was of minor importance." Two days before the Convention adjourned, Gerry stated several of the reasons that would prevent him from signing the Constitution. As reported by Madison, Gerry's objections were: "1, the duration and re-eligibility of the Senate; 2, the power of the House of Representatives to conceal their Journals; 3, the power of Congress over the places of election; 4, the unlimited power of Congress over their own compensation; 5, that Massachusetts has not a due share of representatives allotted to her; 6, that three-fifths of the blacks are to be represented, as if they were freemen; 7, that under the power over commerce, monopolies may be established; 8, the Vice President being made head of the Senate. He could, however, he said, get over all these, if the rights of the citizens were not rendered insecure—first, by the general power of the Legislature to make what laws they may please to call 'necessary and proper;' secondly, to raise armies and money without limit; thirdly, to establish a tribunal without juries, which will be a Star Chamber as to civil cases."

On the final day of the Convention, when he again refused to sign the United States Constitution, Gerry said that he feared that a civil war was likely to result from the existing crisis in the United States. "In Massachusetts, particularly," Madison reported Gerry as saying, "he saw the danger of this calamitous event. In that State there are two parties, one devoted to Democracy, the worst, he thought, of all political evils; the other as violent in the opposite extreme."

Upon returning to Massachusetts from the Convention, Gerry attacked it in a letter to his constituents which said: "My principal objections to the plan are, that there is no adequate provision for a representation of the people; that they have no security for the right of election; that some of the powers of the legislature are ambiguous, and others indefinite and dangerous; that the executive is blended with, and will have an undue influence over the legislature; that the judicial department will be oppressive; that treaties of the highest importance may be formed by the president, with the advice of two-thirds of a quorum in the senate; and that the system is without the security of a bill of rights."

In 1789, Gerry was elected to the U. S. House of Representatives by the people of his district in preference to Nathaniel Gorham, who had signed the Constitution. Gerry served two terms in Congress. Shortly after the opening of the first United

Birthplace of Elbridge Gerry
Marblehead, Massachusetts
Essex Institute Collection

92

States Government, Gerry spoke out strongly for open discussion of all the proposals by the various states for amendments to the Constitution. At the age of forty-eight, he retired from Congress in 1793, having declined re-election.

A commissioner to France

In the early months of the beginning of the administration of President John Adams in 1797, relations with the revolutionary government of France were exceedingly bad, and seemed to be nearing open warfare between the United States and France. In an effort to achieve a peaceful solution, Adams sent three commissioners to France, Charles Cotesworthy Pinckney, John Marshall, and Elbridge Gerry. The first two commissioners were leading Federalists, and Gerry was appointed because he represented the antifederalist Democratic-Republican party. Upon their arrival in France, the American commissioners were insulted by demands for a large loan to France and bribes to certain French officials. The French agents who tried to negotiate the bribe were called X, Y, and Z, so the incident became known as the X Y Z affair. Pinckney and Marshall indignantly left France, feeling that the honor of the United States had been insulted; but Gerry remained at the French capital mistakenly believing that because he was an avowed friend of France he could more successfully conduct negotiations than either Pinckney or Marshall. In May, 1798, James McHenry, Adams' Secretary of War, wrote to George Washington: "Gerry has been playing the double politician and besides a very foolish and hurtful game. He held conversations and correspondencies with Talleyrand, and, in other respects, has conducted himself in the most exceptionable manner."

Praised by John Adams

On the other hand, President Adams felt that Gerry acted absolutely correctly and was responsible for paving the way for ultimate peace with France. Adams wrote of Gerry: "He was nominated and approved, and finally saved the peace of the nation, for he alone discovered and furnished the evidence that X. Y. and Z. were employed by Talleyrand; and he alone brought home the direct, formal, and official assurances, upon which the subsequent commission proceeded, and peace was made."

Upon his return from France, Gerry ran unsuccessfully for governor of Massachusetts several

Lent by Elbridge T. Gerry

Mrs. Elbridge Gerry by John Ramage

times against the Federalist governor Caleb Strong; then in 1810, 1811, and 1812 he won the office of governor, running on the Democratic-Republican ticket. During his last term as governor, the legislature redistricted the state for the advantage of the Democratic-Republican party. One of Gerry's opponents pointed out that one of the new election districts had a shape somewhat like a salamander, and soon cartoons appeared showing the district as a winged beast named a "Gerrymander."

Elected Vice President on Madison ticket

In 1812, Gerry was defeated for re-election as governor by the Federalist candidate Caleb Strong; but the Democratic-Republican members of Congress immediately urged him to accept their nomination as running-mate with James Madison in his campaign for a second term as President. The Madison-Gerry ticket won handily over a Federal party ticket of Mayor DeWitt Clinton of New York for President and Jared Ingersoll of Pennsylvania for Vice-President. Gerry was inaugurated as Vice-President on March 4, 1813, and devoted himself to the work of presiding over the Senate —a task that he had objected to being included in the Constitution at the time it was written.

A year and eight months after taking office, on November 23, 1814, Gerry was in his carriage on the way to the Capitol to preside over the Senate when he was suddenly taken ill and died. The 70-year-old Gerry died almost penniless and was buried at public expense in the Congressional Cemetery in Washington, D.C.

BUTTON GWINNETT of GEORGIA

Best known because his signature is so rare that autograph collectors have paid as much as $22,500 for it, Button Gwinnett died as the result of a duel less than a year after signing the Declaration of Independence. Heavily built and nearly six feet tall, Gwinnett was noted for his terrible temper, which led to the duel.

Gwinnett apparently was born in the year 1735 in Down Hatherley, Gloucestershire, England. Records show that he was baptized on April 10, 1735. His father was a clergyman of Welsh ancestry. Gwinnett became a merchant in Bristol, England; then, in his late twenties, he and his wife, Ann, decided to seek to improve their fortune in America.

Upon coming to America, Gwinnett became a merchant in Charleston, S. C., for several years in the early 1760's. Then, in 1765, he sold his business and used the proceeds to buy St. Catherine's Island off the coast of Georgia, where he established a plantation and built a large mansion.

Gwinnett first entered public life in 1769 with his election to Georgia's colonial legislature, but he won no particular prominence until 1776, when he was elected by the legislature as one of Georgia's delegates to the Continental Congress.

First name signed after Hancock

First taking his seat in Congress on May 20, 1776, Gwinnett was present for the debates on the Declaration of Independence and lent his support to the principle of independence. His name was the first to be signed after that of John Hancock on the engrossed copy of the Declaration. Returning to Georgia late in the summer, Gwinnett was re-elected to Congress, and resumed his seat in Congress at Baltimore in December.

A state constitutional convention had been called for February, 1777, and Gwinnett traveled back to Georgia to attend. He is said to have been the main architect of Georgia's constitution, which provided for a president and a one-house legislature; however, because of the similarity of this state government to that which had already been organized for the state of Pennsylvania, some claims have been made that Gwinnett merely used a model of the Pennsylvania constitution in writing the Georgia constitution.

Shortly after the close of the constitutional convention, Archibald Bulloch, the president of the provincial congress, died, leaving the state without a chief executive; and a committee of the state's leaders appointed Gwinnett to act as president until a meeting of the legislature could be called.

During his brief tenure as chief executive officer of Georgia, Gwinnett created considerable friction between himself and Brigadier General Lachlan McIntosh, who had been appointed by the Continental Congress to raise a brigade of the Continental Army in Georgia. Gwinnett claimed authority over McIntosh's troops because of his office as president of the state. McIntosh disputed the claim because his commission was authorized by Congress. Nevertheless, without McIntosh's knowledge, Gwinnett ordered some of the militia forces to make an attack on East Florida. The defeat of this expedition seemed to prove Gwinnett's lack of military ability.

Issued a challenge to General McIntosh

When the legislature met on the first Monday in May, 1777, Gwinnett offered himself as a candidate for election as chief executive officer of the state, but he was defeated by John A. Treutlen, a candidate he considered much inferior to himself. He blamed his defeat on the failure of the military expedition against Florida, and was particularly sensitive to criticism on that score. McIntosh criticized him before the legislature, and this was the last straw; so he challenged McIntosh to a duel. The story of this duel is contained in a sworn state-

---

BUTTON GWINNETT

1735? Born in Down Hatherley, Gloucestershire, England.

1763? Emigrated to America, settling first in Charleston, S. C.

1769 Member of the colonial legislature of Georgia.

1776-1777 Delegate from Georgia to the Continental Congress; signed the Declaration of Independence.

1777 President and commander in chief of the state of Georgia.

1777 (May 27) Died in Savannah, Ga., of wounds suffered in a duel with General Lachlan McIntosh.

ment that a George Wells made before Judge John Wereat in a later investigation of the death of Gwinnett:

". . . late on the evening of Thursday, the fifteenth, May, inst.,, a written challenge was brought to General McIntosh signed by Button Gwinnett, wherein the said Mr. Gwinnett charged the General with calling him a scoundrel in public convention and desired he would give satisfaction for it, as a gentleman, before sunrise the next morning, in Sir James Wright's pasture behind Colonel Martin's house. To which the gentleman humorously sent answer to Mr. Gwinnett that the hour was rather earlier than his usual, but would assuredly meet him at the place and time appointed with a pair of pistols, as agreed upon with Mr. Gwinnett's second, who had brought the challenge.

"Early the next morning Mr. Gwinnett and his second found the General and his second waiting on the ground, and after politely saluting each other the General drew his pistols to show he was loaded only with single balls, but avoided entering into any conversation but the business on hand. It was then proposed and agreed to that they should go a little lower down the hill, as a number of spectators appeared, and when the ground was chose the seconds asked the distance. Mr. Gwinnett replied whatever distance the General pleases. The General said he believed eight or ten feet would suffice, and they were immediately measured, to which the General desired another step might be added. It was then proposed to turn back to back. The General answered, 'By no means, let us see what we are about,' and immediately each made his stand and agreed to fire as they could. Both pistols went off nearly at the same time when Mr. Gwinnett fell, being shot above the knee and said his thigh was broke. The General was also shot through the thigh and stood still in his place and not thinking his antagonist was worse wounded than himself, as he immediately and afterward declared, asked if he had enough, or was for another shot. To which all objected and the seconds declaring they both behaved like gentlemen and men of honor, led the General up to Mr. Gwinnett and they shook hands and further this deponeth sayeth not."

The forty-two-year-old Gwinnett died of his wounds eleven days later on May 27, 1777. He left no descendants, and his final burial place is unknown, although his body is generally believed to have been interred in Savannah.

During his brief public career, Gwinnett signed his name to very few public documents, and he apparently wrote very few letters. As a result, authentic signatures of this signer of the Declaration of Independence are very rare and have brought unusually high prices from autograph collectors. In 1926, a signature of Gwinnett's as the witness to a friend's will was reported to have been sold to an autograph collector for $22,500. Other Gwinnett signatures have been bought for $6,000.

View of Charleston S.C. circa 1800

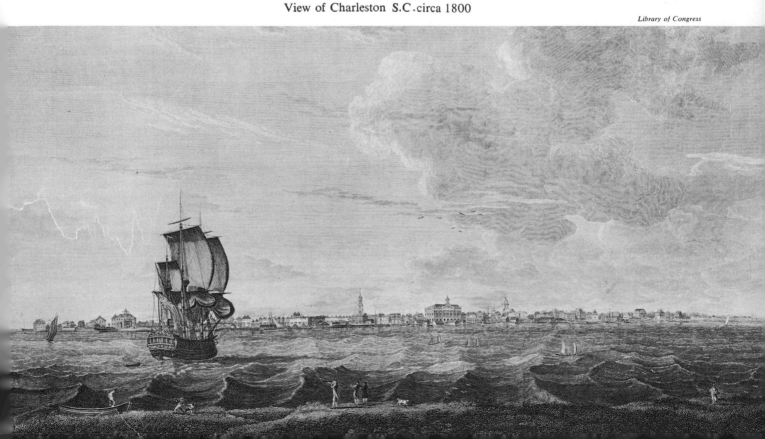

LYMAN HALL of GEORGIA

A New England physician, Lyman Hall helped inspire the patriotism of Georgia by serving in the Continental Congress as the only representative from the colony. He signed the Declaration of Independence, and continued to serve in Congress through five years of the Revolutionary War, even though the British destroyed his home and plantation. After the War, the people of Georgia honored him by electing him to a term as the state's governor.

Lyman Hall was born in Wallingford, Conn., on April 12, 1724. He studied for the ministry at Yale College, and was graduated at the age of twenty-three. He married Abigail Burr of Fairfield, Conn., and after her death he was wed to Mary Osborn, also of Connecticut. He had one son by his second marriage.

From ministry to medicine

Hall gave up the ministry and turned to the study of medicine. After completing his medical studies, Hall settled at Sunbury, Ga., where he established himself in the practice of medicine in 1752.

At the outbreak of the Revolutionary War, the majority of people in Georgia were loyal followers of the King and opposed to the patriotic movement; but St. John's Parish, where Hall lived, was populated by New England families who were sympathetic with the struggle underway in Massachusetts. Therefore, the people of St. John's Parish decided to elect Hall to represent them in the Continental Congress in Philadelphia, even though the rest of Georgia sent no delegates.

Hall presented his credentials to Congress on May 13, 1775, and was permitted to take a seat as a representative of St. John's Parish. Because each colony had only a single vote in the Continental Congress, and because Hall represented only a small portion of Georgia rather than the entire colony, he agreed to give up any voting rights and merely take part in the debates.

The example that Hall had set for Georgia helped cause its provincial congress meeting in July, 1775, to elect a delegation of five members, including Hall, to represent the entire colony in Congress. Hall and two other of the Georgia delegates attended the adjourned meeting of the Continental Congress that convened in September, 1775. However, at this session, the Georgia delegation was disgraced when one of its members, John Joachim Zubly, a Presbyterian clergyman, was denounced as a traitor by Samuel Chase of Maryland. Zubly fled back to Georgia and the protection of the royal governor of the colony.

Hall was re-elected to Congress in 1776, and he was present during the discussions that led up to the adoption of the Declaration of Independence. John Adams referred to Hall and his fellow Georgian, Button Gwinnett, as "a powerful addition to our phalanx." Hall signed the Declaration of Independence with most of the other delegates on August 2, 1776.

Plantation home destroyed

Through 1780, Hall continued to represent Georgia in Congress. British troops destroyed Hall's plantation home in 1778, but his family escaped and he brought them north to be with him.

Hall returned to Georgia in 1782, and the next year he was elected by the legislature as governor of the state. Although he served only one year as governor, Hall instituted programs to help rebuild war-damaged structures and aid the state's recovery from the effects of war.

In 1784, Hall retired from public life, and established a plantation in Burke County, Georgia. Six years later, on October 19, 1790, Hall died at his plantation home at the age of sixty-six. His remains are buried in Augusta, Ga., where a monument was built to his memory and that of George Walton, another Georgia signer of the Declaration of Independence.

LYMAN HALL

1724 (April 12) Born in Wallingford, Conn.
1747 Graduated from Yale College.
1752 Settled in Georgia.
1775 Represented St. John's Parish of Georgia in the second Continental Congress.
1775-1780 Member of Georgia's delegation to Congress; signed the Declaration of Independence.
1783-1784 Governor of Georgia.
1791 (Oct. 19) Died in Burke County, Georgia.

Prospect des großen Plazes gegen der alten ∥ *Vuë de la Rüe grande vers l'Eglise du*
Sud Kirche der Presbiteraner zu Boston. ∥ *Sud Des Presbiterennes a Boston.*

Gravé par François Dav. Habermann.

Se vend à Augsbourg au Negoce común de l'Academie d'Empire des Arts liberaux avec Privilege de Sa Majesté Imperiale et avec Defense m. d'en faire ni la vendre des Copier.

Engraved by FRANCOIS HABERMANN
View of the main street of Boston, 1781

Castle William in Boston Harbor

BATTLE OF SARATOGA,
September 19.th 1777.

JOHN HANCOCK of MASSACHUSETTS

As the President of the second Continental Congress, John Hancock was the first man to sign the Declaration of Independence; and in doing so he won such fame that "John Hancock" became a synonym for the word *signature*. He and Samuel Adams were the leaders of the patriotic movement in Massachusetts, and capturing them was one of the objects of the British troops that clashed with American minutemen at Lexington and Concord in 1775 in the beginning of the Revolutionary War. As one of the richest men of New England, Hancock risked his fortune in the patriotic cause. But his wealth also enabled him to indulge his taste in rich wines and foods, parties and dancing, and other pleasures that hastened his death at the age of fifty-six.

Handsome of face and gracious in manner

Contemporaries described Hancock as appearing to be an old man by the time he was forty-five; although nearly six feet tall, he became thin and stooped, and suffered greatly from gout. A writer who visited him in his home described him thus: "His manners were very gracious, of the old style, of dignified complaisance. His face had been very handsome. His dress was adapted quite as much to be ornamental as useful. Gentlemen wore wigs when abroad, and commonly caps when at home. At this time, (June), about noon, Hancock was dressed in a red velvet cap, within which was one of fine linen, the latter was turned up over the lower edge of the velvet one, two or three inches. He wore a blue damask gown, lined with silk; a white stock, a white satin embroidered waistcoat, black satin small clothes, white silk stockings, and red morocco slippers. It was a general practice in genteel families to have a tankard of punch made in the morning, and placed in a cooler when the season required it. Visitors were invited to partake of it. At this visit Hancock took from the cooler, standing on the hearth, a full tankard, and drank first himself, and then offered it to those present."

Of Puritan background

John Hancock was born on January 23, 1737, in Braintree, Mass., the same village where John Adams had been born a year and a half earlier. His father and grandfather, whose names also were John Hancock, were Puritan clergymen; and young John was born in the Braintree parsonage. When the boy was seven years old, his father died and John was sent to Lexington, Mass., to live with his seventy-three-year-old grandfather. Fortunately, the boy's uncle, Thomas Hancock, a wealthy Boston merchant, took an interest in his education and provided the funds needed to send him to Boston Grammar School and then Harvard College.

After graduating from Harvard at the age of seventeen, John Hancock became a clerk in his uncle's counting house. "And what a school this was!" John Adams later wrote of Hancock's youth. "Four large ships constantly plying between Boston and London, and other business in proportion. He became an example to all the young men of the town. Wholly devoted to business, he was as regular and punctual at his store as the sun in his course." In 1760 Hancock sailed to England for a visit, and was present there for the funeral of King George II and for the coronation of King George III.

JOHN HANCOCK

1737 (Jan. 23) Born in Braintree, Mass.

1754 Graduated from Harvard College.

1764 Inherited a large fortune from his uncle.

1766-1772 Member of the Massachusetts colonial legislature.

1774-1775 President of the Massachusetts provincial congress.

1775-1777 President of the second Continental Congress; first man to sign the Declaration of Independence.

1777-1780 Member of the Continental Congress; signed the Articles of Confederation.

1778 Major general in charge of Massachusetts militia in effort to recapture Rhode Island from the British.

1780-1785 First governor of the state of Massachusetts.

1785-1786 Member of the Congress of the Confederation.

1787-1793 Governor of Massachusetts.

1788 President of the Massachusetts state convention that ratified the United States Constitution.

1793 (Oct. 8) Died in Quincy, Mass.

JOHN HANCOCK AND HIS WIFE, DOROTHY QUINCY HANCOCK
by EDWARD SAVAGE
The Corcoran Gallery of Art

99

The wealthiest merchant in New England at twenty-seven

Shortly after his return from England, the death of his uncle in 1764 left Hancock as heir to the shipping business and an estate of about eighty thousand pounds. At the age of twenty-seven he had become the wealthiest merchant in New England. Soon the people of Boston elected Hancock as a selectman, or member of the town council; and John Adams quotes his cousin Sam Adams as remarking that Boston's citizens had done a wise thing because "they had made that young man's fortune their own."

In 1776, Hancock was elected as one of the representatives from Boston to the general court, or colonial legislature of Massachusetts. The other representatives from Boston were James Otis, Samuel Adams, and Thomas Cushing—all three of whom already were winning prominence as leaders of the Whigs, the patriotic party. Hancock became a member of the Caucus Club, the political organization through which Samuel Adams ran the government of Boston; and it was at a meeting of this club, during a discussion of the best way of getting the British out of Boston, that Hancock is said to have made his famous exclamation: "Burn Boston, and make John Hancock a beggar, if the public good requires it."

A smuggler to avoid taxes

Like many merchants, Hancock engaged in smuggling to avoid British taxes; and, in June, 1768, one of his ships, the *Liberty,* arrived with a cargo of Madeira wine on which Hancock refused to pay the customs duties. The customs officer was held a prisoner on the ship while it was unloaded. In retaliation, customs officers seized the *Liberty;* but an indignant mob of citizens attacked the customs collectors and burned a customs boat. Although Hancock did not personally take part in this riot, his name, as owner of the *Liberty,* became linked with the forces opposing the British administration.

After the Boston Massacre of 1770, Hancock was elected by the citizens of Boston as chairman of a committee that included Samuel Adams and other patriots whose object was to persuade the British governor to withdraw his troops from the town. Both Hancock and Adams won great popularity by the success of their interviews with the governor that resulted in removal of the troops to a fortress in the harbor.

In 1772, during a period of comparative quiet in the patriotic controversy, Hancock accepted appointment by the acting British governor, Thomas Hutchinson, as colonel in charge of a company of cadets that acted as the governor's honor guard. Acting in this capacity, Hancock played an important part in the ceremonies that welcomed the new governor, Lt. Gen. Thomas Gage, to Boston in 1774.

In opposition to quartering British troops

Boston now was suffering under the Coercive Acts under which the British parliament had closed the port in retribution for the "Boston Tea Party," and Hancock took the occasion of the fourth anniversary of the Boston Massacre to remind the citizens of Boston of his patriotism. In an oration on March 5, 1774, Hancock said in part:

"But I gladly quit this theme of death—I would not dwell too long upon the horrid effects which have already followed from quartering regular troops in this town; let our misfortunes instruct posterity to guard against these evils. Standing armies are sometimes (I would by no means say generally, much less universally) composed of persons who have rendered themselves unfit to live in civil society; who are equally indifferent to the glory of a George or a Louis; who, for the addition of one penny a day to their wages, would desert from the Christian cross, and fight under the crescent of the Turkish Sultan; from such men as these, what has not a state to fear? with such as these usurping Caesar passed the Rubicon; with such as these he humbled mighty Rome, and forced the mistress of the world to own a master in a traitor. These are the men whom sceptred robbers now employ to frustrate the designs of God, and render vain the bounties which his gracious hand pours indiscriminately upon his creatures."

As further evidence of his patriotism, Hancock rejected an appointment by the governor as one of his counsellors. This and Hancock's Boston Massacre oration so angered Governor Gage that Hancock was removed as head of the governor's guard, and the company of cadets was disbanded.

A traitor and an outlaw

In October, 1774, Hancock was elected president of the Massachusetts provincial congress of patriots that met in Concord. As such, he was head of the unofficial government of all the colony but

100

LAMB TAVERN, NEWBURY (NOW WASHINGTON) STREET.

Boston, where the British troops maintained the power of the royal governor. In the eyes of Governor Gage, Hancock had become a traitor and an outlaw.

In April, 1775, six months after Hancock's election as president of the provincial congress, British troops were sent out from Boston to capture him and Samuel Adams at Lexington. They were saved by Paul Revere's warning ride, and escaped while the first shots of the Revolutionary War were being fired. Shortly afterward, Governor Gage issued a proclamation offering a pardon to any patriot who would lay down his arms, "excepting only from the benefit of such pardon, Samuel Adams and John Hancock, whose offences are of too flagitious a nature to admit of any other consideration than that of condign punishment."

Hancock had been elected as a member of the Massachusetts delegation to the second Continental Congress, taking his seat in that body early in May, 1775. The session was only about two weeks old when Peyton Randolph, the President of the Continental Congress, was forced to resign in order to return home to Virginia to act as speaker of the house of burgesses in a special session called by the Virginia governor. On May 24, Hancock was unanimously elected to succeed Randolph as President of the Congress.

Frustrated ambition

Events moved swiftly in the spring of 1775 as the delegates from the various colonies studied the means by which they might aid the people of Massachusetts in their struggle against the British government. All were in agreement that an army must be raised, and Hancock believed that he was the logical man to command such a Continental Army. He did not know that John and Samuel Adams had decided that a Virginian, George Washington, should become commander of the army in order to insure the South's participation in the struggle. Therefore, on June 14,

101

when John Adams arose and said that he believed there was only one man who should be considered for the position of commander in chief of the Continental Army, Hancock's face lit with satisfaction, for he was sure he was that man. He could not conceal his disappointment as Adams revealed that Washington was the man he had in mind. "I never saw anyone's expression change as quickly as Hancock's changed," John Adams later wrote in his diary. "Mortification and resentment were expressed as forcibly as his face could exhibit them."

Hancock continued to aspire to military command, and in July, 1775, he wrote to George Washington: "I must beg for the favor that you will reserve some berth for me in such Department as you may judge most proper, for I am determined to act under you if it be to take the firelock and join the ranks as a volunteer." However, Washington replied: "I have to regret that so little is in my power to offer, equal to Colonel Hancock's merits and worthy his acceptance." In the months that followed, Hancock caused Washington no little difficulty by corresponding with various generals under his command and making plans and suggestions without discussing them first with Washington.

In the summer of 1775, Hancock married Dorothy Quincy, daughter of Edward Quincy of Boston. She is said to have been visiting him in Lexington at the time he was alerted by Paul Revere that the British troops were seeking him, and to have fled with him to safety. Hancock and his wife had two children, both of whom died at an early age.

One of two Signers of the first Declaration

At the age of thirty-nine, Hancock rose to his greatest fame with the adoption of the Declaration of Independence. He did not preside over the debate between John Adams and John Dickinson on independence, having given up the chair to Benjamin Harrison, chairman of the committee of the whole of the Continental Congress. But he presided on July 4, 1776, when the delegates approved the Declaration of Independence, and he and Charles Thomson, the secretary of the Congress, were the only two men to sign the original version of the document on that day. Hancock is said to have remarked that he made his signature so bold —nearly five inches long—"so that John Bull could read it without his glasses." The printed version of the Declaration of Independence that was ready

Residence of John Hancock, Beacon Street, Boston

on July 5 and was dispatched to all the provincial congresses and committees of safety in the various colonies also carried only the signature of Hancock attested by Thomson. As a result, John Hancock's name swiftly became second only to that of George Washington as a symbol of freedom in the thirteen states.

After serving as President of the Continental Congress for two and a half years, Hancock resigned this office in October, 1777, because his gout had become so severe that he did not feel he could continue the arduous duties of presiding officer and chief executive of the young republic. However, he continued as a member of the Massachusetts delegation, and in 1778 he signed the Articles of Confederation that officially set up the first United States government.

Commissioned as a Major General

Hancock finally won his opportunity to take a military role in the Revolutionary War when the legislature of Massachusetts commissioned him as a major general of militia in 1778. He was placed in command of about six thousand New England troops that took part in a campaign that was planned to free Rhode Island from British occupation. However, the campaign ended in retreat for the American forces when the French fleet failed to carry out its part of the operation.

When a new constitution was written and adopted in Massachusetts, Hancock took part in the constitutional convention in 1779, and then was elected by the legislature as the state's first governor in 1780. Continuing to serve as governor until 1785, Hancock lived as regally as any of the previous royal governors. His handsomely appointed coach was pulled by six bay horses and he was accompanied by liveried servants. His clothes were embroidered with gold and silver, and he wore gold buttons on his clothes that were engraved with a picture of a sheep under the motto, "You gain more by our lives than our deaths."

Hancock was re-elected as President of Congress in 1785, but did not serve because of illness. He was again elected governor in 1787, an office that he held for the remaining years of his life. He remained closely associated with Samuel Adams throughout this period, for Adams was president of the Massachusetts senate from 1781 to 1788, and then served as lieutenant governor of the state until Hancock's death.

Influenced Massachusetts to ratify the Constitution

Although Hancock did not take part in the Constitutional Convention of 1787, he played an important role in the ratification of the United States Constitution. Because Massachusetts and Virginia were the two most important and largest of the thirteen states, their action on ratification would be extremely influential in deciding whether the Constitution would become the law of the land. The Massachusetts ratification convention met on January 9, 1788. Hancock was elected president of the meeting; however, because he was not ready to commit himself as for or against the Constitution, he did not appear at the convention until January 30, pleading ill health as the excuse for his absence. By this time, Hancock had been persuaded by his friends that Virginia was likely to reject the Constitution, and that if Massachusetts did ratify it, Hancock would become the "only fair candidate for President." When he appeared before the convention, Hancock presented a series of "conciliatory resolutions," including a bill of rights and other proposed amendments to the Constitution; but he persuaded the delegates that the Constitution should be ratified and the resolutions be given later consideration. His influence was great enough to win ratification by a vote of 187 to 168.

Hancock won great popularity among the Federalists as a result of his action, and his contribution was celebrated in a popular ballad written to the tune of "Yankee Doodle" that said in part:

"Then 'Squire Hancock, like a man
    Who dearly loves the nation,
  By a concil'atory plan,
    Prevented much vexation.

"He made a woundy Fed'ral speech,
    With sense and elocution;
  And then the 'Vention did beseech
    T' adopt the Constitution.

"The question being outright put,
    (Each voter independent,)
  The Fed'ralists agreed t' adopt,
    And then propose amendment.

"The other party, seeing then
    The people were against 'em,
  Agreed, like honest, faithful men,

103

JOHN HANCOCK
by J. S. COPLEY

To mix in peace amongst 'em.
Yankee doodle, keep it up!
Yankle doodle, dandy!
Mind the music and the step,
And with the girls be handy."

Disappointment and defeat

When Virginia also ratified the United States Constitution, rather than rejecting it as Hancock had anticipated, his hopes of becoming the first President of the United States under the Constitution swiftly vanished before the popular enthusiasm for Virginia's George Washington. Hancock probably could have had the office of Vice-President if he had wanted it. James Madison wrote to George Washington in November, 1788, that "The public conversation seems to be not yet settled on the Vice-President. Mr. Hancock & Mr. (John) Adams have been most talked of. The former *it is said* rejects the idea of any secondary Station . . ." In a letter to another friend, Madison wrote that Hancock "has declared to his lady, it is said, that she had once been the first in America, & he would never make her the second." In the ensuing electoral college vote, Washington won the presidency unanimously, and Hancock received only a scattering of votes for the vice-presidency, which went to John Adams.

A final encounter with Washington

Hancock, having lost the command of the Continental Army to Washington in 1775 and the office of President of the United States in 1789, had one final losing encounter with Washington. The President made a tour of the New England states in the fall of 1789, and had accepted an invitation to dine with Hancock on the day of his arrival in Boston. Washington assumed that the governor would call on him at his lodgings prior to the din-

ner. When Hancock sent word that his health prevented his making the courtesy call, Washington took this as a slight to his office as President and cancelled the dinner engagement. Hancock sent Lieutenant Governor Samuel Adams and several members of his council to apologize. Washington noted in his diary: "I informed them in explicit terms that I should not see the Governor unless it was at my own lodgings." The next day Hancock had "recovered" sufficiently to travel in his coach to Washington's lodgings, where he had his servants carry him to the President's rooms for the meeting.

While still serving as governor, the fifty-six-year-old Hancock died on October 8, 1793, in Quincy, Mass. The funeral procession was the most impressive that New England had ever seen. It included public officials, the militia, and thousands of citizens. Lieutenant Governor Samuel Adams walked ahead of the coffin and Vice-President of the United States John Adams walked behind the coffin.

John Adams summed up Hancock's career and characteristics in the following words:

"Mr. Hancock had a delicate constitution. He was very infirm; a great part of his life was passed in acute pain. He inherited from his father, though one of the most amiable and beloved of men, a certain sensibility, a keenness of feeling, or, in more familiar language, a peevishness of temper, that sometimes disgusted and afflicted his friends. Yet it was astonishing with what patience, perseverance, and punctuality, he attended to business to the last. Nor were his talents or attainments inconsiderable. They were far superior to many who have been much more celebrated. He had a great deal of political sagacity and penetration into men. He was by no means a contemptible scholar or orator. Compared with Washington, Lincoln, or Knox, he was learned."

View of the Statehouse at Boston, taken from the Mall.

BENJAMIN HARRISON of VIRGINIA

A tall, fat, red-faced man, Benjamin Harrison has been called the Falstaff of the Founding Fathers because of his love for food, wine, and jokes. As a wealthy gentleman farmer, he owned eight plantations and many other tracts of land. As a Virginia political leader, he spent his entire adult life in public office, serving in the colonial and state legislatures, representing Virginia in the Continental Congress, and holding office as governor. A close friend of George Washington, he acted as the commander-in-chief's spokesman in military matters in Congress during the early years of the Revolutionary War. His son, William Henry Harrison, became the ninth President of the United States, and his great-grandson, Benjamin Harrison, became the twenty-third President of the United States.

Benjamin Harrison is believed to have been born in 1726 at his family's estate "Berkeley" in Charles City County, Virginia, but the exact date of his birth is not known. His father, grandfather, great-grandfather, and great-great-grandfather all had been named Benjamin Harrison. While in his teens, Harrison attended the College of William and Mary, but he was not graduated because the death of his father called him home to manage the family's extensive land holdings.

Owner of extensive holdings

The estate which he inherited included thousands of acres of land on the James River, many slaves, and small manufacturing plants and mills. He later constructed his own ship yards to build merchant ships to carry the products of his plantations and mills to Europe. Harrison married Elizabeth Bassett and they had many children, seven of whom survived childhood.

Harrison entered his long career of public service while still in his early twenties when he was elected to the Virginia house of burgesses (the colonial legislature). He was re-elected to this position each year until the Revolutionary War, becoming one of the political leaders of the state and several times serving as speaker of the house of burgesses. In 1764, he was appointed as one of the committee of the house that prepared a petition to the King of England protesting the Stamp Act. In 1773, he became one of the eleven-man committee of correspondence organized to communicate with the other colonies regarding the increasing tyranny of the British.

When the Virginia legislators and the royal governor of the colony came to a parting of the ways in 1774, Harrison became a member of the provincial congress that organized the colony's patriotic government. He also was a member of this body in 1775 and 1776.

Benjamin Harrison
by LAMBDIN *after* TRUMBULL
National Historical Park

BENJAMIN HARRISON

1726? Born in Charles City County, Virginia.

1747?-1774 Member of the Virginia house of burgesses.

1774-1776 Member of the Virginia provincial congress.

1774-1777 Delegate from Virginia to the Continental Congress; signed the Declaration of Independence.

1778-1781 Speaker of the Virginia house of delegates.

1781-1784 Governor of the state of Virginia.

1785-1791 Speaker of the Virginia house of delegates.

1791 (April 24) Died in Charles City County, Virginia

Berkeley
home of Benjamin Harrison

An elder statesman from Virginia

Harrison was elected by the provincial congress as a member of its delegation to the first Continental Congress in 1774, and he continued to be re-elected as a delegate to Congress through 1777. Harrison was an important figure in the early Congresses as one of the elder statesmen of the largest colony. He served as chairman of the committee of the whole of Congress, and was chairman of the board of war and ordinance, the most important congressional committee which was responsible for supervising the Continental Army.

In 1775, Harrison lived in the same house in Philadelphia with George Washington and Peyton Randolph, the president of the Congress, until Washington left for Boston as commander-in-chief of the army and Randolph died. After he was left alone in the house, Harrison lived in a grand manner, dispensing southern hospitality to the delegates from other colonies, and accumulating debts that took him the rest of his life to pay.

As chairman of the committee of the whole,

Harrison presided over the debates on July 1 and 2, 1776, that preceded the adoption of the resolutions calling for independence. An anecdote has been preserved that illustrates Harrison's joviality, even in so serious a matter as the adoption of the Declaration of Independence. The story tells that the delegates were discussing the grim possibility that those who signed the document might well end up being hanged by the British when the corpulent Harrison turned to the short, slender Eldridge Gerry and said, "When the hanging scene comes to be exhibited, I shall have all the advantage over you. It will be over with me in a minute, but you will be kicking in the air half an hour after I am gone."

A fleeing legislature

After retiring from Congress in 1777, the fifty-one-year-old Harrison resumed his seat in the Virginia house of delegates and immediately was elected speaker of the house, a position he held for the next four years. During this period British troops swept through Virginia raiding and plundering, and the legislature with Harrison as its leader was forced to flee from town to town to keep from being captured.

When the governor of Virginia, Thomas Nelson, resigned in 1781, the legislature elected Harrison as governor. He was re-elected twice, serving until 1784. During his governorship, the Revolutionary War was won with the siege of Yorktown, and he was confronted with the many problems of restoring a peacetime economy to his state. Toward the close of his administration he won considerable unpopularity by ordering the militia to demolish the earthworks that had been thrown up during the siege of Yorktown. After completing his administration as governor, Harrison resumed his seat in the state legislature, and again was elected speaker.

Despite his friendship with George Washington, Harrison became one of the leading opponents in Virginia to the ratification of the United States Constitution. He believed that the bill of rights amendments should be incorporated in the Constitution before it should be ratified. He was a member of the Virginia ratification convention in 1788, but, despite his views, a majority of the convention voted in favor of ratification.

In need of financial aid

The state of Harrison's fortune is revealed in a letter that he wrote to Governor William Livingston of New Jersey in 1789, asking for assistance in obtaining a federal appointment:

"The friendship you formerly honoured me with, and the confidence I still have in it, will I hope excuse me to you, for asking the favour of you to assist me with your interest, with the senatorial delegates of your State in Congress, for the appointment of naval officer for the district of Norfolk and Portsmouth in this State. The being a placeman is a line I never expected to walk in, but the distresses brought on me by the ravages and plunderings of the British, have reduced me so low that some prop is necessary, for the comfort of a numerous and valuable family. That I have some claims on the American States, you, my friend, know, as many of my long services were familiar to you; which services, together with my strong attachment to the American cause after my return from Congress marked me out as a peculiar object of British vengeance; and which they did not fail to execute in the most outrageous manner, when the fortune of war put my whole estate in their power. I take the liberty to enclose you a letter to the gentlemen, which you'll be so obliging as to forward to them in any manner you shall please."

When Harrison was re-elected to the legislature in 1791, he and his friends were confident that he would again be elected governor as soon as the legislature met. On the day after the election, Harrison threw a large party at his home with much eating and drinking. Already suffering with gout, Harrison became quite ill during the night and died on April 24, 1791, at the age of about sixty-five.

JOHN HART of NEW JERSEY

A tall, handsome, dark-haired man, John Hart was known as "Honest John" by his friends and neighbors because of his integrity and justice. He was sixty-five years old when he signed the Declaration of Independence and did not live to see the end of the Revolutionary War. Benjamin Rush, a fellow signer of the Declaration of Independence, described Hart as "a plain, honest, well meaning Jersey farmer, with but little education, but with good sense and virtue enough to pursue the true interests of his country."

John Hart was born in Stonington, Conn., in about the year 1711, and moved to New Jersey with his parents while he was still quite young. His father, Edward Hart, was a prosperous farmer who during the French and Indian War raised a company of volunteers called the "Jersey Blues" and marched at their head to Canada where they took part in the Battle of Quebec. Little is known about the education of young John, but apparently he received little if any formal schooling.

He owned and operated a farm of about four hundred acres near Hopewell, N. J. At an early age, he married Deborah Scudder, and they had a family of thirteen children.

"Honest John" the justice of peace

At about the age of forty-four, Hart began his public career as a local justice of the peace in Hunterdon County. Winning his nickname of "Honest John" for his fairness in dealing with the problems brought before his court, Hart was elected to the colonial legislature in 1761 and each year thereafter until 1772. He voted for the resolutions opposing the Stamp Act in 1765, and helped choose New Jersey's delegation to the Stamp Act Congress. Hart also took an active part in the dispute between the colonial legislature and the royal governor, William Franklin, in which the legislature refused to pay British soldiers stationed in the colonies. In 1770, Hart was one of only six legislators willing to vote against pay for the British troops, but the next year the resolution carried.

Hart was a member of the first provincial congress called in New Jersey in 1774 to consider ways to oppose British tyranny and elect delegates to the Continental Congress, and he continued to serve in the provincial congress in 1775 and 1776 as the chairman of such important committees as those of defense and finance. He also became a member of New Jersey's committee of safety, the unofficial patriotic government of the colony in the early days of the Revolution.

In 1776, when the Continental Congress was debating whether the colonies should declare their independence from Great Britain, the delegates which New Jersey had chosen to represent them at the Congress were opposed to independence; so in June the provincial congress appointed a new set of delegates that included John Hart. He voted for independence, and signed the Declaration of Independence with the other delegates on August 2.

Meanwhile, the provincial congress had adopted a state constitution for New Jersey, and Hart was elected as a member of the new state legislature which met in August, 1776, in Princeton, N. J. Hart was chosen as speaker of the house of representatives in the legislature by a unanimous vote.

Located by the Hessians

With the invasion of New Jersey by British troops in 1776, Hart and the other members of the legislature fled from town to town to avoid capture. For weeks at a time he slept in a different bed each night, sometimes sleeping in caves. Hessian mercenaries pillaged his farm and killed his livestock, his wife died, and his children took refuge with neighbors.

William Livingston, who was governor of New Jersey at this time, described the conduct of the

---

JOHN HART

c. 1711 Born in Stonington, Conn.

1761-1772 Member of New Jersey's colonial legislature.

1774-1776 Member of provincial congress of New Jersey.

1775-1776 Member of the New Jersey Committee of Safety.

1776 Delegate to the Continental Congress; signed the Declaration of Independence.

1776-1777 First speaker of the house of representatives in the New Jersey state legislature.

1779 (May 11) Died on his farm near Hopewell, N. J.

British soldiers: "Their rapacity was boundless, their rapine indiscriminate, and their barbarity unparalleled. They have warred upon decrepit age and defenseless youth. They have butchered the wounded asking for quarter, mangled the dying weltering in their blood, refused to the dead the rights of sepulture, suffered prisoners to perish for want of sustenance, and in the age of impiety and barbarism, profaned edifices dedicated to Almighty God."

Hart was re-elected speaker of the house of representatives in the New Jersey legislature when it met in Trenton, N. J., in January, 1777, but soon the illnesses of old age forced him to retire to his farm where he attempted to repair the damages done by the British troops. At the age of about sixty-eight, he died on May 11, 1779.

In 1865, Hart's body was removed from its burial place on his farm to the cemetery of the Baptist church in Hopewell, for which he had deeded the land in 1771. A granite monument was dedicated to his memory and to mark his final resting place.

The Historical Society of Pennsylvania

John Hart (by Deigendesch)

JOSEPH HEWES of NORTH CAROLINA

A well-to-do bachelor merchant and shipowner, Joseph Hewes risked his fortune by helping the patriotic cause and signing the Declaration of Independence. Although reared in the faith of the Society of Friends, he renounced his Quaker beliefs to aid the war against the British. In the Continental Congress, Hewes was in charge of the committee responsible for fitting out the first warships for the American Navy, as such he may be considered the first civilian head of the United States Navy.

Joseph Hewes was born on January 23, 1730, in Kingston, N. J. His parents brought him up as a Quaker, and, as soon as he was old enough, he was apprenticed to a merchant in Philadelphia as a clerk in a countinghouse. When he completed his apprenticeship, Hewes went into business for himself, traveling between New York and Philadelphia.

When Hewes was about thirty years old, he decided to move to North Carolina. He settled at Edenton, N. C., an important trade and shipping center on Albemarle Sound. There, he became a successful merchant with his own fleet of trading ships.

In 1766, at the age of thirty-six, Hewes was first elected to public office, representing his county in the colonial legislature. His success in reflecting the views of his constituents was reflected in his repeated re-election to that body for the next ten years.

As difficulties with Great Britain mounted, Hewes became a member of the patriotic party in the legislature. In 1773, he was appointed a mem-

JOSEPH HEWES
by CHARLES WILLSON PEALE
U. S. Naval Academy

ber of the committee of correspondence to keep in touch with the legislatures of the other colonies to help decide a unified course of action. In 1774, Hewes was appointed as one of North Carolina's three delegates to the first Continental Congress.

Despite the fact that Hewes' fortune was dependent upon trade with Great Britain, he subscribed to the decision of the first Continental Congress to cut off all exports and imports in trade with the British if they did not recognize the rights of the colonists. After the first Congress adjourned in October, 1774, Hewes returned to North Carolina.

Became chairman of the naval committee

The next spring, he again was elected as a delegate to the Continental Congress. He traveled to Philadelphia, arriving there in May with news of the fighting at Lexington and Concord ringing in his ears. A convention of Pennsylvania and New Jersey Quakers had met early in 1775 to denounce the efforts of the Continental Congress, but Hewes broke with his Quaker background to

---

JOSEPH HEWES

1730 (Jan. 23) Born in Kingston, N. J.

1760 Moved to Edenton, N. C.

1766-1775 Member of North Carolina's colonial legislature.

1773 Member of the North Carolina committee of correspondence.

1774-1777 Delegate from North Carolina to the Continental Congress; signed the Declaration of Independence.

1778 Member of the North Carolina state legislature.

1779 Delegate from North Carolina to the Continental Congress.

1779 (Nov. 10) Died in Philadelphia, Pa.

support the war measures voted by the second Continental Congress—he also gave up other Quaker practices, becoming a gay man-of-the-world and learning how to dance. Because of his experience with shipping, Hewes became chairman of the naval committee of Congress and was in charge of building and supplying the first American warships; and, in carrying out these duties, Hewes employed John Paul Jones as a commissioned officer in the Continental Navy, making him the first lieutenant of the *Alfred,* the Continental Navy's first ship.

In 1776, Hewes was present in Congress during the debate on independence. Although he had remained hopeful that some reconciliation might be reached with Great Britain; when he received word that the North Carolina legislature in April had given its delegates the right to "concur with those of the other colonies in declaring independency," Hewes joined John Adams in seeking an immediate declaration of independence. He signed the Declaration of Independence with the other delegates on August 2, 1776.

Hewes remained in North Carolina in 1777 and 1778 looking after his private business; then he was re-elected by the state legislature as a delegate to Congress in 1779. He arrived in Philadelphia in July, but was in ill health and took little part in the business of Congress.

On November 10, 1779, at the age of forty-nine, Hewes died in Philadelphia. He had never married. A state funeral was held in Philadelphia's Christ Church with the members of Congress present, and Hewes' body was buried in Christ Churchyard.

The Announcement of the Declaration of Independence

UNDER ✶ MY ✶ WINGS ✶ EVERY ✶ THING ✶ PROSPERS

A VIEW of NEW ORLEANS TAKEN FROM THE PLANTATION OF MARIGNY

A View of the Towne of York VIRGINIA from the RIVER

View of Portsmouth, New Hampshire, taken from the east shore

THOMAS HEYWARD, JR. of SOUTH CAROLINA

A wealthy Southern aristocrat, Thomas Heyward, Jr., won distinction as a signer of the Declaration of Independence, as an artillery officer in the Revolutionary War, and as a signer of the Articles of Confederation. Captured by the British during the war, he spent about a year in their prison for "dangerous rebels" in St. Augustine, Fla. He was described by a fellow signer of the Declaration, Benjamin Rush, as "an elegant poetical genius."

Born on his father's estate in what is now St. Luke's Parish, South Carolina, Thomas Heyward, Jr., was the eldest son of tobacco planter Daniel Heyward. He was called Junior to distinguish him from various relatives whose names also were Thomas Heyward. His father was determined that he should receive a better education than that of most other planters' sons. After receiving schooling in Greek and Latin, he was placed in the law office of a local attorney; then in his late teens he was sent to London to study law in the Middle Temple, and was admitted to the bar there in 1765 at the age of nineteen. After completing his law studies in England, Heyward spent several years visiting the various countries of Europe.

Returning to South Carolina, Heyward was twenty-five years old when he began practicing law in the colony. Two years later he married Elizabeth Mathewes. They had a happy but short marriage, for Mrs. Heyward died during the Revolutionary War. In 1786, Heyward married again, this time to Susanna Savage. He had several children by each wife.

Heyward was elected to the first patriotic provincial congress in North Carolina which chose delegates for the first Continental Congress. He also became a member of the colony's patriotic committee of safety.

In 1776, Heyward was sent to represent South Carolina in the Continental Congress, arriving there in time to participate in the debate on independence, and to sign his name to the Declaration of Independence. He remained in Congress until 1778, in that year signing the Articles of Confederation.

A particular object for British abuse

Coming home to South Carolina in 1778, Heyward was chosen as a circuit judge to handle both

---

THOMAS HEYWARD, JR.

1746 (July 28) Born in what is now St. Luke's Parish, S. C.

1771 Admitted to the bar to practice law in South Carolina.

1774-1776 Member of the provincial congress.

1775-1776 Member of South Carolina's committee of safety.

1776-1778 Delegate from South Carolina to the Continental Congress; signed the Declaration of Independence.

1778-1789 South Carolina state circuit judge.

1779-1780 Served as a captain of artillery in the militia.

1780-1781 Imprisoned by the British in St. Augustine, Fla.

1782-1784 Member of state legislature.

1785 First president of the Agricultural Society of South Carolina.

1790 Member of state constitutional convention.

1809 (March 6) Died at his estate in what is now St. Luke's Parish, S. C.

Frick Art Reference Library

THOMAS HEYWARD, JR.
by JEREMIAH THEUS, MR. and MRS. JOHN S. HOWKINS, *owners*

Heyward House, Charleston, South Carolina

civil and criminal cases for the new state government. While the British were besieging Charleston, he presided at the trial and conviction of several Loyalists charged with carrying on treasonable correspondence with the British. Heyward became a particular object for British abuse when these prisoners were executed in view of the British forces.

Heyward joined the militia in 1779 as a captain of artillery in the same battalion with Edward Rutledge, another signer of the Declaration of Independence. He fought in several battles, then he and Rutledge both were captured by the British in the fall of Charleston in 1780.

Heyward and Rutledge were imprisoned by the British in St. Augustine, Fla.—a prison reserved for rebels that they considered particularly dangerous. Meanwhile, British forces plundered Heyward's plantation and carried away his many slaves as war booty. After about a year in prison, Heyward and Rutledge were transported to Philadelphia to be exchanged for prisoners held by the American forces. Enroute to Philadelphia by ship, Heyward nearly lost his life when he fell overboard. He saved himself from drowning only by hanging onto the ship's rudder until he was rescued. During this absence from home his wife died.

After returning to South Carolina, Heyward resumed his judge's duties, which he continued to perform until 1789. He was elected to the state legislature in 1782 to 1784, and in 1785 he was elected as the first president of the Agricultural Society of South Carolina. After the adoption of the United States Constitution, Heyward served in 1789 as one of the presidential electors. The next year, he was a member of a state convention that prepared a new state constitution for South Carolina.

At the age of forty-five, Heyward retired to his plantation. He had remarried and had children by his second wife. There, he lived quietly with his family, enjoying the liberty that his efforts had helped win. On March 6, 1809, he died on his family estate where he had been born.

Mrs. Thomas Heyward (Elizabeth Savage)
by Malbone

114

WILLIAM HOOPER of NORTH CAROLINA

A Boston lawyer who received his training under James Otis, the "flame of fire" of the Revolution, William Hooper went to North Carolina to seek his fortune and became one of that state's patriotic leaders. Although he was absent from the Continental Congress during the debate on independence, he arrived in time to vote for and sign his name to the Declaration of Independence.

William Hooper was born in Boston, Mass., on June 17, 1742. His father, a Congregational minister, wanted him to become a clergyman. After attending grammar school, he entered Harvard College at the age of fifteen. In college he was most interested in the study of literature, history, and public speaking. By working hard, he completed the requirements for a bachelor of arts degree in three years and graduated in 1760 at the age of eighteen.

Worked in the law office of James Otis

Rather than follow his father's wishes that he should become a minister, Hooper decided to become a lawyer. He entered the office of James Otis, one of the leading attorneys of Boston, and began studying law. At this time Otis was engaged in a battle with the British administration over the use of search warrants, called writs of assistance, with which Boston merchants were being harassed as British tax agents tried to stamp out smuggling. Hooper undoubtedly was influenced in his think-

ing toward the British government by his association with Otis, who more than any other man aroused the people of Massachusetts to preserve their civil rights.

After being admitted to the bar to practice law in Massachusetts, Hooper decided to go to North Carolina because friends told him there were many fewer lawyers in that colony, and consequently many greater opportunities for a struggling young attorney. In 1767, he married Anne Clark of Wilmington, and settled down in that city. He and his wife had three children, two sons and a daughter.

In 1770-1771, Hooper, who had become deputy attorney general of the colony, took the part of the royal government in its conflict with the North Carolina frontiersmen who called themselves Regulators and were in a state of open rebellion against the governor. Hooper advised that the militia be called out to end the rebellion, and he joined the government forces that defeated the Regulators in the battle of Alamance in 1771.

Worked for the rights of the colonists

Two years later, in 1773, Hooper was elected to the legislature. He took a leading part in an effort to defeat a bill promoted by the friends of the royalist government which would have prevented creditors from attaching the property of persons who were not residents of North Carolina—a bill designed to protect the absentee owners of North Carolina lands who lived in England from paying their debts. Not content with merely speaking against the bill in the legislature, Hooper wrote a series of newspaper essays signed "Hampden" which discussed the rights of the colonists.

In 1774, a provincial congress chose Hooper as the head of the colony's delegation to the first Continental Congress, an office that he continued to hold until 1777. During the second Continental Congress, in 1775, he wrote an address to the people of Jamaica explaining the situation in the American colonies. It said in part:

"That our petitions have been treated with disdain, is now become the smallest part of our complaint: ministerial insolence is lost in ministerial barbarity. It has, by an exertion peculiarly ingen-

---

WILLIAM HOOPER

1742 (June 7) Born in Boston, Mass.

1760 Graduated from Harvard College.

c.1765 Moved to North Carolina to practice law.

1770-1771 As deputy attorney general, helped put down the rebellion of the "Regulators" in western North Carolina.

1773-1774 Member of North Carolina's colonial legislature.

1774-1776 Member of North Carolina's provincial congress.

1774-1777 Delegate from North Carolina to the Continental Congress; signed the Declaration of Independence.

1777-1782 Member of the North Carolina state legislature.

1786 Appointed by Congress to help mediate border dispute between Massachusetts and New York.

1790 (Oct. 14) Died in Hillsboro, N. C.

The Historical Park in Philadelphia

William Hooper *by* J. R. LAMBDIN

on July 4, and to sign his name to the document on August 2. For the rest of 1776 he was active on many committees of the Congress.

Pursued by the British troops

In February, 1777, Hooper obtained leave to return to North Carolina, in order to care for his family and improve his business affairs. He moved his family to a plantation several miles outside Wilmington. British raiders were sent to capture him, but he fled after sending his family back to Wilmington, feeling that it was better for them to live under British occupation than to face the dangers of a fugitive existence. Throughout the rest of the Revolutionary War, Hooper served in the state legislature.

At the end of the war, Hooper moved his family to Hillsboro, N. C., where he resumed the practice of law. In the postwar years, the radical party won control of the state government, and the conservatives, including Hooper, lost prominence in state and national affairs. He was appointed by Congress in 1786 as a mediator in a border dispute between New York and Massachusetts, but commissioners appointed by the two states settled the matter without his assistance. A supporter of the United States Constitution written in 1787, Hooper was defeated in an effort to be elected to the state ratification convention.

All his life Hooper had been plagued by illness, and in the last years of his life he was unable to be very active either in public or personal affairs. On October 14, 1790, at the age of forty-eight, Hooper died in Hillsboro, N. C. About a hundred years later, his body was removed from Hillsboro and reburied at Guilford Courthouse National Military Park where a monument was constructed in his memory.

ious, procured those very measures, which it laid us under the hard necessity of pursuing, to be stigmatized in parliament as rebelious: it has employed additional fleets and armies for the infamous purpose of compelling us to abandon them: it has plunged us in all the horrors and calamities of civil war: it has caused the treasure and blood of Britons (formerly shed and expended for far other ends) to be spilt and wasted in the execrable design of spreading slavery over British America: it will not, however, accomplish its aim: in the worst of contingencies, a choice will still be left, which it never can prevent us from making."

Personal affairs in North Carolina kept Hooper away from the Continental Congress during the spring of 1776, but he arrived in Philadelphia in time to vote for the Declaration of Independence

Virginia State Library
William Brotherhead from Book of the Signers

Residence of Wm. Hooper Wilmington, North Carolina

STEPHEN HOPKINS of RHODE ISLAND

Next oldest to Benjamin Franklin among the signers of the Declaration of Independence, Stephen Hopkins served in public offices from town clerk to governor for more than forty years before the Revolutionary War. His trembling signature on the Declaration of Independence was caused by the infirmities of old age, rather than by any lack of courage; for his hands shook so badly that he always had to hold his right wrist with his left hand whenever he wrote. In his many years of public service, he often held several different political posts at the same time.

Stephen Hopkins was born on March 7, 1707, near Cranston, R. I., in the town of Scituate. The son of a farmer, he received only the most basic kind of education in reading and writing; but he was particularly interested in mathematics, and, like George Washington, learned to be a competent surveyor at an early age. He continued to conduct surveys most of the rest of his life, even after he served as governor.

STEPHEN HOPKINS

1707 (March 7) Born near Cranston, R. I.

1732-1741 Town clerk of Scituate, R. I.

1732-1738 Member of the Rhode Island colonial legislature.

1735-1741 President of the town council of Scituate.

1736-1739 Justice of the peace and judge of the court of common pleas.

1739-1740 Chief justice of the court of common pleas.

1741-1742, 1744-1754 Speaker of the house of representatives in the state legislature.

1750 Helped found the public library in Providence.

1754 Delegate from Rhode Island to the Albany Convention.

1755-1768 Governor of Rhode Island, except for four years during this period.

1765 Chairman of committee opposing the Stamp Act; wrote "The Rights of the Colonies Examined."

1772-1775 Member of the Rhode Island legislature; led in forbidding the importation of slaves.

1774-1776 Delegate from Rhode Island to the Continental Congress; signed the Declaration of Independence.

1775-1776 Chief justice of the superior court of Rhode Island.

1777-1779 Member of the state legislature of Rhode Island.

1778 Delegate to the Continental Congress from Rhode Island.

1785 (July 13) Died in Providence, R. I.

When he was nineteen years old, Hopkins married Sarah Scott, the great-granddaughter of the first Quaker to settle in Providence. Hopkins' father gave the young couple a seventy-acre farm and his grandfather gave them an additional ninety acres. They had seven children before Mrs. Hopkins died in 1753. Two years later, Hopkins married again to Mrs. Anna Smith, a widow.

At the age of twenty-five, Hopkins won his first election to public office, as town clerk of Scituate; and later that same year, 1732, he was elected to represent the town in the colonial legislature. In 1735, he was elected president of the town council of Scituate, holding all three offices at once. In 1736, he added a fourth office to the others he was holding, when he became justice of the peace and judge of the court of common pleas.

A ship-builder and founder of the Providence Library

When he was thirty-four, Hopkins became speaker of the house of representatives in the colonial legislature, an office that he held from 1741 to 1754, except during the year 1743. In 1742, he sold his farm and moved to Providence where he became a shipowner and ship-builder. He also served as chief justice of the superior court from 1751 to 1754. In 1750, he helped found the public library in Providence.

In 1754, Hopkins became one of Rhode Island's delegates to the Albany Convention, the first general meeting of representatives of the American colonies. At this meeting, Benjamin Franklin presented a plan for uniting the colonies, but the idea was not accepted by the British government.

Upon his return from the Albany Convention, the forty-eight-year-old Hopkins was elected governor of Rhode Island in 1755. He served as chief executive officer of the state for nine of the next thirteen years, in 1755-1757, 1758-1762, 1763-1765, and 1767-1768. The political atmosphere of the times was capsulized by Hopkins in the following statement made near the end of his final terms as governor:

'will no good Samaritan come by?'

"When we draw aside the veil of words and professions, when we attend to what is done, not

---

Home of Stephen Hopkins

Photographer: Hirst Milhollen

else can be the cause of our unhappy disputes? What other reason for the continual struggle for superiority and office? What other motive for the flood of calumny and reproach cast on each other? —Behold! the leading men meeting in cabals, and from thence dispersing themselves to the several quarters to delude and deceive the people. The people are called together in tippling-houses, their business neglected, their morals corrupted, themserves deluded; some promised offices for which they are unfit; and those who have disputes with their neighbours are assured of their causes, whether they be right or wrong: those with whom these arts will not prevail, are tempted with the wages of unrighteousness, and offered a bribe to falsify their oath, and betray their country. By these scandalous practices, elections are carried, and officers appointed.—It makes little difference whether the officer who, in this manner, obtains his place, is otherwise a good man, or not; for, put in by a party, he must do what they order, without being permitted to examine the rectitude even of

to what is said, we shall find, in the present age of our country, that liberty is only a cant term of faction, and freedom of speaking and acting, used only to serve private interest and a party.—What his own actions. The unhappy malady runs through the whole constitution: men in authority are not revered, and, therefore, lose all power to do good; the courts of judicature catch the infection, and the sacred balance of justice does not hang even; all complain of the present administration, all cry out the times are hard, and all wish they might grow better; but complaints are weak, wishes are idle, cries are vain, even prayers will be ineffectual, if we do not universally amend:—but no friend, no patriot, will step in, and save the commonwealth from ruin. Will no good Samaritan come by, and pour in the wine and oil into the bleeding wounds of his country?"

Author of an influential pamphlet

In 1765, Hopkins took a leading role in de-

118

nouncing the Stamp Act passed by the British parliament. He was appointed chairman of a committee by the Providence town meeting to draw up a resolution to the colonial legislature detailing the position that should be taken in regard to the Stamp Act. In that same year he wrote a pamphlet titled "The Rights of the Colonies Examined" which reviewed the growing conflict between the British government and the colonies.

For the abolition of slavery

Just before the Revolutionary War, Hopkins became a leading advocate of the abolition of slavery. In 1773, he freed the slaves that he owned, and the next year he prepared a legislative act forbidding the further importation of slaves into Rhode Island. He persuaded the legislature to adopt the act in 1774, the first such anti-slavery legislation adopted in America.

At the outbreak of the Revolutionary War, Hopkins held four important posts. From 1772 to 1779 he represented Providence in the Rhode Island legislature. From 1774 to 1776 he served as a member of Rhode Island's delegation in the Continental Congress. In 1775 he was re-appointed to a term as chief justice of Rhode Island's

State House
Providence, Rhode Island

superior court. He also was a member of Providence's committee of safety.

In the Continental Congress, Hopkins took an active part as a member of many important committees. His experience as a shipowner particularly was put to use on the naval affairs committee; and his brother, Esek Hopkins, was appointed by Congress in 1775 as the first commander in chief of the Continental Navy. He aided John Dickinson in the preparation of the Articles of Confederation; but, unlike Dickinson, he supported and signed the Declaration of Independence. Hopkins did not attend Congress in 1777, but he again served in Congress in 1778.

First chancellor of Brown University

All his life Hopkins had been interested in learning, perhaps because his own education as a boy had been so limited. When Rhode Island College (now Brown University) was founded in 1764, Hopkins became its first chancellor, a position that he held for many years.

After his last term in the legislature in 1779, Hopkins retired in his substantial home in Providence. He died there after a lingering illness at the age of seventy-eight, on July 13, 1785.

STEPHEN HOPKINS

119

FRANCIS HOPKINSON of NEW JERSEY

Although Francis Hopkinson signed the Declaration of Independence and was a respected lawyer and judge, his greatest contribution to the cause of American liberty came in his writing of political satires that helped mold public opinion in favor of the Revolutionary War and the ratification of the United States Constitution. Like Franklin, Jefferson, and several other of the Founding Fathers, Hopkinson was a man of many talents: he was a composer, poet, writer, organist, inventor, painter, and cartoonist, as well as a lawyer and jurist. Some authorities credit Hopkinson with designing the American flag. John Adams described him in a letter to his wife:

Well bred and very social

"At Mr. Peale's painter's room I met Mr. Francis Hopkinson, late a Mandamus Councilor of New Jersey, now a member of the Continental Congress, who, it seems, is a native of Philadelphia; a son of a prothonotary of this country, who was a person much respected. The son was liberally educated, and is a painter and a poet. I have a curiosity to penetrate a little deeper into the bosom of this curious gentleman. He is one of your pretty, little, curious, ingenious men. His head is not bigger than a large apple . . . I have not met with anything in natural history more amusing and entertaining than his personal appearance—yet he is genteel and well bred, and is very social."

Hopkinson's friend and fellow-signer of the Declaration of Independence, Benjamin Rush, described Hopkinson as being "a little below the common size. His features were small, but extremely animated. His speech was quick, and all his motions seemed to partake of the unceasing activity and versatility of the powers of his mind." Rush said of Hopkinson's part in the American Revolution: "The various causes which contributed to the establishment of the independence and Federal Government of the United States, will not be fully traced, unless much is ascribed to the irresistible influence of the ridicule which he poured forth from time to time, upon the enemies of those great political events."

Francis Hopkinson was born in Philadelphia on October 2, 1737, the eldest son of Thomas and Mary Hopkinson, who had emigrated from England only a few years earlier. His father was an Oxford-educated lawyer who served as a jurist in the colonial government of Pennsylvania, was a friend of Benjamin Franklin, and was the first president of the American Philosophical Society when it was founded in 1744. His mother was the niece of the Bishop of Worcester in England.

First to enroll in the University of Pennsylvania

When Francis Hopkinson was fourteen, his father died, leaving him and his six brothers and sisters to the care of his mother. She was an unusually devoted mother, denying herself all luxuries so that her children could obtain the best possible education. Young Francis was the first student enrolled in the academy founded in 1751 by Benjamin Franklin and other Philadelphia citizens; and after this school had been chartered as the College of Philadelphia (now the University of Pennsylvania), Hopkinson was in the first class to graduate in 1757. During his college days, he developed a love for literature and began to write verses; he began to be invited to write poems for weddings, commencements, and other occasions that the customs of the day called upon to be memorialized in poetry.

After completing his college education, the nineteen-year-old Hopkinson began studying law as a clerk in the office of Benjamin Chew, who then was attorney-general of Pennsylvania. After

---

FRANCIS HOPKINSON

1737 (Oct. 2) Born in Philadelphia, Pa.

1757 Graduated from the College of Philadelphia (now the University of Pennsylvania.)

1766-1768 Visited relatives in England.

1776 Delegate from New Jersey to the second Continental Congress; signed the Declaration of Independence.

1779-1789 Judge of the admiralty court of Pennsylvania.

1789 Secretary of the organizational conference of the Protestant Episcopal Church.

1789-1791 Federal circuit court judge in Pennsylvania.

1791 (May 9) Died in Philadelphia.

MRS. FRANCIS HOPKINSON
by C. W. PEALE
The Historical Society of Pennsylvania

several years study, Hopkinson was admitted to the bar and began practicing law in Philadelphia.

Spent fourteen months in England

When Hopkinson was twenty-eight, his mother decided that he should go to England to visit her uncle, the Bishop of Worcester, to attain some of the polish of an English gentleman. It is noteworthy of the position Hopkinson had already attained that the trustees of the College of Philadelphia passed the following resolution in May, 1766, just before his departure: "It was resolved, that as Francis Hopkinson, (who was the first scholar entered in this seminary at its opening, and likewise, one of the first who received a degree in it,) was about to embark for England, and has always done honour to the place of his education by his abilities and good morals, as well as rendered it many substantial services on all public occasions, the thanks of this institution ought to be delivered to him in the most affectionate and respectful manner . . . and wish him a safe and prosperous voyage." Hopkinson enjoyed the fourteen months that he spent in England, living with his uncle, meeting many of the most prominent men of the country, and even having dinner with the prime minister of Great Britain.

Returning to America in 1768, Hopkinson married Ann Borden, a wealthy heiress of Borden-

town, N. J. He moved to New Jersey in order to help manage his wife's estate, and through the influence of his uncle he received appointments as a collector of customs and as a mandamus councilor.

"A Pretty Story"

Despite his position as an official of the royal government, Hopkinson became sympathetic to the patriotic cause, and in 1774 he published a biting satire on the conflict between the colonists and the British government which he entitled "A Pretty Story." This satire was written in the form of an allegory that represented the British King as a nobleman with a large farm. The citizens of the British empire were represented as the nobleman's children, and the British parliament was represented by the nobleman's wife. When the children moved to a distant farm, the "harsh and unconstitutional proceedings" of the nobleman and his wife "irritated" the "inhabitants of the new farm." Hopkinson followed this with another satire in 1776 called "The Prophecy" in which he used Biblical language to forecast the Declaration of Independence.

FRANCIS HOPKINSON
by ROBERT EDGE PINE
The Hopkinson Collection

Designer of the Flag

When the New Jersey legislature imprisoned the royal governor in 1776 and elected a new delegation to represent the colony in the Continental Congress, Hopkinson was one of those elected. He arrived in Philadelphia just in time to hear the debate on Richard Henry Lee's independence resolution. He cast his vote for the Declaration of Independence on July 4, and signed the document with the other delegates on August 2. The following year, he is said to have designed the American flag of stars and stripes.

In recognition of Hopkinson's legal abilities, he was appointed judge of the admiralty of Pennsylvania in 1779. He served in this court for ten years, until the adoption of the United States Constitution ended the jurisdiction of the court.

After the Constitutional Convention had written the United States Constitution, Hopkinson again took up his pen to aid the Federalist cause with humorous essays called "The New Roof" and "Objections to the Proposed Plan of a Federal Government for the United States, on Genuine Principles." In the first, he ridiculed the Anti-Federalists, representing them by a quarrelsome woman who preferred a leaky old roof to one built by a master-architect, and in the latter he represented the Anti-Federalists as convicts in a jail arguing that they were the most knowledgeable people to speak on the subject of freedom and democracy.

Judge of the first federal court

After the organization of the new government of the United States in 1789, President George Washington appointed Hopkinson as a federal circuit judge for eastern Pennsylvania. On November 10, 1789, Hopkinson opened his court—the first federal court to begin operating under the United States Constitution. Also, in 1789, he was secretary of the organizing conference of the Protestant Episcopal Church.

At the age of fifty-three, Hopkinson was stricken with apoplexy while at breakfast in his Philadelphia home on May 9, 1791, and died within two hours. He left a widow and five children. His eldest son, Joseph Hopkinson, became a lawyer, and followed his father as a federal circuit court judge, but became best known as the author of the song "Hail Columbia."

Benjamin Rush summarized Francis Hopkinson's contributions by saying: "He excelled in music and poetry, and had some knowledge in painting. These arts, however, did not monopolize all the powers of his mind; he was well skilled in many practical and useful sciences, particularly mathematics and natural philosophy, and he had a general acquaintance with the principles of anatomy, chemistry, and natural history. But his forte was humour and satire, in both of which he was not surpassed by Lucian, Swift, or Rabelais. These extraordinary powers were consecrated to the advancement of the interests of patriotism, virtue, and science."

View of the TRIUMPHAL ARCH, and the manner of receiving General Washington at Trenton, on his Route to New-York. April 21.st 1789.

SAMUEL HUNTINGTON of CONNECTICUT

The son of a small farmer, Samuel Huntington was a self-made lawyer who rose to become the first President of the United States Congress under the Articles of Confederation. A dignified, aloof man, he served in every important office that the state of Connecticut could offer, spending the last ten years of his life as governor.

Huntington was born on a farm near Windham, Conn., on July 3, 1731. His father was Nathaniel Huntington, a farmer whose ancestors were among the earliest settlers of Connecticut. As a boy, Samuel Huntington received only enough education to learn how to read and write. He spent much of his time doing chores on his father's farm, and when he was old enough he was apprenticed to a cooper to learn how to make barrels. However, the boy was not content to become a farmer or a tradesman, and he educated himself by reading and study in all his spare time. When he completed his apprenticeship at the age of twenty-two, he began studying law; and by the time he was twenty-seven he had been admitted to the bar and was practicing law in Windham.

In 1760, Huntington moved to the larger town of Norwich where there was a greater opportunity for a young lawyer to make a name for himself. He soon began to win cases, and word of his legal abilities spread among the small farmers of the area, who considered him one of their own because of his humble background.

At the age of thirty, Huntington married Marthat Devotion, the daughter of the Reverend Ebenezer Devotion. His younger brother, Joseph, who became a clergyman, married Martha's sister. Although Samuel and Martha Huntington had no children of their own, they later adopted two of Joseph Huntington's children and brought them up as if they were their own. One of these adopted children, also called Samuel Huntington, later became governor of Ohio.

Huntington entered his long career as a public servant at the age of thirty-three when he was elected to represent Norwich in the colonial legislature. For the next twenty years, from 1764 to 1784, he served in the legislature, first in the lower house, then in the governor's council or senate. In 1765, he took on the additional duties of king's attorney, an office that he held until the Revolutionary War ended the colonial government.

An outspoken patriot, Huntington was elected by the legislature in 1775 as a member of Connecticut's delegation to the second Continental

SAMUEL HUNTINGTON

1731 (July 3) Born in Windham, Conn.

1758 Admitted to the bar to practice law.

1764-1775 Member of the lower house of the Connecticut legislature.

1765-1774 King's attorney for Connecticut.

1774-1783 Associate justice of Connecticut's superior court.

1775-1784 Member of the upper house of the Connecticut legislature.

1776-1783 Member of Connecticut's delegation to the Continental Congress; signed the Declaration of Independence and the Articles of Confederation.

1779-1781 President of the Congress.

1784 Chief justice of the superior court of Connecticut.

1785 Lieutenant governor of Connecticut.

1786-1796 Governor of Connecticut.

1796 (Jan. 5) Died in Norwich, Conn.

RES. OF S. HUNTINGTON, NORWICH CONN.

Congress, and he first took his seat in that body in January, 1776. He supported the plans for declaring the colonies independent from Britain, and voted for and signed the Declaration of Independence. Continuing to serve in the Congress throughout most of the Revolutionary War, Huntington also signed the Articles of Confederation in 1778.

Succeeded John Jay as President of Congress

Upon the resignation of John Jay as President of Congress in 1779, Huntington was elected President by his fellow delegates. During his administration, the Articles of Confederation were ratified in 1781 by the last state, Maryland, and went into effect, making Huntington the first President of Congress under the Articles of Confederation. The duties of President were extremely arduous during the Revolutionary War, and finally ill health brought on by overwork forced Huntington to resign in July, 1781. He returned to Connecticut where he resumed his duties as an associate justice of the superior court and as a member of the upper house of the legislature. Although he was re-elected to Congress in 1782, he did not return to that body until the summer of 1783 while it was meeting in Princeton, N. J.

For the rest of his life, Huntington served in the most important state offices in Connecticut. In 1784 he was appointed chief justice of the state's superior court; the next year he was elected lieutenant governor; and the year after that he was elected governor.

Well-liked by the people of Connecticut, Huntington was re-elected governor each year for ten years. When the United States Constitution was written in 1787, he supported his state's ratification of the document and became a leading Federalist. In the presidential election of 1789, he received two electoral votes for President of the United States.

Later in 1795, Huntington became seriously ill with a variety of disorders, and in the final stages of his illness he lost all control of his mind and body. At the age of sixty-four Huntington died on January 5, 1796, at his home in Norwich, Conn.

View in Canaan, between The Green Woods and Salisbury, CONNECTICUT.

THOMAS JEFFERSON of VIRGINIA

In the instructions for his tombstone, Thomas Jefferson wrote that "I wish most to be remembered" as the author of the Declaration of Independence, as the author of the statute of Virginia's religious freedom, and as the Father of the University of Virginia. He made no mention of his many other services and accomplishments: as governor of Virginia, as the first Secretary of State under George Washington, as the second Vice-President of the United States under John Adams, and as the third President of the United States, in which office he doubled his country's size by the Louisiana Purchase.

Jefferson was a many-sided genius who was successful in almost everything he tried as a lawyer, diplomat, political leader, architect, inventor, writer, musician, art collector, and scientist. One of the best descriptions of Jefferson was written by his grandson, Thomas Jefferson Randolph:

"Mr. Jefferson's hair, when young, was of a reddish cast, sandy as he advanced in years—his eye, hazel—dying in his 84th year, he had not lost a tooth, or had one defective; his skin, thin, peeling from his face on exposure to the sun, and giving it a tettered appearance; the superficial veins so weak, as upon the slightest blow, to cause ex-

---

THOMAS JEFFERSON

1743 (April 13) Born at Shadwell in Albemarle County, Virginia.

1757 Inherited the family estate upon the death of his father.

1762 Graduated from College of William and Mary.

1767 Admitted to the bar to practice law.

1769-1775 Member of the Virginia house of burgesses.

1775-1776 Delegate from Virginia to the Continental Congress; wrote and signed the Declaration of Independence.

1776-1779 Member of the Virginia legislature.

1779-1781 Governor of Virginia.

1783-1784 Delegate from Virginia to the Congress of the Confederation.

1784-1785 Representative of Congress in Europe to help negotiate trade treaties.

1785-1789 Minister to France.

1789-1793 Secretary of State of the United States.

1797-1801 Vice-President of the United States.

1801-1809 President of the United States.

1817-1825 Helped found the University of Virginia.

1826 (July 4) Died at Monticello in Albemarle County, Virginia.

---

tensive suffusions of blood, in early life, upon standing to write for any length of time, bursting beneath the skin: it, however, gave him no inconvenience. His countenance was mild and benignant, and attractive to strangers . . .

Never abandoned a plan, a principle, or a friend

"Mr. Jefferson's stature was commanding, six feet two and a half inches in height, well formed, indicating strength, activity, and robust health; his carriage, erect; step firm and elastic, which he preserved to his death; his temper, naturally strong, under perfect control—his courage, cool and impassive—no one ever knew him exhibit trepidation—his moral courage of the highest order—his will, firm and inflexible—it was remarked of him that he never abandoned a plan, a principle, or a friend . . .

"His habits were regular and systematic. He was a miser of his time, rose always at dawn, wrote and read until breakfast, breakfasted early, and dined from three to four—after breakfast read for half an hour in his public rooms or portico, in summer—visited his garden and workshops—returned to his writing and reading till one, when he rode on horseback to three or half past—dined, and gave the evening to his family and company—retired at nine, and to bed from ten to eleven. He said in his last illness, that the sun had not caught him in bed for fifty years. He always made his own fire. He drank water but once a day, a single glass, when he returned from his ride. He ate heartily, and much vegetable food, preferring French cookery, because it made the meats more tender. He never drank ardent spirits or strong wines—such was his aversion to ardent spirits that when, in his last illness, his physician desired him to use brandy as an astringent, he could not induce him to take it strong enough . . .

Recognized strengths and weaknesses in his fellow-men

"His manner was dignified, reserved with strangers, but frank and cordial with his friends; his conversation cheerful, often sportive, and illustrated by anecdotes. He spoke only of the good qualities of men, which induced the belief that he knew little of them, but no one knew them better.

THOMAS JEFFERSON
by Mather Brown, Charles Francis Adams, Jr., *owner*

I had formed this opinion, and on hearing him speak very favorably of men with defects known to myself, stated them to him, when he asked if I supposed he had not observed them, adding others not noted by me, and evincing much more accurate knowledge of the individual character than I possessed, observing, 'My habit is to speak only of men's good qualities.' When he believed that either men or measures were adverse to Republican institutions, he spoke of them with open and unqualified condemnation . . .

"His manners were of that polished school of the Colonial Government, so remarkable in its day — under no circumstances violating any of those minor conventional observances which constitute the well-bred gentleman, courteous and considerate to all persons. On riding out with him, when a lad, we met a Negro who bowed to us; he returned his bow, I did not; turning to me he asked, 'Do you permit a Negro to be more of a gentleman than yourself?'"

On April 13, 1743, Thomas Jefferson was born at Shadwell, his parents' plantation in Albemarle County, Virginia. His father, Peter Jefferson, was descended from one of the early settlers of Jamestown, and his mother, Jane Randolph Jefferson, was a member of the famous Randolph family of Virginia. When Jefferson was nine years old he was sent to a nearby private school to learn the classical languages. When he was fourteen, his father died, leaving him an estate of about two thousand acres and thirty slaves. He continued his studies at another private school near Charlottesville until he was sixteen, and then he entered the College of William and Mary at Williamsburg.

Jefferson spent two years at William and Mary, being graduated in 1762. He later wrote of his time there: "It was my great good fortune, and what probably fixed the destinies of my life, that Dr. William Small, of Scotland, was then professor of mathematics, a man profound in most of the useful branches of science, with a happy talent of communication, correct and gentlemanly manners, and an enlarged and liberal mind."

Patrick Henry spoke as Homer wrote

Upon completing his college work, Jefferson began studying law under George Wythe, who later signed the Declaration of Independence and then became the first professor of law in the United States, at the College of William and Mary. Wythe and Small also introduced Jefferson to Virginia

Governor Francis Fauquier, described by Jefferson as "the ablest man who ever filled the office." The four often met at Fauquier's home to talk and enjoy music, with Jefferson playing the violin. During this time as a law student, Jefferson also visited sessions of the Virginia house of burgesses; and there, in 1765, he was impressed by Patrick Henry's fiery denunciation of the Stamp Act. Jefferson later wrote of this speech by Henry: "He appeared to me to speak as Homer wrote."

In 1767, at the age of twenty-four, Jefferson was admitted to the bar. He practiced law in Williamsburg for the next seven years, until he turned his business over to Edmund Randolph, his cousin, in 1774. He was a successful lawyer, collecting an average income of about three thousand dollars a year. A surviving report of his argument in a case in 1770 reflects the language that he later was to use in the Declaration of Independence. In unsuccessfully trying to win freedom for a slave that was the grandchild of a mulatto, Jefferson said:

"Under the law of nature all men are born free, every one comes into the world with a right to his own person which includes the liberty of moving and using it at his own will. This is what is called personal liberty, and is given him by the author of nature, because necessary for his own sustenance . . ."

Election to the house of burgesses

In 1769, Jefferson won election to the house of burgesses, where he served until the outbreak of the Revolutionary War. When Jefferson began his career as a legislator at the age of twenty-six, he already had won some reputation as a writer, so he was called upon to write the formal reply of the legislature to the opening address of the governor. His first draft was too simply stated to please the leaders of the house, so he wrote it, as he later said, "with amplification enough, and it was accepted." Later in the session, when the governor became angered by an inflammatory petition to the king and dissolved the legislature, Jefferson met in the Apollo Room of the Raleigh Tavern and heard George Washington present the plan for an association to agree to the non-importation of British goods; and on May 18, 1769, he signed his name to the association along with most of the other legislators. Jefferson later wrote of this period:

No alternative but resistance or submission

"The colonies were taxed internally and externally; their essential interests sacrificed to individuals in Great Britain; their legislatures suspended; charters annulled; trials by juries taken away; their persons subjected to transportation across the Atlantic, and to trial by foreign judicatories; their supplications for redress thought beneath answer; themselves published as cowards in the councils of their mother country and courts of Europe; armed troops sent amongst them to enforce submission to these violences; and actual hostilities commenced against them. No alternative was presented, but resistance or unconditional submission. Between these there could be no hesitation. They closed in the appeal to arms."

On January 1, 1772, Jefferson married a widow, Mrs. Martha Wayles Skelton, the daughter of a well-to-do lawyer. By this marriage, he doubled his landed estate. He had started building Monticello in 1770 near his birthplace of Shadwell, and although the new house was only partly finished he took his bride to it because Shadwell had burned the previous year. He and his wife had six children, but only two daughters survived

childhood. After his wife's death in 1782, Jefferson never remarried. One daughter died while he was President, and the other married Thomas Mann Randolph, who became governor of Virginia in 1819 to 1822.

Reared six children of his widowed sister

As relations between the colonies and Great Britain grew worse, Jefferson became more and more convinced that the actions of the various colonies should be coordinated to provide the greatest effective defense against the measures of the British parliament. Early in 1773, he met at the Raleigh Tavern with Patrick Henry, Richard Henry Lee, Francis Lightfoot Lee, and his brother-in-law Dabney Carr (who was married to Jefferson's sister, Martha), and they drew up resolutions to form a committee of correspondence with the other colonies. Jefferson was asked to present the resolutions in the house of burgesses, but he deferred to Carr. The resolutions were approved, and Jefferson was appointed to the committee of

Monticello
home of Thomas Jefferson, the name derived from the Italian.

Drawn Engraved & Published by W. Birch & Son.

Sold by R. Campbell & Co. N⁰ 30 Chesnut Street Philad⁰ 1800   Library of Congress

Preparation for **WAR** to defend Commerce.

The Swedish Church Southwark with the building of the FRIGATE PHILADELPHIA.

References

A A View of one of the Floating Batteries or Gondolas
Built at Cambridge by the Rebels.

B Shews the Manner in which the Entrances into the Works of the
Rebels are clos'd & defended by draw Bridges.

CDE Represent the different kinds of spears in Use in the
Rebel Army.

A. A view of one of the floating batteries or gondolas built at Cambridge by the rebels. B. Shows the manner
in which the entrances into the works of the rebels are closed and defended by draw-bridges.
C, D, E. Represent the different kinds of spears in use in the Rebel army.

correspondence along with ten other legislators. When Carr died only a month later leaving a widow and six children, Jefferson took the entire family to Monticello and reared and educated the children as his own.

A day of fasting in Virginia

In May, 1774, word reached Virginia of the plans to close the port of Boston on June 1 in retaliation for the Boston Tea Party. Immediately, Jefferson, Patrick Henry, the two Lees, and several other legislators "cooked up a resolution," as Jefferson later described it, which called for June 1 to be set aside as a day of fasting in Virginia. This resolution was passed on May 24, and said in part:

"This House, being deeply impressed with apprehension of the great dangers to be derived to British America from the hostile invasion of the city of Boston in our Sister Colony of Massachusetts Bay, whose commerce and harbor are, on the first day of June next, to be stopped by an armed force, deem it highly necessary that the said first day of June be set apart, by the members of this House, as a day of fasting, humiliation and prayer, devoutly to implore the divine interposition, for averting the heavy calamity which threatens destruction to our civil rights and the evils of civil war; to give us one heart and one mind firmly to oppose, by all just and proper means, every injury to American rights; and that the minds of his Majesty and his Parliament, may be inspired from above with wisdom, moderation and justice, to remove from the loyal people of America all cause of danger from a continued pursuit of measures pregnant with their ruin."

Two days later the governor angrily dissolved the house of burgesses, and, just as they had in 1769, the legislators adjourned to the Apollo Room of the Raleign Tavern to discuss their future course of action. After some talk, they passed several resolutions which empowered the committee of correspondence to get in touch with the legislatures of other colonies to urge the calling of a general congress of delegates from all the colonies to decide on a united policy.

"Mr. Jefferson's Bill of Rights"

Jefferson was ill when a convention of Virginia's patriotic legislators was called in August, 1774, but he sent along to his friends a paper that he had prepared entitled, "A Summary View of the Rights of British America, Set Forth in some Resolutions

House in which the Declaration was written.

Intended for the Inspection of the Present Delegates of the People of Virginia, now in Convention." It was soon published and became known as "Mr. Jefferson's Bill of Rights." Addressed to the British king, it said in part:

"Open your breast, sire, to liberal and expanded thought. It behooves you to think and act for your people. The great principles of right and wrong are legible to every reader; to peruse them, requires not the aid of many counsellors. The whole art of government consists in the art of being honest."

Because of his illness, Jefferson was not elected as one of Virginia's delegates to the first Continental Congress; but in the spring of 1775, after he had recovered, he was elected as an alternate to his cousin Peyton Randolph, who was President of the first Continental Congress as well as speaker of the house of burgesses. When Randolph had to return to Virginia in June, Jefferson took his place in the Congress in Philadelphia on June 21. He became a member of John Dickinson's committee that wrote a declaration stating the causes and necessity of taking up arms, and he quickly won a reputation for his "peculiar felicity of expression," as John Adams said.

Drafting the Declaration of Independence

After Richard Henry Lee had presented Congress with his resolutions calling for independence from Great Britain, Jefferson was chosen on June 11, 1776, as chairman of a committee to draw up a declaration of independence. The other members of the committee were John Adams, Benjamin Franklin, Roger Sherman, and Robert R. Livingston. Many years later in a letter to James

Madison, Jefferson summarized the actions of the next several days:

"The Committee of 5 met, no such thing as a subcommittee was proposed, but they unanimously pressed on myself alone to undertake the draught. I consented; I drew it; but before I reported it to the committee, I communicated it separately to Dr. Franklin and Mr. Adams requesting their corrections; because they were the two members of whose judgments and amendments I wished most to have the benefit before presenting it to the Committee; and you have seen the original paper now in my hands, with the corrections of Doctor Franklin and Mr. Adams interlined in their own handwritings. Their alterations were two or three only, and merely verbal. I then wrote a fair copy, reported it to the Committee, and from them, unaltered to Congress."

"An expression of the American mind"

The thirty-three-year-old Jefferson did most of the writing of the Declaration of Independence on a portable writing desk that he had invented. He composed it while sitting in the parlor of the apartment he had rented on the second floor of a brick house at Market and Seventh Streets. Of his composition, Jefferson later said:

"I turned to neither book nor pamphlet while writing it. I did not consider it as any part of my charge to invent new ideas altogether and to offer no sentiment which had ever been expressed before."

He said that he saw his task of writing as:

"Not to find out new principles or new arguments, never before thought of, not merely to say things which had never been said before; but to place before mankind the common sense of the subject, terms so plain and firm as to command their assent, and to justify ourselves in the independent stand we impelled to take. Neither aiming at originality of principle or sentiment, nor yet copied from any particular and previous writing, it was intended to be an expression of the American mind. . . . All its authority rests then on the harmonizing sentiments of the day, whether expressed in conversation, in letters, printed essays, or the

IN CONGRESS, JULY 4, 1776.

The unanimous Declaration of the thirteen united States of America,

When in the Course of human events, it becomes necessary for one people to dissolve the political bands which have connected them with another, and to assume among the powers of the earth, the separate and equal station to which the Laws of Nature and of Nature's God entitle them, a decent respect to the opinions of mankind requires that they should declare the causes which impel them to the separation. —— We hold these truths to be self-evident, that all men are created equal, that they are endowed by their Creator with certain unalienable Rights, that among these are Life, Liberty and the pursuit of Happiness. —— That to secure these rights, Governments are instituted among Men, deriving their just powers from the consent of the governed, —— That whenever any Form of Government becomes destructive of these ends, it is the Right of the People to alter or to abolish it, and to institute new Government, laying its foundation on such principles and organizing its powers in such form, as to them shall seem most likely to effect their Safety and Happiness. Prudence, indeed, will dictate that Governments long established should not be changed for light and transient causes; and accordingly all experience hath shewn, that mankind are more disposed to suffer, while evils are sufferable, than to right themselves by abolishing the forms to which they are accustomed. But when a long train of abuses and usurpations, pursuing invariably the same Object evinces a design to reduce them under absolute Despotism, it is their right, it is their duty, to throw off such Government, and to provide new Guards for their future security. —— Such has been the patient sufferance of these Colonies; and such is now the necessity which constrains them to alter their former Systems of Government. The history of the present King of Great Britain is a history of repeated injuries and usurpations, all having in direct object the establishment of an absolute Tyranny over these States. To prove this, let Facts be submitted to a candid world. —— He has refused his Assent to Laws, the most wholesome and necessary for the public good. —— He has forbidden his Governors to pass Laws of immediate and pressing importance, unless suspended in their operation till his Assent should be obtained; and when so suspended, he has utterly neglected to attend to them. —— He has refused to pass other Laws for the accommodation of large districts of people, unless those people would relinquish the right of Representation in the Legislature, a right inestimable to them and formidable to tyrants only. —— He has called together legislative bodies at places unusual, uncomfortable, and distant from the depository of their public Records, for the sole purpose of fatiguing them into compliance with his measures. —— He has dissolved Representative Houses repeatedly, for opposing with manly firmness his invasions on the rights of the people. —— He has refused for a long time, after such dissolutions, to cause others to be elected; whereby the Legislative powers, incapable of Annihilation, have returned to the People at large for their exercise; the State remaining in the mean time exposed to all the dangers of invasion from without, and convulsions within. —— He has endeavoured to prevent the population of these States; for that purpose obstructing the Laws for Naturalization of Foreigners; refusing to pass others to encourage their migrations hither, and raising the conditions of new Appropriations of Lands. —— He has obstructed the Administration of Justice, by refusing his Assent to Laws for establishing Judiciary powers. —— He has made Judges dependent on his Will alone, for the tenure of their offices, and the amount and payment of their salaries. —— He has erected a multitude of New Offices, and sent hither swarms of Officers to harass our people, and eat out their substance. —— He has kept among us, in times of peace, Standing Armies without the Consent of our legislatures. —— He has affected to render the Military independent of and superior to the Civil power. —— He has combined with others to subject us to a jurisdiction foreign to our constitution, and unacknowledged by our laws; giving his Assent to their Acts of pretended Legislation: —— For quartering large bodies of armed troops among us: —— For protecting them, by a mock Trial, from punishment for any Murders which they should commit on the Inhabitants of these States: —— For cutting off our Trade with all parts of the world: —— For imposing Taxes on us without our Consent: —— For depriving us in many cases, of the benefits of Trial by jury: —— For transporting us beyond Seas to be tried for pretended offences —— For abolishing the free System of English Laws in a neighbouring Province, establishing therein an Arbitrary government, and enlarging its Boundaries so as to render it at once an example and fit instrument for introducing the same absolute rule into these Colonies: —— For taking away our Charters, abolishing our most valuable Laws, and altering fundamentally the Forms of our Governments: —— For suspending our own Legislatures, and declaring themselves invested with power to legislate for us in all cases whatsoever. —— He has abdicated Government here, by declaring us out of his Protection and waging War against us. —— He has plundered our seas, ravaged our Coasts, burnt our towns, and destroyed the lives of our people. —— He is at this time transporting large Armies of foreign Mercenaries to compleat the works of death, desolation and tyranny, already begun with circumstances of Cruelty & perfidy scarcely paralleled in the most barbarous ages, and totally unworthy the Head of a civilized nation. —— He has constrained our fellow Citizens taken Captive on the high Seas to bear Arms against their Country, to become the executioners of their friends and Brethren, or to fall themselves by their Hands. —— He has excited domestic insurrections amongst us, and has endeavoured to bring on the inhabitants of our frontiers, the merciless Indian Savages, whose known rule of warfare, is an undistinguished destruction of all ages, sexes and conditions. In every stage of these Oppressions We have Petitioned for Redress in the most humble terms: Our repeated Petitions have been answered only by repeated injury. A Prince, whose character is thus marked by every act which may define a Tyrant, is unfit to be the ruler of a free people. Nor have We been wanting in attentions to our British brethren. We have warned them from time to time of attempts by their legislature to extend an unwarrantable jurisdiction over us. We have reminded them of the circumstances of our emigration and settlement here. We have appealed to their native justice and magnanimity, and we have conjured them by the ties of our common kindred to disavow these usurpations, which, would inevitably interrupt our connections and correspondence. They too have been deaf to the voice of justice and of consanguinity. We must, therefore, acquiesce in the necessity, which denounces our Separation, and hold them, as we hold the rest of mankind, Enemies in War, in Peace Friends. ——

We, therefore, the Representatives of the united States of America, in General Congress, Assembled, appealing to the Supreme Judge of the world for the rectitude of our intentions, do, in the Name, and by Authority of the good People of these Colonies, solemnly publish and declare, That these United Colonies are, and of Right ought to be Free and Independent States; that they are Absolved from all Allegiance to the British Crown, and that all political connection between them and the State of Great Britain, is and ought to be totally dissolved; and that as Free and Independent States, they have full Power to levy War, conclude Peace, contract Alliances, establish Commerce, and to do all other Acts and Things which Independent States may of right do. —— And for the support of this Declaration, with a firm reliance on the protection of divine Providence, we mutually pledge to each other our Lives, our Fortunes and our sacred Honor.

[signatures]

John Hancock

Button Gwinnett
Lyman Hall
Geo Walton

Wm Hooper
Joseph Hewes
John Penn

Edward Rutledge
Thos Heyward Junr.
Thomas Lynch Junr.
Arthur Middleton

George Wythe
Richard Henry Lee
Th Jefferson
Benj Harrison
Thos Nelson jr.
Francis Lightfoot Lee
Carter Braxton

Robt Morris
Benjamin Rush
Benj. Franklin
John Morton
Geo Clymer
Jas. Smith
Geo. Taylor
James Wilson
Geo. Ross
Caesar Rodney
Geo Read
Tho M: Kean

Samuel Chase
Wm. Paca
Thos. Stone
Charles Carroll of Carrollton

Wm. Floyd
Phil. Livingston
Frans. Lewis
Lewis Morris
Richd. Stockton
Jno Witherspoon
Fras. Hopkinson
John Hart
Abra Clark

Josiah Bartlett
Wm. Whipple
Saml Adams
John Adams
Robt Treat Paine
Elbridge Gerry
Step. Hopkins
William Ellery
Roger Sherman
Saml Huntington
Wm Williams
Oliver Wolcott
Matthew Thornton

elementary books of public right, as Aristotle, Cicero, Locke, Sidney, etc."

After Congress had adopted Lee's independence resolutions on July 2, it took up consideration of Jefferson's draft of the Declaration. Various changes were made in it, a word changed here, a phrase changed there. Jefferson later wrote of this:

"Congress proceeded the same day to consider the Declaration of Independence which had been reported & laid on the table the Friday preceding, and on Monday referred to a committee of the whole. The pusillanimous idea that we had friends in England worth keeping terms with still haunted the minds of many. For this reason those passages which conveyed censures on the people of England were struck out lest they should give them offence. The clause too reprobating the enslaving the inhabitants of Africa was struck out in complaisance to S. Carolina & Georgia, who had never attempted to restrain the importation of slaves & who on the contrary still wished to continue it. Our Northern brethren also, I believe, felt a little tender under those censures, for tho' their people have very few slaves themselves, yet they had been pretty considerable carriers of them to others. The debates having taken up the greater parts of the 2nd, 3rd & 4th days of July, were in the evening of the last, closed; the declaration was reported by the committee, agreed to by the house, & signed by every member except Mr. Dickinson."

While Jefferson was absent in Philadelphia, a convention in Virginia had been drawing up a constitution for the new state. Jefferson wrote his version of what he thought this constitution should be like: forbidding the further importing of slaves, disestablishing the Church of England, and giving women equal rights with men in the inheritance of property. He sent his draft to Virginia in charge of his friend George Wythe, but by the time it got there the delegates already had approved a constitution drawn by George Mason. Jefferson's preample to the constitution was, however, adopted by the convention. Of this preamble, Edmund Pendleton, president of the Virginia convention, wrote to Jefferson in July, 1776:

"I expected you had in the Preamble to our form of Government, exhausted the Subject of Complaint against George 3d & was at a loss to discover what the Congress would do for one to their Declaration of Independence without copying but I find you have acquitted yourselves very well on that score."

Resigned from Congress

Pleading ill health and the necessity of caring for his family, Jefferson resigned from Congress in the fall of 1776. About the same time he declined an appointment by Congress to go to France to aid Benjamin Franklin in negotiating treaties. In October, he took his seat in the Virginia legislature, and devoted his attention to liberalizing the laws of the new state. He particularly pressed through the abolition of the laws on entail and primogeniture which had kept great landed estates passing down from father to eldest son. As a member with George Wythe and Edmund Pendleton, Jefferson helped prepare and revise 126 statutes from 1776 to 1779. He later said of this task:

"In the execution of my part, I thought it material not to vary the diction of the ancient statutes by modernizing it, nor to give rise to new questions by new expressions. The text of these statutes had been so fully explained and defined by numerous adjudications as scarcely ever now to produce a question in our courts. I thought it would be useful also, in all new drafts, to reform the style of the later British statutes and of our own Acts of Assembly; which from their verbosity, their endless tautologies, their involutions of case within case and parenthesis within parenthesis, and their multiplied efforts at certainty, by *saids* and *afore-*

saids, by *ors* and by *ands,* to make them more plain, are really rendered more perplexed and incomprehensible, not only to common readers, but to the lawyers themselves."

The statute for religious freedom

Among the various laws that Jefferson wrote for Virginia, the one he asked most to be remembered by was the statute for religious freedom. Here are words from it that reflect the same ability that he displayed in writing the Declaration of Independence:

"Well aware that the opinions and beliefs of men depend not on their own will, but follow involuntarily the evidence proposed to their minds; that Almighty God hath created the mind free, and manifested his will that free it shall remain by making it altogether insusceptible of restraint;

"—that our civil rights have no dependence on our religious opinions any more than our opinions in physics or geometry; that therefore the proscribing any citizens as unworthy the public confidence by laying upon him an incapacity of being called to offices of trust and emolument unless he profess or renounce this or that religious opinion is depriving him injuriously of those privileges and advantages to which, in common with his fellow-citizens, he has a natural right;

"—that the opinions of men are not the subject of civil government nor under its jurisdiction;

"—and finally that truth is great and will prevail if she is left to herself; that she is the proper and sufficient antagonist to error, and has nothing to fear from the conflict unless by human interposition disarmed of her natural weapons, free argument and debate; errors ceasing to be dangerous when it is permitted freely to contradict them.

"We, the General Assembly, do enact, That no man shall be compelled to frequent or support any religious worship, place or ministry whatsoever, nor shall be enforced, restrained, molested or burdened in his body or goods, nor shall otherwise suffer, on account of his religious opinions or beliefs; but that all men shall be free to profess and by argument to maintain their opinions in matters of religion, and that the same shall in no wise diminish, enlarge or affect their civil capacities."

Other liberal views

The many other bills of Virginia that came from Jefferson's pen included those calling for a free public school system, a free state library, and limi-

tations on the use of the death penalty. Many of the laws he wrote were adopted and some were not. Of this Jefferson wrote:

"Some bills were taken out, occasionally, from time to time, and passed; but the main body of the work was not entered on by the Legislature until after the general peace, in 1785, when, by the unwearied exertions of Mr. Madison, in opposition to the endless quibbles, chicaneries, perversions, vexations, and delays of lawyers and demi-lawyers, most of the bills were passed by the Legislature, with little alteration."

In June, 1779, Jefferson was elected by the legislature to succeed Patrick Henry as governor of Virginia. Much of his time for the next two years was spent in trying to get together money, supplies, and troops to aid the Continental Army. As a result, Virginia was unprepared itself when British troops commanded by Benedict Arnold and Lord Cornwallis invaded the state in 1781. Feeling his own inadequacy to cope with a military defence of Virginia, Jefferson declined re-election and left for his home, Monticello, narrowly avoiding capture by the British. Jefferson later wrote:

"From a belief that, under the pressure of the invasion under which we were then laboring, the public would have more confidence in a military chief, and that the military commander, being invested with the civil power also, both might be wielded with more energy, promptitude and effect for the defence of the State, I resigned the administration at the end of my second year, and General (Thomas) Nelson was appointed to succeed me."

Injury and authorship

Later in 1781, Jefferson was injured in a fall from his horse, and he took advantage of his convalescence to write a book of natural history and philosophy called "Notes on Virginia." In it he set forth his ideas that the best future for America lay in becoming a nation of farmers, and that manufacturing should be left to the European countries. He said:

"The political economists of Europe have established it as a principle that every State should endeavor to manufacture for itself; and this principle, like many others, we transfer to America. . . . But we have an immensity of land courting the industry of the husbandman. Is it best then that all our citizens should be employed in its improvement, or that one half should be called off from that to exercise manufactures and handicraft arts for the others? Those who labor in the earth are the chosen people of God, if ever he had a chosen people, whose breasts he has made his peculiar deposit for substantial and genuine virtue. . . . Corruption of morals in the mass of cultivators is a phenomenon of which no age nor nation has furnished an example. . . . While we have land to labor then, let us never wish to see our citizens occupied at a work-bench, or twirling a distaff . . . for the general operations of manufacture, let our workshops remain in Europe. It is better to carry provisions and materials to work-men there, than bring them to the provisions and materials, and with them their manners and principles. . . . The mobs of great cities add just so much to the support of pure government, as sores do to the strength of the human body. It is the manners and spirit of a people which preserve a republic in vigor. A degeneracy in these is a canker which soon eats to the heart of its laws and constitution."

A personal tragedy

In September, 1782, his beloved wife died, and Jefferson decided to busy himself once again in public affairs to overcome his grief. He accepted an appointment by Congress to go to Paris to aid Benjamin Franklin in negotiating a treaty of peace; before he could embark, however, word came that a preliminary peace treaty had been agreed upon with Great Britain, and Jefferson decided to remain in America. Then, in 1783, the Virginia legislature again elected him to Congress; he took his seat in that body in November; and he served there for the next six months. During this period, Jefferson was chairman of the committee that held hearings on the peace treaty with Great Britain and recommended it to Congress for ratification. He also drafted an act for the organization of the Northwest Territory that later became the basis of the Northwest Ordinance passed in 1787. If Jefferson's draft had been adopted it would have gone far toward preventing the later disputes that led to the Civil War, for his proposal would have forbidden slavery in any new states west of the Appalachians.

Journey to Europe

Congress decided to send another diplomatic representative to Europe in 1784 to join Benjamin Franklin and John Adams in negotiating trade treaties, and Jefferson was chosen for the position.

Taking his oldest daughter, Martha, with him, Jefferson traveled to Paris by way of England, arriving there in August. Franklin decided to return to the United States in 1785, so Jefferson was appointed to replace him as the American minister to France, while Adams was appointed as minister to Great Britain.

Jefferson enjoyed the years that he spent in France, where he saw the beginnings of the French Revolution. He was lionized for his liberal political philosophy and for his erudition in his "Notes on Virginia" that were published in a French-language edition. He negotiated several trade treaties that were favorable to the United States, including the elimination of French tariffs on many of America's most important products such as tobacco and rice. He traveled throughout France, the Netherlands, and Italy, spending much time exploring the living conditions of the peasants. He suggested that his friend the Marquis de Lafayette follow in his footsteps, saying:

"You must ferret the people out of their hovels, as I have done, look into their kettles, eat their bread, loll on their beds, under pretence of resting yourself, but in fact to find if they are soft. You will feel a sublime pleasure in the course of this investigation, and a sublimer one hereafter, when you shall be able to apply your knowledge to the softening of their beds, or the throwing a morsel of meat into their kettle of vegetables."

While Jefferson was in France, the Constitutional Convention met in Philadelphia in 1787 and drafted the United States Constitution. James Madison kept Jefferson informed of the developments and sent him a copy of the completed document. Jefferson approved of the new form of government, although he regretted that it did not contain a Bill of Rights; so much so that he advised that several states should withhold ratification until assurances were made that a Bill of Rights would be added to the Constitution.

An invitation from Washington

Jefferson received a leave of absence to return to the United States in October, 1789, and upon his return home found a letter waiting for him from George Washington asking him to become Secretary of State in his cabinet. He did not receive the offer of the appointment with enthusiasm, and delayed for several months making up his mind whether to accept. Finally, on March 21, 1790, he took office in New York and had his first conference with Washington about the diplomatic affairs of the nation.

In the formative years of the new government, Jefferson and Alexander Hamilton quickly became the leaders of the two opposing forces of thought that evolved into the American two-party system of politics. In 1790, Hamilton as Secretary of the Treasury vigorously promoted the necessity of the federal government's taking over all of the states' war debts and paying them off. But this was opposed by Jefferson and his friends who saw the plan as a move to weaken states' rights. On the other hand, Jefferson and his fellow-Virginians wanted to see the nation's capital moved out of New York City and established in Virginia; but this was opposed by Hamilton who was a New Yorker. The result was the first major example of vote-trading in American politics as Jefferson agreed to have his supporters vote for Hamilton's debt-assumption plan, while Hamilton agreed to find enough votes to move the national capital temporarily to Pennsylvania and permanently to the banks of the Potomac River. Jefferson later claimed that he had been "duped" by Hamilton and "made a tool for forwarding his schemes, not then sufficiently understood by me." In the remaining years of Washington's first term as President, the political issues that persist to this day became clearly drawn between Hamilton's Federalist party and Jefferson's Democratic-Republican party. Jefferson's party supported the Southern States, farm interests, states' rights, a strict interpretation of the Constitution, and a strong belief in democracy. On the other hand, Hamilton's Federalist party supported the Northern States, banking and manufacturing interests, a strong central government, a loose interpretation of the Constitution, and a belief that the voice of the people could not be entirely trusted.

Recognition of the new France

In the spring of 1793, word reached America that the French revolutionists had executed their king and queen, and that France and Great Britain had gone to war. Jefferson urged a policy that would maintain American neutrality in the war while at the same time supporting the French with supplies. Hamilton felt that neutrality should be declared at once and that no aid should be given to the French revolutionary government. Hamilton won an immediate neutrality proclamation, and Jefferson won recognition of the new French

Gen. William Clark
From an original painting by CHESTER HARDING

government and its diplomatic representative, Citizen Genet.

Weary of politics, Jefferson submitted his resignation as Secretary of State in July, 1793; but Washington persuaded him to remain in the Cabinet until the end of the year. Finally, on December 31, 1793, he left the office, being succeeded by his cousin Edmund Randolph, and vowing that he would never "meddle with politics more." He returned to "Monticello" to supervise his plantations, which by now had grown to more than 10,000 acres. Jefferson later wrote of this period of his retirement:

"From 1793 to 1797, I remained closely at home, saw none but those who came there, and at length became very sensible of the ill effect it had upon my own mind, and of its direct and irresistible tendency to render me unfit for society and uneasy when necessarily engaged in it. I felt enough of the effect of withdrawing from the world then, to see that it led to an anti-social and misanthropic state of mind, which severely punishes him who gives into it; and it will be a lesson I shall never forget as to myself."

135

Loss of the Presidency by three electoral votes

After Washington signified in 1796 that he would not accept a third term as President, Jefferson's supporters set about trying to win the presidency for him. When the electoral votes were counted in February, 1797, Jefferson lost the presidency by three votes—the count being 71 votes for John Adams and 68 for Jefferson. Thus, Adams became President and Jefferson became Vice President. In the early part of Adams' administration, the two men were friendly; but as time wore on they broke completely, particularly over such matters as the Alien and Sedition Acts which cut off freedom of speech and freedom of the press for Jefferson's supporters.

The presidential election of 1800 was a hard-fought battle between Jefferson and Adams. Hamilton, the leader of the Federalist party, described Jefferson as "a contemptible hypocrite . . . crafty and persevering in his objects . . . not scrupulous about the means of success, not even mindful of truth." But a falling out between Hamilton and Adams split the Federalist party, with the result that Jefferson and his running-mate Aaron Burr each won 73 electoral votes while Adams won 65. Burr, seeing a chance to win the presidency through the Constitution's defect, refused to withdraw his name as a candidate for President, and the election was given to the House of Representatives to settle. The Federalists, seeing a chance to embarrass Jefferson, dragged the balloting out for weeks, until on the thirty-sixth ballot Jefferson was finally given the office of President and Burr was made Vice President.

The third President

In his inaugural address, on March 4, 1801,

Alexander Hamilton
by JAMES OR ELLEN SHARPLES

Jefferson called for a healing of the political antagonism engendered by the election. "Every difference of opinion," he said, "is not a difference of principle. We have called by different names brethren of the same principle. We are all Republicans —we are all Federalists. If there be any among us who would wish to dissolve this Union, or to change its republican form, let them stand undisturbed as monuments of the safety with which error of opinion may be tolerated where reason is left free to combat it." Jefferson also stated his concept of the best government as that which governs least:

"A wise and frugal government, which shall restrain men from injuring one another, which shall leave them otherwise free to regulate their own pursuits of industry and improvement, and shall not take from the mouth of labor the bread it has earned. This is the sum of good government, and this is necessary to close the circle of our felicities."

The Louisiana purchase

During Jefferson's first term, the United States was more than doubled in size by the acquisition from France of the Louisiana Territory at a cost of about fifteen million dollars. He also sent his Virginia neighbor, Meriwether Lewis, on an expedition with William Clark that gathered the first scientific information about the land stretching from the Mississippi River to the Pacific coast. Toward the end of Jefferson's first term, several of the strongly Federalist New England States plotted to secede from the Union because of their opposition to Jefferson's policies. Aaron Burr was involved in this plan and tried to win the governorship of New York so that he could join it to the seceding New England States, but Alexander Hamilton's denunciation of Burr led to the defeat of the scheme, and ultimately to Hamilton's death in a duel with Burr.

In 1804, Jefferson was overwhelmingly re-elected to the presidency in a race against the Federalist candidate, Charles Cotesworth Pinckney. George Clinton, the governor of New York, replaced Burr as Jefferson's Vice President.

During Jefferson's presidency, Britain and France were again at war, and it called upon all of Jefferson's diplomatic skills to maintain American neutrality. He even succeeded in having Congress pass an Embargo Act in 1807 which forbade the export of any American products, in order to keep American ships in port so that they could not

Meriwether Lewis in Indian Dress
by ST. MEMIN, *from the original*

become involved in the European dispute. But this proved so unpopular with merchants and shipowners that it was repealed and replaced in 1809 with the Non-Intercourse Act that merely forbade any trade with Britain or France and permitted the resumption of shipping to other countries.

Scandal in the second term

The greatest scandal to shake the country during Jefferson's second term was the arrest and trial of Burr on charges of treason, growing out of a new scheme in which he had become involved to attempt to take Spanish territories west of the Mississippi and set up an independent government. Burr was brought to trial in 1807, but won acquittal.

Jefferson declined to run for a third term as President, instead supporting his Secretary of State, James Madison, for the office. After Madison's inauguration in 1809, Jefferson retired to

Monticello, later writing of his feelings that "never did a prisoner released from his chains feel such relief."

In his old age, Jefferson achieved the third of his endeavors by which he wished to be remembered—the founding of the University of Virginia. He selected the place for its campus in Charlottesville, close by Monticello. He was rector, or chairman, of the Board of Visitors, as the governing body of the university was called. He set up the curriculum, planned the buildings, supervised the construction, and chose the instructors; and in 1825 he saw the university open its doors to begin classes with more than a hundred students.

Graceful retirement

After his retirement from the presidency, Jefferson had resumed his cordial relations with John Adams, laying aside the political differences that had made them enemies. The two elder statesmen carried on a long correspondence, then, remarkably, they both died on the fiftieth anniversary of the signing of the Declaration of Independence, July 4, 1826. The 83-year-old Jefferson's last words are said to have been, "I resign myself to my God, and my child (the university) to my country." His body was buried beside that of his wife at Monticello. The Jefferson Memorial, dedicated in Washington, D.C., on the two-hundredth anniversary of his birth, carries on it one of Jefferson's most famous quotations:

"I have sworn upon the altar of God, eternal hostility against every form of tyranny over the mind of man."

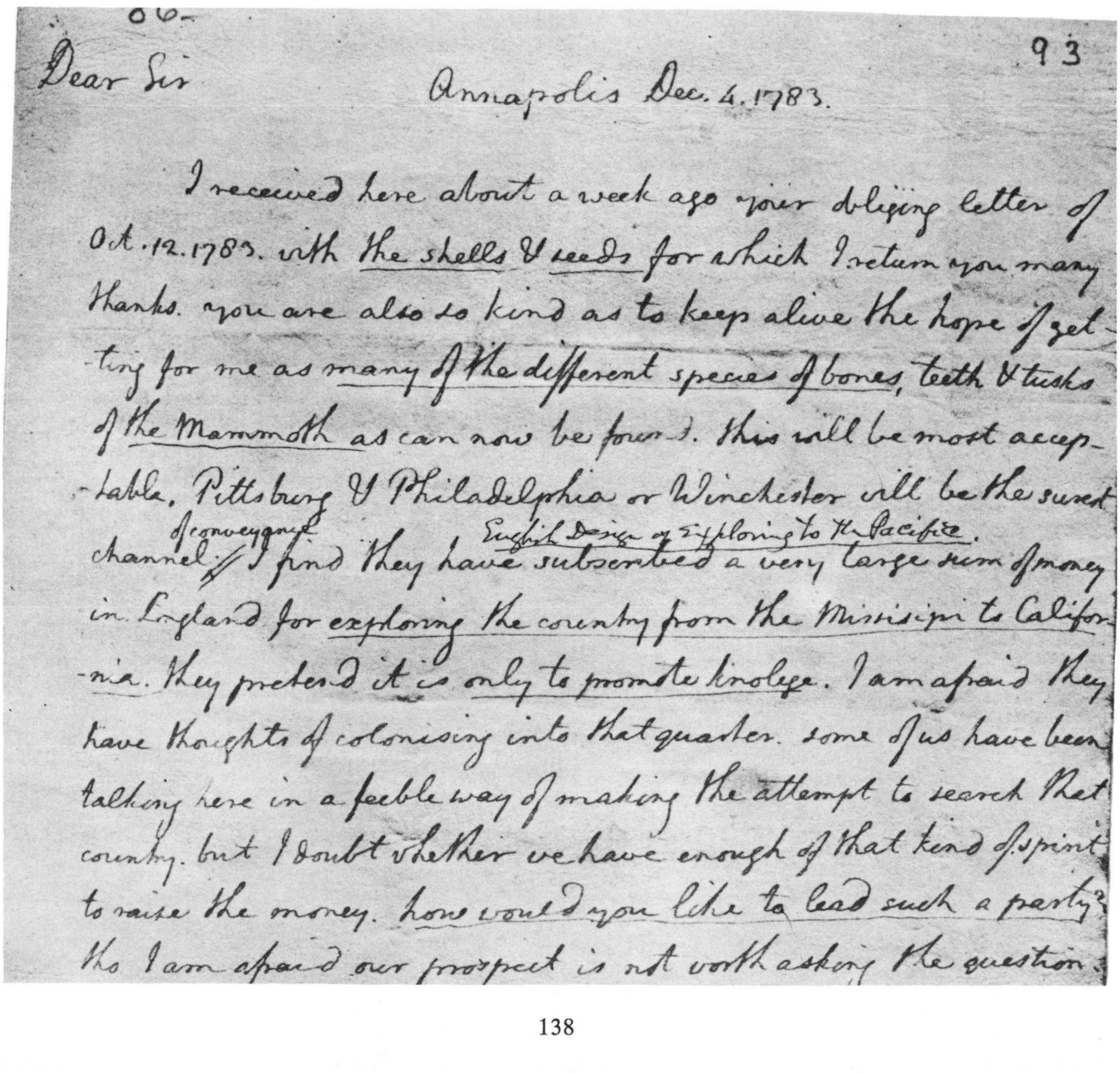

86-

93

Dear Sir   Annapolis Dec. 4. 1783.

I received here about a week ago your obliging letter of Oct. 12. 1783. with the shells & seeds for which I return you many thanks. you are also so kind as to keep alive the hope of getting for me as many of the different species of bones, teeth & tusks of the Mammoth as can now be found. this will be most acceptable. Pittsburg & Philadelphia or Winchester will be the surest channel of conveyance. if I find they have subscribed English design of exploring to the Pacific a very large sum of money in England for exploring the country from the Missisipi to California. they pretend it is only to promote knolege. I am afraid they have thoughts of colonising into that quarter. some of us have been talking here in a feeble way of making the attempt to search that country. but I doubt whether we have enough of that kind of spirit to raise the money. how would you like to lead such a party? tho I am afraid our prospect is not worth asking the question

138

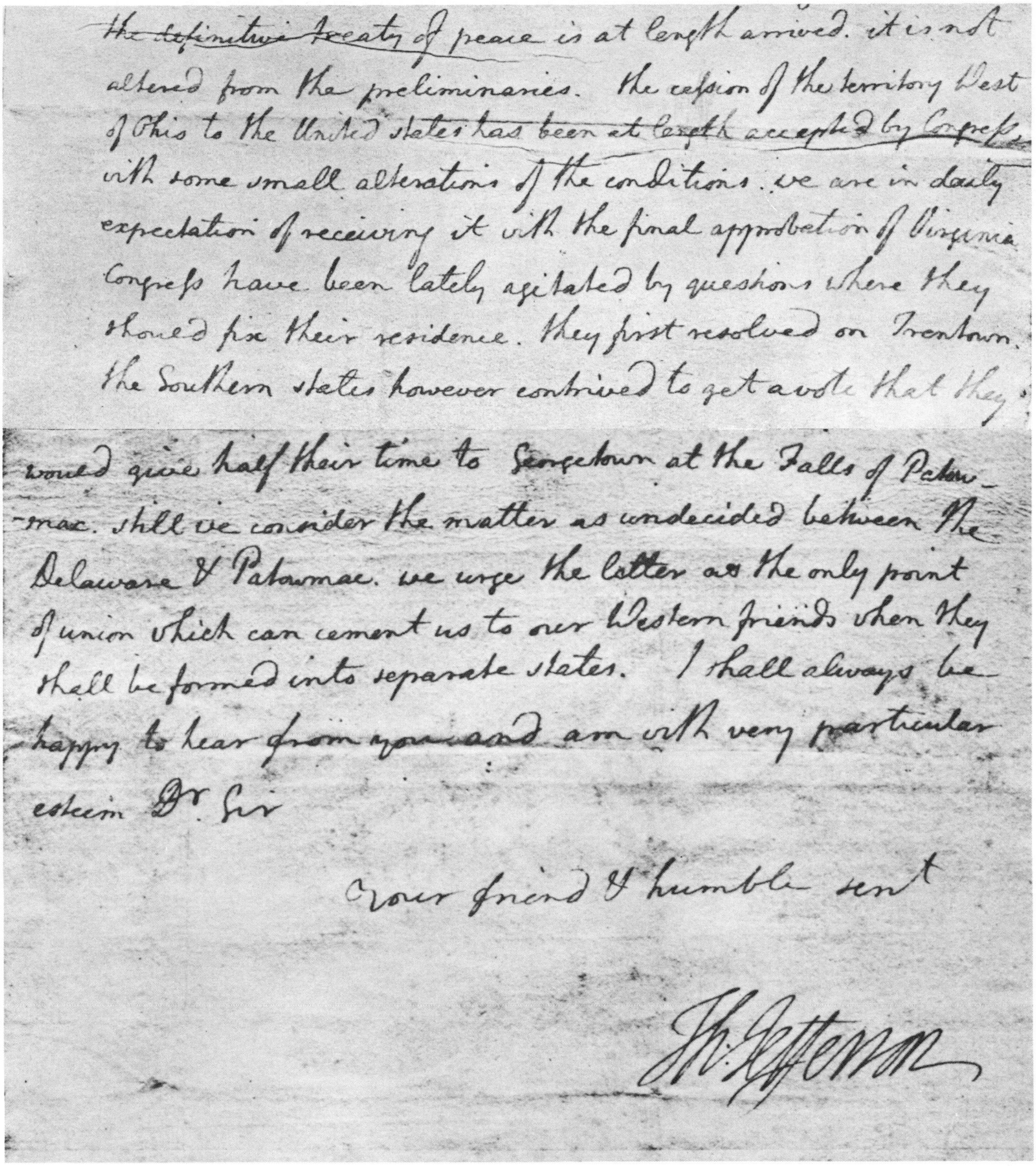

the definitive treaty of peace is at length arrived. it is not altered from the preliminaries. the cession of the territory West of Ohio to the United states has been at length accepted by Congress with some small alterations of the conditions. we are in daily expectation of receiving it with the final approbation of Virginia. Congress have been lately agitated by questions where they should fix their residence. they first resolved on Trentown. the Southern states however contrived to get a vote that they would give half their time to Georgetown at the Falls of Patowmac. still we consider the matter as undecided between the Delaware & Patowmac. we urge the latter as the only point of union which can cement us to our Western friends when they shall be formed into separate states. I shall always be happy to hear from you, and am with very particular esteem Dr Sir

your friend & humble servt

Th: Jefferson

Jefferson's letter to George Rogers Clark.

Washington (c. 1800)

FRANCIS LIGHTFOOT LEE of VIRGINIA

Overshadowed by his older brother Richard Henry Lee, who introduced the resolutions for independence in the Continental Congress, Francis Lightfoot Lee was an equally ardent patriot who made substantial, though less spectacular, contributions to the patriotic cause. He voted for and signed the Declaration of Independence, and he aided in the preparation of and signed the Articles of Confederation; but, in conformance with his middle name, he preferred dancing and a gay social life to weighty matters of state.

Francis Lightfoot Lee was born on October 14, 1734, at the Lee family's estate of Stratford in Westmoreland County, Virginia. His father, Thomas Lee, was one of the most prominent men of the colony. As the fourth oldest of six brothers, young Francis preferred the easy pleasures of life on a southern plantation to the more rigorous formal educations sought by some of his other brothers. For example, his younger brother, Arthur, obtained a medical degree from the University of Edinburgh, then studied law at the Middle Temple in London and was admitted to the bar to practice law in England. All of Francis Lightfoot Lee's education was obtained from private tutors at the family estate.

On the death of his father in 1750, Lee was left a substantial estate in Loudon County, Virginia; and, like most large planters, he became a member of the Virginia house of burgesses (legislature). He served as a burgess representing Loudon County from 1758 to 1768, and representing Richmond County from 1769 to 1776.

Lee remained a bachelor until he was thirty-eight years old; then, in 1772, he married Rebecca Tayloe, the daughter of Colonel John Tayloe, a wealthy plantation owner and race horse fancier of Richmond County. Lee and his bride made the estate Menokin in Richmond County their home. They had no children.

FRANCIS LIGHTFOOT LEE

1734 (Oct. 14) Born at the family estate Stratford in Westmoreland County, Virginia.

1758-1776 Member of the house of burgesses of Virginia.

1775-1779 Delegate from Virginia to the Continental Congress; signed the Declaration of Independence and the Articles of Confederation.

1797 (Jan. 11) Died at his estate Menokin in Richmond County, Virginia.

Noted for his wit and logic

In August, 1775, Lee was elected by Virginia's provincial congress as one of the colony's delegates to the second Continental Congress; and he continued to be re-elected to this office each year until he retired from Congress in 1779. Lee had never learned the art of oratory, and he took little part in the debates in Congress. He apparently made his greatest contributions in the committees of which he was a member. Fellow delegates remarked on his wit and strength of argument in small group discussions. He was present for the discussions on independence, and signed the Declaration of Independence with other delegates on August 2, 1776. He served on John Dickinson's committee that drafted the Articles of Confederation, and he signed his name to that document in 1778.

After his retirement from Congress, Lee spent a short time as a member of the senate of the Virginia state legislature; then he lived the remainder of his life in ease on his plantation. Like George Washington, he was interested in agricultural experimentation, devoting a considerable part of his time to devising ways to improve his crops and livestock. The winter of 1796-1797 was unusually cold in Virginia, and Lee developed a case of pleurisy that ended in his death at the age of sixty-two, on January 11, 1797, at Menokin. His wife became ill at the same time and died within a few days of Lee's death.

Francis Lightfoot Lee

RICHARD HENRY LEE of VIRGINIA

Although he was a wealthy aristocrat from Virginia, Richard Henry Lee believed strongly in abolishing slavery and in the importance of achieving democracy. He thought more like a New Englander than a southern planter, and at one time he said he would like to retire to Massachusetts to get away from the aristocratic atmosphere of the Old South. He introduced the resolution in the Continental Congress calling for independence in 1776; and, if it had not been for the illness of his wife, Lee instead of Jefferson likely would have been called upon to write the Declaration of Independence. An early biographer described Lee's appearance thus:

"His person was tall and well proportioned; his face was on the Roman model; his nose Caesarian; the port and carriage of his head leaning persuasively forward; and the whole contour noble and fine. The eye which shed intelligence over such features, had softness and composure as its prevailing characteristic, till it glowed in debate or radiated in conversation. His voice was clear and melodious, and was modulated by the feeling which swayed his bosom. The progress of time was insensible to those who listened to his conversation, and he entwined himself around the minds of his hearers, fixing his memory on their hearts."

Born in the same county as Washington

Richard Henry Lee was born at his family's estate Stratford in Westmoreland County, Virginia, on January 20, 1732 — a month before George Washington was born in the same county. Lee was one of six brothers, one of whom, Francis Lightfoot Lee, also signed the Declaration of Independence. While in his early teens, Richard Henry Lee was sent to England to be educated at Wakefield academy in Yorkshire, England. The story is told that his older brothers warned him that English schoolboys were likely to try to beat up a young American colonist, so Richard daily trained in boxing with a young slave before sailing to England. While Richard was still in school in England, his father Thomas Lee, then acting governor of Virginia, died; and Richard returned home at the age of nineteen to manage the land and slaves that his wealthy father had left him.

When Lee was twenty-three, he was commissioned as captain of the militia in Westmoreland county, and Lee led his troops to volunteer their services to British General Edward Braddock in the 1755 expedition against the French. Braddock, however, spurned the use of Lee's colonial troops, preferring to believe that the regular British army troops were adequate for the attack he was planning. Lee returned home, bitter at this brush with British arrogance.

Favored abolition of slavery

At the age of twenty-five, Lee began his long political career, being elected justice of the peace for his county. The next year, 1758, he was elected to the Virginia house of burgesses, and continued to serve in that legislative body until it was dissolved at the beginning of the Revolutionary War. In his first speech before the house of burgesses, Lee supported the abolition of slavery:

"As the consequences, sir, of the determination which we must make in the subject of this day's debate, will greatly affect posterity as well as ourselves, it surely merits our most serious attention. If this be bestowed, it will appear both from reason and experience, that the importation of slaves into this colony has been, and will be attended with effects dangerous to our political and moral interest. When it is observed that some of our neigh-

---

RICHARD HENRY LEE

1732 (Jan. 20) Born at the family estate Stratford in Westmoreland County, Virginia.

c.1746-1751 Attended Wakefield academy in Yorkshire, England.

1758-1775 Member of the Virginia house of burgesses.

1774-1775 Member of Virginia's patriotic provincial congress

1774-1779 Delegate to the Continental Congress; wrote the resolution that led to the Declaration of Independence; signed the Declaration of Independence and the Articles of Confederation.

1780-1784 Member of the Virginia state legislature.

1784-1785 President of the Congress of the Confederation.

1785-1789 Delegate to the Congress of the Confederation.

1789-1792 United States Senator from Virginia.

1794 (June 19) Died at his estate Chantilly in Westmoreland County, Virginia.

bouring colonies, though much later than ourselves in point of settlement, are now far before us in improvement, to what, sir, can we attribute this strange but unhappy truth? The reason seems to be this, that with their whites, they import arts and agriculture, while we with our blacks, exclude both. Nature has not particularly favoured them with superior fertility of soil, nor do they enjoy more of the sun's cheering influence, yet greatly have they outstrip us.

"Were not this sufficient, sir, let us reflect on our dangerous vicinity to a powerful neighbour; and that slaves, from the nature of their situation, can never feel an interest in our cause, because they see us enjoying every privilege and luxury, and find security established, not for them, but for others; and because they observe their masters in possession of liberty which is denied to them, they and their posterity being subject for ever to the most abject and mortifying slavery. Such people must be natural enemies, and consequently their increase dangerous to the society in which they live . . .

"Pay regard to the dictates of justice and humanity."

"I have seen it observed by a great writer, that Christianity, by introducing into Europe the truest principles of humanity, universal benevolence, and brotherly love, had happily abolished civil slavery. Let us, who profess the same religion, practise its precepts, and by agreeing to this duty, convince the world that we know and practise our true interests, and that we pay a proper regard to the dictates of justice and humanity."

When the house of burgesses was in session, Lee devoted his attention to managing his plantations, and spent much time studying and reading in his library. He married Anne Aylett, daughter of Colonel William Aylett, a wealthy planter of Westmoreland County. After his first wife's death, Lee married a widow, Mrs. Anne Gaskins Pinckard. He had nine children by his two wives.

When the British parliament began taxing the colonies to support their army of occupation in America, Lee was at first so undecided about the matter that he applied for the position of stamp collector in Virginia. However, discussions with other Virginia leaders, such as Patrick Henry, convinced him of the disastrous implications of the British action; and he became one of the leading opponents of taxation without representation. He won fame for the addresses and memorials that he

RICHARD HENRY LEE
by C. W. PEALE, 1784
National Park Photo Service

wrote to the king and the British parliament opposing the Stamp Act and the Townshend Acts. As an example of his writing of this period, this paragraph is from an article of Lee's published just before the repeal of the Stamp Act:

"And every abandoned wretch, who shall be so lost to virtue and public good, as wickedly to contribute to introduce the said act into this colony, by using stamp paper, or by any other means, will, with the utmost expedition, be convinced, that immediate danger and disgrace shall attend his prostitute purpose."

Early organizer of the committee of correspondence

In 1773, at about the same time Samuel Adams was organizing a committee of correspondence in Massachusetts, Lee introduced a resolution in the house of burgesses in Virginia to establish a similar committee. In later disputes as to whether Adams or Lee thought of the idea first, Christopher Gadsden of South Carolina testified that in 1768 Lee had invited him to become a member of a corresponding society, "the object of which was, to obtain a mutual pledge from the members to write for the public journals or papers of their respective colonies, and to converse with, and inform the people on the subject of their rights and wrongs, and upon all seasonable occasions, to impress upon their minds the necessity of a struggle with Great Britain for the ultimate establishment of independence."

In 1774, the Virginia governor dissolved the house of burgesses because of that body's opposition to the Coercive Acts against Boston. The Virginia legislators then met in a nearby tavern where they adopted an address to the other colonies prepared by Lee which called for a general congress "to deliberate on those general measures which the united interests of America from time to time require." Several months later, when the provincial assembly met again, Lee and Patrick Henry were among the delegates elected to attend the first Continental Congress in Philadelphia.

"Petition to the King"

Lee was a member of all the important committees of the first Continental Congress. When Lee presented a "Petition to the King," the delegates decided that his language was too violent, so it was rewritten by the more conservative John Dickinson of Pennsylvania. Lee also wrote "A Memorial to the People of British America" that was adopted by the Congress. The majority of the delegates to the first Continental Congress of 1774 still were hopeful of placating the British king and parliament, and they refused to approve the following resolution offered by Lee:

"Resolved, that, as we find the reason, declared in the preamble to the act of parliament for raising a revenue in America, to be for supplying the civil government, the administration of justice, and for protecting, defending and securing the colonies, the congress recommend it to those colonies, in which it is not already done, to provide constitutional, competent, and honourable support for the purposes of government and administration of justice; and that as it is quite unreasonable that the mother country should be at the expense of maintaining standing armies in North America for its defence, and that administration may be con-

vinced that this is unnecessary and improper, as North America is able, willing, and, under providence, determined to defend, protect, and secure itself, the congress do most earnestly recommend to the several colonies, that a militia be forthwith appointed and well disciplined, and that it be well provided with proper arms."

"Thrice is he armed who hath his quarrel just"

Lee was present at the meeting of the Virginia assembly in Old Saint John's Church in Richmond in March, 1775, when Patrick Henry thrilled his listeners with his cry of "Give me liberty, or give me death!" Lee supported Henry's argument, that the militia must be armed, with this appeal:

"Admitting the probable calculations to be against us, we are assured in holy writ, that the race is not to the swift, nor the battle to the strong; and if the language of genius may be added to that of inspiration, I will say with our immortal bard:

" 'Thrice is he armed, who hath his quarrel just,
And he but naked, tho' locked up in steel,
Whose conscience with injustice is oppressed.' "

Lee was elected as a delegate to the second Continental Congress in 1775, and he found its spirit of determination more to his liking than that of the congress of 1774. When Washington was unanimously elected as commander in chief, Lee was appointed chairman of the committee that prepared Washington's commission and instructions. Lee wrote a second address to the people of Great Britain that reproached them for their treatment of the colonies. It said in part:

"Yet conclude not that we propose to surrender our property into the hands of your ministry, or vest your Parliament with a power which may terminate in our destruction. The great bulwarks of our Constitution we have desired to maintain by every temperate, by every peaceable means; but your ministers, equal foes to British and American freedom, have added to their former oppressions an attempt to reduce us by the sword to a base and abject submission. On the sword, therefore, we are compelled to rely for protection. Should victory declare in your favor, yet men trained to arms from their infancy and animated by the love of liberty, will afford neither a cheap nor easy conquest. Of this at least we are assured, that our struggle will be glorious, our success certain; since even in death we shall find that freedom which in life you forbid us to enjoy."

The landing of the British Forces in the Jerseys on the 20th of
November, 1776, under the command of the Rt. Hon. Lieut. Gen. Earl Cornwallis.

(from an original drawing, which is supposed to have been done by Lord Rawdon, who served at the time as engineer
officer on Cornwallis's staff. Purchased from the estate of the Marquis of Hastings, grandson of the General.)

View in THIRD STREET, *from Spruce Street* PHILADELPHIA.

Drawn, Engraved & Published by W. Birch & Son Neshaminy Ferry.

Stratford birthplace of Richard Henry Lee and Francis Lightfoot Lee From MANSIONS OF VIRGINIA, by Waterman
Photo by ARTHUR E. SCOTT

Lee's resolution for independence

In the spring of 1776, the Virginia assembly authorized its delegates in Philadelphia to urge Congress to declare the colonies free of Great Britain, and on June 7, 1776, Lee introduced his famous resolution:

"Resolved

"That these United Colonies are, and of right ought to be, free and independent States, that they are absolved from all allegiance to the British Crown, and that all political connection between them and the State of Great Britain is, and ought to be, totally dissolved.

"That it is expedient forthwith to take the most effectual measures for forming foreign Alliances.

"That a plan of confederation be prepared and transmitted to the respective Colonies for their consideration and approbation."

"Why do we longer delay?"

In concluding the speech in which he introduced this resolution, Lee eloquently said:

"Why, then, sir, why do we longer delay? Why still deliberate? Let this happy day give birth to an American republic. Let her arise, not to devastate and to conquer, but to re-establish the reign of peace and of law. The eyes of Europe are fixed upon us; she demands of us a living example of freedom, that may exhibit a contrast, in the felicity of the citizen, to the ever-increasing tyranny which desolates her polluted shores. She invites us to prepare an asylum, where the unhappy may find solace, and the persecuted repose. She entreats us to cultivate a propitious soil, where that generous plant which first sprung and grew in England, but is now withered by the poisonous blasts of Scottish tyranny, may revive and flourish, sheltering under its salubrious and interminable shade all the unfortunate of the human race. If we are not this day wanting in our duty, the names of the American legislators of 1776 will be placed by posterity at the side of Theseus, Lycurgus, and Romulus—of the three Williams of Nassau, and of all those whose memory has been, and ever will be, dear to virtuous men and good citizens."

Seconded by John Adams

John Adams of Massachusetts seconded Lee's resolution, but John Dickinson of Pennsylvania and Robert R. Livingston of New York opposed the measure, feeling that there was no need to call for independence as long as any possibility remained of a reconciliation with Great Britain. So Congress, on June 10, decided to postpone further consideration of the resolution until July 1, but meanwhile to appoint a committee to write a declaration of independence. That same day, Lee received word from Virginia that his wife was seriously ill, and he decided to return home, leaving his fellow-delegate from Virginia, Thomas Jefferson, to fill his place on the committee to write the declaration.

Lee was absent from the Continental Congress when his resolution and the Declaration of Independence were adopted, but Jefferson sent him a copy of his original draft of the Declaration, noting, "You will judge whether it is the better or worse for the critics." Lee returned to the Congress later in the summer, and signed the Declaration of Independence on September 4, 1776.

In 1777, Lee obtained a leave of absence from Congress to return home and fight charges made against him that he was a Tory and disloyal to the patriotic cause. These charges had grown out of the report that he was refusing to accept rent payments in colonial money from the tenants on his land and instead insisting that the rents be paid in produce. After an inquiry into the matter by the Virginia legislature, he was cleared of the charges.

Hopeful of a wise and free republican government

After receiving the thanks of the legislature for his services, Lee returned to Congress where he served on many important committees and signed the Articles of Confederation. It was during this period that he wrote to Samuel Adams expressing admiration for the democratic attitude of New England as opposed to the aristocracy of the South: "Independently of a general principle of philanthropy, I feel myself interested in the establishment of a wise and free republican government in Massachusetts, where yet I hope to finish the remainder of my days. The hasty, unpersevering, aristocratic genius of the south suits not my disposition, and is inconsistent with my views of what must constitute social happiness and security."

For a short while in 1778, Lee took the field of battle as commander of the militia of Westmoreland County, although he was somewhat handicapped because he had lost the use of one hand in a hunting accident. He and his troops skirmished with British forces ravaging the Virginia countryside.

Served as president of Congress

During the remaining years of the Revolutionary War, Lee remained in Virginia and served in the state legislature; then in 1784 he was again appointed to Congress, and there was elected President. After serving honorably for a year as the nation's chief executive, he retired from that office, but continued to be elected as a delegate from Virginia until the Congress of the Confederation expired with the ratification of the United States Constitution.

Constitution not democratic enough

Lee declined to serve in the Constitutional Convention of 1787; and, after the United States Constitution had been written, he opposed its ratification with the power of his pen in a series of articles

Engraved by W. A. Wilmer from the large print by Mr Edwin after the original Portrait by G. Stuart

JAMES MADISON.

The City of
RICHMOND Metropolis of VIRGINIA.

Engraved by Fred.ᵏ Bossler

called "Letters from the Federal Farmer." These articles were written with restraint but firm conviction that the Constitution was not democratic enough. "Every man of reflection must see," he wrote, "that the change now proposed, is a transfer of power from the many to the few." He believed that the Constitution was drafted as a result of a contest for power between two minority parties, neither representing the great mass of the people:

"One party is composed of little insurgents, men in debt, who want no law, and who want a share of the property of others; these are called levellers, Shaysites, &c. The other party is composed of a few, but more dangerous men, with their servile dependents; these avariciously grasp at all power and property; you may discover in all the actions of these men, an evident dislike to free and equal government, and they go systematically to work to change, essentially, the forms of government in this country; these are called aristocrats, &c. Between these two parties is the weight of the community: the men of middling property, men not in debt on the one hand, and men, on the other, content with republican governments, and not aiming at immense fortunes, offices and power. In 1786, the little insurgents, the levellers, came forth, invaded the rights of others, and attempted to establish governments according to their wills. Their movements evidently gave encouragement to the other party, which, in 1787, has taken the political field, and with its fashionable dependents, and the tongue and the pen, is endeavouring to establish in a great haste, a politer kind of government. These two parties . . . are really insignificant, compared with the solid, free, and independent part of the community."

With the aid of Patrick Henry, the Virginia legislature elected Lee as one of the state's first United States Senators under the new Constitution in 1789, defeating James Madison, the "Father of the Constitution." In the United States Senate, Lee took an active role in obtaining the amendments to the Constitution that secured the rights to the people and to the states that he felt were essential to a more democratic government.

A severe case of the gout forced Lee to resign from the Senate in 1792, and he returned to his estate, Chantilly, in Westmoreland County, Virginia. He died there at the age of sixty-two on June 19, 1794.

FRANCIS LEWIS of NEW YORK

The only native-born Welshman among the signers of the Declaration of Independence, Francis Lewis was a wealthy 63-year-old New York merchant in the summer of 1776. He was a dedicated patriot and he paid heavily to support the cause of liberty. During the Revolutionary War, British troops destroyed his Long Island mansion, imprisoning and torturing his wife. The war swept away his fortune, but Lewis lived to see the British beaten and to see two of his fellow signers—John Adams and Thomas Jefferson—become Presidents of the United States.

Lewis was born March 21, 1713, in Landaff, Wales, where his father was an Episcopal clergyman. Orphaned at the age of four or five years, he was cared for by a maiden aunt for several years. Next, he was sent to live with relatives in Scotland. Finally, his mother's brother, who was Dean of St. Paul's in London, took charge of the boy's education. Lewis was placed in Westminster school, where he became a good classic scholar.

Upon completing school, Lewis entered the counting-room of a merchant in London. He served a regular clerkship and acquired an extensive knowledge of commerce.

Tiring of the counting-room and eager to make a fortune, Lewis decided to try his luck in the American colonies. With the proceeds of a modest inheritance, he purchased a cargo of goods for trading and sailed to America. He successfully traded his goods in New York and Philadelphia and established a partnership with a prominent New Yorker, Edward Annesley. He soon married his partner's sister, Elizabeth Annesley. The couple had seven children, four of whom died during infancy.

A merchant traveller

As a trader, Lewis had many adventures and became one of the most widely-traveled of the men who signed the Declaration. He visited most of the countries of Europe, including two trips to Russia. He was shipwrecked twice on the coast of Ireland.

During the French and Indian War, Lewis acted as an agent to supply the British troops with clothing. While on a mission to Fort Oswego, N. Y., in 1756, he was captured by the French. Legend has it that he saved his scalp from the Indian allies of the French because the Indians believed he was speaking their tongue when he talked to them in his native Welsh. In any event, Lewis was sent to France as a prisoner. Upon his release several years later, the colonial government repaid his services by giving him a land grant.

In the 1760's, as the British government began to encroach on the rights of the American people, Lewis gave firm support to the patriotic cause. He joined the Sons of Liberty, an organization dedicated to resisting British force with force. Lewis was elected as a member of the New York delegation to the Stamp Act Congress in 1765. This Congress helped force the British parliament to repeal the Stamp Act.

In April, 1775, Lewis was appointed a mem-

FRANCIS LEWIS

FRANCIS LEWIS

1713 (March 21) Born in Landaff, Wales.

1738 Immigrated to New York.

1756. Captured by the French at Fort Oswego, N. Y., during the French and Indian War.

1765 New York delegate to the Stamp Act Congress.

1775-1779 New York delegate to the Continental Congress.

1802 (Dec. 31) Died in New York City at the age of 89.

A Perspective View of the City Hall in New York taken from Wall Street

ber of the New York delegation to the Continental Congress. In December he was appointed to a committee to try to establish a navy for the colonies.

Lewis did not take a prominent part in the drafting of the Declaration. He was present on July 4, 1776, when it was adopted, but he was forced to abstain from the voting because the New York delegation had not received authorization to approve the document. When word came that the New York legislature approved the Declaration, Lewis happily signed it on August 2.

Home destroyed and wife imprisoned

A few months after the adoption of the Declaration, British cavalry raided Lewis' Long Island home. The British troops destroyed all Lewis' property and carried off his wife. It is said that the British treated Mrs. Lewis with unusual cruelty, presumably because of her husband's prominence in the patriotic cause. Mrs. Lewis was a British prisoner for nearly two years, until George Washington arranged a prisoner-exchange to free her. Her health was severely impaired during her imprisonment by the British.

The business experience that Lewis had accumulated in his many years as a trader was put to good use during his four years of service in the Continental Congress. He aided particularly in the purchase of clothing for the army, in the importation of arms and ammunition, and in contracting for provisions. As a member of the committee of claims, which was appointed to put the accounts of the government in order, his professional knowledge was especially valuable.

On April 27, 1779, Lewis obtained a leave of absence from Congress and this appears to have ended his congressional career. Several months later, in December, 1779, Lewis was appointed a commissioner for the board of admiralty, apparently his last public office.

In his declining years, Lewis took pride in the achievements of his son Morgan Lewis (1754-1844), who had served as an officer during the Revolutionary War, rising to become chief of staff to General Horatio Gates. After the war, Morgan Lewis became chief justice of New York from 1801 to 1804 and then became governor of New York from 1804 to 1807.

Francis Lewis died at the age of 89, on December 31, 1802, not living to see his son become governor. The body of Francis Lewis is buried in the graveyard of Trinity Church on Wall Street in New York.

PHILIP LIVINGSTON of NEW YORK

A wealthy New York City merchant and politician, Philip Livingston helped found the Whig party to oppose British control of the colonies. As a conservative patriot, he tried to avoid open rebellion with Great Britain; but when war came he supported it in every way he could. He was not present during the debate on the adoption of the Declaration of Independence, but he was proud to sign his name to it. Sixty years old at the time of the signing, Livingston died less than two years later—before Independence had been won and at a period when it looked as though the British would win the Revolutionary War.

A terrible tempered aristocrat

A portly aristocrat, Livingston had an irritable temper that made him a terror to those that faltered in the line of personal virtue or patriotic duty. His dignified, austere manner made it difficult for strangers to approach him. Yet he was tender and affectionate to his family and friends. His reserve led him to prefer reading to conversation, and, as a result, he had a broad understanding of many fields of knowledge.

Livingston was a member of one of New York's great land-holding families. In the 1680's, his Scottish grandfather, Robert Livingston, had received a land grant of about 160,000 acres, called Livingston Manor, that covered most of what is now Duchess and Columbia counties. The land made Robert Livingston and his descendants one of the wealthiest families in the colony.

Philip Livingston was born in Albany on Jan. 15, 1716. His father, also called Philip, had inherited the wealth of Livingston Manor. Young Philip was the fourth of six brothers who distinguished themselves in colonial business and government. After being graduated from Yale in 1737, he decided to go into business in New York City. An older brother, Peter, had already achieved success there as a merchant. Philip married Christina Ten Broeck, member of another wealthy New York clan, and they reared a family of five sons and three daughters.

Helped found Columbia University

At the age of 38, Livingston began a political career that extended for twenty-five years. In 1754, he was elected one of the seven aldermen of New York City—then a town of about 10,000 persons. For nine years, Livingston served as an alderman. During this period, he helped found the New York City library and King's College, now Columbia University. From 1759 to 1769, Livingston represented New York City in the colonial assembly.

As Britain tried to impose more taxes and controls on the colonies, Livingston became a leader of New York's conservative patriots. In 1764, in a speech directed at New York's royal lieutenant-governor, he expressed his views this way: "We

Philip Livingston by Benjamin West

PHILIP LIVINGSTON

1716 (Jan. 15) Born in Albany, N. Y.

1754-1763 Alderman in New York City.

1759-1768 Member of the New York colonial assembly.

1768 Speaker of the New York colonial assembly.

1774-1778 New York delegate to the Continental Congress.

1777 Elected state senator in first New York state legislature.

1778 (June 12) Died in York, Pa., at the age of 62, while serving in the Continental Congress.

hope your honor will join with us in an endeavor to secure that great badge of English liberty, of being taxed only with our own consent, to which we conceive all his majesty's subjects at home and abroad equally entitled to."

Livingston's views led to his appointment as one of the delegates to the Stamp Act Congress in 1765. This meeting of the delegates from nine of the colonies forced Great Britain to slow down for a few years on its demands.

In New York's election in 1768, the conservative patriots, or Whigs as they began to be called, won a majority in the colonial assembly. Livingston, as leader of the Whigs, was named speaker of the assembly. Soon, Livingston set the assembly to drawing up resolutions asserting the rights of the colonies against the usurpation of power by the British parliament. Angered, the royal governor dissolved the assembly in December.

Rejected by the Tories

New elections were called in New York in 1769. This time, the Tories, who were favorable to the British crown, won a majority in the colonial assembly. When Livingston, who had declined to run in New York City, attempted to take a seat

Mrs. Philip Livingston
(Christina Ten Broeck) *by* BENJAMIN WEST

representing Livingston Manor, the Tories refused to seat him. This temporarily ended his role in public office.

For the next several years, Livingston devoted

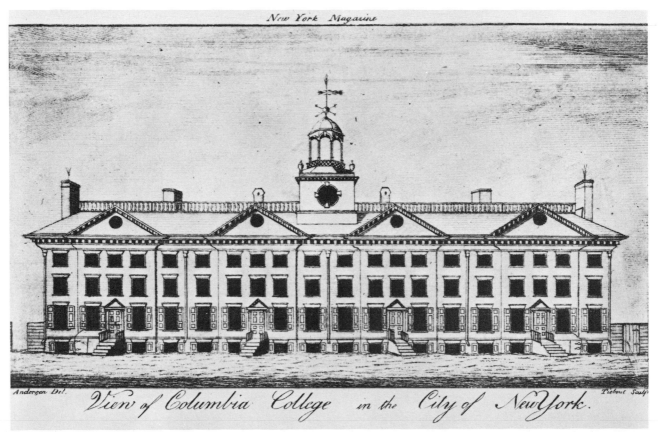

View of Columbia College in the City of New York.

much attention to his business and to civic affairs. He helped found the New York City chamber of commerce in 1770. The next year he helped establish the city's first hospital, serving on its board of governors.

As the clouds of the revolution began to gather, Livingston was chosen as a member of the New York delegation to the First Continental Congress in 1774. He took a distinguished part, serving on the committee to prepare an address to the subjects of the British king. At the conclusion of the Congress, he was appointed as a member of the Continental Association, which was set up to boycott trade with Great Britain.

Fighting had already broken out in Massachusetts by the time the Second Continental Congress convened in 1775. Livingston was a delegate, as were his brother, William, and his cousin, Robert R. Livingston. William Livingston left the Congress before the adoption of the Declaration of Independence in order to take command of the New Jersey militia. Robert R. Livingston, who did not believe the time was ripe for the adoption, also had left the Congress before it took action. Philip Livingston, too, was absent from Congress during June and July of 1776, but he returned in August to sign the Declaration of Independence.

While serving in Congress, Livingston continued to take an active part in civic and colonial politics in New York. In April, 1775, he was appointed president of a provincial congress assembled in New York. On Feb. 1, 1776, he was unanimously chosen a member of the colonial general assembly. In April, 1777, a constitution for the state of New York was adopted, and the next month, Livingston was chosen as a state senator under the new state constitution.

Livingston continued to serve in the Continental Congress as a member of the New York delegation in 1777 and 1778. He was appointed to the board of treasury and as a member of the marine committee.

Although he was in poor health in 1778, Livingston forced himself to attend the Congress because of the critical state of the war. The British had taken Philadelphia, and the Congress had been forced to flee to York, Pa. On June 12, 1778, Livingston died at the age of 62. His body was buried in York that same day with the members of Congress attending the funeral in mourning.

Home of Philip Livingston

Library of Congress, Homes of America, Lamb
Photo by Arthur E. Scott

THOMAS LYNCH, JR. of SOUTH CAROLINA

The next to youngest man to sign the Declaration of Independence, Thomas Lynch, Jr., was only three-and-a-half months older than Edward Rutledge of South Carolina, the youngest signer. Although Lynch had been elected as a delegate to the Continental Congress, it was not so much on his own merit as it was to enable him to care for his ailing father, whose seat he took. He did not live to see the end of the Revolutionary War, dying at sea while taking a voyage for his health to the West Indies.

Thomas Lynch, Jr., was born at his father's plantation Hopsewee on the Santee River in Prince George's Parish, South Carolina, on August 5, 1749. His father, Thomas Lynch, Sr., was one of the influential political leaders of the colony, and one of the wealthiest planters. His mother, Elizabeth Alston Lynch, died while he was a small child, and he was placed in the Indigo Society School in Georgetown, S. C., to receive his basic education.

A graduate of Cambridge University

His father was determined that young Lynch should follow in his own political footsteps and that he should receive the best possible education to help him do so. Therefore, when the boy was still only twelve, he was sent to Eton school in England. After completing a classical education at Eton, he was graduated from Cambridge University. Then, continuing to follow his father's plan even though he had no desire to become a lawyer, he undertook the study of law at the Middle Temple in London.

After an absence of ten years from America,

THOMAS LYNCH, JR.

1749 (Aug. 5) Born at his father's plantation in Prince George's Parish, South Carolina.

1762-1772 Studied in England; graduated by University of Cambridge; admitted to study law in the Middle Temple.

1775 Commissioned a captain in the militia.

1776 Delegate to the Continental Congress from South Carolina; signed the Declaration of Independence.

1779 Lost at sea when his ship disappeared enroute to the West Indies.

Lynch returned to South Carolina about the year 1772. He told his father that he found the law distasteful and that he had no desire to practice at the bar, so his father deeded to him one of his largest plantations on the Santee River to provide him with a means of livelihood. Shortly after his return from England, he married Elizabeth Shubrick, whose sister later married Edward Rutledge.

Commissioned as captain in South Carolina militia

In 1775, Lynch accepted a commission as captain in the South Carolina militia. His father, then serving as a delegate in the Continental Congress, opposed his acceptance of the commission and asked him to come to Philadelphia where he might receive a commission of a higher rank in the Continental Army; but young Lynch replied to his father that "his present commission was fully equal to his experience."

In July, 1775, Lynch and Charles Cotesworth Pinckney, who was at that time also a captain in the militia, set out on a recruiting campaign. Unused to the exposure and rough living necessitated by this trip, Lynch became ill with a lingering fever that plagued him the remainder of his life.

Appointed to succeed his father

Having recovered sufficiently from his illness to resume his military duties late in 1775, Lynch now received word that his father had been stricken with paralysis in Philadelphia and had resigned as a delegate to the Continental Congress. His commanding officer, Christopher Gadsden, refused to grant him leave to go to his father's bedside; but the political influence of his father's friends won him an appointment by the legislature as a delegate to succeed his father, thus excusing him from further military duty.

Arriving in Philadelphia in the spring of 1776, Lynch took part in the discussions among the South Carolina delegates as to whether or not they should support the idea of independence from Britain. Finally, after delaying the vote on independence in hope that they could receive more instructions from the legislature, Lynch and the other South Carolinians decided to vote for independence.

After signing his name to the Declaration of Independence on August 2, 1776, Lynch started home to South Carolina with his sick father. In Annapolis, Md., the elder Lynch suffered another paralytic stroke and died.

Lost at sea with his wife

Lynch took no further part in public affairs, retiring to his plantation to nurse his health. In the autumn of 1779, acting on the advice of a physician, Lynch decided to travel to the West Indies, and there seek a neutral ship that would take him to Europe where he might find a cure for his fevers. He and his wife set sail near the end of the year 1779. The ship never was heard from again, and was believed to have been sunk in a storm with the loss of all those aboard.

Thomas Lynch, Jr. Miniature by John Ramage

The State House at Columbia, South Carolina
View taken from Rive's Tavern, May, 1794
Photo from WASHINGTON'S SOUTHERN TOUR, 1791, by ARCHIBALD HENDERSON
© Houghton Mifflin Company, The Riverside Press, Cambridge, Mass.

THOMAS McKEAN of DELAWARE

A tall, dignified lawyer, Thomas McKean was one of the most patriotic and hardest-working of the Founding Fathers, holding public office for more than fifty years in the period before, during, and after the Revolutionary War. He was the only delegate to the first Continental Congress of 1774 who continued to serve regularly until the peace treaty with Great Britain was approved in 1783. During this time, he signed the Declaration of Independence and the Articles of Confederation, and in 1781 he was elected President of the Congress—the highest office in the nation. He was chief justice of Pennsylvania for twenty-two years and then governor for nine years.

Thomas McKean was born on March 19, 1734, in New London, Pa. He was the son of William McKean, who had immigrated to Pennsylvania from Ireland. In his teens, Thomas McKean was tutored in academic subjects by the Reverend Francis Allison, and then became a student of law under the tutelage of David Finney, a relative of his mother. When he was about twenty, McKean began practicing law in Pennsylvania and Delaware.

McKean began his long public career at the age of twenty-two, being appointed in 1756 as

deputy attorney general to handle the prosecution of cases in Sussex County, Delaware. In 1757, he was appointed clerk of the lower house of the Delaware legislature, an office that he held for two years. In 1762, he was elected as a member of the lower house of the legislature from New Castle County, Delaware, and he continued to win election as the representative of this county for seventeen years, finally declining to serve any longer in 1779.

The same year that he was first elected to the Delaware legislature, the twenty-eight-year-old McKean married Mary Borden, the oldest daughter of Joseph Borden of Bordentown, N.J. By this marriage he became the brother-in-law of Francis Hopkinson who later became one of his fellow signers of the Declaration of Independence. McKean and his wife had six children before her death in 1773. The next year he re-married, this time, Sarah Armitage of Newcastle, Del., and the second marriage resulted in five more children.

Helped establish principle of state equality in senate

In 1765, McKean was elected by the Delaware legislature as one of its delegates to the Stamp Act Congress in New York. At the outset of this meeting, McKean suggested and the Congress adopted as a form of procedure that each colony should have one vote on each measure to come before it. This was the basis for the equal voice of each colony or state that was later followed in the Continental Congress, the Congress of the Confederation, and in the Senate under the United States Constitution. The Congress agreed on a declaration of rights that had been written by John Dickinson, a petition to the king, and memorials to the British parliament, all calling for repeal of the Stamp Act. At the close of the congress on October 24, several members, refused to sign the proceedings. When McKean pressed Ruggles to explain his reluctance to sign, the president said that "it was against his conscience." At this, McKean made such a sarcastic speech on the subject of "conscience" that Ruggles challenged him to a duel in front of the Congress; but Ruggles left New York for Boston before dawn the next day without carrying out the duel.

THOMAS McKEAN

1734 (March 19) Born in New London, Pa.

c.1754 Began practicing law in Delaware and Pennsylvania.

1756-1757 Deputy attorney general in Sussex County, Delaware.

1757-1758 Clerk of the lower house of the Delaware legislature.

1762-1779 Member of the Delaware legislature.

1765 Delegate to the Stamp Act Congress from Delaware.

1772-1773 Speaker of the house of representatives of the Delaware legislature.

1774-1783 Delegate from Delaware to the Continental Congress; signed the Declaration of Independence and the Articles of Confederation.

1776 Chairman of the committee of safety for Pennsylvania.

1777 Acting president of Delaware.

1777-1799 Chief justice of the state of Pennsylvania.

1781 President of the Congress of the Confederation.

1799-1808 Governor of Pennsylvania.

1817 (June 24) Died in Philadelphia, Pa.

**MRS. THOMAS McKEAN (SARA ARMITAGE),
WITH DAUGHTER**
by Charles Willson Peale, 1757
Peter Dechert—PDA

First court to ignore the Stamp Act

McKean began his career as a justice in 1765 when he was appointed as a justice of the peace and to the court of common pleas for New Castle County. His court is believed to be the first in the colonies that ordered its officers to ignore the British Stamp Act and to use unstamped paper for their documents. McKean also continued to rise in popularity among his fellow-legislators, and in 1772 and 1773 was elected speaker of the house of representatives in the Delaware legislature.

In 1774, the Delaware legislature elected McKean as one of its delegates to the first Continental Congress, and he continued to be re-elected as a congressional representative of Delaware for the next nine years. Meanwhile, McKean moved to Philadelphia and began to take an active part in the patriotic movement in that state. In June, 1776, he was president of a provincial convention held at Carpenter's Hall in Philadelphia that recommended that the Continental Congress adopt a Declaration of Independence. He also had been elected colonel of a militia regiment and chairman of the committee of safety of Pennsylvania.

When the Continental Congress met as the committee of the whole to consider Richard Henry Lee's resolution for independence on July 1, 1776, McKean and George Read were the two delegates from Delaware who were present. McKean favored independence and, at this time, Reed did not, so Delaware's vote was split and could not be registered in favor of independence. McKean sent a message to the third Delaware delegate, Caesar Rodney, then in Dover, Del., urging him to hurry to Philadelphia. Rodney heeded McKean's plea, riding day and night, and arrived in time to support McKean in registering Delaware's vote for the Declaration of Independence on July 4.

Wrote the constitution for Delaware

A few days after the Declaration of Independence had been adopted, McKean marched at the head of his battalion of militia to Perth Amboy, N. J., for the support of General George Washington's army. Immediately after this tour of military duty, McKean was called to Dover, Del., as a member of a convention to adopt a constitution for Delaware. Upon his arrival, a committee called upon McKean and asked him to write the constitution, and it is said that he stayed up all night writing the document and presenting it to the convention at ten o'clock the next morning where it was unanimously adopted. He became speaker of the Delaware house of representatives under the new constitution.

Last man to sign the Declaration of Independence

Because of the various activities in which McKean was engaged in the latter part of 1776, he was not present on August 2, 1776, when the Declaration of Independence was signed by most of the delegates to the second Continental Congress. It is not known exactly when he did sign it, but he apparently was the last man to do so, sometime in 1781. During his lifetime some question was raised as to whether McKean actually had signed the document; and in September, 1796, he wrote a letter endeavoring to explain what had happened: "Modesty should not rob any man of his just honour, when by that honour, his modesty cannot be offended. My name is not in the printed journals of congress, as a party to the Declaration of Independence, and this, like an error in the first concoction, has vitiated most of the subsequent publications, and yet the fact is, that I was then a member of congress for the state of Delaware, was personally present in congress, and voted in favour of independence on the fourth of July, 1776, and signed the Declaration after it had been engrossed on parchment, where my name, in my own handwriting, still appears."

On July 28, 1777, the executive council of the state of Pennsylvania appointed McKean as chief justice of that state, a position he continued to occupy for the next twenty-two years. However, during the first part of his tenure as chief justice of Pennsylvania he was more occupied with duties in Delaware than he was in Pennsylvania. On September 13, 1777, British troops captured President John McKinly of Delaware, and McKean was made acting president for the next several months. Later, McKean wrote to John Adams about this period of his life:

"Hunted like a fox by the enemy"

"I have had my full share of the anxieties, cares and troubles of the present war. For some time, I was obliged to act as president of the Delaware state, and as chief justice of this: General Howe had just landed, at the head of the Elk river, when I undertook to discharge these two important trusts. The consequence was, to be hunted like a fox by the enemy, and envied by those who ought to have been my friends. I was compelled to remove my family five times in a few months, and, at last, fixed them in a little log-house on the banks of the Susquehanna, more than a hundred miles from this place: but safety was not to be found there, for they were soon obliged to remove again, on account of the incursions of the Indians."

McKean had been a member of John Dickinson's committee that wrote the first draft of the Articles of Confederation in 1776, and he signed his name to the document as a delegate from Delaware on February 22, 1779. However, the Articles did not become effective until 1781 because of delays in ratification by Maryland. As a result, McKean became the first man to be elected President of the Congress under the Articles of Confederation on July 10, 1781.

First president under the Confederation

While McKean served as President of the Congress of the Confederation, he had the honor of

THOMAS McKEAN AND SON
by CHARLES WILLSON PEALE, 1757
Peter Dechert—PDA

receiving from George Washington the news of the surrender of Cornwallis at Yorktown. The dispatch was delivered to him about three o'clock in the morning of October 22, 1781, and the night-watchman who had guided Washington's messenger to McKean's residence began crying through the streets: "Past three o'clock and Cornwallis is taken!" But other matters during his presidency were not so pleasant; the newspapers were full of articles questioning the legality of his continuing as chief justice of Pennsylvania; so in November, 1781, McKean resigned as President of Congress.

During the twenty-two years that McKean served as chief justice of Pennsylvania, he was called upon to make many difficult decisions and was often the target of political attacks. During the Revolutionary War, he presided at the treason trials of Loyalists and upheld their death sen-

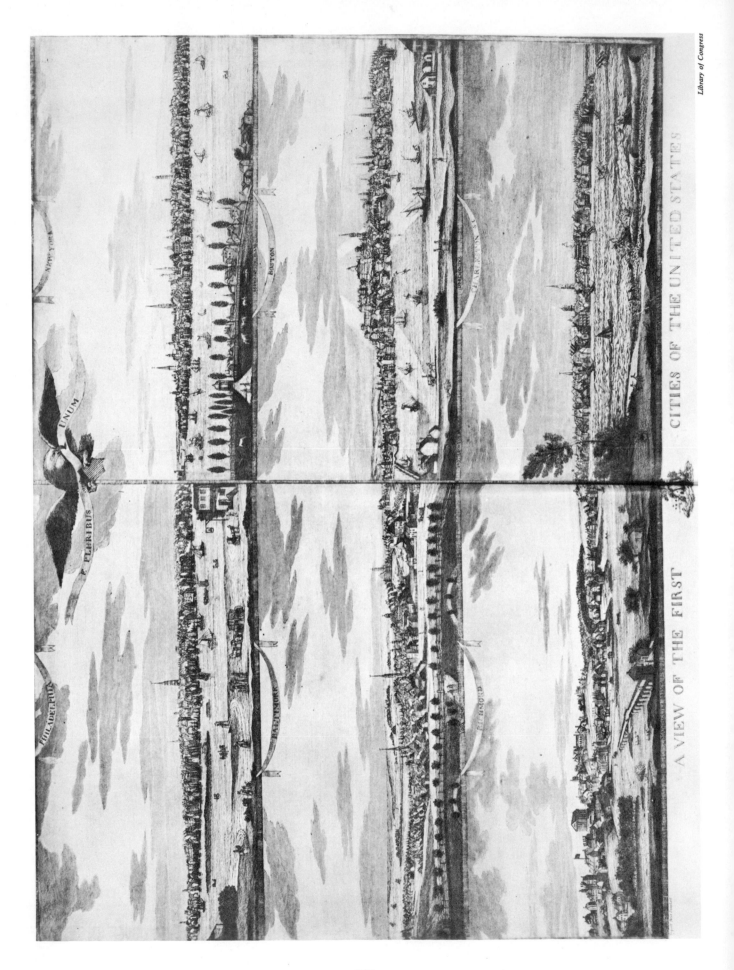

A VIEW OF THE FIRST CITIES OF THE UNITED STATES

tences. On the other hand he did not let patriotism sway his regard for the law, for he upheld the right of those accused of treason to exercise writs of habeas corpus in the face of a popular outcry that he should not do so. He also clashed with the officers of the Continental Army in his insistence that the war should not interfere with his orders that military officers be brought before his court in regard to civil actions. A justice of the supreme court of Pennsylvania who served after McKean had retired from the bench said of him: "Chief Justice McKean was a great man: his merit in the profession of the law, and as a judge, has never been sufficiently appreciated. It is only since I have been upon the bench, that I have been able to conceive a just idea of the greatness of his merit. His legal learning was profound and accurate . . ."

Best system the world has seen

McKean was not a member of the Constitutional Convention that wrote the United States Constitution, but he was elected to the Pennsylvania state ratification convention that approved it in 1787. He told this convention: "I have gone through the circle of office, in the Legislature, Executive, and Judicial departments of government; and from all my study, observation, and experience, I must declare, that from a full examination and due consideration of this system, it appears to me the best the world has yet seen. I congratulate you on the fair prospect of its being adopted, and am happy in the expectation of seeing accomplished what has long been my ardent wish, that you will hereafter have a salutary permanency in magistracy and stability in the laws."

Credited with fostering public education

In 1789, McKean was elected to the Pennsylvania state constitutional convention that revised that state's government. He was elected chairman of the committee of the whole, and as such he was unable to take much part in the debates. However, he is credited with the inclusion in the state constitution of the provision that free public education be provided for the poor.

At the age of sixty-five, McKean was elected governor of Pennsylvania and resigned as chief justice. He ran on the ticket of Thomas Jefferson's Democratic-Republican party, and was elected three times to three-year terms from 1799 to 1808. McKean received considerable criticism because he turned out of appointive office almost everyone who was not a member of his political party. He mentioned this in a letter to Thomas Jefferson, saying: "It is, at least, imprudent to foster spies continually about oneself. I am only sorry that I did not displace ten or eleven more; for it is not right to put a dagger in the hands of an assassin." Some efforts were made in 1803 to talk McKean into running for Vice President at the next national election, but he declined the honor. In 1807 and 1808 McKean's political opponents made efforts to impeach him on grounds that he considered "the constitution and the laws as mere instruments of executive convenience, and of so ductile a character as to be moulded into any shape at the suggestion of passion, ambition, or interest." The Pennsylvania house of representatives indefinitely postponed consideration of a committee report recommending impeachment, and no action was taken.

"I shook hands with the world"

At the age of seventy-four, McKean retired to private life in 1808. In a letter to John Adams a few years later he described his retirement: "Three years ago I shook hands with the world, and we said farewell to each other: the toys and rattles of childhood would, in a few years more, be, probably, as suitably to me, as office, honour, or wealth; but (thank God,) the faculties of my mind are, as yet, little, if any thing impaired, and my affections and friendships remain unshaken. Since my exemption from official and professional duties, I have enjoyed a tranquility, never (during a long, protracted life,) heretofore experienced; and my health and comforts are sufficient for a moderate man."

McKean made one more brief appearance as a public man when in 1814 he was elected at the age of eighty as chairman of a town meeting that had been called in Philadelphia to discuss what preparations might be made for defense against a possible invasion of the city by British troops in the War of 1812. McKean called upon the citizens to lay aside personal differences warning them "that there were then but two parties, our country and its invaders." The meeting then set about without further political discussion making plans for the city's defense.

McKean was eighty-three years old when he died in Philadelphia on June 24, 1817. His body was interred in the cemetery of the Presbyterian church in Philadelphia.

ARTHUR MIDDLETON of SOUTH CAROLINA

The wealthiest of the landed aristocrats who represented South Carolina at the signing of the Declaration of Independence, Arthur Middleton was such an idealist that he refused the governorship of South Carolina because he believed the legislature was acting illegally in offering it to him. He willingly gave up a life of ease and luxury to work for the patriotic cause during the Revolutionary War, but as soon as it was over he retired to the management of his rice and indigo plantations with their hundreds of slaves.

Arthur Middleton was born at his family's estate, Middleton Place, on the Ashley River near Charleston, S. C., on June 26, 1742. He was the son of Henry Middleton, who was president of the first Continental Congress at its close in 1774, and who ranked with George Washington and Charles Carroll as one of the three wealthiest men in the colonies. His grandfather, whose name also was Arthur Middleton, had headed a revolution in 1719 that had overthrown the power of the proprietors and made South Carolina a royal colony.

Educated in Europe

At the age of about twelve, Arthur Middleton was sent to England for his education. He attended the lower schools of Hackney and Westminster, and entered the University of Cambridge when he was eighteen. After obtaining his bachelor of arts degree from Cambridge, he toured Europe for two years studying the culture of various countries.

Returning to South Carolina in about the year 1766, Middleton married Mary Izard. About a year after their marriage, Arthur Middleton and his wife began an extensive tour of Europe that lasted for several years. They had nine children. Their oldest son, Henry Middleton, who was born in London, later became governor of South Carolina. In 1773, Arthur Middleton and his family came back to South Carolina and took up their residence at Middleton Place, which his father had given to him.

Middleton plunged into the efforts being made by local patriots to assert their rights in the face of the high-handed actions of the British government. In April, 1775, Middleton was appointed by the provincial congress to a five-man secret committee charged with preparing the defenses of the colony, and two months later he was made a member of the colony's committee of safety, which became the unofficial executive government of South Carolina at the onset of the Revolution.

Early in 1776, Arthur Middleton served on a committee of the provincial congress that drew up a new state constitution for South Carolina. Shortly after that, his father, Henry Middleton, resigned as a delegate to the Continental Congress because of ill health, and Arthur was elected to the legislature to take his place. Middleton arrived in Philadelphia in time to support the movement for independence. He continued to serve as a delegate to Congress in 1777, but took little part in the debates.

Declined the governorship of South Carolina

Middleton was put to an unusual test of his ethics in 1778. The legislature of South Carolina adopted a new constitution that spring, and John Rutledge, the governor, resigned in protest that the legislature did not have the power to change the state constitution without going to the people for their approval. Without his knowledge, the legislature elected Middleton to fill the vacancy as governor. But as soon as he learned of the legislature's action, Middleton declined to serve for the same reasons given by Rutledge in resigning.

ARTHUR MIDDLETON

1742 (June 26) Born at his father's estate, Middleton Place, on the Ashley River near Charleston, S. C.

1754-1766 Studied in Europe; graduated from the University of Cambridge.

1775-1776 Member of the provincial congress of South Carolina.

1775-1776 Member of the committee of safety of South Carolina.

1776-1777 Delegate from South Carolina to the Continental Congress; signed the Declaration of Independence.

1778 Declined election as governor of South Carolina.

1780-1781 Captured by the British and imprisoned at St. Augustine, Fla.

1781-1782 Delegate from South Carolina to the Congress of the Confederation.

1787 (Jan. 1) Died and was buried at Middleton Place near Charleston, S. C.

HIGH STREET FROM NINTH STREET, PHILADELPHIA

Drawn, Engraved & Published by W. Birch & Son.

Sold by R. Campbell & Cᵒ. Nᵒ. 30 Chesnut Street Philadᵃ. 1799

PENNSYLVANIA HOSPITAL in PINE STREET, PHILADELPHIA

Drawn Engraved & Published by W. Birch & Son

Sold by R. Campbell & C.º Nº 50. Chesnut Street Philadª 1799

HON. ARTHUR MIDDLETON, HIS WIFE, MARY IZARD, AND SON, HENRY
by BENJAMIN WEST. HENRY MIDDLETON DRINKER, *owner*
Frick Art Reference Library

When the British conquered Charleston, S. C., in 1780, Middleton was captured and sent to prison in St. Augustine, Fla., and his estate — Middleton Place was pillaged. After about nine months' imprisonment, Middleton's release was arranged by an exchange of prisoners, and he was taken to Philadelphia and freed. Middleton immediately was appointed as one of South Carolina's delegates to the Continental Congress, serving there for the remainder of 1781 and during the year 1782.

When word came from Europe that a temporary peace treaty had been approved and that a permanent peace was in prospect, Middleton retired from Congress to rejoin his family in South Carolina for the first time in two years. However, Middleton was to enjoy his retirement for only a few years. In November, 1786, he became ill with a fever that did not respond to treatment, and at the age of forty-four he died on January 1, 1787. His body was interred at Middleton Place.

LEWIS MORRIS of NEW YORK

A member of the landed aristocracy of New York, Lewis Morris was the third and last lord of the manor of Morrisania, an estate of about two thousand acres of farmland in what is now the borough of the Bronx of New York City. With everything to lose and nothing to gain, Morris signed the Declaration of Independence in the knowledge that liberty is more important than property.

Lewis Morris was born at Morrisania on April 8, 1726. Both his father and grandfather, the first two lords of the manor, also had been named Lewis Morris. He had three younger brothers who became famous in their own right: Gouverneur Morris, who signed the United States Constitution and became a U. S. Senator; Richard Morris, who became chief justice of the state of New York; and Staats Morris, who became a major general in the British army.

After receiving his early education from tutors, Morris was sent to Yale College at the age of sixteen. Four years later, in 1746, he was graduated with a bachelor of arts degree.

Lewis Morris
by John Wollaston

National Gallery of Art

The tall, handsome Morris was widely sought after as a husband for the eligible daughters of New York society, and in 1749 he married Mary Walton, daughter of a wealthy merchant. They had six sons and four daughters. On his father's death in 1762, Morris inherited the huge estate, and his time was absorbed with managing its large-scale agricultural operations.

The New York provincial congress elected Morris in 1775 as a member of its delegation to the Continental Congress. He took his seat there in May, shortly after fighting had begun in Massachusetts at the battles of Lexington and Concord. Before George Washington was designated commander in chief, Morris served on a committee with Washington as chairman which studied ways in which the colonies might supply an army. Morris also was sent to western Pennsylvania in an effort to convince the Indians on the western frontier to join forces with the colonists in resisting the British.

A brigadier general in the New York militia

Morris was again elected as a delegate to Congress in 1776, and in that same year he accepted a commission as a brigadier general in the New York militia. During the debates and votes on independence in the Congress, Morris was absent in New York on military duty; but after the New York provincial congress approved independence on July 9, 1776, Morris returned to Congress in time to sign the Declaration of Independence with the other delegates on August 2. He retired from the Continental Congress in 1777 to devote him-

---

LEWIS MORRIS

1726 (April 8) Born at the family estate Morrisania now in the Bronx, N. Y.

1746 Graduated from Yale College.

1775-1777 Delegate from New York in the Continental Congress; signed the Declaration of Independence.

1776-1783 General in the New York militia.

1777-1790 Member of the senate in the New York legislature.

1788 Member of state convention that ratified the United States Constitution.

1798 (Jan. 22) Died at Morrisania.

Morrisania home of Lewis Morris

Mary Walton Morris
by John Wollaston

self to his military duties, and his brother Gouverneur Morris was elected in his place.

During the years of the Revolutionary War, the British occupied Morrisania, and Morris was forced to live on the generosity of friends. He rose to the rank of major general in the militia, primarily concerning himself with the problems of recruiting troops and obtaining military supplies. During this period, he also served as a member of the senate of the New York legislature.

After the war, Morris devoted most of his time to rebuilding his estate, although he continued to serve in the New York state senate until 1790. As an ardent Federalist, he was an influential member of the state convention that ratified the United States Constitution in 1788. He also was a candidate for the U. S. Senate in 1789, but was defeated by the Anti-Federalist lower house of the state legislature.

The declining years of his life were spent in serenity and comfort at Morrisania. At the age of seventy-one, he died there on January 22, 1798, and his body was entombed in the family vault on the estate.

163

ROBERT MORRIS of PENNSYLVANIA

Morris House, Washington's Headquarters
5442 Main Street, Philadelphia, Pa.
Essex Institute Collection

The wealthiest merchant in Philadelphia, Robert Morris was given almost dictatorial powers during the greatest crisis of the Revolutionary War. When Congress fled Philadelphia in 1776, fearing British capture of the city, Morris was left as chairman of a committee of three to carry out the executive powers of the revolutionary government. By pledging his personal credit, Morris succeeded in giving Washington the decisive support needed to win his first victory by crossing the icy Delaware on the day after Christmas, 1776, to defeat the Hessian mercenaries at Trenton, N. J.

Certainly one of the real leaders of his era

Known as "The Financier" and regarded by many as second in importance only to Washington in winning the Revolutionary War, Morris insured Washington's final victory at Yorktown by using his personal credit to obtain the necessary supplies for the Continental Army. Morris also won distinction as being one of the two men, Roger Sherman being the other, to sign all three of the most important documents of the Revolutionary Era—

the Declaration of Independence in 1776, the Articles of Confederation in 1778, and the United States Constitution in 1787. When Morris lost his fortune in his old age and had been jailed for debt, Washington showed his lasting gratitude by taking the unusual expedient of having dinner in prison with his fallen friend.

Robert Morris was born in Liverpool, England, on January 31, 1734. His father was a well-to-do merchant who moved to America and established himself in the tobacco trade at Oxford, Md. When Robert was thirteen, his father sent for him, and he traveled by himself to the American colonies. Shortly after his arrival, he was sent to school in Philadelphia under a teacher by the name of Annan. Less than a year later, Morris wrote his father, "I have learned, sir, all that he could teach me." But before any further provision could be made for the boy's education, his father was killed in an unfortunate accident in which he was wounded in the shoulder by a cannon shot in celebration of the arrival of one of his ships.

A prosperous young gentleman

Left an orphan at the age of fifteen, Morris became an apprentice clerk to one of Philadelphia's

---

ROBERT MORRIS

1734 (Jan. 31) Born in Liverpool, England.

1747 Came to America.

1754-1793 Partner of Thomas Willing as a Philadelphia merchant.

1775 Appointed member of Pennsylvania's committee of safety.

1775-1778 Delegate from Pennsylvania to the Continental Congress; signed the Declaration of Independence and the Articles of Confederation.

1779-1780 Member of the Pennsylvania legislature.

1781-1784 Superintendent of finance and agent of marine for the Congress of the Confederation.

1781 Founded the Bank of North America at Philadelphia.

1785-1786 Member of the Pennsylvania legislature.

1786 Delegate of Pennsylvania to the Annapolis Convention.

1787 Member of Pennsylvania delegation to the Constitutional Convention; signed the United States Constitution.

1789-1795 United States Senator from Pennsylvania.

1798-1801 Jailed for debt after losing his fortune in land speculations.

1806 (May 8) Died in Philadelphia.

164

ROBERT MORRIS
by C. W. PEALE, 1782
Independence National Historical Park Collection

leading merchants, Charles Willing. Applying himself diligently to the tasks assigned him in the counting house, Morris won the respect of his employer. At the age of twenty, Morris became a partner in the firm of Willing, Morris & Company with his master's eldest son, Thomas Willing. Morris made several trips on the firm's ships. On one of the voyages he was captured by the French, winning his freedom by his dexterity in repairing a watch. The firm prospered under Morris' guidance, and by the time of the Revolutionary War it was the leading mercantile enterprise in Philadelphia, a partnership that lasted thirty-nine years, until 1793.

On March 2, 1769, Morris married Mary White, daughter of Colonel Thomas White of Maryland, and sister of William White, who was to become the first Episcopalian bishop in America (1786). Morris and his wife had five sons and two daughters.

The advent of war

Although Morris had signed the non-importation agreement of the colonies in 1765 during the Stamp Act crisis, he had taken no extremely active part in political affairs until 1775. He was presiding at a holiday dinner in honor of Britain's patron St. George on April 23, 1775, when the festivities were interrupted by the arrival of a messenger with news of the battles of Lexington and Concord. In the excitement that followed, tables and chairs were overturned as the guests made a hasty exit to arrange their affairs for the war that everyone knew he was sure to follow, making a mockery of the motto "Reconciliation" that hung on the wall of the hall where the celebration was being held.

In his first election to political office, Morris was chosen by the Pennsylvania legislature in November, 1775, as one of its delegates to the Continental Congress. After taking his seat in Congress, Morris was appointed chairman of the secret committee responsible for obtaining arms and ammunition from abroad, and he became a member of other important committees, including the maritime committee that was in charge of developing a navy for the war effort.

Opposed independence on July 1, 1776

In June, 1776, Morris sided with John Dickinson and the majority of Pennsylvania delegates who opposed Richard Henry Lee's independence resolutions. Morris felt that the time was not ripe

Maj. Gen. John Sullivan
(Showing the uniform of an officer during the Revolutionary War)

to declare independence, although John Adams ascribed Morris' action to "timidity." Morris voted against Lee's resolutions in the Committee of the Whole on July 1. But, when the issue of independence came before Congress on July 2, Morris and Dickinson stayed away from the meeting, thus enabling Benjamin Franklin, James Wilson, and John Morton to cast Pennsylvania's vote in favor of independence. Morris' business partner, Thomas Willing, was one of the delegates who voted against independence. Morris also abstained from voting for the Declaration of Independence on July 4, 1776. He later explained his position in a letter to General Horatio Gates in which he said: "The business of all America seems to be making constitutions. It is the fruits of a certain premature declaration, which you know I always opposed. My opposition was founded on the evil consequences I foresaw, and the present state of several of the colonies justifies my apprehension." Despite his opposition, Morris was reelected to Congress by the Pennsylvania legislature later in July, and he signed the Declaration of Independence with most of the other delegates on August 2, 1776.

A personal loan to finance Washington's army

When the British invaded New Jersey late in 1776 and seemed to be threatening the attack of Philadelphia, Congress decided to flee to Baltimore, leaving Morris as chairman of a committee composed of himself, George Clymer, and George Walton with powers to execute any necessary business to keep the war going. In December, Washington wrote to Morris that he was considering an offensive, but that he could not possibly undertake it without increased financial assistance. The story is told that Morris was walking home from his counting house with Washington's problem on his mind when he met a wealthy Quaker friend who asked him what news there was. "The most important news," Morris is said to have replied, "is that I require a certain sum in specie, and that you must let me have it. Your security is to be my note and my honour." The friend replied, "Robert, thou shall have it." The money from this loan is said to have been used by Washington in winning his important surprise victory over the Hession soldiers on the day after Christmas, 1776.

After the return of Congress to Philadelphia in March, 1777, the committee of three was disbanded, and Morris became a member of the committee of commerce and of the committee of finance. He continued to be re-elected to Congress, the last time being in December, 1777. He signed the Articles of Confederation as one of Pennsylvania's delegates in July, 1778.

Accused and vindicated

Henry Laurens, the President of Congress, raised charges in 1778 that Willing, Morris & Company had been making unwarranted profits in dealing with war supplies because of Morris's inside information on government operations. A congressional committee was appointed to investigate the charges in January, 1779; but Morris was able to vindicate his actions, and the committee and Congress voted to approve his conduct.

Morris served as a member of the Pennsylvania legislature in 1779 and 1780, and during this period continued to aid the American cause with pledges of his personal credit and by obtaining important supplies for the army through his mercantile contacts. Richard Peters, a member of the congressional board of war, described an incident by which Morris secured a much needed supply of lead for bullets:

"In 1779 or 1780, two of the most distressing years of the war, General Washington wrote to me a most alarming account of the prostrate condition of the military stores, and enjoined my immediate exertions to supply the deficiencies. There were no musket-cartridges but those in the men's boxes, and they were wet; of course, if attacked, a retreat, or a rout, was inevitable. We (the board of war) had exhausted all the lead accessible to us, having caused even the spouts of houses to be melted, and had offered, abortively, the equivalent in paper of two shillings specie per pound for lead. I went, in the evening of the day on which I received this letter, to a splendid entertainment, given by Don Juan Mirailles, the Spanish minister. My heart was sad, but I had the faculty of brightening my countenance, even under gloomy disasters; yet it seems *then* not sufficiently adroitly. Mr. Morris, who was one of the guests, and knew me well, discovered some casual traits of depression. He accosted me in his usual blunt and disengaged manner: 'I see some clouds passing across the sunny countenance you assume; what is the matter?' After some hesitation, I showed him the general's letter, which I had brought from the office, with the intention of placing it at home in a private cabinet. He played with my anxiety,

MRS. ROBERT MORRIS
by C. W. PEALE, 1782
Independence National Historical Park Collection

which he did not relieve for some time. At length, however, with great and sincere delight, he called me aside, and told me that the Holkar privateer had just arrived at his warf, with *ninety tons of lead,* which she had brought as ballast. It had been landed at Martinique, and stone ballast had supplied its place; but this had been put on shore, and the lead again taken in. 'You shall have my half of this fortunate supply; *there* are the owners of the other half' (indicating gentlemen in the apartment). 'Yes, but I am already under heavy personal engagements, as guarantee for the department, to those, and other gentlemen.' 'Well,' rejoined Mr. Morris, 'they will take your assumption with my guarantee.' I, instantly, on these terms, secured the lead, left the entertainment, sent for the proper officers, and set more than one hundred people to work, during the night. Before morning, a supply of cartridges was ready, and sent off to the army. I could relate many more such occurrences."

The bleak winter of 1780-81

The winter of 1780 to 1781 was one of the bleakest for the patriotic cause. Benedict Arnold, a trusted American general, had been exposed as a traitor. Pennsylvania and New Jersey troops had mutinied. The Continental Army was desperate for supplies. And the treasury of the Continental Congress was nearly bankrupt with its paper money almost worthless. Washington wrote in May, 1781:

"Instead of having magazines filled with provisions, we have a scanty pittance scattered here and there in the several states: Instead of having the various articles of field equipage ready to deliver, the quarter-master-general is but now applying to the several states (as the dernier resort) to provide these things for their troops respectively: Instead of having a regular system of transportation established upon credit, or funds in the quartermaster's hand to defray the contingent expenses of it, we have neither the one nor the other; and all that business, or a great part of it, being done by military impressment, we are daily and hourly oppressing the people, souring their tempers, and alienating their affections: Instead of having the regiments completed to the new establishments, scarce any state in the union has, at this hour, one eighth part of its quota in the field; and there is little prospect that I can see, of ever getting more than one half. In a word, instead of having every thing in readiness to take the field, we have noth-

The Hon. Sir Willm Howe K.^t
BATH,
Commander in Chief of all his Majesty's Forces in Am...

ing; and, instead of having the prospect of a glorious offensive campaign before us, we have a bewildered and gloomy prospect of a defensive one, unless we should receive a powerful aid of ships, land troops, and money, from our generous allies: and these at present are too contingent to build upon."

A pledge of his private credit

To help bring order out of the economic chaos, Morris accepted in May, 1781, the appointment

Excellency George Washington Esq.

ever study to avoid and prevent. I must therefore request that you will immediately use your best skill, judgment, and industry, in purchasing, on the lowest terms you can, one thousand barrels of sweet, sound flour, and in sending it forward to camp in the most expeditious and least expensive manner that you can contrive. To obtain this flour readily and on good terms, I know you must pledge your private credit, and as I have not the money ready, although the means of raising it are in my power, I must also pledge myself to you, which I do most solemnly, as an officer of the public; but lest you should, like some others, believe more in private than in public credit, I hereby pledge myself to pay you the cost and charges of this flour in hard money.

"I will enable you most honourably to fulfill your engagements. My character, utility, and the public good, are much more deeply concerned in doing so than yours is."

To strengthen his ability to obtain needed supplies and money, Morris arranged in June, 1781, to be appointed by the Pennsylvania legislature as their agent to requisition supplies and taxes requested of the state by Congress. Armed thus with both federal and state powers, Morris set about supplying the needs of the army.

Financing the attack at Yorktown

In August, 1781, Morris met with Washington at his headquarters to discuss a proposed attack against the British forces in New York City. He was there when Washington received the disappointing news that the French fleet would be unable to aid in the attack on New York, and instead planned to put into Chesapeake Bay. Washington then devised the plan to attack Cornwallis in Virginia; and Morris agreed to support the campaign with his personal credit. In the next several weeks he issued notes of more than a million dollars for the purchase of guns, ammunition, and supplies. He also negotiated a $200,000 loan of hard money from the French. Washington made Morris' Philadelphia home his headquarters in September when his troops marched through the capital on the way to Yorktown and the victory that in effect concluded the Revolutionary War.

A national government without means of taxation

In the next several years Morris fought a losing battle to shore up the national economy which labored under the impossible situation of a national

of Congress as Superintendent of Finance, and threw the immense prestige of his personal fortune into bolstering up the national treasury. Typical of the actions that he immediately embarked upon was a letter that he wrote to a New Jersey merchant on May 29, 1781, in which he said:

"It seems that General Washington is now in the utmost necessity for some immediate supplies of flour, and I must either undertake to procure them, or the *laws of necessity must be put in force* (a threat to seize the provisions), which I shall

169

government that could not levy taxes and states that refused to pay the obligations imposed upon them. He succeeded in establishing the first national bank, the Bank of North America, which acted as a lending agent to the national government. Morris wrote pleading letters and threatening letters to the states, all to little avail. In October, 1782, he wrote to the states:

"It is a mighty fashionable thing to declaim on the virtue and sufferings of the army, and it is a very common thing for those very declaimers to evade, by one artifice or another, the payment of those taxes which alone can remove every source of complaint. Now, sir, it is a matter of perfect indifference by what subterfuge this evasion is effected, whether by voting against taxes, or, what is more usual, agreeing to them in the first instance, but taking care, in the second, to provide no competent means to compel a collection; which cunning device leaves the army at last, as a kind of pensionary upon the voluntary contributions of good whigs, and suffers those of a different complexion to skulk and screen themselves entirely from the weight and inconvenience . . . my credit has already been on the brink of ruin; if that goes, all is gone."

"It was my duty to be honest"

In January, 1783, Morris wrote a letter of resignation to Congress in which he denounced the irresponsible fiscal policies of the states and said that as an honest man he could no longer associate himself with a position in which he constantly was piling up debt on which there were no efforts toward repayment. To General Nathaniel Greene he wrote:

"I felt the consequences of my resignation on public credit; I felt the probable derangement of our affairs; I felt the difficulties my successor would have to encounter; but still I felt, above all things, that it was my duty to be honest. This first and highest principle has been obeyed. I do not hold myself answerable for consequences. These are to be attributed to the opposers of just measures, let their rank and station be what it may. I expect much obloquy for my conduct, because this is what I know to be the reward for any conduct whatever, which is right. To the slander I am indifferent, and still more indifferent about the attempts to question the services I have rendered."

Obligations ignored by the states

Despite his wishes, however, Congress per-

suaded Morris to stay on in charge of finances throughout 1783 and most of 1784. During this period, the states continued to make little effort to pay their obligations to the national treasury and as a consequence America's credit fell to zero in European countries. When he finally left office on November 1, 1784, Morris published an appeal that forecast the need for an overhaul of the Articles of Confederation and the establishment of a strong national government. He wrote:

"The inhabitant of a little hamlet may feel pride in the sense of separate independence. But if there be not one government, which can draw forth and direct the efforts, the combined efforts of United America, our independence is but a name, our freedom a shadow, and our dignity a dream. To you, fellow citizens, these sentiments are addressed by one who has felt their force. In descending from that eminence on which your representatives had placed him, he avoids the shafts which calumny had aimed. He has no longer, therefore, any *personal* interest in those jealousies and distrusts which have embarrassed his administration, and may prove your ruin. He no longer asks confidence in himself. But it is his duty to declare his sincere opinion, that if you will not repose in the members of that general federal government which you yourselves have chosen, that confidence and those powers which are necessary, you must, and you will, (in no very distant period,) become the dupes of European politics. What may be the final event, time only can discover; but the probability is, that, first divided, then governed, our children may lament, in chains, the folly of their fathers. May heaven avert these evils, and endow us with wisdom so to act, as may best promote the present and future peace, prosperity, and happiness, of our country."

Presented with the sword of John Paul Jones

Throughout the entire period from 1781 to 1784, Morris also had served as agent of marine for the Congress. As such he was in charge of the affairs of the Continental Navy, and was a particular friend of John Paul Jones, whose heirs later presented Morris with the gold-mounted sword Jones had received from Louis XVI of France. In regard to his administration of naval affairs, Morris remarked: "I could have wished that this task had fallen to the lot of some other person. I could have wished to bestow on this subject an attention undissipated by other cares. But it is now

John Paul Jones

some time since I have learned to sacrifice to the public service, my ease, my wishes, and my inclinations."

In 1785, the Pennsylvania legislature annulled the charter of the Bank of North America, and, in an effort to get the charter reinstated, Morris ran for and won election to the legislature along with his friends George Clymer and Thomas FitzSim-ons. They succeeded in getting the bank re-chartered in 1786.

Rebuilding his fortune

Meanwhile, Morris was rebuilding his fortune. He was one of the earliest American merchants whose ships engaged in trade with China, and his ship the *Empress* was the first American vessel to enter the port of Canton. His firm, Willing, Morris

& Company, also won a monopoly on the tobacco trade with France. His house was the finest in Philadelphia, and his country home was equally luxurious; for example, he was said to have been the first to have a hot house for growing flowers and the first to have an ice-house for keeping food fresh. The parties and the dinners that he and his wife held were the center of Philadelphia society.

In his belief that the federal government had to be strengthened if the independence of the colonies were to be preserved, Morris accepted appointment of the Annapolis Convention as one of Pennsylvania's delegates in 1786, and then was elected by the legislature as a member of Pennsylvania's delegation to the Constitutional Convention in 1787. When Washington arrived in Philadelphia to attend the Convention, he accepted Morris' invitation to stay at his home during the meeting. On the opening day of the Convention, May 25, Morris nominated Washington as President of the meeting. James Madison's record of the debates in the Constitutional Convention indicate that Morris took no part in the discussions other than seconding a motion at one point to allow United States Senators to serve for life "during good behavior." However, it would be unrealistic to assume that a man of Morris' stature, and particularly a man at whose home Washington stayed throughout the meeting, did not have a considerable effect upon the writing of the United States Constitution. On the Sunday before the signing of the Constitution, Washington and Morris apparently had a private celebration at The Hills, Morris' lavish country home on the Schuylkill River. Then, on September 17, Morris signed the United States Constitution with most of the other delegates.

After the Constitution had been ratified, the Pennsylvania legislature in 1788 elected Morris as one of that state's two United States Senators to the first Congress of the United States. Morris was among the handful of Senators in New York City when Congress was supposed to convene on March 4, 1789, and he waited until enough Senators arrived to make a quorum on April 6. Later in April, Morris returned to Philadelphia to welcome George Washington to that city; he played host to the President-elect at his home; and then accompanied him to New York for the inauguration. In May, Mrs. Morris hosted Martha Washington in Philadelphia, and then traveled with the first lady to New York.

Although some biographies have said that Morris turned down an appointment by Washington as Secretary of the Treasury and instead recommended Alexander Hamilton, this could hardly have been so because Morris' position as a Senator would have precluded his accepting appointment created by the Congress of which he was a member. However, it is likely that Washington often sought his advice, for he and Morris were close friends; and Morris' partner, Thomas Willing, was appointed as president of the first Bank of the United States when it was created.

Morris played an important role in the maneuvers in Congress that resulted in the national capital's being moved from New York City to Philadelphia in 1790. Morris' home in Philadelphia became the presidential mansion, being described by Washington as "the best single House in the City." Washington leased this house from Morris, but required that additions be made to it in order to accommodate his large staff.

Financial disaster and debtor's prison

Even before Morris completed his term as Senator, there were signs that his financial empire was beginning to weaken. He owned millions of acres of western land in New York, Pennsylvania, Georgia, South Carolina, and Virginia, as well as some 7,000 city lots in the new federal city that was to become Washington, D.C. Although he was in the process of constructing a huge new mansion in Philadelphia that was commonly called "the palace," he was having trouble making payments on his loans. When land values collapsed after Washington left the presidency, Morris was wiped out and fled to his country home to stave off his creditors. But in February, 1798, Morris was sent to debtor's prison in Philadelphia. Nine months later, when Washington visited Philadelphia as commander in chief of the new United States Army, he had dinner in prison with Morris the day after he had had dinner with President John Adams in Morris' former home.

After his release from prison in August, 1801, Morris lived in obscurity on an annuity of fifteen hundred dollars a year that his wife received from Gouverneur Morris. He had a bad case of asthma and could relieve his attacks of coughing only by violent exercise at pumping water. Worn by his affliction and discouraged by his loss of wealth and position, the 72-year-old Morris died on May 8, 1806.

JOHN MORTON of PENNSYLVANIA

The first man to die after signing the Declaration of Independence, John Morton joined with Benjamin Franklin and James Wilson to cast Pennsylvania's crucial vote for independence. Although he was a powerful political figure in Pennsylvania, being speaker of colony's house of representatives, even some of his close friends turned against him for supporting the severence of all ties with Great Britain. On his death-bed, Morton is said to have cried out, "Tell them that they will live to see the hour, when they shall acknowledge it to have been the most glorious service that I ever rendered to my country."

John Morton was born in 1724 in Ridley township, near Chester, Pa. His father, whose name also was John Morton, died before the boy was born. His mother, Mary Richards Morton, after a period of mourning, married an Englishman named John Sketchley.

His step-father reared John Morton as though the boy were his own son. Although young John had only a few months of formal schooling, Sketchley, who was a surveyor, taught him mathematics and surveying.

Upon reaching manhood, Morton became a farmer and supplemented his income by surveying. He married Ann Justis of Delaware, and they reared a family of three sons and five daughters.

Outspoken opponent of British taxing policies

When he was about thirty-two years old, Morton was elected to the colony's legislature, where he continued to serve for twenty years. As an outspoken opponent of the British parliament's efforts to tax the colonies against their will, Morton was elected by the legislature as a delegate to the Stamp Act Congress held in New York City in 1765. Upon the death of the sheriff of Delaware County in 1766, the governor appointed Morton to the post; and in the next election the people of the county elected him to a three-year term as sheriff. In 1772, the house of representatives elected him speaker, an office that he continued to hold until 1776.

After fighting began at Lexington and Concord in Massachusetts, a volunteer militia battalion was formed in Delaware County, and Morton was offered the commission of colonel to command the volunteers. He declined the commission, however, because about this time he had been appointed as an associate justice of the supreme court of Pennsylvania.

Cast the crucial Pennsylvania vote for independence

Morton's greatest service to his country came as a delegate from Pennsylvania to the Continental Congress. The legislature elected him as one of its delegates to the first Continental Congress in 1774, and repeatedly re-elected him until his death. In

---

JOHN MORTON

1724 Born in Ridley township, Pennsylvania.

1756-1776 Representative in the Pennsylvania legislature; speaker of the house from 1772-1776.

1765 Delegate from Pennsylvania to the Stamp Act Congress.

1766-1769 Sheriff of Delaware County, Pennsylvania.

1774-1777 Delegate from Pennsylvania to the Continental Congress; signed the Declaration of Independence.

1777 (April) Died in Chester, Pa.

John Morton Miniature by Pierre Eugene du Simitiere

the debate on independence, John Dickinson of the Pennsylvania delegation led the opposition to a complete break with Great Britain, and he was supported by three other members of the delegation — Robert Morris, Charles Humphreys, and Thomas Willing. On July 2, when the resolution for independence came to a vote, Dickinson and Morris were absent. In the Pennsylvania delegation, Willing and Humphreys continued to oppose independence, while Benjamin Franklin and James Wilson favored it. This left the deciding vote to Morton, and he cast his lot with independence, thus preserving the unanimity of the colonies on this crucial question.

Because Pennsylvania had many Quakers who opposed the militant action of the Continental Congress, Morton suffered much abuse for his actions in voting for independence and for signing the Declaration of Independence. Many old friends and political supporters turned against him, and it was believed that this preyed on his mind and helped lead to his early death. He became ill with a high fever in the spring of 1777, and died in April at about the age of fifty-three. His body was buried in the cemetery of the church of St. James in Chester, Pa., where he was a member.

Home of John Morton

174

THOMAS NELSON of VIRGINIA

An affable fat man described by John Adams as "alert and lively for his weight," Thomas Nelson rode to Philadelphia in May, 1776, with the resolution of Virginia that called upon the Continental Congress to declare the colonies free of Great Britain; then he stayed to vote for independence and to sign the Declaration of Independence. He threw his fortune and his ability into winning the Revolutionary War, and as governor and commander in chief of Virginia he aided George Washington in the siege of Yorktown. The money that he spent and the loans that he guaranteed to help the war effort left his family deeply in debt upon his death.

Directed fire on his own house

The story is told that, during the siege of Yorktown, Nelson observed that his own mansion in the town was the only one that had not been struck by the American artillery. Upon inquiring why, he was told that the cannoneers had been asked to respect the governor's property, even though it was being used as Cornwallis' headquarters. Nelson urged that it be fired upon at once, and had the pleasure of seeing British officers flee from his house as it was struck by cannonballs.

Thomas Nelson was born on December 26, 1738, at his parents' town house in Yorktown, Pa. He was the oldest son of William Nelson, a wealthy merchant and landowner who served as acting governor of Virginia in 1770 to 1771. When the boy was fourteen, he was sent to England to school. There, he first attended Hackney preparatory school, then enrolled in Trinity College at Cambridge University. After an absence from America of eight years, the twenty-two-year-old Nelson returned home to Yorktown in 1761.

The year after returning home, Nelson married Lucy Grymes, the daughter of a plantation owner of Middlesex County. Nelson's father gave him valuable plantation lands and a town house in Yorktown; and the young couple settled down to enjoy a life of ease. In the years that followed, they had eleven children.

Opposed the British for closing Boston port

When Nelson was twenty-six years old, he entered public life, winning election to the Virginia house of burgesses. He continued to serve in the legislature until it was dissolved by Governor Dunmore in 1774 for passing resolutions opposing the British parliament for closing the port of Boston. Nelson was among the burgesses who immediately adjourned to a tavern, passed further inflammatory resolutions, and called on the other colonies to join in a Continental Congress.

He was elected to the Virginia provincial con-

THOMAS NELSON

1738 (Dec. 26) Born at Yorktown, Va.

1753-1761 Educated in England; attended Trinity College of the University of Cambridge.

1765-1774 Member of the house of burgesses of Virginia.

1774-1776 Member of the provincial congress of Virginia.

1775-1777, 1779 Delegate to the Continental Congress; signed the Declaration of Independence.

1777-1781 Commander-in-chief of the militia of Virginia.

1781 Governor of Virginia.

1789 (Jan. 4) Died at his farm of Offly in Hanover County, Virginia.

Essex Institute Collection

Nelson Mansion, Yorktown, Virginia

gress of patriots in 1774 and 1775. He recognized that body's growing antagonism to the British administration. When the provincial congress decided to raise troops for the protection of the colony, Nelson was elected as a colonel to command one of three regiments being formed. But the next month, in August, 1775, the provincial congress elected Nelson as one of Virginia's delegates to the Continental Congress, so he resigned his commission and hurried off to Philadelphia.

Suffered a lapse of memory

Nelson served in the Continental Congress from September, 1775, until the summer of 1777. During the spring of 1776, he was in Virginia attending a session of the provincial congress, when he introduced a resolution calling on the delegates in the Continental Congress to declare the colonies independent. When the Virginia legislators adopted his resolution, Nelson rode with it to Philadelphia. There it provided the basis of Richard Henry Lee's independence resolutions that led to the Declaration of Independence. While serving in the Continental Congress in 1777, Nelson was stricken with a severe headache that caused a lapse of memory; although he endeavored to carry on his duties, his illness did not improve, and he finally obtained a leave of absence and returned to Virginia.

In August, 1777, after being home only a short while, Nelson again was called to public duty. A large British fleet had been sighted off the coast of Virginia, and it was feared that an invasion was about to be launched. In preparation for the expected attack, Governor Patrick Henry appointed Nelson brigadier general and commander-in-chief of the Virginia militia. Only a few hundred militiamen had been mustered for the colony's defense, when the British fleet sailed off for an attack on Philadelphia, and Nelson was able to return to civilian life.

"I will pay my debts like an honest man."

Having been elected to the Virginia legislature in 1776, Nelson was present at a session in October in which a law was passed confiscating British property. In the debate on this legislation, Nelson angrily opposed it, pointing out that it was unfair to British merchants who had extended credit to the colonists, and who could not be held accountable for the acts of the British parliament. "I hope the bill will be rejected," Nelson declared, "but

Courtesy of Dr. John Randolph Page

Thomas Nelson, Jr. as a very young boy
Photo by Arthur E. Scott by Mason Chamberlin

whatever be its fate, by God, I will pay *my* debts like an honest man."

In March, 1778, the Continental Congress urged the states to encourage the raising of troops of light cavalry to serve at their own expense to aid in the war effort, and, when Nelson heard of the request, he immediately set about organizing and outfitting a troop of about seventy horsemen with himself as commanding officer. Nelson led his troop north, reaching Baltimore in July, and arriving in Philadelphia in August. Meanwhile, the British had retreated from Pennsylvania, and Congress decided that the volunteer cavalrymen were not needed, passing the following resolution on August 8, 1776:

"Whereas, in pursuance of the recommendations of congress of March the second, a volunteer corps of cavalry from the state of Virginia, under the command of the honourable General Nelson, are now in this city, on their way to the army, under the command of General Washington: and, whereas, the removal of the enemy from this state renders the employment of this corps at present unnecessary:

"Resolved, That it be recommended to the said corps to return, and that the thanks of congress be given to the honourable General Nelson and the officers and gentlemen under his command, for their brave, generous, and patriotic efforts in the cause of their country."

Paid the troops out of his own pocket

Nelson disbanded the troops, providing sufficient money from his own pocket for their journey

Schröckenvolle Feuersbrunst welche zu Neu Yorck von denen Americanern in der Nacht vom 19. Herbst Monath 1776. angeleget worden, wodurch alle Gebäude auf der West Seite der neuen Börse binauf der Broock brent bys an das Königl Kollegii mehr als 1600 Häuser, die Dreyfaltigkeit Kirche, die Lutherische Kappelle u. die armen Schule in Asche verwandelt worden.

Representation du Feu terrible à Nouvelle Yorck que les Americains ont allumé pendant la Nuit du 19 Septembre 1776 par le quel ont été brulés tous les Batiments du Côté de l'Est a droite de Borse dans la Rue de Broock jusqu'au Collège du Roi et plus que 1600. Maisons avec l'Eglise de la St.e Trinité la Chapelle Lutherine et l'Ecole des pauvres.

Se vend à Augsbourg au Negoce artium de l'Academie Impériale d'Empire des Arts à Augsbourg avec Privilege de Sa Majesté Imperiale et avec Defense ou sous Peine de ne vendre les Copies.

Engraved by FRANCOIS HABERMANN—*Library of Congress*

(Translation)

A representation of the terrible fire in New York, lighted by the Americans during the night of September 19, 1776, in which all of the buildings on the West side, to the right of the (Stock) Exchange, on Broock Street up to the King's College, as well as more than 1600 houses, the Church of the Holy Trinity, the Lutheran Chapel, and the School for the Poor, were burned.

NEW YORK.

New York Harbor circa 1800

home. Although his efforts to aid the army had been in vain, the outdoor activity had restored his health.

In 1779, Nelson accepted the election of the legislature to another term in the Continental Congress. He served from February to April, but again was struck down by illness and forced to return home.

Borrowed money in his own name for the cause

At the urging of Congress, the Virginia legislature set out to borrow two million dollars in the spring of 1780—the money to be given to the continental treasury to help buy provisions for the French fleet that was expected to help end the war. Nelson set about endeavoring to raise the money for the legislature, but on every hand he received the following reply from those he asked for loans: "We will not lend the government a shilling—but we will lend you, Thomas Nelson, all we can possibly raise." With that, Nelson made the loans in his own name, and turned the money over to the government, receiving in return securities that later turned out to be worthless.

The British generals Benedict Arnold and Lord Cornwallis attacked Virginia in 1781, and, Governor Thomas Jefferson's term coming to an end that year, he declined re-election, recommending that a military man be made governor to better defend the state. As a result, Thomas Nelson was elected by the legislature as governor and commander in chief of Virginia's military forces.

Reinforcements from France

During his administration as governor, British forces swept from one end of Virginia to the other, causing great destruction and completely disorganizing the state's government. Nelson was forced to take extraordinary powers to seize supplies for his troops and put up even token opposition. But in August, 1781, Nelson received pleasing words from George Washington:

"The arrival of the Count de Grasse with a formidable fleet and corps of land forces in the Chesapeake (which may every moment may be expected) will, I flatter myself (with proper exertions on our part) give a moral certainty of succeeding in the great object now in contemplation."

French Officers.

Eng⁴ by D.C.Hinman, from the original painting by Col.Trumbull, in the Gallery at Yale College.

Each figure is accurately copied from the original Portrait.

American Officers.

SURRENDER OF LORD CORNWALLIS, AT YORKTOWN, VA. OCT. 19ᵗ 1781.

No.1.Gen.Lincoln: 2.Gen.O'Hara representative of Cornwallis: 3,Washington:4,Gen.Knox: 5,Baron Steuben.— 6, Count Rochambeau: 7.Duke de Lauzun.

Entered according to act of Congress in the year 1844 by D.C.Hinman, in the Clerk's office of the Dist.t of Conn.

177

The Surrender of Lord Cornwallis

Washington was referring to the plan that had been conceived to trap Lord Cornwallis and a large British army at Yorktown; and in September American and French forces closed in on Yorktown with Nelson commanding three Virginia brigades of about three thousand militiamen. When Cornwallis surrendered his eight thousand British troops in October, Nelson reported to the Virginia delegation in the Continental Congress: "This blow must be a decisive one, it being out of the power of Great Britain to replace such a number of good troops." In the general orders of October 20, 1781, General Washington mentioned Nelson's part in the successful operation:

"The general would be guilty of the highest ingratitude, a crime of which he hopes he shall never be accused, if he forgot to return his sincere acknowledgments to his excellency, Governor Nelson, for the succours which he received from him and the militia under his command, to whose activity, emulation, and bravery, the highest praises are due. The magnitude of the acquisition will be ample compensation for the difficulties and dangers which they met with so much firmness and patriotism."

Resigned from the office of governor

Nelson remained in office as governor only a month after the siege of Yorktown. On November 20, 1781, he wrote to the speaker of the Virginia legislature: "The very low state of health to which I am reduced, and from which I have little expectation of soon recovering, makes it my duty to resign the government, that the state may not suffer for want of an executive." His fellow-signer of the Declaration of Independence, Benjamin Harrison, was elected as his successor.

Almost immediately upon his retirement, petitions were sent to the legislature accusing Nelson of having acted illegally during his term of office by issuing warrants and taking supplies for the troops. But the legislature absolved him of blame with the following resolution:

"An act to indemnify Thomas Nelson, Esquire, late governor of this commonwealth, and to legalize certain acts of his administration. Whereas, upon examination, it appears that previous to and during the siege of York, Thomas Nelson, Esquire, late governor of this commonwealth, was compelled by the peculiar circumstances of the state and army, to perform many acts of government without the advice of the council of state, for the purpose of procuring subsistence and other necessaries for the allied army under the command of his excellency General Washington; be it enacted that all such acts of government, evidently productive of general good, and warranted by necessity, be judged and held of the same validity, and the like proceedings be had on them as if they had been executed by and with the advice of the council, and with all the formalities prescribed by law. And be it further enacted, that the said Thomas Nelson, Esquire, be, and he hereby is, in the fullest manner, indemnified and exonerated from all penalties and dangers which might have accrued to him from the same."

Nelson never again served in public office. He was elected as a delegate to the Constitutional Convention in 1787, but he declined to serve. His fortune and his health had both been shattered by the war. On January 4, 1789, at the age of fifty, Nelson died at the small farm of Offly in Hanover county to which he had retired.

PRO. PATRIA.

WILLIAM PACA of MARYLAND

Described by a contemporary as a man of "respectability and legal dignity," William Paca was a Maryland signer of the Declaration of Independence who won friends easily and was even liked by his political opponents. As the first governor of Maryland after the Revolutionary War, Paca made the social life of Annapolis whirl with his balls and receptions. He spent his last years as a federal district judge, appointed to that office by President George Washington even though he had opposed ratification of the United States Constitution.

William Paca was born on October 31, 1740, at his family's estate near Abingdon, Md. His father, John Paca, was a large landowner. After receiving his early education by tutors, he was sent to the College of Philadelphia where he obtained his bachelor of arts degree.

At the age of nineteen, Paca began studying law under Stephen Bordley, an Annapolis attorney; and while he was still a law clerk he married Mary Chew, the daughter of a wealthy family of Ann Arundel county. She died after only a few years, and in 1777 Paca married Anne Harrison of Philadelphia. He had five children by his first wife, but only one survived childhood. His second wife had one child who also died at an early age.

Studied law in England

Before being admitted to the bar, Paca also went to London for a short while to study law at the Inner Temple; then he returned to Annapolis and began practicing law there in 1764. Through his father's friends, and because of his own abilities, Paca soon established himself as a talented lawyer.

In 1768, Paca began his career of public service with election to the Maryland colonial legislature, where he continued to serve until the beginning of the Revolutionary War. Paca became a close associate of Samuel Chase in 1771 in opposing efforts by the Maryland governor to make laws by proclamation, even though they had not been approved by the legislature. When the governor proclaimed a list of fees to be collected by public officials,

---

WILLIAM PACA

1740 (Oct. 31) Born near Abingdon, Maryland.

1759 Graduated from the College of Philadelphia.

1764 Admitted to the bar to practice law in Maryland.

1768-1774 Member of the colonial legislature of Maryland.

1774-1779 Delegate from Maryland to the Continental Congress; signed the Declaration of Independence.

1777-1779 Member of the Maryland state senate.

1778-1780 Chief judge of the general court of Maryland.

1780-1782 Chief judge of the circuit court of appeals in admiralty.

1782-1785 Governor of Maryland.

1789-1799 Federal district judge for Maryland.

1799 (Oct. 13) Died at his estate in Talbot County, Maryland.

Old Wye Country home of William Paca

Original etching by DON SWANN

Paca and Chase led a crowd of citizens to the public gallows, where the proclamation was "hanged" in a mock ceremony, then buried in a coffin under the gallows. All during the mock execution, Paca fired guns from a model sailing schooner that he had brought with him.

In 1774, Paca was elected as a delegate from Maryland to the first Continental Congress, which attempted to reconcile the difficulties with the British king and parliament; and he continued to be elected to subsequent sessions of the Continental Congress until 1779. In the spring of 1776, the Maryland delegates worked under a restriction by the legislature that prevented them from voting for independence. Paca and Chase aroused the people of Maryland to bring pressure on their legislators. Finally, on June 28, 1776, the Maryland patriotic convention released the restrictions on the congressional delegates, and Paca was freed to vote for independence and to sign the Declaration of Independence.

Throughout his service as a congressional delegate, Paca remained quite active in the local affairs of Maryland. He was a member of the committee of safety that planned the military defenses of the state. He served in the convention in 1776 that drew up Maryland's first state constitution, and he was elected as a member of the state senate under the new constitution for the period 1777 to 1779.

Paca's judicial career began in 1778 with his appointment as chief judge of the superior court of Maryland. Two years later he was appointed by the Congress of the Confederation as the chief judge of the court of appeals in admiralty cases.

A handsome widower, popular with the ladies

In 1782, the legislature of Maryland elected Paca governor, an office that he held for three years. During his term, the Revolutionary War came to an end, and he was involved in all the difficulties of helping his state return to a peacetime economy. As a handsome widower in his middle forties, Paca was a popular governor, particularly with the ladies. He held many balls and receptions that were the center of the gay social life of Annapolis. During this period, he also aided in the establishment of Washington College at Chestertown, Maryland.

After the Constitutional Convention had written the new United States Constitution, Paca opposed its ratification at the Maryland convention

GOVERNOR WILLIAM PACA
PEABODY INSTITUTE COLL., ON DEPOSIT AT MARYLAND
HISTORICAL SOCIETY, BALTIMORE
Frick Art Reference Library

in 1788. But, when ratification had been effected, Paca accepted an appointment from President George Washington in 1789 as a federal district judge for Maryland. Before making this appointment, Washington wrote to James McHenry for his opinion of Paca, and received McHenry's reply that Paca would "carry much respectability and legal dignity into the office." Paca continued to serve as a federal judge until he died at the age of fifty-eight, on October 13, 1799, at his estate Wye Hall in Talbot County, Maryland.

ROBERT TREAT PAINE of MASSACHUSETTS

At the time he signed the Declaration of Independence, Robert Treat Paine was 45-years-old and was recognized as the leading lawyer of Massachusetts. He served in public office for thirty years, devoting all his talent and energy to the cause of Independence.

A thin-lipped Puritan, Paine had little toleration for those who did not live up to his standards. He believed firmly that those who broke his code should be punished. When his poet son, also named Robert Treat Paine, married an actress against his father's wishes, the elder Paine completely cut himself off from the youth.

Paine was born in Boston on March 11, 1731. His father was a school teacher who also had been pastor of a church in Weymouth, Mass., for a few years. His mother was the daughter of a clergyman. He received his early education at the Boston Latin School. Then, at the age of 14, he entered Harvard College. He was graduated in 1749 at the age of 18.

His parents wanted him to become a clergyman, so Paine took up the study of theology. He served as a chaplain with New England troops in the French and Indian War in 1755. He also occasionally preached in the pulpits of regular clergy in and around Boston.

Decides to study law

It is not too clear what made Paine change his mind about becoming a clergyman, but in any event he decided to become a lawyer. Having heard of Benjamin Pratt, a distinguished lawyer in New York, he decided to go to New York to study law under Pratt. Because his parents could not afford to send him money for his support, Paine kept himself alive during his law apprenticeship by teaching school on the side. Finally, he was admitted to the bar in 1759. He first established a law office in Boston. Then he moved to Taunton, Mass., to practice. About this time he married Sally Cobb and in the following years they had eight children.

As the conflict began to mount between the people of Massachusetts and the British governor in the 1760's, Paine took an active part as a patriot. He attended a convention called the people in 1768 to protest the royal governor's closing of the legislature of the colony.

In 1771 Paine won greater prominence when he was chosen by the people of Boston as special prosecutor in the case against the British soldiers who had killed five persons in the Boston Massacre. In this case he opposed John Adams, who was one of the lawyers for the defense. Paine succeeded in winning manslaughter convictions against two of the soldiers.

Paine was chosen to represent the town of Taunton in the Massachusetts General Court (legislature) from 1773 to 1775. In this critical period, the members of the legislature soon began to realize that they had only two possible courses of action: one, to submit to British tyranny, or, two, to use open opposition with military force. Paine was a member of a committee of the legislature that recommended calling the First Continental Congress to determine the feelings of the other colonies.

"The Objection Maker"

As one of Massachusetts' five delegates, Paine attended the Continental Congress from 1774 to 1778. Because he argued against so many proposals in the Congress, he was given the nickname of "The Objection Maker." He, along with many other patriots, had hoped that a show of united action by the colonies would be sufficient to cause Great Britain to return the rights to the colonies

---

ROBERT TREAT PAINE

1731 (March 11) Born in Boston, Mass.

1749 Graduated from Harvard College.

1773-1775 Representative in the Massachusetts legislature.

1774-1778 Massachusetts delegate to the Continental Congress.

1777-1778 Member of the Massachusetts house of representatives.

1777-1790 Attorney general of Massachusetts.

1779 Member of the Massachusetts constitutional convention.

1790-1804 Justice of the Supreme Court of Massachusetts.

1804 Elected a counsellor of the state of Massachusetts.

1814 (May 11) Died in Boston at the age of 83.

without any need for military action. But the outbreak of fighting in 1775 ended such hopes. Paine became chairman of a congressional committee empowered to contract for the manufacture of guns and bayonets. He also did considerable work to encourage the production of gunpowder. When the Declaration of Independence was prepared, Paine voted for it and signed it.

While continuing to serve in the Continental Congress in 1777 and 1778, Paine also filled some of the important offices in the government of the state of Massachusetts. He served as a member of the state house of representatives in 1777 and 1778, acting as speaker of the house part of the time. He was appointed attorney general of Massachusetts in 1777 by unanimous vote of both houses of the legislature.

An active Federalist

For the next thirteen years, Paine devoted much of his time to the work of being state attorney general. But many other activities were demanded of him. In 1779, he became a member of the council, the upper house of the Massachusetts legislature. This same year, he also was elected as a delegate to a convention to draw up a new constitution for the

THE OLD SOUTH.

ROBERT TREAT PAINE
from a sketch by SAVAGE

state of Massachusetts. In 1780, he helped found the American Academy of the Arts and Sciences.

In the debate over the adoption of the United States Constitution, Paine was an active Federalist. He supported both Washington and Adams and employed his considerable influence in favor of their administrations.

From 1790 to 1804, Paine held the office of justice of the Supreme Court of Massachusetts. He resigned at the age of 73 because he was troubled by deafness and his age made it difficult to travel the hundreds of miles necessary to follow the court's circuit. On resigning the office of justice, he was elected a counsellor of the state of Massachusetts for the year 1804.

For the final ten years of his life, Paine lived in quiet retirement. His memory remained remarkably keen and he enjoyed discussing the many great events that he had lived through. He died in Boston on May 11, 1814, at the age of 83.

JOHN PENN of NORTH CAROLINA

A self-educated lawyer, John Penn moved to North Carolina just a year before the outbreak of the Revolutionary War, but was almost immediately recognized as one of the patriotic leaders of that state. He served as a North Carolina delegate in the Continental Congress for five years, signing both the Declaration of Independence and the Articles of Confederation. At the height of the fighting in North Carolina in 1780, he was given almost dictatorial power to help defend the state from the marauding British troops.

John Penn was born in Caroline County, Virginia, on May 17, 1741, the son of Moses Penn and Catharine Taylor Penn. His father was a small plantation owner, and, either from lack of money or neglect, the boy received little education—not more than two or three years of country schooling.

Educated himself through extensive reading

When Penn was eighteen, his father died leaving him with only a small inheritance and no training for a career or profession. He conceived the idea of teaching himself to become a lawyer, and began studying the law books in the personal library of a relative, Edmund Pendleton, who was then a local justice of the peace but later became one of Virginia's leading statesmen. Penn worked so diligently at his studies that by the time he was

John Penn
Miniature by Charles Willson Peale

twenty-one, he was sufficiently qualified to be admitted to the bar to practice law in Virginia.

The year after he began to practice law, Penn married Susannah Lyme. They had three children, and lived in modest circumstances as he struggled to build a law practice.

In 1774, Penn decided to move to North Carolina, where he had heard there were greater opportunities for a young man of talent. He settled in Granville County, and his pleasant personality and ability quickly made him a leader of the patriotic cause.

Served five years in the Continental Congress

The year after he had moved to North Carolina, the provincial congress elected him as one of its delegates to the Continental Congress. He took his seat in the Congress in Philadelphia in October, 1775, and continued to serve in this capacity to the year 1780. During this period, he was a member of many congressional committees, but was noted for his reticence in taking part in debates. He signed his name to the Declaration of Independence with the other delegates on August 2, 1776, and he signed the Articles of Confederation in 1778.

Penn returned to North Carolina in 1780 in time to aid in its defense against the invasion of British forces led by Lord Cornwallis. As a member of the state's board of war, Penn was given almost dictatorial powers to aid the state in the emergency. He used these powers with discretion, helping supply the militia and guerilla forces that defeated the British and forced them to retreat before the year was over.

For the few remaining years of his life, Penn

JOHN PENN

1741 (May 17) Born in Caroline County, Virginia.

1762 Admitted to the bar to practice law in North Carolina.

1774 Moved to Granville County, North Carolina.

1775-1780 Delegate to the Continental Congress from North Carolina; signed the Declaration of Independence and the Articles of Confederation.

1780 Member of the board of war of North Carolina.

1788 (September) Died at his estate near Stovall, N. C.

A View of the Sea & Beach, from M.r James Newbolds Plantation, near Indian River.

lived in Granville County, North Carolina, building up his law practice, and enjoying life with his family from whom he had been separated during most of the war years. At the age of forty-seven, he died at his home near Stovall, N. C., and was buried on his own estate. About a hundred years later, his body was moved to Guilford Courthouse National Military Park, where it was re-interred with that of William Hooper, a fellow-signer of the Declaration of Independence.

To the Right Honourable, George Dunk Earl of Halifax First Lord Commissioner, and to the Rest of the Right Honourable and Honourable Commissioners, for TRADE and PLANTATIONS.

GEORGE READ of DELAWARE

One of the six Founding Fathers who signed both the Declaration of Independence and the United States Constitution, George Read had been an official of the British colonial government for a dozen years before the Revolutionary War. He refused to vote for the Declaration of Independence, but once it had been approved, he risked his fortune by signing it. At the Constitutional Convention he believed so deeply in a strong national government that he proposed that the President be given the power to appoint the members of the United States Senate. He became one of Delaware's first United States Senators under the Constitution, and in the last years of his life he was chief justice of the Delaware supreme court. One of his great-grandsons, John Meredith Read, Jr., described him as follows:

"As a lawyer, a patriot, a senator, and a judge, he was alike unpretending, consistent, dignified, and impartial. His other peculiar characteristics were an inflexible integrity of motive; a cool determination of purpose; and an invincible perseverance in the conclusions of his judgment . . .

His manners were dignified, and his dignity may sometimes have bordered upon austerity. He avoided trifling occupations, disliked familiarity, and could not tolerate the slightest violation of good manners, for which he was himself distinguished. A strict and consistent moralist, he granted no indulgence to laxity of principle in others; and he was remarkably adverse to that qualified dependence which an obligation necessarily produces. Notwithstanding an exact attention to his expenditure, which he never permitted to exceed his income, his pecuniary liberality was very extensive. Mr. Read was above the middle size, erect, and dignified in his demeanour; and he was remarkable for attention to personal arrangements. In fine, he was an excellent husband, a good father, an indulgent master, an upright judge, a just man, and a fearless patriot."

A classmate of Thomas McKean and Hugh Williamson

George Read was born on September 18, 1733, at his father's plantation near North East in Cecil County, Maryland. His father, John Read, was the

GEORGE READ
by THOMAS SULLY, after R. E. PINE,
MRS. HARMON RUMPELLY READ COLLECTION
The Historical Society of Delaware, Wilmington

GEORGE READ

1733 (Sept. 18) Born on his father's plantation near North East, Md.
1753 Admitted to the bar to practice law.
1763-1744 Attorney general for the crown for Delaware.
1765-1780 Member of the Delaware legislature.
1774-1779 Delegate from Delaware to the Continental Congress; signed the Declaration of Independence.
1776 President of the Delaware state constitutional convention.
1777-1778 Acting president of Delaware.
1782-1789 Judge of the court of appeals in admiralty cases.
1786 Delegate from Delaware to the Annapolis Convention.
1787 Member of the Constitutional Convention; signed the United States Constitution.
1789-1793 United States Senator from Delaware.
1793-1798 Chief justice of Delaware.
1798 (Sept. 21) Died at New Castle, Del.

son of a wealthy Irish family, and his mother, Mary Howell Read, was Welsh. While George Read was a small boy, his family moved to another large estate in New Castle County, Delaware, where he spent his boyhood. He received his early education in a school at Chester, Pa., and then was sent to New London, Pa., for academic instruction under the Reverend Francis Allison. At Allison's school, Read's classmates included his future fellow-signer of the Declaration of Independence Thomas McKean and his future fellow-signer of the Constitution Hugh Williamson. When Read was seventeen, he was sent to Philadelphia where he began the study of law in the office of attorney John Moland. There he became a close friend of John Dickinson, later known as the "Penman of the Revolution," who was a fellow law student under Moland.

At the age of nineteen, Read was admitted to the bar to practice law in 1753. He established his office at New Castle, Del., and slowly built a reputation as a skillful lawyer. Early in 1763 he married an attractive widow, Mrs. Gertrude Ross Till, the daughter of the pastor of the Anglican Church in New Castle. One of his wife's brothers was John Ross, the attorney general of Pennsylvania and Delaware. Just three months after the marriage Ross arranged for Read to replace him as attorney general for Delaware, an office Read held until the Revolutionary War. Also by this marriage he became a brother-in-law of George Ross, who later became a fellow-signer of the Declaration of Independence. Read and his wife had five children.

In 1765, he was elected to the Delaware legislature where he continued to serve for the next fifteen years. Despite his position as attorney general, an official of the royal government, Read supported the viewpoint of the colonists in their struggles with the British government.

First favored moderation over independence

He was elected by the legislature as one of its delegates to the first Continental Congress in 1774, and he continued to represent Delaware in Congress during much of the Revolutionary War. When Richard Henry Lee proposed his resolution in June, 1776, calling for independence of the colonies from Great Britain, Read felt strongly that the time was not ripe for such a declaration. His negative on independence caused a split vote in the Delaware delegation until Caesar Rodney arrived to join Thomas McKean in voting for the resolution. From then on, Read supported independence and signed his name to the Declaration of Independence with most of the other delegates on August 2, 1776.

When Delaware called a state constitutional convention in September, 1776, Read was elected president of the meeting that approved an independent government for the state. He was offered the presidency of the state under the new constitution, but declined that position, accepting instead the vice presidency so that he could continue to serve in Congress.

Nearly taken by the British

When John McKinley, the president of Delaware, was captured by the British in September, 1777, Read was in Philadelphia. On his way home to Delaware with his family, Read narrowly escaped McKinley's fate. He and his family were crossing the Delaware river in a boat that went aground some distance from the Delaware shore. A nearby British warship sent a boatload of sailors to investigate, but Read convinced the boatswain in charge that he was merely a country gentleman trying to return home with his family, so the British sailors helped carry the women, children, and baggage ashore. Upon his arrival in Delaware,

Mrs. George Read *by* R E. PINE

187

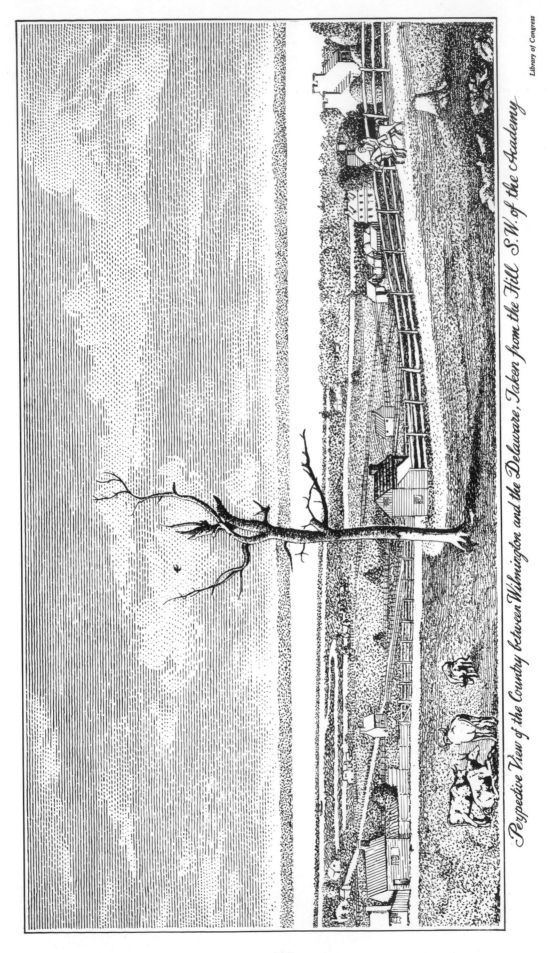

Perspective View of the Country between Wilmington and the Delaware, Taken from the Hill S.W. of the Academy

Read became acting president of the state, taking over from Thomas McKean who had held the government reins until Read could get there. Read served as president until Caesar Rodney was elected to the office in 1778.

In 1782, Read was appointed by the Congress to the Confederation as a judge of the court of appeals in admiralty cases. He served on this bench until the court was abolished by the new federal government in 1789.

Read had been critical of the Articles of Confederation when they were adopted, feeling they soon would have to be revised to strengthen the national government. He therefore gladly accepted election by the Delaware legislature as a delegate to the Annapolis Convention that was presided over by his old friend John Dickinson. After the Annapolis meeting recommended the calling of a convention of all the colonies, Read was elected as a Delaware delegate to the Constitutional Convention of 1787.

Read was present from the opening day of the Constitutional Convention on May 25, 1787. James Madison, who kept notes on the debates in the Federal Convention, reported that on June 7, Read made one of the most unusual proposals concerning the selection of senators under the new Constitution: "Mr. Read proposed 'that the Senate should be appointed by the Executive magistrate, out of a proper number of persons to be nominated by the individual Legislatures.' He said, he thought it his duty to speak his mind frankly. Gentlemen he hoped would not be alarmed at the idea. Nothing short of this approach towards a proper model of government would answer the purpose, and he thought it best to come directly to the point at once. His proposition was not seconded nor supported."

Believed in a single national government

Repeatedly during the Convention, Read rose to speak on the subject of the need of a national government, as opposed to a federal government. He believed strongly that all state governments should be abolished in favor of a single strong national government. For example, Madison's report of Read's speech on June 29, says: "He should have no objection to the system if it were truly national, but it has too much of a federal mixture in it. The little States, he thought, had not much to fear . . . He was not, however, so selfish as not to wish for a good General Govern-

ment. In order to obtain one, the whole States must be incorporated. If the States remain, the representatives of the large ones will stick together and carry everything before them. The Executive, also, will be chosen under the influence of this partiality, and will betray it in his administration. These jealousies are inseparable from the scheme of leaving the States in existence. They must be done away . . ."

After signing the United States Constitution with most of the other delegates on September 17, 1787, Read returned to Delaware. His urging aided Delaware's becoming the first state to ratify the Constitution. In October, 1788, the Delaware legislature elected Read as one of the state's U. S. Senators under the new Constitution.

Read served a little more than four years as a Senator, from 1789 to 1793. He was a member of the Federalist party and strongly supported President Washington and Vice President John Adams. He resigned as Senator in September, 1793, when he was appointed chief justice of the supreme court of Delaware.

For five years Read presided over the highest court in Delaware. His experience and ability were respected by the lawyers of the state, and his decisions were regarded as landmarks in the development of law and order in the post-revolutionary period.

At the age of sixty-five, Read died on September 21, 1798, at his mansion on the bank of the Delaware River near New Castle, Del. His grandson, John Meredith Read, became chief justice of Pennsylvania; and his great-grandson John Meredith Read, Jr., became a distinguished diplomat, archaeologist, and historian.

CAESAR RODNEY of DELAWARE

Caesar Rodney won fame by riding seventy miles by night and by day through wind and rain to reach Philadelphia in July, 1776, in time to break a tie in the Delaware delegation in the Continental Congress so that the vote of the colonies on independence would be unanimous. One of the few Founding Fathers who was a bachelor, Rodney was handicapped by a severe cancer of the face that he concealed by wearing a green silk scarf as a veil. But despite this disease, he was quite active throughout the Revolutionary War both as a general and as chief executive officer of his state.

John Adams wrote this description after meeting him: "Caesar Rodney is the oddest-looking man in the world; he is tall, thin and slender as a reed, pale; his face is not bigger than a large apple, yet there is sense and fire, spirit, wit, and humor in his countenance."

He was born near Dover, Del., on October 7,

1728. His father was a well-to-do planter who died while Caesar Rodney was still a boy. His mother, who guided his education at home, was the daughter of an Anglican minister. He inherited his father's entire estate, and as soon as he was old enough, he took charge of managing the plantation.

A delegate to the Stamp Act Congress

When he was thirty years old, Rodney entered public life with his election as high sheriff of Kent County, Delaware; and, at the end of his term of office in that position, he became justice of the peace. Journals of the colonial legislature show that he was a member of that body in 1761, although he may have been a legislator much earlier. He was elected by the legislature as a delegate to the Stamp Act Congress that met in New York City in 1765.

Rodney continued to serve in the legislature until the Revolutionary War, actively supporting the most liberal party. In the late 1760's, when a bill taxing the import and export of slaves was being discussed, Rodney supported an amendment to prohibit completely the importation of slaves into Delaware, but did not win enough of a following to pass the amendment. In October, 1769, Rodney was elected speaker of the lower house of the legislature, and somewhat later he became chairman of Delaware's committee of correspondence.

As speaker of the house, Rodney called a meet-

A French Frigate

CAESAR RODNEY

1728 (Oct. 7) Born near Dover, Del.

1758 Elected high sheriff of Kent County, Delaware.

1761-1776 Member of the Delaware colonial legislature; for several years speaker of the house.

1765 Delegate to the Stamp Act Congress.

1774 Chairman of Delaware's first patriotic convention of delegates.

1774-1776 Delegate from Delaware to the Continental Congress; signed the Declaration of Independence.

1775-1777 Brigadier general in command of Delaware's militia.

1778-1781 President of Delaware.

1782-1783 Elected to Congress, but did not serve because of ill health.

1784 (June 29) Died at his estate near Dover, Del.

ing of the colony's legislators as a patriotic convention in August, 1774, to consider how Delaware might aid the citizens of Boston, suffering under British retaliation for the Boston Tea Party. Rodney was elected chairman of the patriotic convention. The convention elected him as a delegate to the first Continental Congress in 1774, and re-elected him to the second Continental Congress in 1775.

A diligent leader

Rodney was absent from Congress during much of 1775, for he had been appointed brigadier general in command of Delaware's militia and also was a member of the colony's committee of safety. Because there were so many Loyalists in Delaware, Rodney had a difficult time finding enough volunteers; but he worked at his task so diligently that Delaware's troops became noted for their discipline and loyalty.

Late in June, 1776, while Rodney was in Dover, he received a message from his fellow congressional delegate Thomas McKean that urged him to come to Philadelphia at once because the Delaware delegation was split on the question of independence, and Rodney's vote was needed to break the tie. He immediately ordered his horse saddled and rode as fast as he could go along the seventy miles of mud roads that lay between Dover and Philadelphia. He arrived fatigued, but, while still wearing his spurs and riding clothes, he cast his tie-breaking vote to insure unity of the colonies in the cause of independence. Rodney remained in Philadelphia long enough to sign the Declaration of Independence on August 2, and then he returned to his military duties in Delaware.

Fought in aid of Washington at Philadelphia

In the fall of 1776, the conservative party won control of the provincial convention, and Rodney was not re-elected to Congress, although he remained a member of the committee of safety and continued to command the militia. He served in the field with his troops in the winter fighting of 1776 to 1777, sharing their hardships and winning their respect. In the spring of 1777, he put down an uprising in Sussex County, Delaware, and later that year he and his troops aided George Washington's army in its futile defense of Philadelphia.

In 1778, Rodney was elected by the legislature as President of Delaware, an office that he held for four years. These were difficult years for Delaware and for Rodney. The British repeatedly raided the Delaware coast and were supported by the large numbers of Loyalists in the State.

Because the cancerous condition of his face had grown constantly worse, Rodney declined to accept re-election as chief executive officer of Delaware in 1782. To honor him, the legislature elected him as a delegate to Congress in 1782 and 1783, even though his condition did not permit him to serve. On June 29, 1784, Rodney died at the age of fifty-five and was buried on his plantation near Dover, Del. About a hundred years later, his body was re-interred in Christ Episcopal Churchyard in Dover. A statue of Rodney represents the state of Delaware in Statuary Hall in the Capitol in Washington, D.C.

RES. OF CÆSAR RODNEY
Poplar Grove near Dover Delaware

191

GEORGE ROSS of DELAWARE

The next most popular man in Pennsylvania to Benjamin Franklin, George Ross made his reputation as a lawyer on the western frontier. He signed the Declaration of Independence and is said to have been a member of a secret committee with George Washington that employed his niece by marriage, Betsy Ross, to make the first United States Flag of stars and stripes. A handsome, witty man, Ross enjoyed good living, but paid the penalty for it by dying of gout before the end of the Revolutionary War.

Ross was born on May 10, 1730, in Newcastle, Delaware. His father, whose name also was George Ross, was an Episcopal clergyman. The boy moved with his family to Pennsylvania when the Reverend Ross became assistant rector of Philadelphia's Christ Church. Young George was tutored by his father in Latin and Greek, and then, when he was about eighteen, he began studying law under his older brother John who was practicing in Philadelphia.

Completing his law studies, Ross was admitted to the bar to practice law in Pennsylvania in 1750; but he soon decided that there were too many lawyers in Philadelphia for him to make a good living. He moved to Lancaster, Pa., then on the western frontier. He served as king's prosecutor for twelve years, and built a large legal practice. During this period, he married Anne Lawler of Lancaster, and they had a family of two sons and a daughter.

In 1768, Ross was elected to the Pennsylvania legislature, and he continued to be re-elected to this assembly until the early years of the Revolutionary War. He took an active part in the legislature, looking out for the rights of the western settlers in their constant troubles with the Indians.

A conservative in politics

Ross was elected by the legislature as a member of Pennsylvania's delegation to the first Continental Congress in 1774. There, he supported the conservative views of John Dickinson, in the belief that by petitions and addresses the British king and parliament could be persuaded to give up their tyrannical measures toward the colonies.

GEORGE ROSS
by Benjamin West, 1760
Fackenthal Library, Franklin & Marshall College

In 1775, Ross was appointed to Pennsylvania's committee of safety, which acted for some time as the unofficial executive branch of the colony's government, planning defense measures, raising the militia, and generally preparing for war.

Ross was not a delegate to the Continental Con-

GEORGE ROSS

1730 (May 10) Born in Newcastle, Del.
1750 Admitted to the bar to practice law in Pennsylvania.
1768-1776 Member of the Pennsylvania legislature.
1774 Delegate from Pennsylvania to the first Continental Congress.
1776 Vice-president of the Pennsylvania state constitutional convention.
1776-1777 Delegate from Pennsylvania to the Continental Congress; signed the Declaration of Independence.
1779 Admiralty judge of the state of Pennsylvania.
1779 (July 14) Died in Philadelphia, Pa.

An explanation on the prospect draught of the Fort William and Mary on Piscataqua River in yᵉ Province of New Hampshire on the Continent of America ____ a The new made powder house. b The new made centry boxe c The new made lodgings for officers & Men d The new made blockhouse & dungeon e The new made fresh water well f A pipe coming thro' the Pallisados for the Queens ship, to water g The Sally port fort to have correspondency with the well h Blockade Sea thᵗ Port i The old guard house k The Piscataqua River l the new flag staff m Part of the provinces of Maine n Justice Peperils Jaresens house O The Town of new Castle on the Great Island F the church G The Ministers house R Justice Atkinson house Sᵗ The Province gally Capt Cyprian Southack Commander

1. Mistic River 2. Charlestown Point where the British Troops landed the 17 June 3. Redout of the Rebels 4. Noodles Island 5. Hog Island 6. Boston Harbour
7. The Dykes 8. Boston North 9. Mops Hill and Battery which played on the Rebels Redout on Bunkers Hill the 17 of June 10. Beacon Hill 11. The Somerset

Boston

gress during the spring of 1776 while independence was being debated. But, when only three of Pennsylvania's delegates voted for independence, the legislature decided to replace the other five members of the delegation with patriots who were ready to sacrifice everything for liberty. Ross was one of the new delegates elected to the Continental Congress in July, and, although he had not voted for the Declaration of Independence, he signed it with the other delegates on August 2, 1776. One of his fellow-signers of the Declaration was George Read, his brother-in-law, who had married his sister Gertrude Ross.

A member of the committee to commission the flag

In June, 1776, during a visit of George Washington to Philadelphia, Ross is said to have been a member of a committee that included Washington, Robert Morris, and others that commissioned Betsy Ross to make the first flag of stars and stripes. Betsy Ross was the widow of George Ross's nephew, John Ross, who had been killed earlier in the year while serving in the militia. According to tradition, Betsy Ross made the flag, following a design sketched by Washington. Whether the tradition is completely accurate, it certainly is true that Betsy Ross made many flags for the United States government, for ships, and for patriotic organizations.

The popularity that Ross had with his fellow legislators was demonstrated in 1776, when as a member of the state constitutional convention, he was elected vice president to serve with Benjamin Franklin, who was elected president of the conven-

MRS. GEORGE ROSS
by BENJAMIN WEST, 1760
Fackenthal Library, Franklin & Marshall College

tion. Ross played an important part in drawing up the new Pennsylvania constitution.

In January, 1777, he became ill with the gout as a result of his fondness for rich food and wine, and he retired from public office. By the spring of 1779, he had recovered sufficiently to accept an appointment as an admiralty judge for Pennsylvania, but his health permitted him to serve in this office for only a few months. He died at the age of forty-nine, on July 14, 1779, in Philadelphia.

Library of Congress

BENJAMIN RUSH
Courtesy: Henry Francis du Pont Winterthur Museum

194

BENJAMIN RUSH of PENNSYLVANIA

The leading American physician of his time, Benjamin Rush established the first free medical clinic in the United States and set an example for other doctors in caring for the poor during two great yellow fever epidemics in Philadelphia. He also was one of Pennsylvania's leading patriots at the beginning of the Revolutionary War and signed the Declaration of Independence. He was a close friend of both John Adams and Thomas Jefferson, but he was critical of George Washington, both as a commanding general and as President.

Rush also was a prolific writer on medical subjects, politics, morals, philosophy, and contemporary affairs. He wrote against slavery, liquor, and tobacco; he wrote the first American textbook on chemistry; he wrote an analysis of mental illness; and his letters and autobiographical writings provide historians with many insights into the life of his times. "It is a matter of wonder," wrote Dr. David Ramsey, a contemporary physician-historian, "how a physician who had so many patients to attend, a professor who had so many pupils to instruct, could find leisure to write so much, and at the same time so well."

Graduated from college at fourteen

Benjamin Rush was born on December 24, 1745, in Byberry township northeast of Philadelphia. His great-grandfather, who had been a cavalry officer in Oliver Cromwell's army, had emigrated to Pennsylvania in 1683. His father, John Rush, a farmer, died while Benjamin was a baby. To provide money for his education his mother went to work in Philadelphia. At the age of nine, he was sent to an academy in West Nottingham, Md., run by his uncle, Samuel Finley, a Presbyterian minister who later became president of the College of New Jersey (now Princeton University). After about four years at his uncle's academy, Rush then attended the College of New Jersey and was graduated from that institution in 1760 when he was only fourteen.

Six years of uninterrupted study

The youthful Rush next plunged into the study of medicine. For the next six years he worked under the direction of Dr. John Redman, a Philadelphia physician so dedicated to his profession that Rush later recorded that during the entire period no more than two days were uninterrupted from the demands of his medical practice. During this time Rush had his first encounter with yellow fever when an epidemic of that disease occurred in Philadelphia in 1762. In a day when most American doctors began practicing medicine after a few years study with an older physician, Rush was determined to learn all that could be learned about his profession; so in 1766 he travelled to Europe to study at the medical school of the University of Edinburgh in Scotland.

BENJAMIN RUSH

1745 (Dec. 24) Born in Byberry township, near Philadelphia, Pa.

1760 Graduated from the College of New Jersey (now Princeton University).

1760-1766 Studied medicine in Philadelphia.

1766-1768 Studied at University of Edinburgh, Scotland, and received degree of Doctor of Medicine.

1768-1769 Studied medicine in London and Paris.

1769 Became professor of chemistry at the College of Philadelphia (now the University of Pennsylvania).

1776 Member of Pennsylvania patriotic congress; helped write a declaration of independence which the meeting urged the Continental Congress to adopt.

1776 Elected by Pennsylvania legislature as delegate to the Continental Congress; signed the Declaration of Independence.

1777 Appointed physician-general of military hospitals for the middle department of the Continental Army.

1783 Became a staff member of the Pennsylvania Hospital.

1786 Established the first free medical clinic in the United States.

1787 Member of the Pennsylvania convention that ratified the United States Constitution.

1789 Appointed professor of the theory and practice of medicine at the College of Philadelphia.

1789-1790 Member of Pennsylvania state constitutional convention.

1791 Appointed professor of medicine at the University of Pennsylvania.

1793 Worked tirelessly in the yellow fever epidemic that killed about 4,000 persons in Philadelphia.

1797-1813 Served as Treasurer of the United States Mint.

1798 One of few physicians who remained in Philadelphia during another severe yellow fever pidemic.

1813 (April 19) Died in Philadelphia.

While Rush was in Scotland, his uncle, the Reverend Finley, died while holding the office of president of the College of New Jersey. The trustees of the school asked Rush to aid in persuading John Witherspoon, then a Presbyterian minister in Paisley, Scotland, to take the presidency of the institution. Frank Stockton, a trustee of the school, also traveled to Great Britain to talk with Witherspoon. Rush particularly used his charm on Mrs. Witherspoon who was fearful of exposing her young family to the dangers of Indians in America. Rush and Stockton were successful in their mission of getting Witherspoon to New Jersey, and only ten years later all three put their signatures to the Declaration of Independence. Rush's friendship with Stockton also led in 1776 to his marriage to Stockton's sixteen-year-old daughter Julia.

Study in London and Paris

After receiving the degree of Doctor of Medicine from the University of Edinburgh in 1768, Rush went to London where he spent the winter visiting hospitals and attending medical lectures. The story is told that during this period, when the movement toward revolt was growing in the American colonies, Rush attended a debate in which a British orator declared "if the Americans possessed cannon, they had not even a ball to fire," causing Rush to retort that "if the Americans possessed no cannon balls, they could supply the deficiency by digging up the skulls of those ancestors who had courted expatriation from the old hemisphere, under the vivid hope of enjoying more ample freedom in the new." From London, Rush went on to visit hospitals in Paris during the summer of 1769, and then he returned home.

Published the first American textbook on chemistry

At the age of twenty-three, Rush set up practice as a physician in Philadelphia. His extensive education and his charming manner soon won him patients from older more established doctors. He also was honored in 1769 by being appointed as professor of chemistry at the College of Philadelphia (now the University of Pennsylvania), and the next year he published *A Syllabus of a Course of Lectures on Chemistry,* the first American textbook on chemistry.

Suggested the title Common Sense

In the years immediately preceding the Revolutionary War, when the light of patriotism did not burn so brightly in Pennsylvania as it did in Massachusetts and Virginia, Rush played a leading role in the patriotic movement. He encouraged Thomas Paine to write his essay that stirred American opposition to Great Britain and suggested its title, *Common Sense.* He rode out on horseback to meet the Massachusetts delegates to the first Continental Congress in 1774, and established a lasting friendship with John Adams. In June, 1775, although Rush was not a member of the Continental Congress, he was invited to attend the dinner celebrating George Washington's election as commander in chief of the Continental Army. Rush wrote of this occasion: "General Washington rose from his seat, and with some confusion thanked the company for the honor they did him. The whole company instantly rose and drank the toast standing. This scene, so unexpected, was a solemn one. A silence followed it, as if every heart was penetrated with the awful but great events which were to follow the use of the sword of liberty which had been put into General Washington's hands by the unanimous voice of his country."

Helped draft a declaration of independence

In June, 1776, when most of the Pennsylvania delegation to the Continental Congress was op-

Henry Francis Winterthur Museum

Mrs. Benjamin Rush *by* CHARLES WILLSON PEALE

196

posing independence for the colonies, Rush was a member of a Pennsylvania provincial convention in which he moved the appointment of a committee to write a report urging the colony's congressional delegates to support independence. Rush was appointed to the committee, along with James Smith and Thomas McKean, and he helped draft a declaration adopted by the convention that anticipated in many details the Declaration of Independence itself.

In July, 1776, after the Continental Congress had adopted the Declaration of Independence despite the objections of such Pennsylvania delegates as John Dickinson, Rush was elected by the Pennsylvania legislature as one of its new delegates to Congress. Thus, he was present on August 2, when the engrossed copy of the Declaration of Independence was presented to Congress, and he added his signature with most of the delegates even though he had not had the opportunity to vote for the Declaration.

Appointed physician-general for middle department

Rush was appointed physician-general of military hospitals for the middle department of the Continental Army in April, 1777. He attended the American wounded in the battles of Princeton and Brandywine. After the latter battle, the British were unable to care for wounded American troops within the territory they held, and they permitted Rush and other physicans to enter their lines to provide the needed medical care. Rush wrote of this experience: "I was much struck in observing the difference between the discipline and order of the British and Americans . . . I lamented this upon my return. It gave offense and was ascribed to fear and to lack of attachment to the cause of my country."

Advocated demotion of George Washington

Apparently partly as a result of his experience during this trip behind enemy lines, Rush became associated with the "Conway cabal," the group that believed Washington should be replaced as commander in chief by Horatio Gates, the victor at the Battle of Saratoga. Early in 1778, Patrick Henry sent Washington an anonymous letter he had received from York, Pa., where Congress was then meeting, which said in part: "The northern army has shown us what Americans are capable of doing, with a General at their head. The spirit of the southern army is no way inferior to

THE HONBLE Horatio Gates

the spirit of the northern. A Gates, a Lee, or a Conway would in a few weeks render them an irresistible body of men." Although the letter was not signed, it carried an injunction that it "must be thrown in the fire." Washington recognized the handwriting, and wrote back to Henry identifying the writer of the letter as Rush, whom he painfully pointed out "has been elaborate and studied in his professions of regard for me, and long since the letter to you." Shortly after this, Rush resigned his post with the army when he failed to win the support of Congress in an effort to reorganize the military hospitals. He held no further military position during the course of the Revolutionary War, and he received no federal appointment until after Washington had left the presidency. He continued to feel bitter toward Washington for many years, and even attributed the yellow fever epidemic of 1798 to the wrath of God over such matters as the public "worship" of Washington, saying: "We ascribe all the attributes of the Deity to the name of General Washington. It is considered by our citizens as the bulwark of our nation. God would cease to be what He is, if he did not visit us for these things."

Established first free medical clinic in America

In the years following the Revolutionary War, Rush won a greater and greater reputation as a physician and an educator. In 1783 he became a staff member of the Pennsylvania Hospital, which he helped to found. Three years later he established the first free medical clinic in the United State to care for patients too poor to pay for medical care. He became professor of the theory and

"SHIPPEN MANSION" RES. OF Dr. B. RUSH.

practice of medicine at the College of Philadelphia in 1789; two years later, after that institution had become the University of Pennsylvania, he took on the additional professorship of the institutes of medicine and of clinical practice; and in 1796 he was appointed as the university's professor of physics. When Rush first began teaching medicine at the university, he had a class of about twenty students; but by the time he delivered his last lectures in the winter of 1813 to 1814, he had more than four hundred students. He expressed his ideals as a physician in one of his lectures when he said:

"I was an advocate for principles in medicine."

"Medicine without principles is an humble art, and a degrading profession. It reduces the physician to a level with the cook and the nurse, who administer to the appetites and the weaknesses of sick people. But directed by principles, it imparts the highest elevation to the intellectual and moral condition of man. In spite, therefore, of the obloquy with which they have been treated, let us resolve to cultivate them as long as we live. This, gentlemen, is my determination as long as I am able to totter to this chair; and if a tombstone be afforded after my death to rescue my humble name for a few years from oblivion, I ask no further addition to it, than that 'I was an advocate for principles in medicine.'"

One certain preventative, "fly from it"

Rush became world famous by his devotion to his profession during the yellow fever epidemic that broke out in Philadelphia in August, 1793, and resulted in the deaths of about 4,000 persons. He identified the first case of the disease on August 19, as a "bilious remitting yellow fever." Six days later the Philadelphia College of Physicians met, appointing Rush to draw up a program to control the spread of the fever. When his rules warning against the visiting of sick persons were printed in Philadelphia newspapers on August 28, the frightened public began fleeing from the capital city. Rush wrote to his wife the next day saying: "I have advised all the families that I attend, that can move, to quit the city. There is but one preventative that is certain, and that is 'to fly from it.'" He developed a treatment that consisted of frequent bleedings of his patients combined with the use of strong laxatives that became known as "Rush's thunderbolts." Other physicians advised rest, cold baths, and wine, and described Rush's treatment as "certain death." But Rush stayed to treat rich and poor patients alike, while his colleagues died or fled, until at one point in the epidemic it is said that only two other doctors remained in the city to aid him in attending the thousands of stricken persons.

"Prayers were heard by heaven"

Rush himself became ill from the disease. The story is told that while he was recovering, he had a dream that a crowd of poor persons had gathered in front of his house asking him to help their friends and families and that he was about to turn away when a poor woman ran forward, crying out: "Oh, Doctor! Don't turn away from the poor! You were doomed to die of the yellow fever; but the prayers of the poor were heard by heaven, and have saved your life!"

Five years later, in August, 1798, yellow fever again struck Philadelphia. It again resulted in the deaths of nearly four thousand persons, and again Rush stayed at his post while many other prominent physicians fled the city. Medical controversies were renewed over the proper treatment of the disease, but Rush's position and reputation were now secure. He later was sent presents from the King of Prussia and the Czar of Russia in honor of his service.

Treasurer of the United States Mint

Rush continued to maintain a close interest in the political affairs of his country. In 1787, he wrote newspaper articles supporting the United States Constitution, and he was a member of the Pennsylvania convention that ratified the Constitution. He also was a member of the Pennsylvania state constitutional convention in 1789 and helped James Wilson write a new constitution for Pennsylvania. He carried on considerable correspondence with both John Adams and Thomas Jefferson; and, since he leaned toward Jefferson's political views, he sometimes passed along to Jefferson "inside information" about Adams's political activities. At the beginning of Adams's term as President in 1797, Rush was appointed Treasurer of the United States Mint in Philadelphia, an office that he continued to hold under Presidents Jefferson and James Madison.

At the age of sixty-seven, on April 19, 1813, Rush died in Philadelphia. He and his wife, Julia, had had thirteen children, the most famous of whom, Richard Rush, served as a cabinet officer under three Presidents.

Bridewell, and Charity School, Broadway, opposite Chamber Street, Philadelphia, February, 1808.

EDWARD RUTLEDGE *of* SOUTH CAROLINA

As the youngest man to sign the Declaration of Independence, Edward Rutledge won a place in history, even though his attendance at the Continental Congress was more the result of his brother John's political influence than it was of his own merit. He served a short time as an artillery captain during the Revolutionary War, but was captured by the British and spent months as a prisoner. Prematurely bald, Rutledge was badly crippled by the gout when he died at the age of fifty while serving as governor of the State of South Carolina.

Edward Rutledge was born in Charleston (then Charles Town), S. C., on November 23, 1749. He was the youngest of seven children of Dr. John Rutledge and Sarah Hext Rutledge. When Edward was only a year old, his father died. His early education was provided by private tutors, and when he was old enough he went to work as a clerk in the office of his brother John Rutledge, the leading attorney in Charleston.

Studied law in London

At the age of nineteen, Edward Rutledge was sent to England to study law at the Middle Temple in London, where John Rutledge had also studied. His brother John wrote to him, admonishing him, "I hope that whatever you attempt you will make yourself completely master of; for nothing makes a person so ridiculous as to pretend to things which he does not understand; and it will not be sufficient for a man, in such a case, to rest satisfied, because he may pass as a complete scholar among those with whom he may have to do in general, who, perhaps, may know little about the matter; such a one may meet sometime with his superiors, and in what situation will he then be?"

Married into great wealth

When he returned from England in 1773, Edward Rutledge was admitted to the bar to practice law, and he married Henrietta Middleton, daugh-

Charleston, South Carolina, in 1780

ter of the wealthiest planter in South Carolina. By this marriage, Edward automatically became the richest man in his family, because he received from the Middletons a dowry worth about 70,000 pounds. After the death of Henrietta Rutledge, Edward married Mary Shubrick Eveleigh, a widow who had once been his childhood sweetheart. Rutledge had three children by his first wife, but his second marriage was childless.

In 1774, the twenty-four-year-old Edward Rutledge was elected to the colonial legislature through the arrangements of John Rutledge. Later in that same year he was elected by the legislators as a representative to the first Continental Congress along with his brother John and his father-in-law Henry Middleton. The trip to the convention in Philadelphia was something of a family party, for all three men took their wives.

The acid tongue of John Adams

The sharp-tongued John Adams of Massachusetts took a dim view of the rich young gentleman from the South, describing him thus:

"Young Ned Rutledge is a perfect Bob-o-Lincoln—a swallow, a sparrow, a peacock; excessively vain, excessively weak, and excessively variable and unsteady; jejeune, inane, and puerile."

This diatribe no doubt was caused by young Rutledge's following the lead of his conservative elder brother and father-in-law, both of whom were still convinced that America's problems with Great Britain could be solved without an outright rebellion. In a letter to a friend in South Carolina, young Rutledge discussed his own impressions of the Continental Congress, apparently referring to Christopher Gadsden, another member of the South Carolina delegation who was the most vio-

Edward Rutledge

EDWARD RUTLEDGE

1749 (Nov. 23) Born in Charleston, S. C.

1773 Admitted to the bar to practice law in South Carolina.

1774-1777 Delegate from South Carolina to the Continental Congress; signed the Declaration of Independence.

1779 Served as captain of artillery in the Revolutionary War.

1780-1781 Prisoner of the British.

1782-1798 Served in South Carolina state legislature.

1798-1800 Governor of South Carolina.

1800 (Jan. 23) Died in Charleston, S. C.

lent agitator for liberty in the colony:

"I long to tell you what we have done, but am prevented, from silence having been imposed upon us all, by consent, the first week in congress. This, however, I may say, that the province will not be able to account for our conduct until we explain it, though it is justifiable upon the strictest principles of honour and policy. Don't be alarmed; we have done no mischief, though I am sure, if, Mr. ———— had had his way, we should. But you may thank your stars you sent prudent men; and I trust that the youngest is not the least so. The gentleman to whom you have alluded is, if possible, worse than ever; more violent, more wrong-headed. But I do not mean to censure others; sufficient for me if I pursue a right line, and meet with the approbation of my countrymen."

A change of heart

Both Edward and John Rutledge were again elected as delegates to the second Continental Congress in 1775; but John left Edward to represent his interests in Philadelphia while he returned to South Carolina, wrote a state constitution, and was elected president of the state. When Richard Henry Lee of Virginia presented his resolutions for independence to the Congress on June 7, 1776, Edward Rutledge was undecided how South Carolina should vote upon the matter, so at his behest a decision on independence was postponed until July 1. Meeting in committee of the whole on July 1, Rutledge and the other South Carolinians voted against independence; but the next day Rutledge changed his mind and voted for Lee's independence resolutions. On July 4 he voted in favor of the Declaration of Independence, and he signed it with the other delegates on August 2. In a letter to his brother John written on July 9, Edward mentioned what had happened in the following offhand manner: "Enclosed also is a very important Declaration which the King of Great Britain has at last reduced us to the necessity of making . . . All the colonies . . . were united . . ."

Wily Ben Franklin

In August, 1776, Rutledge was appointed by Congress along with John Adams and Benjamin Franklin to meet with the British commander Lord Howe in New York at his request to discuss the possibility of a peace settlement. The negotiations were fruitless, but in later years Rutledge enjoyed telling an anecdote about Franklin that occurred at the time. According to the story, Franklin offered the British sailors who took them back from Howe's headquarters a handful of gold and silver coins for their trouble, but the officer in charge would not let the soldiers accept it. When Rutledge later asked Franklin why he had done this, the witty old statesman replied, "As these people are under the impression that we have not a farthing of hard money in the country, I thought I would convince them of their mistake: I knew, at the same time, that I risked nothing by an offer which their regulations and discipline would not permit them to accept."

A prisoner of war

Rutledge returned to South Carolina in 1777 and became a captain in an artillery battalion. He was taken prisoner by the British in the siege of Charleston in 1780, and was sent to St. Augustine, Fla., where "dangerous" rebels were held. After about a year in the prison, he was taken to Philadelphia and freed in an exchange of prisoners.

After his return to South Carolina, he was elected to the state legislature in 1782 and every year thereafter for the next sixteen years. He became a law partner of Thomas Pinckney, who served as governor in 1787 to 1788, and his fortune prospered. In 1798, he retired from his law practice. That same year, he was elected governor of South Carolina as a Federalist.

Rich. Lord Viscount H

In the last years of his life, Rutledge had become quite fat because of his love of good food and wine. He also was afflicted by gout to such an extent that he could walk only with the use of a cane. On January 23, 1800, while still serving as governor, Rutledge died in Charleston at the age of fifty.

ROGER SHERMAN of CONNECTICUT

Described by John Adams as "one of the most sensible men in the world" and by Thomas Jefferson as "a man who never said a foolish thing in his life," Roger Sherman won the unusual distinction of being the only one of the Founding Fathers to help prepare and sign four of the most important documents of the Revolutionary Era: the Articles of Association in 1774, the Declaration of Independence in 1776, the Articles of Confederation in 1778, and the United States Constitution in 1787.

A plain-spoken, plain-dressing Puritan, Sherman began his adult life as a hard-working cobbler. He taught himself law, and then served as a judge, Connecticut legislator, representative in Congress, and finally as a United States Senator. A modest man, he was not given to flights of oratory in the legislative halls, but when he spoke his words were listened to because of his reputation for common sense. Adams wrote of him:

"The honourable Roger Sherman was one of the most cordial friends which I ever had in my life. Destitute of all literary and scientific education but

---

ROGER SHERMAN

1721 (April 19) Born in Newton, Mass.

1743 Moved to New Milford, Conn., where he worked as a cobbler.

1745 Appointed county surveyor.

1754 Admitted to the bar to practice law.

1755-1761 Member of the Connecticut legislature.

1759-1761 Judge of the court of common pleas of Litchfield County.

1765 Judge of the court of common pleas of New Haven County.

1766-1785 Member of the governor's council of Connecticut.

1766-1789 Judge of the superior court of Connecticut.

1766-1776 Treasurer of Yale College.

1774-1781 Delegate from Connecticut to the Continental Congress; signed the Declaration of Independence and the Articles of Confederation.

1781-1789 Delegate from Connecticut to the Congress of the Confederation.

1784-1793 Mayor of New Haven, Conn.

1787 Member of the Constitutional Convention; signed the United States Constitution.

1789-1791 Representative from Connecticut in the United States Congress.

1791-1793 U. S. Senator from Connecticut.

1793 (July 23) Died in New Haven, Conn.

---

such as he acquired by his own exertions, he was one of the most sensible men in the world. The clearest head and the steadiest heart. It is praise enough to say, that the late Chief Justice (Oliver) Ellsworth told me that he had made Mr. Sherman his model in his youth. Mr. Sherman . . . was one of the soundest and strongest pillars of the revolution."

Roger Sherman was born in Newton, Mass., on April 19, 1721. His father, William Sherman, was a small farmer and shoemaker whose ancestors had come to America in 1634. Young Roger received little more education than being taught how to read and write, but his father also taught him the trade of making shoes.

Walked a hundred miles with his cobbler's tools

When his father died in 1741, Sherman was 19 years old, and the responsibility of caring for his younger brothers and sisters fell to him. He worked at his trade as a cobbler in Newton for about two years; and then in 1743 he decided to move the family to New Milford, Conn., where his older brother was working. The story is told that Sherman walked the entire distance of more than a hundred miles to New Milford, carrying a bag of shoemaker's tools on his back.

Sherman was ambitious and he enjoyed reading, so it is not hard to imagine him working at his cobbler's bench in New Milford with a book propped up before him. He was particularly interested in mathematics. His knowledge led him to receive an appointment as surveyor for Litchfield County in 1745, a position that supplemented his regular income with welcome cash that was needed to help pay for the education of his younger brothers, who later became clergymen. Sherman carried his own mathematical education further than most colonial surveyors, for he also learned to make astronomical observations that he submitted to an almanac that was published in New York in 1748.

In 1749, when Sherman was twenty-eight, he married Elizabeth Hartwell of Stoughton, Mass. They had seven children before she died in 1760. Sherman later married a second time—Rebecca Prescott of Danvers, Mass. By his second marriage he had eight children.

ROGER SHERMAN
by RALPH EARL, gift of ROGER SHERMAN WHITE

As a surveyor, Sherman was thrown into contact with various landholders who were involved in disputes with each other; and, since many of these disputes ended in a court of law, it was natural that Sherman became interested in learning more about the law. Before long he was able to draw up legal papers that were as good as those prepared by practicing lawyers, and at the age of thirty-three, in 1754, Sherman was admitted to the bar to practice law.

In 1755, Sherman began his long political career in which he was to serve Connecticut and his country for the rest of his life. That year he was appointed as a local justice of the peace, and he also was elected to the lower house of the Connecticut legislature. In 1759 he received an appointment as judge of the court of common pleas of Litchfield County, a position that he held for two years.

The death of his first wife, and a belief that he would be able to obtain a larger law practice in a bigger town led Sherman to move his family to New Haven, Conn., in 1761, when he was forty years old. He again was appointed as justice of the peace, and soon was elected to represent New Haven in the colonial legislature. In 1765, he was appointed judge of the court of common pleas for New Haven County.

Gained three important offices

At the age of forty-five, in 1766, Sherman won three important offices that he held simultaneously for many years. He was elected as a member of the governor's council, the upper house of the Connecticut legislature, an office that he held for nineteen years, until 1785. He was appointed judge of the superior court of Connecticut, a position in which he served for the next twenty-three years. And he was appointed treasurer of Yale College, an office that he continued in until the Revolutionary War.

As the disputes with Great Britain over taxation drew toward a climax in the 1770's, Sherman took a firm stand in support of colonial rights. When the first Continental Congress convened in Philadelphia in 1774, Sherman was sent as one of Connecticut's four delegates. John Adams, who met Sherman at this time, recorded his impressions of the Connecticut delegate in his diary: "He is between fifty and sixty, a solid, sensible man. He said he read Mr. Otis' 'Rights,' etc., in 1764, and

thought he had conceded away the rights of America. He thought the reverse of the Declaratory Act was true, namely, that the Parliament of Great Britain had authority to make laws for America in no case whatever." With views such as this, Sherman naturally approved and signed the first Continental Congress's Articles of Association that called for the boycott of the exportation or importation of trade with Great Britain.

Connected with ordnance, treasury, and navy committees

Sherman served almost continuously in Congress for the rest of his life, being absent from that body only when he was ineligible to serve because of Connecticut's laws that required rotation of office. The respect held for his judgment was evidenced by the important committees on which he served, including the board of war and ordnance that directed the war effort, the maritime committee that was concerned with building a navy, and the board of treasury to raise money for the war.

As a leading advocate of independence from Great Britain, it was logical that in June, 1776, Sherman was appointed to the committee to draft the Declaration of Independence. Jefferson later recalled this of his association with Sherman: "I served with him in the old congress in the years 1775 and 1776: he was a very able and logical debater in that body, steady in the principles of the revolution, always at the post of duty, much employed in the business of committees, and, particularly, was of the committee of Dr. Franklin, Mr. J. Adams, Mr. Livingston, and myself, for preparing the Declaration of Independence. Being much my senior in years, our intercourse was chiefly in the line of our duties. I had great respect for him." Although there is no direct evidence of specific changes that Sherman introduced in the writing of the famous document, it can be assumed that his common sense helped formulate some of its passages. He voted for the Declaration of Independence on July 4, and signed it with most of the other delegates on August 2, 1776.

In 1776, Sherman also was a member of John Dickinson's committee that drafted the Articles of Confederation. After Dickinson left the Congress, Sherman helped push the Articles of Confederation through to conclusion. He signed this document as a delegate from Connecticut in 1778, although this constitution did not go into effect until Maryland's ratification in 1781.

FORTIFYING BREED'S HILL IN THE NIGHT JUNE 16. 1775.

Vol.I. p. 467

(From the original drawing in the possession of the publishers)

Throughout the Revolutionary War, Sherman divided his time between serving in Congress, sitting on the superior court bench of Connecticut, serving in the upper house of the Connecticut legislature, and sitting as a member of the governor's committee of safety. In 1783, Sherman and a fellow superior court judge, Richard Law, were chosen by the legislature to revise the statutes of Connecticut into a simplified code of laws. The next year, in 1784, the citizens of New Haven honored Sherman by electing him their mayor, and continued him in that office for the rest of his life.

The "Connecticut Compromise"

When the national government was in the process of breaking down because of the weaknesses of the Articles of Confederation, Sherman was chosen in 1787, at the age of sixty-six, as one of Connecticut's delegates to the Constitutional Convention in Philadelphia. Sherman was a particularly active and important member of the convention, and his name has become best known for the "Connecticut Compromise" that included a series of proposals to reconcile the differences between the large and small states on the provisions for representation in Congress. Sherman, who rarely made long speeches, discussed at length on June

20, 1787, his feelings about the discord in the convention; as reported by James Madison:

"He admitted two branches to be necessary in the State Legislatures, but saw no necessity in a confederacy of States. The examples were all of a single council. Congress carried us through the war, and perhaps as well as any government could have done. The complaints at present are, not that the views of Congress are unwise or unfaithful, but that their powers are insufficient for the execution of their views. The national debt, and the want of power somewhere to draw forth the national resources, are the great matters that press. All the States were sensible of the defect of power in Congress. He thought much might be said in apology for the failure of the State Legislatures, to comply with the Confederation. They were afraid of leaning too hard on the people by accumulating taxes; no *constitutional* rule had been, or could be observed in the quotas; the accounts also were unsettled, and every State supposed itself in advance, rather than in arrears. For want of a general system, taxes to a due amount had not been drawn from trade, which was the most convenient resource. As almost all the States had agreed to the recommendation of Congress on the subject of an impost, it appeared clearly that they were willing to trust Congress with power to draw a revenue from trade. There is no weight, therefore, in the argument drawn from a distrust of Congress; for money matters being the most important of all, if the people will trust them with power as to them, they will trust them with any other necessary powers. Congress, indeed, by the Confederation, have in fact the right of saying how much the people shall pay, and to what purpose it shall be applied; and this right was granted to them in the expectation that it would in all cases have its effect. If another branch were to be added to Congress, to be chosen by the people, it would serve to embarrass. The people would not much interest themselves in the elections, a few designing men in the large districts would carry their points; and the people would have no more confidence in their new representatives than in Congress.

Individual distinctions of states important to happiness

He saw no reason why the State Legislatures should be unfriendly, as had been suggested, to Congress. If they appoint Congress, and approve of their measures, they would be rather favourable and partial to them. The disparity of the States in point of size he perceived was the main difficulty. But the large States had not yet suffered from the equality of votes enjoyed by the smaller ones. In all great and general points, the interests of all the States were the same. The State of Virginia, notwithstanding the equality of votes, ratified the Confederation without even proposing any alteration. Massachusetts also ratified without any material difficulty, &c. In none of the ratifications is the want of two branches notices or complained of. To consolidate the States, as some have proposed, would dissolve our treaties with foreign nations, which had been formed with us, as *confederated* States. He did not, however, suppose that the creation of two branches in the Legislature would have such an effect. If the difficulty on the subject of representation cannot be otherwise got over, he would agree to have two branches, and a proportional representation in one of them, provided each State had an equal voice in the other. This was necessary to secure the rights of the lesser States; otherwise three or four of the large States would rule the others as they please. Each State, like each individual, had its peculiar habits, usages, and manners, which constituted its happiness. It would not, therefore, give to others a power over this

happiness, any more than an individual would do, when he could avoid it."

A spirit of compromise

Sherman personalized the spirit of compromise of the convention, for he gave up many of the things that he believed would make a sound government in order to achieve agreement. He believed that the people should not vote directly for members of Congress, and he believed that the President should be elected by Congress; but, even though the final draft of the United States Constitution did not agree with these ideas, he signed it with most of the other delegates on September 17, 1787.

Sherman supported the Constitution with a series of essays published in newspapers over the signature "A Citizen." He then attended the state ratification convention along with the other two Connecticut delegates to the Constitutional Convention, Samuel Johnson and Oliver Ellsworth. The newspaper *Connecticut Courant* reported the effect of their speeches to the ratification convention: "All the objections to the Constitution vanished before the learning and eloquence of a Johnson, the genuine good sense and discernment of

Trinity Church
(New York)

207

a Sherman, and the Demosthenean energy of an Ellsworth."

Advocate of states rights

In 1789, Sherman was elected by Connecticut to the new United States House of Representatives. At the age of sixty-eight, Sherman was the oldest man in the new Congress. Sherman now took a leading role in the preparation of the Bill of Rights amendments to the Constitution. His views on the matter were published widely throughout the colonies in an essay signed "A Citizen of New Haven" in which he said in part:

"The immediate security of the civil and domestic rights of the people will be in the government of the particular states. And as the different states have different local interests and customs, which can be best regulated by their own laws, it would not be expedient to admit the federal government to interfere with them, any further than is necessary for the good of the whole . . .

Experience will test the Constitution

"On the whole, will it not be best to make a fair trial of the Constitution, before any attempts are made to alter it? It is now become the only frame of government for the United States, and must be supported and conformed to, or they will have no government at all as confederated states. Experience will best shew whether it is deficient or not; on trial it may appear that the alterations proposed are not necessary, or that others not yet thought of may be necessary. Every thing that tends to disunion, ought to be carefully avoided. Instability in government and laws, tends to weaken a state,

and render the rights of the people precarious. The Constitution which is the foundation of law and government ought not to be changed without the most pressing necessity. When experience has convinced the people in general, that alterations are necessary, they may be easily made, but attempting it at present may be detrimental, if not fatal to the union of the states, and to their credit with foreign nations."

After Madison proposed the Bill of Rights amendments in Congress and suggested that they be incorporated in the body of the Constitution, Sherman, as a member of the congressional committee to study the amendments, objected to rewriting sections of the Constitution to incorporate the amendments by saying, "We might as well endeavor to mix brass, iron, and clay, as to incorporate such heterogeneous articles; the one contradictory to the other . . . it is questionable whether we have the right to propose amendments in this way. The constitution is the act of the people, and ought to remain entire. But the amendments will be the act of the State Governments." Sherman then recommended the procedure of adopting the proposals as amendments when they had been ratified by three-fourths of the state legislatures. Sherman also was a member of the joint House-Senate conference committee that drew up the final version of the Bill of Rights amendments.

When Samuel Johnson resigned as United States Senator in 1791, the Connecticut legislature elected Sherman to fill the vacancy. He continued to serve as a Senator until his death at the age of seventy-two on July 23, 1793, in New Haven, Connecticut.

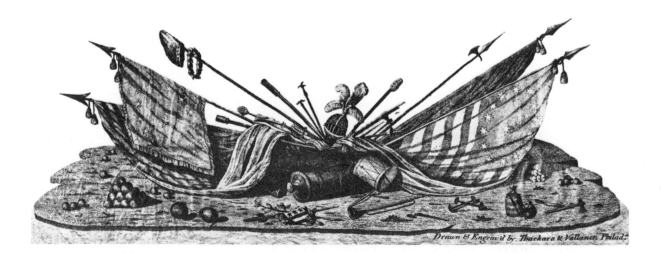

Drawn Engraved & Published by W. Birch & Son.

Sold by R. Campbell &Cᵒ. Nᵒ. 30. Chesnut Street Philadᵃ. 1799.

South East CORNER of THIRD, and MARKET Streets
PHILADELPHIA

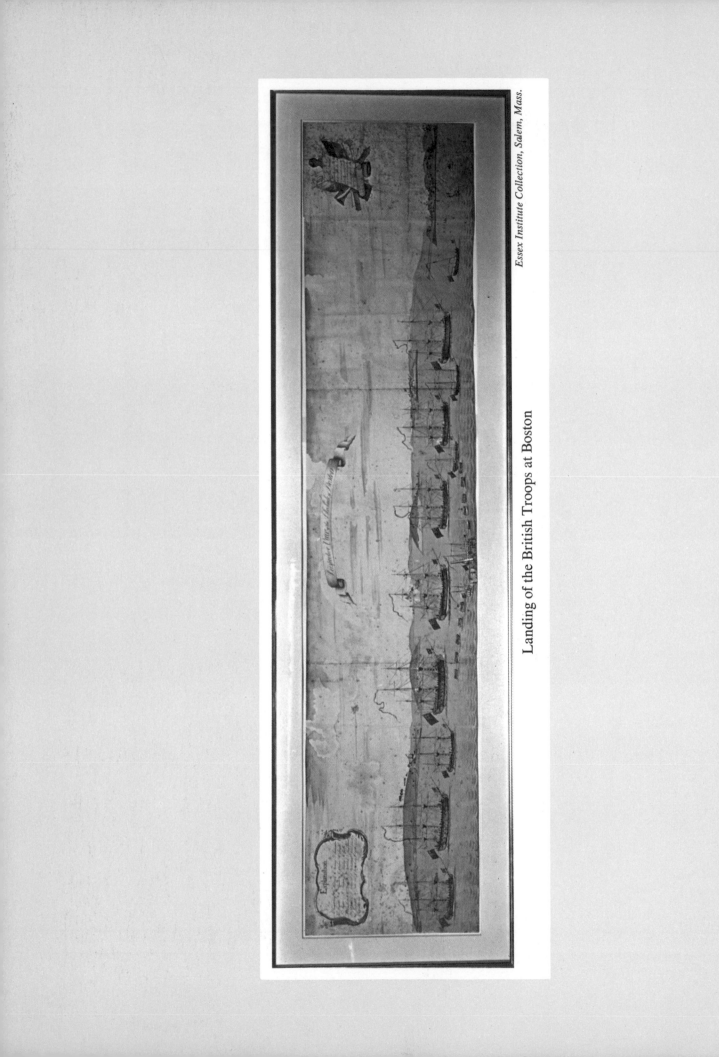

Landing of the British Troops at Boston

JAMES SMITH of PENNSYLVANIA

Irish-born James Smith was an enthusiastic patriot long before most of his fellow-Pennsylvanians. He raised the first company of volunteer soldiers to defend the colony against the British. He served in the Continental Congress as a replacement for one of the Pennsylvania delegates who refused to vote for the Declaration of Independence, and Smith signed the Declaration. He was a lawyer, an ironworks owner, and a humorist who like to tell racy jokes; but relatively little is known about him because a fire destroyed the papers in his office shortly before his death.

The exact year that James Smith was born in northern Ireland is not known, because he kept the date of his birth a closely guarded secret; however, it is believed he was born about the year 1719. His parents brought him to America when he was about ten years old, and the family settled on a farm in York County.

Smith attended the College of Philadelphia (now the University of Pennsylvania), and then took up the study of law. About this time he also learned surveying. After completing his education, Smith settled in Cumberland County where he combined the careers of lawyer and surveyor. He later moved to York, Pa., where he was the only lawyer in town. He married Eleanor Armor of New Castle, Delaware, and they had three sons and two daughters.

JAMES SMITH

c.1719 Born in northern Ireland.

1729 Came to America with his parents.

1774 Delegate to convention of patriots in Philadelphia.

1774 Raised the first company of volunteer soldiers in Pennsylvania for defense against the British.

1775-1776 Member of the Pennsylvania patriotic conferences; helped write a declaration calling for the independence of Pennsylvania.

1776 Member of the Pennsylvania state constitutional convention.

1776-1778 Delegate to the Continental Congress; signed the Declaration of Independence.

1780 Member of the Pennsylvania state legislature.

1781 Judge of the Pennsylvania high court of errors and appeals.

1782 Appointed brigadier general of Pennsylvania volunteers.

1806 (July 11) Died in York, Pa.

In 1774, a convention of citizens was called in Philadelphia to study what might be done to aid the people of Boston who were suffering under the Coercive Acts of the British parliament, and Smith was selected as one of the delegates from York to attend the meeting. The majority at the convention were not war-like, and the resolutions they adopted were mild and conciliatory.

Raised the first company of voluteers

Smith, however, apparently was not convinced of the likelihood of peace, for when he returned home to York he set about raising the first company of volunteers to prepare for the defense of Pennsylvania. He was elected captain of the company. When enough volunteers had joined his militia company to make it a regiment, Smith was elected colonel.

Again in 1775 and 1776, Smith served as a delegate to Pennsylvania patriotic conventions held in Philadelphia. In June, 1776, the majority of Pennsylvania's delegates to the Continental Congress opposed the resolution for independence introduced by Richard Henry Lee. As guidance to the delegates in Congress, the Pennsylvania patriotic convention of which Smith was a member adopted a resolution calling for independence for

The R. W. Norton Art Gallery, Shreveport, Louisiana
Photography by Menasco Studio, Shreveport
James Smith Miniature by Jeremiah Theus

Pennsylvania. Smith was a member of the committee that drafted this independence resolution, along with Benjamin Rush and Thomas McKean.

In July, 1776, a convention was called to draft a state constitution for Pennsylvania, and Smith was elected as a delegate from York. On July 20, Smith was elected as a delegate to the Continental Congress to replace one of the Pennsylvanians who had opposed the Declaration of Independence. Although Smith had not had an opportunity to vote for the Declaration, he signed the engrossed copy on August 2 along with most of the other delegates. Smith continued to serve in Congress until 1778, although he withdrew for several months in 1777 in order to put his private affairs in order in York.

Became brigadier general

After retiring from Congress in 1778, Smith remained out of public office for a year, and then accepted election for a single term in the Pennsylvania state assembly in 1780. The following year he was appointed briefly a judge of the Pennsylvania high court of errors and appeals. In 1782, he received an appointment as brigadier general in the Pennsylvania militia.

In his old age, Smith continued to practice law and took an active interest in state and national politics as a member of the Federalist party, but he served only in local public service in York. An early biographer described him during this period as "social, jocular, and friendly . . . the life of all conviviality . . . with a store of rich and diverting anecdote that was inexhaustible and unequalled." A fire in his office in 1805 destroyed his valuable collection of letters from Benjamin Franklin, Samuel Adams, and others. On July 11, 1806, Smith died at his home in York, and his body was buried in the cemetery of the Presbyterian church. His gravestone marked his age at death as ninety-two, but it is believed he was closer to eighty-seven.

Library of Congress

Courthouse, York, Pennsylvania
Old print from Magazine of American history
Photo by Arthur E. Scott

RICHARD STOCKTON of NEW JERSEY

The first signer of the Declaration of Independence to be captured by the British, Richard Stockton received unusually cruel punishment by the British that hastened his death before the end of the Revolutionary War. As one of the first graduates of the College of New Jersey (now Princeton University), Stockton became a trustee and loyal alumnus, and, in that capacity, persuaded John Witherspoon to come to America from Scotland to become president of the college—an event that resulted in Witherspoon's becoming one of the Founding Fathers of the United States.

Richard Stockton was born at his family's estate near Princeton, N. J., on October 1, 1730. He was the eldest son of John Stockton, a wealthy landowner. As a boy he was sent to a private school in West Nottingham, Md. When he was seventeen years of age he entered the College of New Jersey, at that time located at Newark, N. J., with Aaron Burr, Sr., as president of the college. In 1748, Stockton was a member of the first class to graduate from the college.

Next, Stockton undertook the study of the law under the guidance of David Ogden of Newark, N. J., who was considered the leading lawyer of New Jersey. One of his fellow students was Elias Boudinot, who later was President of the Congress of the Confederation and signed the peace treaty

---

RICHARD STOCKTON

1730 (Oct. 1) Born at his family's estate near Princeton, N. J.

1748 Graduated from College of New Jersey (now Princeton University).

1754 Admitted to the bar to practice law in New Jersey.

1766-1767 Visited England, Scotland, and Ireland; convinced John Witherspoon he should come to America to become president of the College of New Jersey.

1768-1774 Member of the executive council of New Jersey.

1774-1776 Associate justice of the supreme court of New Jersey.

1776 Delegate to the Continental Congress; signed the Declaration of Independence.

1776-1777 Captured and imprisoned by the British in New York City.

1781 (Feb. 28) Died at his estate near Princeton, N. J.

---

of 1783 between the United States and Great Britain. Stockton and Boudinot became brothers-in-law when Stockton married his friend's sister, Annis Boudinot, and later Boudinot married Stockton's own sister. Stockton and his wife had six children. One of their daughters, Julia, married Benjamin Rush, a signer of the Declaration of Independence.

At the age of twenty-three, Stockton was admitted to the bar to practice law in New Jersey. A tall, dignified man, Stockton soon built a large law practice that increased his fortune. He enjoyed sports, being an excellent horseman and swordsman. He and his wife entertained in a lavish style at his large mansion.

Persuaded John Witherspoon to come to America

As a trustee of the College of New Jersey, Stockton set off for the British Isles in 1766 to interview possible candidates for a new president for the college. In 1767, he persuaded John Witherspoon, a Scottish Presbyterian minister, to accept the position. In this project Stockton was aided by Benjamin Rush, then a medical student at the University of Edinburgh.

After returning to America, Stockton was appointed in 1768 as a member of the governor's executive council. There, he served under William Franklin, who was the natural son of Benjamin Franklin and the royal governor of New Jersey. Most of the members of the council were very conservative and unswervingly loyal to the king; so, when Stockton became convinced there could be no reconciliation between the colonies and the British government, he withdrew from the council. Stockton was appointed as an associate justice of the supreme court of New Jersey in 1774.

William Franklin, son of Ben Franklin, imprisoned

In June, 1776, the provincial congress of New Jersey arrested Governor Franklin and imprisoned him. Shortly afterward, they elected a new delegation to the Continental Congress who would express a more patriotic view—Stockton and Witherspoon both were elected as members of this delegation.

Richard Stockton
by John Wollaston

Princeton University

Mrs. Richard Stockton
attributed to Copley, Benbridge, or Blackburn

The Art Museum of
Princeton University

Stockton and the other New Jersey delegates arrived in Philadelphia in time to hear the debate between John Adams and John Dickinson on July 1, 1776, which was concerned with whether the Congress should adopt the independence resolutions offered by Richard Henry Lee of Virginia. In these debates, Stockton called Adams "the Atlas of American Independence." Stockton voted for the Declaration of Independence on July 4, and signed his name to it with the other delegates on August 2.

At the first meeting of the state legislature under the new state constitution, in August, 1776, Stockton and William Livingston were the two main candidates for governor, and they each received the same number of votes on the first ballot. However, Stockton's friends were persuaded to agree to the election of Livingston as governor, and in turn Stockton was unanimously elected chief justice of the state. However, when informed of the election, Stockton declined to serve.

In September and October of 1776, Stockton and George Clymer were appointed by the Continental Congress to a committee to inspect the northern Continental Army. This tour carried them through upper New York State, and upon their return they were able to report to Congress on ways that the northern army could be strengthened.

Jailed by the British

With the invasion of New Jersey by British troops, Stockton returned to Princeton and removed his family to safety. However, on November 30, 1776, a traitor led British troops to his hiding place where he was dragged out of bed in the middle of the night and carried off to jail in Amboy, N. J. He later was taken on to New York City and thrown into jail as a common criminal.

As soon as the Continental Congress heard of the treatment he had been given, the following resolution was passed: "Whereas congress hath received information that the honourable Richard Stockton, of New Jersey, and a member of this congress, hath been made a prisoner by the enemy, and that he hath been ignominiously thrown into a common jail, and there detained: Resolved, that General Washington be directed to make immediate inquiry into the truth of this report, and if he finds reason to believe it well founded, that he send a flag to General Howe remonstrating against this departure from that humane procedure which has marked the conduct of these states to prisoners who have fallen into their hands; and to know of General Howe whether he chooses this shall be

212

The Stockton Mansion, New Jersey.

the future rule for treating all such, on both sides, as the fortune of war may place in the hands of either party."

"The fear of God is the beginning of wisdom"

By the time Stockton's release was obtained in an exchange of prisoners, his health had been seriously impaired by the brutal treatment he had received. He returned to his estate to find that the British had burned his library and private papers, had stolen his livestock, and had plundered his property. On top of all these discouragements, Stockton was stricken with cancer. He died in pain at his home near Princeton at the age of fifty, on February 28, 1781. In his will, he set forth his faith that had sustained his life:

"As my children will have frequent occasion of perusing this instrument, and may probably be particularly impressed with the last words of their father, I think it proper here, not only to subscribe to the entire belief of the great and leading doctrines of the Christian religion, such as the being of a God, and the universal defection and depravity of human nature, the divinity of the *Person,* and the completeness of the redemption purchased by the Blessed Saviour; the necessity of the operations of the divine spirit, of divine faith accompanied with an habitual virtuous life, and the universality of the divine providence; but also, in the bowels of a father's affection, to charge and exhort them to remember that 'the fear of God is the beginning of wisdom.'"

213

THOMAS STONE of MARYLAND

A tall, thin, pale lawyer, Thomas Stone signed the Declaration of Independence and was on the committee of the Continental Congress that wrote the Articles of Confederation. He declined to serve in the Constitutional Convention because of the critical illness of his wife, and after her demise, he grieved to death in four months.

Thomas Stone was born in 1743 at his family's plantation in Charles County, Maryland. His father was David Stone, a wealthy landowner. The family was descended from William Stone who had served as governor of Maryland from 1648 to 1655, but was overthrown by a revolt of Puritans. As a boy, Thomas Stone rode twenty miles on horseback to and from school each day, and by the time he was in his early teens he had obtained a sound education in the Latin and Greek languages.

The older brother inherited the family estate

At his father's death, the law of primogeniture awarded the family estate to an older brother, Samuel; and Thomas was left only his good name and a thirst for learning. He borrowed enough money to go to Annapolis, Md., where he began the study of law under an attorney by the name of Thomas Johnson. At the age of twenty-one, Stone was admitted to the bar, and began practicing law in Frederick, Md. Two years later, in 1766, he returned to Charles County and continued the practice of law there.

In 1771, Stone married eighteen-year-old Margaret Brown of Charles County, who brought him a thousand pound dowry. The young couple were extremely devoted to each other and soon had a family of three children. They settled on a farm near Port Tobacco, Md., which he called Habre-de-Venture.

Stone was elected by the provincial congress of Maryland as a member of the second Continental Congress of 1775, where he continued to serve until 1777. At the age of thirty-three, he was the youngest member of the Maryland delegation to vote for the Declaration of Independence and sign it in 1776. Stone served on many important committees in Congress, particularly on that which drew up the Articles of Confederation.

Upon his retirement from Congress, Stone was elected as a member of the Maryland state senate, and served in that body until his death. A fellow-member in the Maryland state senate described Stone as follows:

A talented writer

"He was most truly a perfect man of business; he would often take the pen and commit to paper, all the necessary writings of the senate, and this he would do cheerfully while the other members were amusing themselves with desultory conversation; he appeared to be naturally of an irritable temper, still he was mild and courteous in his gen-

The Baltimore Museum of Art

The Hon. Thomas Stone
by ROBERT EDGE PINE

THOMAS STONE

1743 Born in Charles County, Maryland.

1764 Admitted to the bar to practice law in Maryland.

1775-1777 Represented Maryland in the Continental Congress; signed the Declaration of Independence.

1777-1787 Member of the Maryland state senate.

1783-1784 Delegate to the Congress of the Confederation; acting president of the Congress for several days.

1787 (Oct. 5) Died in Alexandria, Va.

eral deportment, fond of society and conversation, and universally a favourite from his great good humour and intelligence; he thought and wrote much as a professional man, and as a statesman, on the business before him in those characters; he had no leisure for other subjects; not that he was unequal to the task, for there were few men who could commit their thoughts to paper with more facility or greater strength of argument. There was a severe trial of skill between the senate and the house of delegates, on the subject of confiscating British property. The senate for several sessions unanimously rejected bills passed by the house of delegates for that purpose; many, very long and tart, were the messages from one to the other body, on this subject; the whole of which, were on the part of the senate, the work of Mr. Stone, and his close friend and equal in all respects, the venerable Charles Carroll of Carrollton."

Stone was elected to the Congress of Confederation in 1783, while it was meeting in Annapolis. During this session, he was elected acting president of the Congress for a short period toward the end; but he declined re-election to the Congress in 1784.

Left his estate to his eldest son

During the next several years, Stone devoted himself to continued service in the state senate and to his legal practice which he had moved to Annapolis. In the senate, he wrote and introduced a bill which abolished the right of primogeniture, which had deprived him of any part of his father's estate; but, interestingly enough, when he wrote his own will, he followed primogeniture, leaving his estate to his eldest son.

Although he was elected as a delegate to the Constitutional Convention, he refused to serve because of the critical illness of his wife. In 1776, while visiting him in Philadelphia, she had been inoculated for smallpox because several cases had been discovered in the capital. At that time, the practice of inoculation was a risky procedure, and Mrs. Stone had become quite ill, remaining an invalid since that time. In June, 1787, she died at the age of thirty-four. Grief-stricken, Stone retired to his farm in Charles County.

After several melancholy months, Stone accepted the advice of his physicians that he should take a trip abroad to recover his spirits. In preparation for the voyage, he went to Alexandria, Va.; but, while awaiting the sailing of a ship at that port, he died suddenly at the age of forty-four, on October 5, 1787. His body was returned to his farm Habre-de-Venture for burial.

Habre de Venture home of Thomas Stone *photo by* RODNEY McCOY MORGAN

GEORGE TAYLOR of PENNSYLVANIA

An Irish immigrant who came to America as a bound servant, George Taylor won his place in history by signing the Declaration of Independence even though he had not had the opportunity of voting for it. Illness forced Taylor to retire from public affairs, and he died before the Revolutionary War was won.

George Taylor was born in Ireland in 1716, and is believed to have been the son of a clergyman. Taylor is believed to have begun the study of medicine before deciding to seek his fortune in America.

When he was about twenty, Taylor took passage on a ship sailing to the colonies. Because he had no money, he agreed to become a bound servant to pay for his passage. When he arrived in Philadelphia, an ironmaker by the name of Savage bought his services and put him to work at his mill in Durham, Pa., a village near Easton, Pa. His first job was shoveling coal into the furnaces, but he was not strong enough for this rough work and soon was made a clerk to handle the accounts.

Married the widow of his master

After the death of his master, Taylor married the widow, Mrs. Anne Taylor Savage, and thus became owner of the ironworks. By hard work and good fortune, he increased the size of the business, and soon built a large home in nearby Northampton, Pa.

Elected to the colonial legislature of Pennsylvania from 1765 to 1770, Taylor took part in the debates over the British Stamp Act of 1765 and the efforts of the legislature to have the British parliament end the powers of the proprietary government in Pennsylvania. He served on the legislative committee that drew up an address to the king thanking him for the repeal of the Stamp Act.

In the years immediately preceding the Revolutionary War, Taylor kept busy improving the business of his ironworks and serving as a county judge. Then, when word of the fighting in Massachusetts reached Pennsylvania, Taylor threw himself into preparations for the defense of the colony. He was elected a colonel in his county's militia. In October, 1775, he was elected to the colonial legislature, and then to the provincial congress where he became one of the group of patriots who believed that independence should be declared as soon as possible.

Signed the Declaration though not present to vote

In 1776, only three out of the eight members of the Pennsylvania delegation to the Continental Congress voted in favor of the Declaration of Independence, and so on July 20, the provincial legislature decided to replace the five delegates who had opposed independence. Because of his patriotism, Taylor became one of the new Pennsylvania delegates to the Continental Congress. Although he had not been present on July 4 to vote for it, Taylor signed the Declaration of Independence on August 2.

The legislature elected Taylor in 1777 as a member of Pennsylvania's first Supreme Executive Council, the chief executive body of the state under its new constitution. He served only a short while, as illness forced him to resign.

Taylor spent his last years in sickness and loneliness. His wife and their only child had died before the beginning of the war. He moved to Easton, Pa., to be closer to his ironworks where he devoted himself as much to his business as his health would allow. Finally, at the age of about sixty-five, Taylor died at his home in Easton on February 23, 1781.

GEORGE TAYLOR

1716 **Born in Ireland.**

1736 **Came to America as a bound servant to an iron manufacturer.**

1754 **Married his master's widow and became manager of the ironworks.**

1764-1770 **Member of the Pennsylvania colonial legislature.**

1775-1776 **Member of the Pennsylvania provincial congress.**

1776-1777 **Delegate from Pennsylvania to the Continental Congress; signed the Declaration of Independence.**

1777 **Member of Pennsylvania's first Supreme Executive Council.**

1781 **(Feb. 23) Died in Easton, Pa.**

MATTHEW THORNTON of NEW HAMPSHIRE

A dark-eyed Irishman, Matthew Thornton signed the Declaration of Independence, although he did not become a member of the Continental Congress until four months after independence had been declared. Like his fellow-signer from New Hampshire, Josiah Bartlett, Thornton was a physician. Thirty years before the Revolutionary War he had served as a military surgeon with British colonial troops that attacked French forces in Nova Scotia.

A noted storyteller

He was noted as a wit who particularly enjoyed puns, satires, and humorous fables. An early biographer said of him: "He exhibited the very essence of hilarity and humour, in the infinite variety of his stories, and his mode of narrative, which was particularly inviting. In this rational pastime, he never descended to vulgarity, but afforded general amusement, while he instructed the minds, and improved the morals, of his hearers: like the great Franklin, whom he, in many traits of character, resembled, he illustrated his sentiments by fable; in which he displayed a peculiar and original talent. His inventive powers in exercises of this nature were quick and judiciously directed; he frequently commenced a fictitious narrative for the amusement of his auditors, and, like an Eastern storyteller, continued it for the space of an hour, supported solely by instantaneous invention. His posture, and manner of narrating, were as peculiar as the faculty itself; when he placed his elbows upon his knees, with his hands supporting his head, it was the signal for the *erectis auribus* of the assembly. Their attention became instantly arrested and irresistibly fixed upon the narrative; the curious incidents of which were evolved in the most masterly manner. Commencing with a slow articulation, and a solemn countenance, he gradually proceeded in his tale, casting, at intervals, his black and piercing eyes upon the countenance of his hearers, to detect the emotions excited in their breasts, and pausing to observe its full effects."

Matthew Thornton was born in Ireland in about the year 1714, the son of James Thornton. When he was about three or four years old, his parents immigrated to Massachusetts, bringing him with them. The Thornton family first settled in Wiscasset (now in Maine), and later moved to Worcester, Mass. After receiving a preparatory education, Thornton was sent to Leicester, Mass., where he studied medicine under a physician named Grout. When he was about twenty-six years old, he began practicing medicine in Londonderry, N. H.

In 1745, British colonial troops launched an

MATTHEW THORNTON

c.1714 Born in Ireland.

c.1718 Came to America with his parents.

1740 Began practicing medicine in Londonderry, N. H.

1745 Took part in the first Battle of Louisbourg in Nova Scotia as a surgeon with New Hampshire militia.

1775 President of the first patriotic provincial congress of New Hampshire.

1776 Speaker of the general assembly of the New Hampshire legislature.

1776-1778 Delegate to the Continental Congress; signed the Declaration of Independence.

1776-1782 Associate justice of the superior court of New Hampshire.

1785 Member of the senate of the state of New Hampshire.

1803 (June 24) Died in Newburyport, Mass.

RES. OF MATTHEW THORNTON.

VIEW OF THE OLD-HOUSE, IN DEERFIELD, WHICH ESCAPED THE CONFLAGRATION WHEN THAT TOWN WAS DESTROYED IN 1704

attack on the French in Nova Scotia, and Thornton joined the expedition as a surgeon for a unit of about five hundred New Hampshire militia. Thornton took part in the siege of the French at Louisbourg which resulted in the surrender of that fortress in June, 1745. It has been stated as proof of his medical abilities that only six members of the New Hampshire troops that were under his care died of sickness during the expedition. Thornton remained an officer in the militia, and had attained the rank of colonel by the time of the Revolutionary War.

After the Battle of Louisbourg, Thornton returned to Londonderry, N. H., where he gradually built a large and profitable medical practice. He married Hannah Jack, and they had five children.

Thornton was a member of New Hampshire's colonial legislature in the years preceding the Revolutionary War, taking part in the patriotic agitation against the various tax measures the British parliament tried to impose on the colonies. Therefore, it was natural that in 1775, after the outbreak of fighting in Massachusetts, he was elected president of the provincial congress of New Hampshire and chairman of the colony's committee of safety to raise troops and arms. He helped prepare a constitution for the state, and then in January, 1776, was elected speaker of the house of representatives of the new state legislature. Perhaps Thornton's

use of satire against his colleagues was responsible for his not having been elected as the first president of the state under the new constitution, for that office went to Meshech Weare.

In the fall of 1776, Thornton was elected by the legislature as one of New Hampshire's delegates to the Continental Congress. He took his seat in that body in November, more than four months after the Congress had voted independence; however, because his feelings of patriotism were so strong, the sixty-two-year-old Thornton obtained permission to sign his name to the Declaration of Independence on November 19, 1776.

Although Thornton continued to be re-elected to serve in the Continental Congress until 1778, he spent much of that time in New Hampshire attending to his duties as an associate justice of the superior court of the state—an office he held from 1776 to 1782. At the age of seventy-one, Thornton held his last public office, serving as a member of the president's council, or senate, of the state.

In his old age, Thornton retired to a farm he owned near Merrimack, N. H. Although he was afflicted with palsy, he continued to be active to his death, exchanging visits with his friends and relatives. At the age of eighty-nine, he died on June 24, 1803, while visiting one of his daughters in Newburyport, Mass. His body was returned to New Hampshire, and was buried at Merrimack.

GEORGE WALTON of GEORGIA

A carpenter's apprentice who taught himself to be a lawyer, George Walton became a leader of the patriotic movement in Georgia. He was the youngest of the three Georgia delegates who signed the Declaration of Independence, and after that he won the highest honors his state could bestow—serving twice as governor, as chief justice, and as U.S. Senator.

George Walton was born near Farmville, Va., in 1741. His parents were too poor to send him to school, so at an early age he was apprenticed to a carpenter. His master forced him to work from sunrise to sunset and refused to give him a candle that he might read by at night, so Walton collected wood scraps from the carpentry work and burned them in the evening while he read borrowed books.

When he was about twenty-eight-years-old, Walton moved to Savannah, Ga., and there he persuaded an attorney by the name of Henry Young to let him study in his office. Finally, in 1774, he was admitted to the bar to practice law in Georgia. Although his patron, Young, was a determined loyalist to the King of England, Walton had associated himself with various Georgians who were sympathetic to the struggle against the British being waged in Massachusetts.

Establishing a committee of correspondence

In July, 1774, Walton and three other patriots signed their names to a newspaper notice calling upon the citizens of Savannah to meet "at the Liberty Pole at Tondee's tavern" to discuss what action might be taken to support the people of Boston in their resistance to British tyranny. The only positive action decided by this meeting was the setting up of a committee of correspondence with the other colonies, of which Walton was a member.

A larger meeting of patriots was called in Savannah in January, 1775, and Walton became the secretary of this provincial congress. But, again, the people of Georgia were not sufficiently aroused to take any further action than dispatching a petition to the King of England, similar in nature to that sent by the first Continental Congress in 1774.

After St. John's Parish, Georgia, elected Lyman Hall as a delegate to the Continental Congress

---

GEORGE WALTON

1741 Born near Farmville, Va.

1774 Admitted to the bar to practice law in Georgia.

1775 President of the Georgia Committee of Safety.

1776-1781 Member of Georgia's delegation to the Congress.

1778 Captured by the British while serving as a colonel in the Georgia militia.

1779-1780 Governor of Georgia.

1783-1789 Chief Justice of Georgia.

1789-1790 Governor of Georgia.

1790-1795 Judge of the superior court of Georgia.

1795-1796 U.S. Senator from Georgia.

1799-1804 Judge of the superior court of Georgia.

1804 (Feb. 2) Died in Augusta, Ga.

Yale University Art Gallery
George Walton
by CHARLES WILLSON PEALE

Vue de la Ville de Savannah, du Camp, des Tranchées et de L'attaque Octobre 1779.

City of Savannah, October, 1779
Showing the camp, the trenches, and the attack

early in 1775, the provincial congress decided to follow suit. In July, 1775, the Georgia patriots elected a five man delegation to the Congress to represent the entire colony; and in February, 1776, Walton was elected to replace one of the delegates to Congress who had proven to be a Loyalist traitor.

On the executive committee

Walton took his place in the Continental Congress in time to vote for independence and sign his name to the Declaration of Independence. Because of his small physical build, some of the delegates believed that Walton was the youngest signer of the document, even though he was actually thirty-five years old. However, Walton won the respect of his fellow members of the Congress, most of whom were far wealthier and better educated. When Congress, fearing a British attack, left Philadelphia for Baltimore in December, 1776, Walton was appointed with George Clymer and Robert Morris as a committee to remain in Philadelphia and carry out executive functions.

Walton continued to serve in Congress until 1778, at which time he was appointed a colonel in the militia of Georgia. He took part in the battle for Savannah, was wounded in the leg, and captured by the British. After being held prisoner about nine months, he won his freedom in an exchange for a British navy captain in September, 1779.

The Georgia legislature elected Walton as governor in October, 1779, an office that he filled until he returned to Congress as a delegate in May, 1780. While Walton was governor, a forged letter over the signature of the speaker of the Georgia house of representatives was sent to Congress urging the removal of General Lachland McIntosh. McIntosh accused Walton of complicity in the affair, but Walton fortunately escaped the fate of his fellow signer of the Declaration of Independence, Button Gwinnett, who was killed in a duel with the general several years earlier. Walton served his final term in the Congress in 1780 and 1781; then, after George Washington's victory at the Battle of Yorktown, he retired to resume the practice of law.

Appointed chief justice of Georgia

In January, 1783, Walton returned to public life when the legislature appointed him as chief justice of the state. Immediately after this appointment, documentary evidence was presented to the legislature regarding the forged letter concerning General McIntosh, and the legislature passed a resolution censuring Walton for his earlier conduct as governor. At the same time, the legislature suggested that an order should be given to the state's attorney general to prepare a case against Walton if the facts warranted. Apparently, the legislature was ducking its responsibility, for, as chief justice, Walton himself would have had to issue the order to the attorney general.

Walton continued to serve as chief justice of his state until 1789, when he was elected governor again, this time on the Democratic-Republican ticket. After completing a one-year term as governor in 1790, he became a judge of the state's superior court, an office that he held almost continuously for the rest of his life. In November, 1795, he was appointed by the governor as U.S. Senator to take the place of James Jackson, who had resigned; but Walton filled this office only until February, 1796, when the legislature elected Josiah Tatnall to complete the rest of Jackson's unexpired term. On February 2, 1804, at the age of sixty-three, Walton died at his home, "Meadow Garden," in Augusta, Ga.

Vernet pinxit.

VÛE DU PORT DE SAVANAH
DANS L'AMÉRIQUE

Port of Savannah
(c. 1800)

WILLIAM WHIPPLE of NEW HAMPSHIRE

A former slave-ship captain, William Whipple signed the Declaration of Independence, and then fought in the Revolutionary War as a brigadier general of New Hampshire militia. Troubled by a heart ailment, he spent the last few years of his life as an associate justice of the superior court of his state, but he died before the United States Constitution had been written or ratified.

Whipple was born on January 14, 1730, in Kittery, then in Massachusetts, but now in Maine. After attending public school in Kittery, he went to sea as a boy and rapidly rose to become a ship's captain while still in his twenties. He sailed in the profitable West Indies trade carrying rum and slaves; and, by the time he was twenty-nine, he had saved enough money to retire from the sea.

From sea captain to merchant

In 1760, he went into business as a merchant in Portsmouth, N. H., in partnership with his brother in the firm William and Joseph Whipple. The business prospered, and he became one of the leading citizens of the town. Whipple married his cousin, Catherine Moffatt of Portsmouth. They had one child who died in infancy.

Whipple represented the town of Portsmouth in the provincial congress of patriots that met in Exeter, N. H., in 1775. There, he was elected to the provincial committee of safety that acted as the executive body to manage the government of the colony until the state constitution was adopted. In January, 1776, under the new state constitution, Whipple was elected by the state house of representatives as a member of the twelve-man executive council to act as adviser to the president of the state.

Later in 1776, Whipple was elected by the New Hampshire legislature as a member of the state's delegation to the Continental Congress. He was present during the debates concerning independence, and on August 2, 1776, he signed the Declaration of Independence. He continued as a member of Congress until 1779, serving on such committees as those on marine and business affairs where his background as a sailor and merchant were put to best use.

Participated in the Battle of Saratoga

From time to time, Whipple left Congres to take part in the military affairs of the Revolutionary War, because he had been appointed brigadier general in charge of one of New Hampshire's two

RES. OF GENᵗ Wᵐ WHIPPLE

WILLIAM WHIPPLE

1730 (Jan. 14) Born in Kittery, Me.
1775 Member of the provincial congress of New Hampshire; member of New Hampshire's committee of safety.
1776 Member of the first executive council of the state of New Hampshire.
1776-1779 Delegate to the Continental Congress; signed the Declaration of Independence.
1777-1778 Fought in the Revolutionary War as a brigadier general of the New Hampshire militia.
1780-1784 Member of the New Hampshire legislature.
1782-1784 Receiver of finances for Congress in New Hampshire.
1782 President of a court of commissioners to settle a land dispute between Connecticut and Pennsylvania.
1782-1785 Associate justice of the superior court of New Hampshire.
1785 (Nov. 28) Died in Portsmouth, N. H.

brigades of militia. Whipple and his troops took part in the Battle of Saratoga under General Horatio Gates in October, 1777. Upon the surrender of British General John Burgoyne, Gates appointed Whipple as one of the two officers to arrange the capitulation, and then he chose Whipple to escort the British prisoners to camp near Boston.

The story is told that on the way to the Battle of Saratoga Whipple had a Negro slave with him whose name was Prince, and that he told his slave that if the occasion arose he expected him to fight bravely for his country. Prince is said to have replied, "Sir, I have no inducement to fight; but if I had my liberty, I would endeavor to defend it to the last drop of my blood." At that, Whipple gave his slave his freedom on the spot.

From July to September, 1778, Whipple and his militia troops served under Major General John Sullivan in an unsuccessful effort to recapture Rhode Island from the British. During this period of military duty, Whipple is said to have narrowly missed death when a British cannonball smashed through his headquarters.

Declined the post of Commissioner of the Admiralty

In 1780, Whipple was appointed by Congress as a commissioner of the board of admiralty, but he declined the appointment, writing: "I am confident that your wishes, that I would accept the office you mentioned, are founded on the best principles, viz. the public good; though I am not altogether so clear that you would not be mistaken. No doubt some other person may be found that will fill the place much better; at least this is my sincere wish, for I have nothing more at heart than our navy. The official account of my appointment did not reach me till some time in January, although the letter was dated the 27th November; this may account for my answer's being so long delayed: indeed, I took a fortnight to consider the matter before I gave my answer, and I assure you considered it very maturely; and, in casting up the account, I found the balance so greatly against it, that I was obliged, on the principle of self-preservation, to decline."

However, that same year, Whipple accepted election to the state legislature; and two years later, in 1782, he became receiver of finances for the state of New Hampshire. In the latter office, Whipple's duties were to receive money from the state and send them to Congress for use in paying the costs of the war. This was an extremely thankless job, for money was scarce in New Hampshire, and the state legislators were reluctant to send any money to Philadelphia. Whipple attempted to resign, but was persuaded to remain in the position when Robert Morris, the superintendent of finance, wrote to him in August, 1783: "If a number of competitors would appear, I am well persuaded that you would not have accepted. Your original motives must continue to exist, until the situation of our affairs shall mend. Persist, then, I pray you, in those efforts which you promised me, and be persuaded that the consciousness of having made them will be the best reward. If this is not the case, I have mistaken your character." Finally, in 1784, Whipple succeeded in collecting three thousand dollars from New Hampshire and sent it to Morris, then in July of that year he resigned.

From 1782 until his death, Whipple served as an associate justice of the superior court of New Hampshire. During this period, in July, 1782, he also served briefly as president of a court of commissioners appointed by Congress that settled a dispute between Connecticut and Pennsylvania over lands lying in the Wyoming Valley region. During the last several years of his life, Whipple suffered from a heart ailment that made it difficult to carry out his duties as a circuit court judge. In the autumn of 1785, his heart disorder became so severe that he was confined to his home in Portsmouth, and he died there at the age of fifty-five on November 28, 1785.

WILLIAM WILLIAMS of CONNECTICUT

A taciturn and reserved man, William Williams had studied to be a Congregational minister, but became a merchant instead. For nearly fifty years, he served in a variety of public offices, and usually in at least three at the same time. During the Revolutionary War, he resigned his commission as a colonel in the militia in order to become a delegate to the Continental Congress and sign the Declaration of Independence.

Williams was born in Lebanon, Conn., on April 8, 1731. His ancestors had settled in Roxborough, Mass., in 1630, and both his grandfather and his father were ministers. When he was sixteen years old, he was sent to Harvard College. He was graduated four years later in 1751. He then returned to Lebanon where he studied theology with his father.

In 1755, early in the French and Indian War, he was appointed a member of the staff of his uncle, Colonel Ephraim Williams, the founder of Williams College, who was commander of the frontier posts west of the Connecticut River. After his uncle was killed by a French and Indian ambush near Lake George, N. Y., he returned home and took no further part in the fighting.

Decided to be a merchant instead of a minister

The experience fighting the French and Indians apparently changed Williams's mind about becoming a minister, because he went into business as a merchant in Lebanon and then began his long career of government service. At the age of twenty-five, he was elected town clerk, an office that he held for the next forty-five years. At about the same time, he was elected to represent Lebanon in the Connecticut legislature where he subsequently was elected clerk and then speaker of the house of representatives. He also served as a judge most of his life; first, as a justice of the peace, and then as a probate judge and as county judge for Windham County. In addition to all these public duties, Williams also was a selectman, or town council member, in Lebanon for most of his life.

When he was forty years old, Williams married Mary Trumbull, the daughter of Jonathan Trumbull, who at that time was governor of Connecticut. He and his wife had three children.

As relations with Great Britain deteriorated, Williams was appointed as colonel in command of one of Connecticut's regiments of militia in 1773. After the fighting began in Massachusetts in 1775, he became a member of Connecticut's council of safety that planned the defense of the state.

RES. OF Wᴹ WILLIAMS

WILLIAM WILLIAMS

1731 (April 8) Born in Lebanon, Conn.

1751 Graduated from Harvard College.

1755 Served in the French and Indian War.

1756-1801 Town clerk of Lebanon, Conn.

c.1756-1804 Member of the Connecticut legislature.

c.1764-1804 Probate judge and county judge for Windham County, Connecticut.

1773-1776 Colonel in the militia.

1775-1778 Delegate to the Continental Congress; signed the Declaration of Independence.

1783-1784 Delegate to the Congress of the Confederation.

1788 Member of Connecticut state ratification convention for United States Constitution.

1811 (Aug. 2) Died in Lebanon, Conn.

View of New York

View of the town of New Castle from the River Delaware

In October, 1775, Williams was elected by the legislature as a member of Connecticut's delegation to the Continental Congress. He attended Congress for the discussions over whether or not to break all ties with Great Britain, supported the movement for independence, and signed the Declaration of Independence with other delegates on August 2, 1776. He continued to serve in the Congress until 1778, writing many letters to keep his father-in-law, Governor Trumbull, informed of what was going on in the nation's capital. He also served a term in the Congress of the Confederation from 1783 to 1784.

Solicited supplies from four thousand residents

Williams has been described as being devoted to the American cause "by pure and disinterested patriotism." When the fortunes of war were running against George Washington, and his army was almost out of supplies, Williams is said to have visited the homes of every one of Lebanon's four thousand residents to beg for help for the troops, collecting more than a thousand blankets and many clock weights that could be melted into lead for bullets.

After the United States Constitution had been written in 1787, Williams became one of its strong advocates. He was elected to the Connecticut state ratification convention, and voted for approval of the Constitution in 1788.

At the age of seventy-three, Williams resigned from his many public offices because his health and his hearing were failing. He retired to Lebanon and died there at the age of eighty, on August 2, 1811. An early biographer described him thus:

"His person was of the middle stature and remarkably erect and well-proportioned: in his youth, his features were handsome; his hair and eyes were black; his nose aquiline; his face round; and his complexion fair. His temper was naturally ardent, but his exertions to attain the command over it were, in some degree, crowned with success. He possessed, however, during his whole life, a redundancy of spirit and vehemence of expression, which frequently created in himself strong and sorrowful feelings."

GEN. STARK AT BENNINGTON.

JAMES WILSON of PENNSYLVANIA

Scottish-born James Wilson was one of the six Founding Fathers who signed both the Declaration of Independence and the United States Constitution. As the leading lawyer in Philadelphia, Wilson played an important role in writing both the United States Constitution and the Pennsylvania state constitution. He became an associate justice of the first Supreme Court of the United States; but he did not use judicial deliberation in his private affairs, for he speculated in thousands of acres of western lands bought for him by the discredited William Blount and his brothers, and in the last years of his life he described himself as hounded "like a wild beast" by his creditors.

"His mind was one blaze of light."

"James the Caledonian," as he was sometimes called, was a tall, serious man, and so near-sighted that he wore thick glasses. Benjamin Rush, a fellow-signer of the Declaration of Independence, said of Wilson: "His mind, while he spoke, was one blaze of light. Not a word ever fell from his lips out of time, or out of place, nor could a word be taken from or added to his speeches without injuring them."

The son of a well-to-do farmer, Wilson was born on September 14, 1742, near St. Andrews, Scotland. After completing his grammar school education, Wilson attended in turn the universities of St. Andrews, Glasgow, and Edinburgh.

At the age of twenty-three, Wilson decided to seek his fortune in America. He arrived in New York City in 1765, at the height of the colonial uproar over the British parliament's Stamp Act. Early in 1766 he arrived in Philadelphia, and obtained a position teaching Latin at the College of Philadelphia (now the University of Pennsylvania). Then, deciding that the swiftest road to success lay in the law, he began studying to be an attorney in the offices of John Dickinson, the "Penman of the Revolution."

After being admitted to the bar to practice law in 1767, Wilson moved to Carlisle, Pa., and developed a substantial legal practice. He married Rachel Bird, daughter of a well-to-do ironworks owner, and they had six children before she died in 1786. Later, he married Hannah Gray, the daughter of a Boston merchant. He had one child by his second wife.

A colonel in command of the militia

Wilson took an active part in Pennsylvania's patriotic movement in the years leading up to the Revolutionary War. He won particular notice in 1774 for a pamphlet he wrote that was entitled *Considerations of the Nature and Extent of the Legislative Authority of the British Parliament*, and that same year he was a member of Pennsylvania's patriotic provincial convention that elected delegates to the first Continental Congress. Wilson was nominated as a delegate, but was defeated through the efforts of a Philadelphia lawyer who later turned Loyalist and joined the British during the Revolutionary War. Wilson returned to Carlisle from the convention, and was chosen colonel in command of the militia of Cumberland County —a commission that he never exercised in active military service.

JAMES WILSON

1742 (Sept. 14) Born near St. Andrews, Scotland.
1765 Emigrated to America.
1766 Taught Latin at the College of Philadelphia.
1766-1767 Studied law under John Dickinson and admitted to the bar.
1774-1775 Member of the Pennsylvania provincial convention.
1775-1777 Delegate to the second Continental Congress; signed the Declaration of Independence.
1779-1782 Advocate general of France in the United States.
1781 Appointed a director of the Bank of North America.
1782-1783 Delegate from Pennsylvania to the Congress of the Confederation.
1785-1787 Delegate to Congress.
1787 Delegate from Pennsylvania to the Constitutional Convention; signed the United States Constitution.
1787 Member of Pennsylvania state ratification convention.
1789-1790 Member of the Pennsylvania state constitutional convention; helped write the new state constitution.
1789-1798 Associate justice of the Supreme Court of the United States.
1790-1791 First professor of law at the College of Philadelphia (now the University of Pennsylvania).
1798 (Aug. 21) Died at Edenton, N.C., while serving in federal circuit court.

A political rebuff

In 1775, after fighting had begun at Lexington and Concord in Massachusetts, Wilson was elected as one of Pennsylvania's delegates to the second Continental Congress. He became a member of the board of war and of dozens of other important committees. When Congress took up the question of independence in July, Wilson voted for the Declaration of Independence, even though John Dickinson, his old law mentor, opposed it; and he signed the engrossed copy of the document with other delegates on August 2, 1776. Wilson's political opponents charged that he had been one of the delegates who opposed independence, and in 1777 he received a letter from his friend Robert Morris warning him: "I am told our assembly do not intend you shall be in the new list of delegates. I am too busy to attend, or I would contest the matter warmly; although I well know, that the honesty, merits, and ability which you possess in so eminent a degree, would not be sufficient plea against the previous determination of a strong party; for that, I am told, is the case. However, you will enjoy your family and friends at home, if you are deprived of the opportunity of continuing those services to your country, which she so much needs, and which, if I mistake not, she will feel the want

of, until better men, in better times, shall call you forth again." Later, in 1777, Morris' forecast came true, as the Pennsylvania assembly replaced Wilson with one of his political opponents.

Name French advocate general in America

With the British capture of Philadelphia in September, 1777, Wilson moved to Annapolis, Md., remaining there for nearly a year. After the retreat of the British in 1778, Wilson returned to Philadelphia and made it his permanent home from then on. He became recognized as the leading member of the bar in Philadelphia, and in 1779 the French government appointed Wilson as its advocate general in America, an office that he held until he resigned it in 1782 because of a disagreement over his salary. Meanwhile, Wilson also had been appointed a director of the Bank of North America that had been developed by Robert Morris to handle the finances of the United States government.

Wilson used his legal talents to defend various Philadelphians who were charged with treason. He also acted as lawyer for some of the wealthiest merchants of the city who were refusing to sell food and other necessities at the prices fixed by a town meeting. As a result, in October, 1779, placards were posted throughout the city that threatened banishment to New York for Wilson, Morris, and others of his friends and clients. Those who had been threatened armed themselves and gathered at Wilson's large brick mansion, which soon became known as Fort Wilson. A mob of workmen and militia formed around the house, brought up two cannons, and began firing. Those in the house fired back. Two members of the mob and one man in the house were killed before a troop of cavalry arrived and restored order. Wilson left the city for a time after this incident, returning only when public feeling had become calmer.

When John Dickinson became President of the executive council of Pennsylvania in 1782, Wilson was again elected by the Pennsylvania legislature as a delegate to the Congress of the Confederation, serving for about a year. He was re-elected to Congress in 1785 to 1787, after Benjamin Franklin succeeded Dickinson as President of Pennsylvania.

Advocated popular elections of Congress and the President

The time had now come when Wilson was to perform his greatest service to his country—as a delegate to the Constitutional Convention of 1787. Throughout the convention, he acted as a spokesman for the aged and feeble Benjamin Franklin, reading Franklin's speeches for him. Throughout the convention, Wilson was one of the strongest advocates for popular election of the members of Congress and the President, and he began to sound

this theme before the convention was a week old. James Madison reported that on May 31:

"Mr. Wilson contended strenuously for drawing the most numerous branch of the Legislature immediately from the people. He was for raising the federal pyramid to a considerable altitude, and for that reason wished to give it as broad a basis as possible. No government could long subsist without the confidence of the people. In a republican government, this confidence was peculiarly essential. He also thought it wrong to increase the weight of the State Legislatures by making them the electors of the National Legislature. All interference between the general and local government should be obviated as much as possible. On examination it would be found that the opposition of States to Federal measures had proceeded much more from the officers of the States than from the people at large."

A member of the Constitutional drafting committee

In July, Wilson was appointed to the important committee of detail chaired by John Rutledge which drafted the Constitution in very nearly the same form as was finally approved. Wilson wrote a draft of the Constitution which was severely edited and revised by Rutledge. Wilson then copied and polished this version, and it was distributed to the delegates for their further consideration on August 6, 1787. After another month of consideration, the delegates approved and signed the United States Constitution on September 17, after

Residence of James Wilson
Southwest corner, Third and Walnut Streets, Philadelphia

hearing Wilson read Franklin's dramatic plea for unanimity.

Best form of government ever offered

Next, Wilson was elected to Pennsylvania state convention to consider the Constitution, and has been credited with swaying the delegates to vote for ratification on December 12, 1787, because of his powerful oratory. In part, he told the state convention:

"It is neither extraordinary nor unexpected that the constitution offered to your consideration should meet with opposition. It is the nature of man to pursue his own interest, in preference to the public good; and I do not mean to make any personal reflection, when I add, that it is the interest of a very numerous, powerful, and respectable body to counteract and destroy the excellent work produced by the late convention. All the officers of government, and all the appointments for the administration of justice, and the collection of the public revenue, which are transferred from the individual to the aggregate sovereignty of the states, will necessarily turn the stream of influence and emolument into a new channel. Every person, therefore, who either enjoys, or expects to enjoy, a place of profit under the present establishment, will object to the proposed innovation; not, in truth, because it is injurious to the liberties of his country, but because it affects his schemes of wealth and consequence. I will confess, indeed, that I am not a blind admirer of this plan of government, and that there are some parts of it which, if my wish had prevailed, would certainly have been altered. But, when I reflect how widely men differ in their opinions, and that every man (and the observation applies likewise to every state), has an equal pretension to assert his own, I am satisfied that anything nearer to perfection could not have been accomplished. If there are errors, it should be remembered, that the seeds of reformation are sown in the work itself, and the concurrence of two-thirds of the congress may, at any time, introduce alterations and amendments. Regarding it, then in every point of view, with a candid and disinterested mind, I am bold to assert, that it is the *best form of government which has ever been offered to the world*."

Wilson was chosen to make the main oration at a huge Fourth of July celebration in Philadelphia in 1788 to hail the ratification of the United States Constitution. The next year, he was elected to a state constitutional convention where he was appointed to the committee to draft the document and did the major share of the work in writing this state constitution that went into effect in 1790.

Named Associate Justice of U. S. Supreme Court

On April 21, 1789, Wilson wrote to President George Washington suggesting that he should be appointed Chief Justice of the United States. But when Washington appointed the members of the Supreme Court the following September, Wilson was named as an associate justice, while the office of Chief Justice went to John Jay. Wilson attended the first session of the Supreme Court in February, 1790. That same year, Wilson was appointed as the first professor of law at the College of Philadelphia, the same school where he had briefly taught Latin on his arrival in the American colonies twenty-four years earlier. Wilson also took students into his Philadelphia law office; and one of the most notable of these was Bushrod Washington, the nephew of George Washington.

Financial setback in land speculation

Like his close friend Robert Morris, Wilson became deeply involved in land speculation. He bought thousands of acres of western land, borrowing huge sums of money to do so. Much of this land was purchased for him by the Blount brothers, the most famous of whom was William Blount, a fellow-signer of the United States Constitution who was impeached by the House of Representatives and was expelled from the United States Senate in 1797. With the collapse of land values, Wilson fell into serious debt, and only his office as an associate justice of the Supreme Court saved him from total disgrace.

Under the laws existing in the early years of the new federal government, the associate justices of the Supreme Court acted as circuit judges, traveling about to hold court in various states. While serving in the capacity of a federal circuit judge, the fifty-five-year-old Wilson died on August 28, 1798, in Edenton, N.C., at the home of Associate Justice James Iredell. His body was buried in Edenton, but more than a hundred years later it was moved to Philadelphia and re-interred in Christ Churchyard there. Interestingly, the vacancy on the Supreme Court caused by Wilson's death was filled by President John Adams with the appointment of Wilson's former law student — Bushrod Washington.

JOHN WITHERSPOON of NEW JERSEY

The only clergyman to sign the Declaration of Independence, John Witherspoon was no stranger to revolutions against the English, having taken part in an unsuccessful one in Scotland in the 1740's. Witherspoon had been induced to leave Scotland where he was a leading Presbyterian minister to come to America in 1768 as president of the College of New Jersey (now Princeton University). Although he was of medium height and rather stout, an early biographer described him as having "more of what is called *presence,* than almost any other man . . . excepting Washington." A scholar, as well as a theologian and a patriot, Witherspoon coined the word *Americanism* in a magazine article discussing differences between the use of the English language in England and the United States.

A direct descendant of John Knox

John Witherspoon was born in the parish of Yester, near Edinburgh, Scotland, on February 5,

1723. He was a direct descendant of John Knox, the founder of Protestantism in Scotland, and his father was a Presbyterian clergyman. After attending public school in Haddington, Witherspoon was sent to the University of Edinburgh when he was fourteen. He was graduated from that institution four years later in 1742. He continued his studies in theology until he was twenty-one.

In 1745, he accepted an invitation from the people of the parish of Beith to become their pastor. In that same year he became involved in the efforts of the Highlanders of Scotland to restore to the throne Charles Edward Stuart, whom they called "Bonnie Prince Charlie." Witherspoon was captured by the English in the Battle of Falkirk, early in 1746, but was released after a short imprisonment.

An interesting coincidence

Witherspoon remained as pastor at Beith until 1757, when he was called to take the pastorate in the manufacturing town of Paisley. His growing reputation as a minister and a writer became known in America, and in 1767 Richard Stockton, a trustee of the College of New Jersey, made a special trip to the British Isles to persuade him to accept the presidency of the college. His wife, Elizabeth Montgomery Witherspoon, was reluct-

REVEREND JOHN WITHERSPOON
by C. W. PEALE
Independence National Historical Park Collection

JOHN WITHERSPOON

1723 (Feb. 5) Born in the parish of Yester, near Edinburgh, Scotland.

1742 Graduated from the University of Edinburgh.

1745-1757 Presbyterian minister at Beith, Scotland.

1745-1746 Took part in the Highlanders's revolt in support of Bonnie Prince Charlie and was captured by the English.

1757-1768 Presbyterian pastor at Paisley, Scotland.

1768 Came to America with his wife and their five children.

1768-1794 President of the College of New Jersey (now Princeton University).

1776 Member of the New Jersey provincial congress that imprisoned Governor William Franklin.

1776 Member of the state constitutional convention.

1776-1782 Delegate from New Jersey to the Continental Congress; signed the Declaration of Independence and the Articles of Confederation.

1789 Moderator of the first General Assembly of the Presbyterian Church in the United States.

1794 (Nov. 15) Died at his home Tusculum near Princeton, N. J.

View upon the Road from New-Windsor, towards Morris Town *JERSEY.*

ant to go to the "uncivilized" colonies. But Benjamin Rush, who was then a medical student at the University of Edinburgh, helped induce her to agree to go. By an interesting coincidence, Witherspoon, Stockton, and Rush all signed the Declaration of Independence.

In August, 1768, Witherspoon, with his wife and their five children, arrived at Princeton, N. J., to become the sixth president of the College of New Jersey. His reputation and ability brought to the college many new students, including James Madison, who later became known as the "Father of the Constitution."

Already bitter at the British government because of its treatment of the Scottish people after the defeat of Bonnie Prince Charlie, Witherspoon quickly joined in with the patriotic groups opposing the British tyranny in the colonies. He took part in the revolutionary committees and conventions in New Jersey that brought about the arrest of New Jersey's royal governor, William Franklin, in 1776.

"Not only ripe but rotting"

Witherspoon and his friend Stockton both were elected delegates to the Continental Congress in June, 1776, arriving in Philadelphia just in time to hear the debate over independence between John Adams and John Dickinson. When it was remarked that the colonies were "not yet ripe for a declaration of independence," Witherspoon is said to have replied, "In my judgment, sir, we are not only ripe, but rotting." As might have been expected, Witherspoon voted for independence. He signed the Declaration of Independence with the other delegates on August 2. During 1776, Witherspoon also took part in the provincial congress that wrote a constitution for the state of New Jersey.

Throughout the years of the Revolutionary War, Witherspoon was one of the most influential members of the Congress. He served on the powerful board of war and also on the secret committee that handled foreign relations. His friend and fellow-signer of the Declaration of Independence, Stockton, had been captured by the British and subjected to unusually cruel punishment, Witherspoon is believed to have authored the resolution of Congress in 1778 that declared in part:

Vindicating the rights of humanity

"While the shadow of hope remained that our enemies could be taught by our example, to respect those laws which are held sacred among

231

civilized nations, and to comply with the dictates of a religion which they pretend, in common with us, to believe and revere, they have been left to the influence of that religion and that example. But since their incorrigible dispositions cannot be touched by kindness and compassion, it becomes our duty, by other means, to vindicate the rights of humanity — We, therefore, the congress of the United States of America, do solemnly declare and proclaim, that if our enemies presume to execute their threats, or persist in their present career of barbarity, we will take such exemplary vengeance as shall deter others from a like conduct. We appeal to that God who searcheth the hearts of men, for the rectitude of our intentions; and in his holy presence declare, that as we are not moved by any light and hasty suggestions of anger or revenge, so, through every possible change of fortune, we will adhere to this our determination."

Delay augments the difficulty

In 1778, Witherspoon signed the Articles of Confederacy as a delegate from New Jersey. He also lectured the remaining states who were holding up ratification of the Articles, saying: "If, at present, when the danger is yet imminent, when it is so far from being over, that it is but coming to its height, we shall find it impossible to agree upon the terms of this confederacy, what madness is it to suppose that there ever will be a time, or that circumstances will so change as to make it even probable, that it will be done at an after season? Will not the very same difficulties that are in our way, be in the way of those who shall come after us? Is it possible that they should be ignorant of them, or inattentive to them? Will they not have the same jealousies of each other, the same attachment to local prejudices, and particular interests? So certain is this, that I look upon it as on the repentance of a sinner; every day's delay, though it adds to the necessity, yet augments the difficulty, and takes from the inclination."

In 1779, Witherspoon turned the active administration of the College of New Jersey over to his son-in-law, the Reverend Samuel Smith, who had married Witherspoon's oldest daughter, Ann. He gave up his house on the Princeton campus to his daughter and her husband, and moved to a country home, Tusculum.

First use of the term "Americanism"

While still a member of Congress in 1781, Witherspoon wrote a series of articles in the *Pennsylvania Journal and Weekly Advertiser* in which he discussed the use of the English language by Americans. He coined the term *Americanism* in one of the articles, and said of it:

"I understand an use of phrases or terms, or construction of sentences, even among people of rank and education, different from the use of the same terms or phrases, or the construction of similar sentences in Great Britain. It does not follow, from a man's using these, that he is ignorant, or his discourse upon the whole inelegant; nay, it does not follow in every case that the terms or phrases used are worse in themselves, but merely that they are of American and not of English growth. The word *Americanism,* which I have coined for the purpose, is exactly similar in its formation and significance to the word *Scotticism.*"

A surprise ending

After retiring from Congress in 1782, Witherspoon devoted most of his attention to restoring the College of New Jersey and attempting to improve it. Late in 1783, he traveled to England in an effort to raise funds for the support of the college, but he returned in 1784 with the mission a failure.

A leader of the Presbyterian Church, he helped organize and presided over the opening session of the first General Assembly of the church in 1789. His essays and his sermons on theological subjects were widely read.

Near the end of his life, Witherspoon created considerable controversy among his students, faculty, and friends, when, his first wife having died, he married a twenty-three-year-old widow, Mrs. Ann Dill. He was nearly seventy at the time of his marriage, but he and his second wife had two daughters.

During the last two years of his life, Witherspoon became totally blind; but he continued to give sermons, even though he had to be led to the pulpit. At the age of seventy-one, on November 15, 1794, Witherspoon died at his home near Princeton.

OLIVER WOLCOTT of CONNECTICUT

Dividing his time almost equally between civil and military affairs, Oliver Wolcott, an energetic Connecticut Yankee, was one of the most ardent patriots who helped win Independence. He had no part in writing the Declaration of Independence, being absent at the time of its discussion and adoption; but, when he found time to return to Congress after aiding in the military defense of New York, he proudly signed the Declaration.

Wolcott was a tall man with a dignified, military bearing. Although he was modest, he was firm and tenacious in his opinions and freely expressed them. He loved books and read widely in medicine, law, science, history, and literature.

He was born Nov. 26, 1726, in Windsor, Conn. He was the youngest son of Roger Wolcott, who served as colonial governor of Connecticut from 1751 to 1754. Oliver received a good education, being graduated from Yale College at the head of his class in 1747.

At the time of his graduation, the British were fighting the French in Canada in what was called King George's War. Wolcott received a commission as captain in the army from the governor of New York. He raised a company of men and marched to the defense of the northern frontier with Canada. When the war ended in 1748, Wolcott's company was disbanded and he returned to Connecticut.

Pursuit of medicine and law

Next, Wolcott took up the study of medicine under his brother, Dr. Alexander Wolcott. But, be-fore he could establish a practice, he was appointed in 1751 as sheriff of Litchfield County. He then began to study law.

He married Laura Collins, of Guilford, Conn., in 1755. Too little is known about the wives of many of the Founding Fathers, but Mrs. Wolcott must have been a remarkable person. With her husband absent from home almost continuously during the period of the Revolutionary War, she managed their small farm, reared their five children, and preserved their estate. They remained devotedly married until her death in 1795.

Beginning in 1774, Wolcott served for twelve years as a member of the state council, or upper house, of the Connecticut general assembly. At the same time, he held office as chief judge of the court of common pleas of Litchfield County and as judge of the court of probate for Litchfield County.

Wolcott was appointed by the Continental Congress in July, 1775, as one of the commissioners

---

OLIVER WOLCOTT

1726 (Nov. 26) Born in Windsor, Conn.

1747 Graduated from Yale College.

1747-1748 Captain in the army during King George's War with the French in Canada.

1751 Appointed sheriff of Litchfield County, Conn.

1774-1786 Member of the upper house of the Connecticut general assembly.

1776-1778 Represented Connecticut in the Continental Congress.

1776-1780 Major general in command of militia troops during the Revolutionary War.

1780-1784 Represented Connecticut in the Continental Congress.

1786-1796 Lieutenant-governor of Connecticut.

1796-1797 Governor of Connecticut.

1797 (Dec. 1) Died at East Windsor, Conn., at the age of 71.

OLIVER WOLCOTT
by RALPH EARL

Residence of Oliver Wolcott

of Indian affairs for the northern department. His task was to try to induce the Indians to remain neutral during the Revolutionary War. At the same time, he worked effectively to help settle boundary disputes between Connecticut and Pennsylvania and between Vermont and New York. Wolcott exerted considerable influence on the frontier settlers and these colonies, winning their support for the idea of Independence. After the Revolutionary War in 1784 to 1785, he again was appointed an Indian commissioner, this time to help draw up peace terms with the Iroquois Indians who had sided with the British in the war.

Wolcott was appointed in 1775 as a member of the Connecticut delegation to the Continental Congress. He first took his seat there in January, 1776. Becoming ill in June, he returned to Connecticut while discussions were in progress concerning the Declaration of Independence.

From captain to major general

Meanwhile, Wolcott had continued to serve in the Connecticut militia, rising grade by grade from captain to major general. In 1776, he was appointed to lead fourteen regiments of the Connecticut militia to aid in the defense of New York City. After he had joined his force with the Continental Army in New York, he returned to Congress where he signed the Declaration of Independence on Sept. 4, 1776. He accompanied the Congress when it moved to Baltimore during the winter of 1777.

Wolcott was kept busy recruiting units of militia in Connecticut during the summer of 1777. That fall he commanded a force of several thousand militia aiding General Horatio Gates in his victory over British General John Burgoyne at Saratoga, N. Y.

Congress was meeting in York, Pa., when Wolcott resumed his seat in that body in 1778. In the summer of 1779, he commanded a division of militia defending the Connecticut sea coast against a British invasion. His service with the militia continued to occupy him during most of 1780. Except for the year 1779, Wolcott continued to represent Connecticut in the Continental Congress until 1784.

After the war, Wolcott was one of the most respected and popular men in his state. From 1786 to 1796 he was annually elected as Connecticut's lieutenant-governor. During the discussions over the adoption of the United States Constitution, Wolcott gave it his enthusiastic support as a member of the Federalist party. His son, Oliver Wolcott, Jr., also had risen to distinction, serving as Secretary of the Treasury under Presidents George Washington and John Adams.

In 1796, Connecticut gave Wolcott its highest honor, electing him governor. While still holding this office, he died on Dec. 1, 1797, at East Windsor, Conn., at the age of 71.

MRS. OLIVER WOLCOTT (LAURA COLLINS)
by RALPH EARL, HON. ROGER WOLCOTT, *owner.*
SUBJECT'S MAIDEN NAME IS GIVEN AS LORRAINE COLLINS BY
THE OWNER

GEORGE WYTHE of VIRGINIA

George Wythe, the man who taught Thomas Jefferson to be a lawyer, signed the Declaration of Independence with a special pride in the work of his famous student. Later, with Jefferson's assistance, Wythe became the first professor of law in the United States, at the College of William and Mary. He also served more than twenty-five years as a judge in Virginia courts. At the age of eighty, he was poisoned, possibly by a grand-nephew who had grown tired of waiting to inherit his fortune. Thomas Jefferson wrote of his beloved teacher:

Thomas Jefferson's praise

"No man ever left behind him a character more venerated than George Wythe. His virtue was of the purest kind; his integrity inflexible, and his justice exact; of warm patriotism, and devoted as he was to liberty, and the natural and equal rights of men, he might truly be called the Cato of his country, without the avarice of the Roman; for a more disinterested person never lived. Temperance and regularity in all his habits, gave him general good health, and his unaffected modesty and suavity of manners endeared him to every one. He way of easy elocution, his language chaste, methodical in the arrangement of his matter, learned and logical in the use of it, and of great urbanity in debate. Not quick of apprehension, but with a little time, profound in penetration, and sound in conclusion. In his philosophy he was firm, and neither troubling, nor perhaps trusting any one with his religous creed, he left to the world the conclusion, that that religion must be good which could produce a life of such exemplary virtue.

"His stature was of the middle size, well formed and proportioned, and the features of his face, manly, comely, and engaging. Such was George Wythe, the honour of his own, and model of future times."

Wythe was born in 1726 at Back River in Elizabeth County, Virginia, near Yorktown. His father was a well-to-do plantation owner and his mother was an unusually well-educated woman of the Quaker faith. His mother tutored him in Latin, Greek, and other subjects, so that by the time he was in his teens he had obtained an excellent education. The death of both his father and mother while he was still a boy left him to look out for himself; particularly so because his father died without a will, and the law of primogeniture gave the entire estate to an older brother.

After attending the College of William and Mary, Wythe became a law clerk to one of his uncles, and in about 1750 he was admitted to the bar to practice law in Virginia. He married Ann Lewis, but she died after about a year. Later, he re-married. His second wife was Elizabeth Talia-

George Wythe Miniature by Henry Benbridge

GEORGE WYTHE

1726 Born at Back River, Va.

1752-1768 Member of the house of burgesses of Virginia.

1768-1775 Clerk of the house of burgesses of Virginia.

1775-1776 Delegate from Virginia to the second Continental Congress; signed the Declaration of Independence.

1776 Helped write the constitution for the state of Virginia; appointed to committee to revise the laws of Virginia.

1777 Speaker of the house of delegates of the Virginia legislature.

1778-1786 Judge of the Virginia court of chancery.

1779-1786 First professor of law in America, at the College of William and Mary.

1786-1806 Chancellor of the state of Virginia.

1806 (June 8) Died at Richmond, Va.

George Wythe House

ferro of Williamsburg. The large brick house in which Wythe and his wife lived has been restored in Williamsburg.

When he was about twenty-six years old, Wythe was elected to the Virginia house of burgesses, where he continued to serve until the Revolutionary War ended that legislative body. Wythe represented the College of William and Mary in the house of burgesses, and became the personal adviser to the acting governor of the colony, Lieutenant Governor Francis Fauquier. By the time he was in his forties, fellow-lawyers in Williamsburg described Wythe as "second to none of the

profession with us." In 1768, Wythe was elected to succeed John Randolph in the influential position of clerk of the house of burgesses.

Taught Thomas Jefferson

Like most prominent attorneys, Wythe took aspiring students into his office and helped them prepare for a career in the law. Thomas Jefferson was one of his students from 1762 to 1767. Other prominent men who were his students included John Marshall, James Monroe, and Henry Clay.

Wythe was elected by the Virginia provincial congress in 1775 as one of the delegates to the second Continental Congress. He was present on June 7, 1776, when Richard Henry Lee presented his resolution for independence, and he aided Lee and John Adams in arguing for it. Later that month he returned to Virginia to aid in writing a constitution for the state, taking with him the draft of a constitution that Thomas Jefferson had prepared; thus, he was not present in July when the Continental Congress voted for independence. However, he went back to Philadelphia later that summer and added his name to the Declaration of Independence on August 27, 1776.

In November, 1776, Wythe was appointed to a committee of distinguished Virginia lawyers, that also included Jefferson, to revise the laws of the state to conform with the change in government. In the next year and a half this committee revised and sent to the legislature one hundred and twenty-six bills, covering all the English and Colonial laws in force prior to the Revolutionary War.

Wythe was elected speaker of the house of delegates of the Virginia state legislature in 1777, but he retired from that office later that same year when Governor Patrick Henry appointed him as one of the three judges of the high court of chancery of Virginia.

First American law professor

Through the efforts of Thomas Jefferson, the College of William and Mary in 1779 established the first professorship of law at any American college and Wythe was named to fill this chair. He held this professorship until 1786 when he was appointed chancellor of the courts of Virginia and moved to the new state capital of Richmond.

Wythe was a member of the distinguished Virginia delegation headed by George Washington that was sent to the Constitutional Convention in Philadelphia in 1787. On the opening day of the Convention, Wythe was appointed chairman of the committee on rules; but after preparing the rules and having them approved, he left the Convention and returned to Virginia.

Decided that the courts could hold a law unconstitutional

Wythe's most important opinion as a judge came in a case that he heard before the Court of Appeals of Virginia in November, 1782, in which he established the precedent, later used by the United States Supreme Court, that the courts could hold a law to be unconstitutional. In his opinion he stated:

"Nay, more, if the whole legislature, an event to be deprecated, should attempt to overleap the bounds prescribed to them by the people, I, in administering the public justice of the country, will meet the united powers, at my seat in this tribunal; and, pointing to the constitution, will say to them here is the limit of your authority; and hither shall you go, but not further."

George Washington appointed Wythe as a federal district court judge in 1789, but he declined the appointment, preferring to remain as chancellor of the courts of Virginia. During Washington's second administration, Wythe became one of the leaders of the Anti-Federalist party in Virginia, particularly opposing the Jay Treaty with Great Britain.

During the Revolutionary War, British troops had seized most of the slaves from Wythe's plantations, carrying them off as plunder; and in the latter part of his life Wythe freed his remaining slaves, providing for them in his will.

At the age of eighty, on June 8, 1806, Wythe died at his home in Richmond from drinking a cup of coffee that had been poisoned with arsenic. Because he was childless, Wythe had bequeathed the bulk of his estate to his grand-nephew, George Wythe Sweney; but a few days before his death, Wythe changed the will, mentioning the suspicious death of one of his freed Negroes who would have benefitted by his will, and cutting Sweney out of the will altogether. Sweney was brought to trial and acquitted of the murder of Wythe, but the suspicion continued to linger that justice had miscarried.

Patrick Henry

PATRICK HENRY of VIRGINIA

Called the "Firebrand of the Revolution," red-haired Patrick Henry roused Virginia to the dangers of British tyranny in the same way that James Otis and Samuel Adams stirred the early spirit of patriotism in Massachusetts. Ten years before the Revolutionary War, Henry's Virginia resolutions against the Stamp Act and his speech supporting the resolutions were denounced as treason. Then, only a few weeks before the fighting began at Lexington and Concord, in a voice "like the thunder out of the clear sky," Henry uttered the rallying motto of the Revolution: "Give me liberty, or give me death!"

Second only to George Washington in popularity in Virginia, Henry became the first governor and the political boss of the largest of the first thirteen states. He strongly opposed ratification of the United States Constitution, believing that it took away too many rights from the people and from the states. But after the new United States government had been organized, Henry became a Federalist, supporting George Washington and John Adams against the Democratic-Republican policies of Thomas Jefferson and James Madison. Because of old age and sickness, Henry turned down offers by Washington to become Secretary of State or Chief Justice of the United States.

Of Scotch descent

Patrick Henry was born May 29, 1736, on his step-brother's plantation, "Studley," in Hanover County, Virginia. He was the second oldest son in a family of nine children of John and Sarah Henry. His father had emigrated from Scotland several years earlier and had improved his fortune by marrying Sarah Winston Syme, a "portly, handsome dame" and widow of a well-to-do planter. Her son by her first marriage, John Syme, was heir to "Studley." Patrick Henry's uncle, whose name also was Patrick Henry, was rector of the local parish of the Church of England. Young Patrick was baptized in his uncle's church, although his mother was a Presbyterian.

The boy grew up at his father's plantation, "Mount Brilliant." He went to a country school for a few years, where he learned his three R's. Then his father tutored him in "a little Latin and less Greek." But the boy was much more interested in hunting, fishing, and playing the fiddle than he was in studying. An early biographer described him as spending most of his time in idleness, lying "along under the shade of some tree that overhung the sequestered stream, watching for hours, at the same spot, the motionless cork of his fishing-line, without one encouraging symptom of success, and without any apparent source of enjoyment, unless he could find it in the ease of his posture, or in the illusions of hope, or, which is most probable, in the stillness of the scene and the silent workings of his own imagination."

Failed in his first business

When Patrick Henry was fifteen years old, he went to work as a clerk in a general store; and the next year his father set him up in business as a partner with his older brother, William, in a store. But neither of the boys had much of a head for business, so before many months had passed the store had to be written off as a failure.

At the age of eighteen Patrick Henry fell in love and married Sarah Shelton, the daughter of a poor farmer. The families of the bride and groom provided them with a farm of several hundred acres and a half dozen slaves, but Patrick Henry was no better a farmer than he had been a storekeeper. For two years he tilled the land, then gave it up and again tried his hand as a storekeeper. About this time, young Thomas Jefferson met

PATRICK HENRY

1736 (May 29) Born at "Studley" in Hanover County, Virginia.
1760 Admitted to the bar to practice law.
1765-1775 Member of the Virginia House of Burgesses.
1774-1776 Member of the Virginia revolutionary conventions.
1774-1775 Member of the Virginia delegation to the Continental Congress.
1776-1779 Governor of Virginia.
1780-1784 Member of the Virginia legislature.
1784-1786 Governor of Virginia.
1786-1790 Member of the Virginia legislature.
1788 Member of the Virginia ratification convention; led opposition to the United States Constitution.
1796 Elected governor of Virginia, but declined to serve.
1799 Elected to the Virginia legislature.
1799 (June 6) Died at "Red Hill" in Charlotte County, Virginia.

1. Front View of the State-House &c. *at* ANNAPOLIS *the Capital of* MARYLAND.

Henry at a party at the home of Colonel Nathaniel West Dandridge and noted that "his manners had something of coarseness in them; his passion was music, dancing, and pleasantry."

Admitted to the bar in six months

In 1760, when he was twenty-four, Patrick Henry suddenly tired of being a ne'er-do-well storekeeper. He was deeply in debt, had several children to support, and realized that there was more to life than hunting with a hound dog, catching a trout, or playing a fiddle. Surprisingly, he decided to become a lawyer. In a period of six weeks intensive study he prepared for his bar examinations, and then impressed the attorneys who examined him sufficiently that he was granted a license to practice law. Now, he moved his family into the Hanover tavern which his father-in-law had just purchased. There, he hung up his shingle as an attorney-at-law, and in the long intervals when he had no law clients he helped out the innkeeper. Patrick's father, John Henry, was then the presiding judge of the county court in Hanover, and this no doubt helped the young man obtain cases, for in the first three years of his law practice he is said to have handled more than a thousand suits.

Statewide recognition

Henry won his first state-wide renown as a lawyer in 1763 in what became known as the "Parsons' Cause." At this time in Virginia, the Church of England was the established church, and the annual payment to its ministers was fixed by law at 16,000 pounds of tobacco. Normally, tobacco was worth two pence a pound or less, but in years when the crop failed tobacco became much more valuable. As an aid to the tobacco growers, the Virginia House of Burgesses had passed a law in 1758 that permitted all payments normally figured in tobacco to be paid in cash for the equivalent of two pence a pound. The angered clergymen had appealed to the British king with the result that in 1759 the law was declared null. In 1763, the Reverend James Maury of Hanover County brought suit demanding damages because he had been paid his annual salary in cash instead of the more valuable tobacco, and twenty-seven-year-old Patrick Henry was named as the defense lawyer for the officials who had collected the tax. The suit came before a jury in Hanover on December 1, 1763, with John Henry as presiding judge. There was no question of law as to the validity of Maury's case, the jury was only to fix the damages. But when the eloquent Patrick Henry addressed the jury of farmers and pointed out to them the injustice of the king having ruled as invalid a law that had been passed by the Virginia legislature, the jury nodded their heads in agreement and awarded the Reverend Maury only one penny for damages. Maury sadly wrote to a fellow-clergyman: "After the court adjourned (Henry) apologized to me for what he had said, alleging that his sole view in engaging in the cause, and in saying what he had, was to render himself

Gravé par Balth. Frederic Leizalt

Salem.

Eine Stadt im Engelländischen America, in der Grafschaft Essex; | Vne Ville de l'Amerique Angloise dans le Comté d'Essex, elle
welche von den Engelländern 1629. erbauet worden. und 2. Hafen | fut bâtie par les Anglois en 1629. et a deux Ports, l'un pour
hat, einen für den Sommer, und einen für den Winter. | l'Eté. et l'autre pour l'Hyver.

Se vend à Augsbourg au Negoce commun de l'Academie Imperiale d'Empire dai A-s libereaux avec Privilege de Sa Majesté Imperiale et avec Defense ni d'en faire ni de vendre les Copie.

(Translation)   Engraved by Balthasar Friedrich Leizalt—Library of Congress

Salem

A town of English America, in Essex County, built by the English in 1629,
which has two ports, one for summer and the other for winter.

Collection des Prospects.

Prospect von Boston gegen der Bucht | Vue de Boston vers le Cale
am Hafen. | du Port.

Se vend à Augsbourg au Negoce même de l'Académie Imperiale d'Empire des Arts libéraux avec Privilege de Sa Majesté Imperiale, et avec Défense n'y en faire ni d'en faire ni de vendre les Copies.

Gravé par François Xav. Habermann.

(Translation)   Engraved by Francois Habermann–Library of Congress

View of Boston toward the bay of the port

popular. You see, then, it is so clear a point in this person's opinion that the ready road to popularity here is to trample under foot the interests of religion, the rights of the church, and the prerogatives of the Crown."

Elected to the House of Burgesses

Patrick Henry had won the popularity that Maury said he sought, so much so that adjoining Louisa County, where he did not live, elected him to the House of Burgesses in the spring of 1765. Henry took his seat in the colonial legislature on May 20, 1765—a poorly-dresed frontier lawyer in an assemblage of Virginia's wealthiest aristocrats.

The session of the House of Burgesses was nearly over and nearly two-thirds of the legislators had already left for home, when a copy of the new Stamp Act just passed by the British parliament arrived from London. The legislators adjourned into a committee of the whole to consider what action they should take in regard to the stiff new tax law. On his twenty-ninth birthday, May 29, Henry rose and dramatically presented a series of inflammatory resolutions that he had written on the end-sheet of an old law book "alone, unadvised and unassisted." These resolutions are believed to have been as follows:

Resolutions opposing the Stamp Act

"Resolved—

"That the first Adventurers and settlers of this his Majesty's Colony and Dominion brought

Interior of Saint John's Church

with them and transmitted to their Posterity and all other his Majesty's Subjects since inhabiting in this his Majesty's said Colony, all the Privileges, Franchises and Immunities that have at any Time been held, enjoyed, and possessed by the People of Great Britain.

"That by two royal Charters, granted by King James the first the Colonists aforesaid are declared entitled to all the Privileges, Liberties and Immunities of Denizens and natural-born Subjects, to all Intents and Purposes as if they had been abiding and born within the Realm of England.

"Resolved—

"That the Taxation of the People by themselves or by Persons chosen by themselves to represent them, who can only know what Taxes the People are able to bear, and the easiest Mode of raising them, and are equally affected by such Taxes themselves, is the distinguishing Characteristic of British Freedom and without which the ancient Constitution cannot subsist.

"Resolved—

"That his Majesty's liege People of this most ancient Colony have uninterruptedly enjoyed the Right of being thus governed by their own Assembly in the article of their Taxes and internal Police, and that the same hath never been forfeited or in any other way given up, but hath been constantly recognized by the Kings and People of Great Britain.

"Resolved—

"Therefore, That the General Assembly of this Colony have the only and sole exclusive Right and Power to lay Taxes and Impositions upon the Inhabitants of this Colony and that every Attempt to vest such Power in any Person or Persons whatsoever, other than the General Assembly aforesaid, has a manifest Tendency to destroy British as well as American Freedom."

"If this be treason, make the most of it."

Upon the submission of these resolutions a warm debate followed. Other representatives from Virginia's frontier counties welcomed the audacity of their young colleague, while the more conservative leaders of the eastern colonies of Virginia saw that their leadership of the House of Burgesses was being threatened by a country bumpkin. The first four resolutions passed by narrow majorities with but a few minor changes. But Henry knew that the opposition leaders were most anxious to prevent passage of the final and strongest resolution, so in support of it he rose to make one of his greatest orations. Thomas Jefferson, then a law student in Williamsburg, heard the address and later recalled that Henry "appeared to me to speak as Homer wrote." After denouncing the Stamp Act as an unprincipled attempt by the British parliament to exercise powers that were inherently the right of the Virginia people, Henry reached the climactic close of his speech in which he declared:

"Tarquin and Caesar each had his Brutus, Charles the First his Cromwell, and George the Third—"

At this point he was interrupted by a cry of "Treason!" from John Robinson, the speaker of the House of Burgesses; a cry that was picked up by other conservative legislators. Pausing only long enough to create a more dramatic effect, Henry thundered the conclusion:

". . . and George the Third may profit by their example! If this be treason make the most of it!"

The resolution was approved by the committee of the whole by a vote of twenty to nineteen. The meeting then adjourned to the next day when the resolutions would be taken up by the legislators sitting as the House of Burgesses. Jefferson reported that he heard the angry Peyton Randolph exclaim: "By God, I would have given 500 guineas for a single vote!"

The next day, by a parliamentary maneuver, the certificate of Henry's recent election was brought into question before the House in order to prevent his making any further speeches. But when the resolutions were taken up, they again passed by the same narrow margin. At the close of the day's session, Henry concluded that the main business of the meeting was over and headed home to Hanover.

But with Henry absent on May 31, the conservative leaders called for new votes on the resolutions. This time the first four passed, but the fifth was defeated and wiped off the record book. When the resolutions reached Virginia's Governor Francis Fauquier, he called the remaining burgesses into session, then ordered the house dissolved, requiring new elections before it could meet again.

"Practice virtue thyself, and encourage it in others."

Henry later left among his private papers for the executors of his estate a copy of these resolutions against the Stamp Act, of which he said, "I

Home of Patrick Henry

determined to venture, and alone, unadvised and unassisted, wrote the within." He then summarized his views as to the results of his action:

"Upon offering them to the house, violent debates ensued. Many threats were uttered, and much abuse cast on me, by the party for submission. After a long and warm contest, the resolutions passed by a very small majority, perhaps of one or two only. The alarm spread throughout America with astonishing quickness, and the ministerial party were overwhelmed. The great point of resistance to British taxation was universally established in the colonies. This brought on the war which finally separated the two countries, and gave independence to ours. Whether this will prove a blessing or a curse, will depend upon the use our people make of the blessings which a gracious God hath bestowed on us. If they are wise, they will be great and happy. If they are of a contrary character, they will be miserable. Righteousness alone can exalt them as a nation. Reader! whoever thou art, remember this; and in thy sphere practise virtue thyself, and encourage it in others.—P. Henry."

Stamp Act repealed by Parliament

Because the Virginia House of Burgesses had been dissolved, there was no opportunity for that colony's representatives to take part in the Stamp Act Congress that convened in New York City in October, 1765. But sentiment against the stamp tax was so great in Virginia as a result of Henry's resolutions and dramatic speech, that the governor did not dare enforce the law, and it was repealed by the British parliament before the House of Burgesses met again in 1766. Governor Fauquier wrote of the temper of the Virginians at the time that "if the least Injury was ofered to him (Henry) they'd stand by him to the last Drop of their blood. some of them muter betwixt their teeth, let worst Come to the worst we'l Call the french to our sucour."

In the years that followed, Henry continued to be re-elected to the House of Burgesses, winning greater prestige both politically and as a lawyer. In 1768, George Washington's close friend and adviser George Mason wrote of Henry that "had he lived in Rome about the time of the first Punic War, when the Roman people had arrived at their meridian glory, and their virtue not tarnished, Mr. Henry's talents must have put him at the head of that glorious commonwealth."

JOIN, or DIE.

We hear that the General Assembly of this Province have voted the Sum of Ten Thousand Pounds to be given to the King's Use at this Time; and also Five Hundred Pounds, to be given in Behalf of this Province, as a Present to the Indians of the Six Nations at the Treaty proposed to be held at Albany in June next.

Captain Cotton, from Barbados, advises, that off of Guadaloupe he was boarded by a French Guard de Coast, who, after asking him some Questions, and trying his Rum, Sugar, &c. left him, and went on board Capt. Lowther, of and for this Place from the same Island, of whom there is no Account since.

Part of First Page of *Pennsylvania Gazette*, May 9, 1754,

Travelled with Washington to the first Continental Congress

As the crisis between the colonies and Great Britain deepened, Henry was the rallying point for the patriotic forces of Virginia. In 1773, he was elected to the colony's committee of correspondence to keep in touch with the patriotic movement in the other colonies. Then, the next year, he joined with Thomas Jefferson, Richard Henry Lee, Francis Lightfoot Lee, George Mason, and several others in preparing a resolution declaring a day of fasting to memorialize the oppressive measures enacted by the British parliament against Boston. Upon the passage of this resolution, the royal governor, Lord Dunmore, dissolved the House of Burgesses. The first Virginia patriotic convention was called in August, 1774, where Henry was elected as one of Virginia's seven-man delegation to the first Continental Congress. On the last day of August, Henry set out in company with George Washington to the Philadelphia meeting.

Favored proportional representation

At the opening session of the Congress, Henry exercised his eloquence in a plea that each colony should have a vote proportional to its population, thus giving the larger colonies a dominant role in the meeting. The high point was his declaration: "I am not a Virginian, but an American." Although the delegates from the smaller colonies applauded this sentiment, they did not wish to give up their equality, so it was decided to give each colony a single vote. Henry received a second set-back when the Congress, on October 21, rejected an address to the King which he had prepared, and added John Dickinson of Pennsylvania to his committee to tone it down and make it more conservative. A few days later he left the Congress, before it had concluded its business, and returned to Virginia.

At the second patriotic convention of Virginia, called in March, 1775, at Richmond, Henry electrified the delegates by calling for a resolution "that this Colony be immediately put in a posture of defense; and that _____ be a committee to prepare a plan for the embodying, arming and disciplining such a number of men as may be sufficient for that purpose." Using his great powers of speech, Henry then hammered home to the Virginians the necessity of preparing for war. Although Henry did not write out a copy of his speech, an early biographer, William Wirt, pieced together what he believed to have been this famous address from the recollections of men who had heard it, as follows:

"Mr. President, it is natural to man to indulge in the illusions of hope. We are apt to shut our eyes against a painful truth—and listen to the song of that siren, till she transforms us into beasts. Is this the part of wise men, engaged in a great and arduous struggle for liberty? Are we disposed to be of the number of those who, having eyes, see not, and having ears, hear not, the things which so nearly concern their temporal salvation? For my part, whatever anguish of spirit it may cost, I am willing to know the whole truth; to know the worst and to provide for it.

"Let us not deceive ourselves."

"I have but one lamp by which my feet are guided; and that is the lamp of experience. I know of no way of judging of the future but by the past. And judging by the past, I wish to know what there has been in the conduct of the British ministry for the last ten years to justify those hopes with which gentlemen have been pleased to solace themselves and the House? Is it that insidious smile with which our petition has been lately received? Trust it not, sir; it will prove a snare to your feet. Suffer not yourself to be betrayed with a kiss. Ask yourself how this gracious reception

The desk used in the signing of the Declaration of Independence.

of our petition comports with those warlike preparations which cover our waters and darken our land. Are fleets and armies necessary to a work of love and reconciliation? Have we shown ourselves so unwilling to be reconciled that force must be called in to win back our love? Let us not deceive ourselves, sir. These are the implements of war and subjugation—the last arguments to which kings resort.

I ask gentlemen, sir, what means this martial array, if its purpose be not to force us to submission? Can gentlemen assign any other possible motives for it? Has Great Britain any enemy in this quarter of the world, to call for this accumulation of navies and armies? No, sir, she has none. They are meant for us; they can be meant for no other. They are sent over to bind and rivet upon us those chains which the British ministry have been so long forging.

"And what have we to oppose to them? Shall we try argument? Sir, we have been trying that for the last ten years. Have we anything new to offer upon the subject? Nothing. We have the subject up in every light of which it is capable; but it has been all in vain. Shall we resort to entreaty and humble supplication? What terms shall we find which have not been already exhausted? Let us not, I beseech you, sir, deceive ourselves longer. Sir, we have done everything that could be done to avert the storm which is now coming on. We have petitioned—we have remonstrated—we have supplicated—we have prostrated ourselves before the throne, and have implored its interposition to arrest the tyrannical hands of the ministry and parliament. Our petitions have been slighted; our remonstrances have produced additional violence and insult; our supplications have been disregarded; and we have been spurned with contempt from the foot of the throne. In vain, after these things, may we indulge the fond hope of peace and reconciliation.

"We must fight."

"There is no longer any room for hope; If we wish to be free—if we mean to preserve inviolate those inestimable privileges for which we have been so long contending—if we mean not basely to abandon the noble struggle in which we have been so long engaged, and which we have pledged ourselves never to abandon until the glorious object of our contest shall be obtained—we must fight!—I repeat it, sir, we must fight; an appeal to arms and to the God of Hosts is all that is left us!

"They tell us, sir, that we are weak—unable to cope with so formidable an adversary. But when shall we be stronger? Will it be the next week or the next year? Will it be when we are totally disarmed, and when a British guard shall be stationed in every house? Shall we gather strength by irresolution and inaction? Shall we acquire the means of effectual resistance by lying supinely on our backs and hugging the delusive phantom of hope, until our enemy shall have bound us hand and foot? Sir, we are not weak, if we make a proper use of those forces which the God of nature hath placed in our power. Three millions of people armed in the holy cause of liberty, and in such a country as that which we possess, are invincible by any force which our enemy can send against us. Besides, sir, we shall not fight our battles alone. There is a just God who presides over the destinies of nations, and who will raise up friends to fight our battles for us. The battle, sir, is not to the strong alone; it is to the vigilant, the active, the brave. Besides, sir, we have no election. If we were base enough to desire it, it is now too late to retire from the contest. There is no retreat but in submission and slavery! Our chains are forged. Their clanking may be heard on the plains of Boston? The war is inevitable—and let it come! I repeat it sir, let come!

"Give me liberty or give me death."

"It is vain, sir, to extenuate the matter. Gentlemen may cry, peace, peace—but there is no peace. —The war is actually begun! The next gale that sweeps from the north will bring to our ears the clash of resounding arms! Our brethren are already in the field! Why stand we here idle? What is it that gentlemen wish? What would they have? Is life so dear, or peace so sweet, as to be purchased at the price of chains and slavery? Forbid it, Almight God! I know not what course others may take; but as for me, give me liberty, or give me death!"

Stunned by this torrent of oratory, the Virginia representatives approved the resolution, naming Henry as head of a committee of twelve, including George Washington, to organize military forces for the defense of the colony. Before the convention adjourned, Henry was again chosen as one of the delegates to the second meeting of the Continental Congress set for May in Philadelphia.

Not quite a month later, on the night of April 20, 1775, Virginia Governor Dunmore ordered a party of British marines to seize the colony's supply of gunpowder and carry it aboard a warship. When Henry learned of this, and at about the same time heard of the outbreak of fighting at Lexington and Concord in Massachusetts, he assembled the militia of Hanover County and began marching at their head toward Williamsburg to force the governor to return the powder or pay the colonists for it. Before Henry and his troops could reach Williamsburg, Governor Dunmore prudently approved sending Henry a bill of exchange for the value of the powder. Upon receiving the money, Henry marched his men back to Hanover County. But Dunmore, determined to have the last word, issued a proclamation on May 6, declaring that "a certain Patrick Henry, of the County of Hanover, and a number of deluded followers" were in effect traitors, and warning all persons "upon their allegiance, not to aid, abet, or give countenance to the said Patrick Henry, or any other persons concerned in such unwarrantable combinations; but, on the contrary, to oppose them and their designs by every means; which designs must otherwise inevitably involve the whole country in the most direful calamity, as they call for the vengeance of offended majesty, and the insulted laws to be exerted here to vindicate the constitutional authority of governments."

When Henry left for the meeting of the Continental Congress on May 11, he was accompanied by an armed guard of followers until he safely got out of Virginia. He took his seat in the Philadelphia meeting about May 17. Henry aided in the establishment of a Continental Army for the colonies and the selection of Washington as commander-in-chief. After accepting this post, Washington told his friend: "Remember, Mr. Henry, what I now tell you: from the day I enter upon the command of the American armies, I date my fall, and the ruin of my reputation."

Not fitted for military role

When the Virginia patriotic convention met again in Richmond in July, 1775, Henry was appointed commander of the colony's troops. However, he was no more fitted for a military role than he had been for that of a storekeeper or farmer, running into many difficulties and arguments with the Virginia committee of safety. Washington had heard of these problems, and in a private letter to a friend written in March, 1776, he commented: "I think my countrymen made a capital mistake when they took Henry out of the Senate to place him in the field; and pity it is that he does not see this and remove every difficulty by a voluntary resignation." But, unknown to Washington, Henry had arrived at the same conclusion, had turned down a colonel's commission offered by Congress, and had resigned his Virginia command.

Elected governor of Virginia

Henry now resumed his political career. He was elected to the Virginia patriotic convention held in Williamsburg in the spring of 1776, and was a member of the committee that drew up the state's first constitution and bill of rights. The convention then elected Henry as Virginia's first governor. He and his council were inaugurated on July 5, the day after the Congress in Philadelphia had adopted the Declaration of Independence.

About this time, Henry's wife, Sarah, who had borne him six children, died after several years of illness. After a period of a year's mourning, Henry married again, this time in 1777 to Dorothea Dandridge, the daughter of Nathaniel West Dandridge, a well-to-do plantation owner of Hanover County. Henry and his second wife had nine children.

In 1778, Henry was instrumental in revealing to Washington Benjamin Rush's complicity in the "Conway Cabal," the clique that was endeavoring to replace Washington with Major General Horatio Gates as commander-in-chief. Henry relayed to Washington a derogatory anonymous letter that was obviously in Rush's handwriting. A short time later, Henry wrote Washington of his feelings about the men criticizing him at this low ebb in the war:

"While you faced the armed enemies of our liberty in the field, and by the favor of God have been kept unhurt, I trust your country will never harbor in her bosom the miscreant, who would ruin her best supporter. I wish not to flatter; but when arts, unworthy honest men, are used to defame and traduce you, I think it not amiss but a duty to assure you of that estimation in which the public hold you . . ."

Relinquished the governorship to Thomas Jefferson

After being re-elected governor in 1777 and 1778, Henry gave up the office in 1779, because of a provision in the state constitution that limited a governor's administration to three successive years and forbade his resuming the office for a period of six more years. After turning the governorship over to his successor, Thomas Jefferson, Henry retired to an estate of nearly 10,000 acres, called "Leatherwood," that he had recently purchased in southern Virginia's Henry County, which had been named for him during his administration. During the remaining years of the Revolutionary War, Henry served in the state legislature.

In 1784, as soon as Henry was again eligible for the governorship, the legislature again elected him to the state's highest office. Henry supported an unusual bill in the legislature which was intended to end ill feeling between the Indians and the settlers by encouraging intermarriage of the races, but the bill failed shortly after Henry assumed the governorship. He also exhibited his humanity in his charitable view toward the return to Virginia of loyalists who fled during the revolutionary War. After serving for two years during this administration, Henry declined re-election in 1786 on grounds that the governor's salary was not sufficient to support his large family. He again returned to his seat in the legislature, and resumed his profitable law practice.

Opposed ratification of the Constitution

Although the legislature elected him as a delegate to the Constitutional Convention in 1787 with the second highest number of votes to Washington, he declined to serve, later explaining his action by saying, "I smelt a rat." When the United States Constitution had been drafted and signed, Henry became the leader of the opposition to its ratification at the Virginia convention in Richmond in June, 1788. He told the convention he did not like even the opening words of the new plan of government:

". . . give me leave to demand, what right had they to say, 'We the people?' My political curiosity, exclusive of my anxious solicitude for the public welfare, leads me to ask, who authorized them to speak the language of 'We the people,' instead of, 'We the states?' States are the characteristics and the soul of a confederation. If the states be not the agents of this compact, it must be one great consolidated national government, of the people of all the states. . . . The people gave them no power to use their name. . . . You must, therefore, forgive the solicitation of one unworthy member, to know what danger could have arisen under the present confederation, and what are the causes of this proposal to change our government."

A challenge to a duel

When Edmund Randolph, who had succeeded Henry as governor and who had refused to sign the Constitution at the convention in Philadelphia, took the floor of the Virginia convention in support of the Constitution, Henry attacked him by saying that he found it "strange and unaccountable" that Randolph should have changed his mind. Randolph leaped to his feet and hotly replied that Henry's remarks were outside the pale of "parliamentary decency" and that "if our friendship must fall—let it fall, like Lucifer, never to rise again." Before the day was over, Henry challenged Randolph to a duel, but friends settled the dispute without blood being drawn.

The ratification convention dragged on for nearly a month, while the rest of the nation watched to see what the largest state would finally do. Henry took the floor again and again to argue that the Constitution would deny the states and the people the rights they had fought for. But, in the end, Henry's power of eloquence was not sufficient to overcome the reasoned arguments of James Madison and Edmund Randolph—the convention voted 89 to 79 in favor of ratification.

Defeating James Madison

Henry, who was the political boss of Virginia, took vengeance on Madison by defeating his bid in the legislature for a seat as one of Virginia's first United States Senators. Then he gerrymandered the election districts of the states in an unsuccessful effort to defeat Madison in his race for U. S. Representative. Washington in a letter to Madison in November, 1788, summed up Henry's role in the legislature: "The whole proceedings of the Assembly, it is said may be summed up in one word, to wit, that the Edicts of Hr. H——— are enregistered with less opposition by the majority of that body, than those of the Grand Monarch are in the Parliaments of France. He has only to say let this be Law, and it is Law."

After his last administration as governor, Henry had acquired a large plantation in Charlotte County called "Red Hill." There he lived with his large family, leaving it only to attend sessions of the legislature or to argue cases in court. His fame as a lawyer continued to grow, and he won new renown in the federal courts where he became an authority in international law. In 1791, he retired from the legislature to devote full time to his family and his law practice.

Declined appointment as Secretary of State

Henry and Thomas Jefferson had fallen out during the Revolutionary War because Henry had been critical of Jefferson's administration as governor; therefore, in the 1790's, as Jefferson became more powerful politically as the head of the Democratic-Republican party, Henry became more sympathetic to the views of the Federalist party. Jefferson commented that Henry was "all tongue without either head or heart." In October, 1795, President Washington offered Henry the post of Secretary of State, which had been vacated by the dismissal of Edmund Randolph who was suspected of betraying state secrets to France. Henry declined the appointment, commenting, ". . . I have bid adieu to the distinction of federal and anti-federal ever since the commencement of the present government." A few months later Washington again put out feelers to find out if Henry would accept appointment as Secretary of War or as Chief Justice, but apparently received no acceptance from the retired master of "Red Hill." The next year, in 1796, the Virginia legislature again elected Henry as governor, but he declined the election because of illness.

A favor to Washington

In 1799, Washington called upon Henry one last time for support, and this time the old orator responded. Washington had become deeply concerned with the state of political affairs in Virginia, where the legislature had recently passed resolutions attempting to nullify the federal Alien and

Sedition Acts. Washington feared this was the beginning of a chain of events that could lead to the destruction of the federal government. On January 15, he wrote to Henry asking him to become a Federalist party candidate for the state legislature in order to put the "weight of character and influence" into the fight against the destructive Democratic-Republican forces of Jefferson and Madison. Henry consented, remarking in part: "My children would blush to know that you and their father were contemporaries, and that when you asked him to throw in his mite for the public happiness, he refused to do it."

In the last few months of his life, Henry received a further honor when he was nominated by President John Adams in February, 1799, to serve as a diplomatic envoy to the French Republic on a mission to attempt to prevent a war that threatened between the two nations. But Henry was forced to decline this appointment from fear that his health would not permit an extended trip overseas.

"I am but a poor worm of the dust."

Henry made his last election speech at Charlotte Court House, Virginia, in March, 1799, where he debated with young John Randolph, who was making his first appearance as a candidate for Congress on the Democratic-Republican ticket. William Wirt, an early biographer of Henry, tells an anecdote concerning this last appearance of the old patriot. It seems a Baptist preacher was distressed that such a large crowd was following Henry and called to them, "Mr. Henry is not a god!" Hearing the remark, Henry is said to have replied: "No, no, indeed, my friend; I am but a poor worm of the dust—as fleeting and unsubstantial as the shadow of the cloud that flies over your fields, and is remembered no more." The magic of his name won Henry the election. But before he could take his seat in the legislature, the sixty-three-year-old Henry died at "Red Hill" on June 6, 1799.

JAMES OTIS of MASSACHUSETTS

If Samuel Adams is considered the Father of the Revolution, then James Otis must be regarded as its grandfather. He fulfilled the same role in Massachusetts that Patrick Henry did in Virginia ... denouncing the leaders of the British parliament in speeches and pamphlets that rallied the people of his colony to a sense of resistance to tyranny. John Adams described Otis as a "flame of fire" who more than a dozen years before the battles of Lexington and Concord left his hearers "ready to take up arms."

Suffered a beating that deranged him

Unfortunately, the American cause lost Otis's abilities before the Revolution actually got underway. He was attacked by a British customs collector in 1769, and the beating left him mentally deranged. He lived on throughout the Revolutionary War, and died by a stroke of lightning the same year that a peace treaty was signed granting the United States its independence.

James Otis was born on February 5, 1725, in West Barnstable, Massachusetts. His father, grandfather, and great-grandfather all had been prominent lawyers, jurists, and political leaders of the colony. His father, whose name also was James Otis, served as speaker of the lower house of the colonial legislature in the early 1760's and then was chief justice of the colony's court of common pleas until the outbreak of the Revolutionary War.

Young James received his early education under the guidance of a Congregational clergyman, the Reverend Jonathan Russell. He then was sent to Harvard College, where he undoubtedly became acquainted with Samuel Adams, who was a student there at the same time. The eighteen-year-old Otis was graduated from Harvard in 1743. For

---

JAMES OTIS

1725 (Feb. 5) Born in West Barnstable, Mass.
1743 Graduated from Harvard University.
1748 Admitted to the bar to practice law.
1761-1771 Member of the Massachusetts legislature.

James Otis

1765 **Delegate from Massachusetts to the Stamp Act Congress.**
1769 **Received brain damage in a fight with a British customs commissioner.**
1783 **(May 23) Killed by lightning at Andover, Mass.**

the next year and a half he took graduate work in classic literature. Next, he devoted himself to the study of the law under one of the colony's leading attorneys, Jeremiah Gridley.

When Otis was twenty-three, in 1748, he was admitted to the bar and began practicing law in Plymouth, Massachusetts. But after a few years he moved to Boston to take advantage of the greater need for lawyers in that prosperous port city. When he was thirty, he married Ruth Cunningham, the daughter of a merchant.

Resigned appointment as the King's attorney

Otis was in his thirties when he first asserted himself as a popular leader in Boston. By 1760 he had won appointment as advocate general, or king's attorney, for the colony's court of admiralty—an appointment undoubtedly secured by the political influence of his father, who was then speaker of the lower house of the Massachusetts legislature. But Otis resigned this office because he refused to aid the royal government in its use of writs of assistance, a kind of search warrant used by the king's customs officers to hunt for smuggled goods among the warehouses of Boston merchants.

The chief justice of Massachusetts ordered a court hearing in February, 1761, to determine the legality of the writs of assistance. Otis and another prominent lawyer, Oxenbridge Thacher, under-

took the case for the Boston merchants, while Jeremiah Gridley, Otis's former law teacher, acted as king's attorney in defense of the writs. John Adams, then a young attorney who had been practicing law for only three years, attended the court hearings and was deeply affected by them. He later described them as "a moral spectacle more affecting to me than any I have ever since seen upon the stage, to observe a pupil treating his master with all the deference, respect, esteem and affection of a son to a father, and that without the least affectation; while he baffled and confounded all his authorities, confuted all his arguments, and reduced him to silence."

Otis won the case with powerful arguments based upon the principles of liberty. Daniel Webster later wrote of Otis's plea: "Unquestionably it was a masterly performance. No flighty declamation about liberty, no superficial discussion of popular topics, it was a learned, penetrating, convincing, constitutional argument, expressed in a strain of high and resolute patriotism." More than fifty years after sitting in the Boston courtroom and listening to Otis, John Adams wrote:

The birth of American independence

". . . Otis was a flame of fire! With a promptitude of classical allusions, a depth of research, a rapid summary of historical events and dates, a profusion of legal authorities, a prophetic glance of his eye into futurity, and a torrent of impetuous eloquence, he hurried away everything before him. American independence was then and there born; the seeds of patriots and heroes were then and there sown. . . . Every man of a crowded audience appeared to me to go away, as I did, ready to take arms against writs of assistance."

A few months after the writs of assistance case, Otis decided to run for the legislature. One of Otis's early biographers described a dialogue that reputedly took place between Otis and a Boston politician "of great shrewdness and capacity"—the conversation is mostly revealing of the fact that politics has changed relatively little over hundreds of years.

Otis: They talk of sending me to the next General Court (legislature).

Politician: You will never succeed in the General Court.

Otis: Not succeed! and why not, pray?

Politician: Why, Mr. Otis, you have ten times the learning, and much greater abilities than I have, but you know nothing of human nature.

Otis: Indeed, I wish you would give me some lessons.

Politician: Be patient, and I will do so with pleasure. In the first place, what meeting (church) do you go to?

Otis: Dr. Sewall's (the pastor of the Old South Church).

Politician: Very well; you must stand up in sermon time—you must look devout and deeply attentive. Do you have family prayers?

Otis: No.

Politician: It were well if you did. What does your family consist of?

Otis: Why, only four or five commonly, but at this time I have, in addition, one of Dr. Sewall's saints, who is a nurse of my wife.

How to succeed in politics

Politician: Ah! that is the very thing: you must talk religion with her in a serious manner; you must have family prayers at least once while she is in your house. That woman can do you more harm, or more good, than any other person; she will spread your fame throughout the congregation. I can also tell you, by way of example, some of the steps I take. Two or three weeks before an election comes on, I send to the cooper and get all my casks put in order; I say nothing about the number of hoops. I send to the mason, and have some job done to the hearths or the chimneys; I have the carpenter to make some repairs in the roof or the wood-house; I often go down to the ship-yards about eleven o'clock, when they break off to take their drink, and enter into conversation with them. They all vote for me.

The importance of legislative consent

Otis won election to the legislature, and there he quickly came into conflict with the governor, Francis Bernard. When the governor and his council appropriated money for the maintenance of an armed sloop without first obtaining the consent of the house of representatives, Otis drew up a protest for the lower house. In it he accused the governor and council of "taking from the House their most darling privilege, the right of originating taxes." He then added: "No necessity can be sufficient to justify a house of representatives, in giving up such a privilege; for it would be of little consequence to the people, whether they were subject to George or Louis, the king of Great Britain, or the French king, if both were arbitrary, as both

would be, if both could levy taxes without Parliament." When Otis read this statement, the conservative members of the house cried: "Treason! Treason!" When the governor insisted that the final sentence be deleted from the remonstrance, the house of representatives gave in to the demand.

The rights of the people versus the government

Upon the adjournment of the legislature in 1762, Otis published a pamphlet entitled "A Vindication of the Conduct of the House of Representatives of the Province of Massachusetts Bay." In this publication, Otis set the stage for the future important writings of the Revolutionary period, differentiating between the rights of the people and the arbitrary invasion of these rights by the royal government. "No government," he said, "has a right to make hobby horses, asses and slaves of the subject; nature having made sufficient of the two former, for all the lawful purposes of man, from the harmless peasant in the field, to the most refined politician in the cabinet, but none of the last, which infallibly proves they are unnecessary." John Adams wrote the following about this booklet by Otis:

"How many volumes are concentrated in this

Bostonians paying the Exciseman.

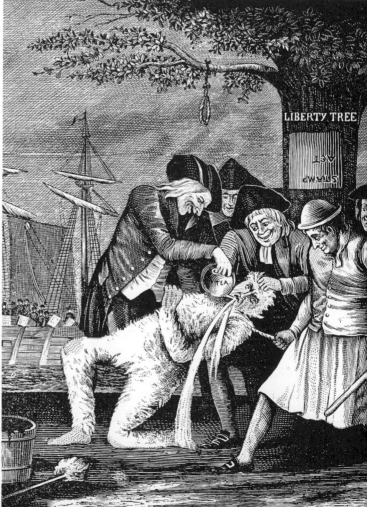

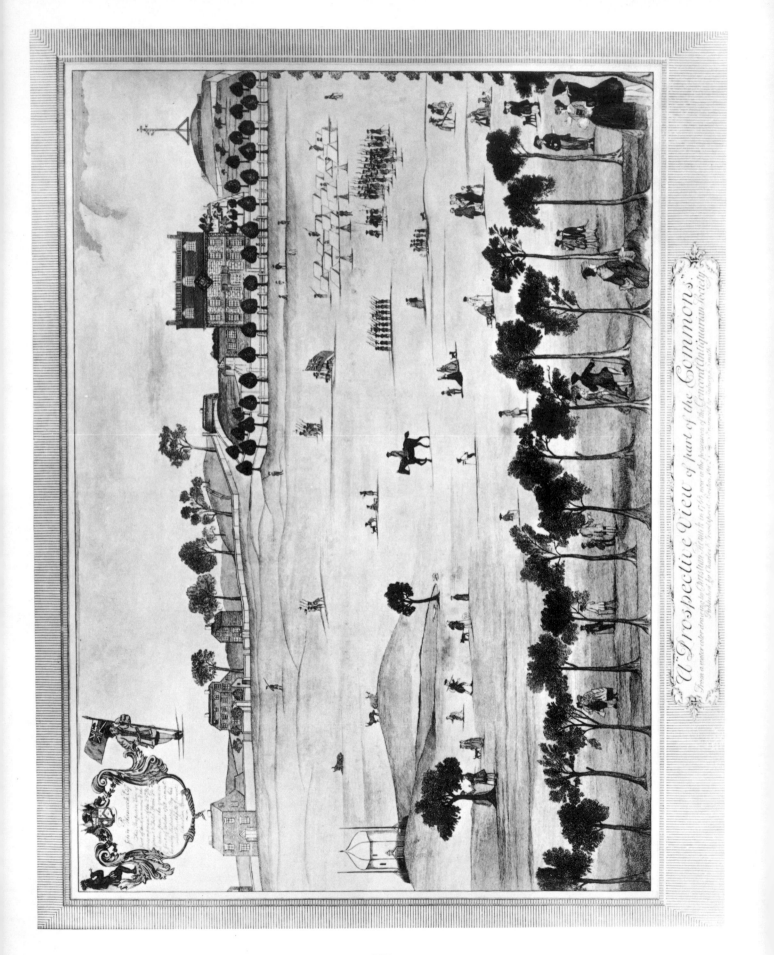

View) of the Town of BOSTON from Breeds Hill in CHARLESTOWN.

little fugitive pamphlet, the production of a few hurried hours, amidst the continual solicitation of a crowd of clients; for his business at the bar at that time was very extensive, and of the first importance, and amidst the host of politicians, suggesting their plans and schemes, claiming his advice and directions. Look over the Declaration of Rights and Wrongs, issued by Congress in 1774. Look into the Declaration of Independence in 1776. Look into . . . all the French constitutions of government, and to cap the climax, look into Mr. Thomas Paine's Common Sense, Crisis, and Rights of Man; what can you find that is not to be found in solid substance in this Vindication of the House of Representatives?"

"The King can do no wrong"

In 1764, Otis published another pamphlet called, "The Rights of the British Colonies Asserted and Proved." This publication is revealing of the conflict in the colonial mind, for in it Otis reasserts the rights of the people, and then, with sarcasm so thick that English tories took him literally, Otis stated: "It is a maxim, that the king can do no wrong; and every good subject is bound to believe his king is not inclined to do any. We

are blessed with a prince who has given abundant demonstrations, that in all his actions, he studies the good of his people, and the true glory of his crown, which are inseparable. It would therefore be the highest degree of impudence and disloyalty, to imagine that the king, at the head of his parliament, could have any but the most pure and perfect intentions of justice, goodness and truth, that human nature is capable of. . . . There would be an end of all government, if one or a number of subjects, or subordinate provinces should take upon them so far to judge of the justice of an act of parliament, as to refuse obedience to it. If there was nothing else to restrain such a step, prudence ought to do it, for forcibly resisting the parliament and the king's laws is high treason. Therefore let the parliament lay what burdens they please on us, we must, it is our duty to submit and patiently bear them, till they will be pleased to relieve us."

After the British parliament passed the Stamp Act in 1765, Otis was chosen as head of a Massachusetts delegation to attend a meeting of representatives of the various colonies in New York City "to consult together on the present circumstances of the Colonies, and the difficulties to which they are and must be reduced by the operation of the acts of Parliament, for levying duties and taxes on the Colonies; and to consider of a general and united, dutiful, loyal, and humble representation of their condition to his Majesty and to the Parliament, and to implore relief." At this meeting, Otis was thrown into close association with John Dickinson of Pennsylvania and John Rutledge of South Carolina, both of whom were to help write the United States Constitution more than twenty years later. Otis had come to the Stamp Act Congress demanding that the colonies be represented in the British parliament, but he bowed to the more conservative wishes of the delegates from the other colonies. He signed their watered-down declarations and petitions, to the disgust of his fire-eating friend Sam Adams, who had not attended the Congress, but who had hoped for more forceful action by the colonial delegates.

Too outspoken for the governor

The Massachusetts house of representatives chose Otis as speaker in 1766, but Governor Bernard vetoed the choice because of Otis's outspoken opposition to the government's policies. The next year, Otis and Sam Adams prepared a circular letter to the legislatures of the other colonies proposing that they cooperate in opposition to the Townshend Act taxes recently enacted by parliament. The British government demanded that the Massachusetts legislature rescind the resolution that adopted the circular letter. In the debate that followed, Otis ridiculed the British cabinet ministers and nobility as "the very frippery and foppery of France, the mere outsides of monkeys." Stirred by Otis's oratory, the Massachusetts legislature refused to repeal the circular letter by a vote of ninety-two to seventeen.

While British troops were stationed in Boston to help the colonial governor maintain himself in power, Otis made speech after speech in opposition to the military occupation. Learning that Governor Bernard and his tax collectors were sending letters to the British government denouncing him as a traitor, Otis decided to publish an advertisement in the *Boston Gazette* on September 4, 1769, in which he declared that he was "determined at all events to bear true and faithful allegiance."

He went on to ask that the British ministers in London should "pay no kind of regard to any of the abusive representations of me or of my country" that were being sent by Governor Bernard or by his customs collectors.

Severely injured in a brawl

The next evening after the advertisement had appeared, Otis stepped into the British Coffee House where he encountered John Robinson, one of the custom collectors whom he had denounced. An argument swiftly developed, and Robinson struck Otis with a heavy cane or the flat of a sword. Someone put out the lights, and in the brawl that followed Otis was severely wounded in the head. Otis's friends brought suit for him against Robinson, and he was awarded damages of two thousand pounds, a huge sum; but Otis refused to accept the money declaring, "It is absolutely impossible that I should take a penny from a man in this way, after an acknowledgment of his error."

Unable to exert leadership

Although Otis continued to be elected to the legislature for the following two years, the head-wound had left him mentally deranged and unable to exert his leadership. John Adams wrote of encountering Otis at a club meeting in January, 1770:

"Otis is in confusion yet; he loses himself; he rambles and wanders like a ship without a helm; attempted to tell a story, which took up almost all the evening; the story may at any time be told in three minutes, with all the graces it is capable of, but he took an hour. I fear he is not in his perfect mind. The nervous, concise, and pithy were his character till lately; now the verbose, roundabout, and rambling, and long-winded."

His remaining years were spent at a farm near Andover, Mass. Some time before his death, he told his sister: "I hope when God Almighty, in his righteous providence, shall take me out of time into eternity, that it will be by a flash of lightning." This wish was granted on May 23, 1783, when lightning struck him while he stood inside the farmhouse. The fifty-eight-year-old Otis died instantly.

IN CONGRESS, JULY 4, 1

The unanimous Declaration of the thirteen united States of

When in the Course of human events it becomes necessary for one people to dissolve the political bands which have

assume among the powers of the earth, the separate and equal station to which the Laws of Nature and of Nature's God entitle them, a decent respect to the

should declare the causes which impel them to the separation. ———— We hold these truths to be self-evident, that all men are created equal

certain unalienable Rights, that among these are Life, Liberty and the pursuit of Happiness. — That to secure these rights, Governments are in

the consent of the governed. — That whenever any Form of Government becomes destructive of these ends, it is the Right of the People to alter

foundation on such principles and organizing its powers in such form, as to them shall seem most likely to effect their Safety

established should not be changed for light and transient causes; and accordingly all experience hath shewn, that

to which they are accustomed. But when a long train of

right, it is their duty, to throw off such Government,

which shall have been previously ascertained, by law; and to be informed of the nature

for obtaining witnesses in his favor, and to have the assistance of counsel for his

Article the ninth In suits at common law, where the value in controversy shall exceed twenty dollars, t

any Court of the United States, than according to the rules of the common law.

Article the tenth Excessive bail shall not be required, nor excessive fines imposed, nor cruel and un

eleventh The enumeration in the Constitution, of certain rights, shall not be construed to de

twelfth The powers not delegated to the United States by the Constitution, nor prohibited

Frederick Augustus Muhlenberg

John Adams

In Convention Monday September 17th 1787.

Present

The States of

New Hampshire, Massachusetts, Connecticut, Mr. Hamilton from New York, New Je
Maryland, Virginia, North Carolina, South Carolina and Georgia.

Resolved,

That the preceding Constitution be laid before the United States in Con
this Convention, that it should afterwards to a Convention of Delegates, chosen in each
for that each Convention assenting to, and

Congress OF THE United State

begun and held at the City of New-York, on

Wednesday the fourth of March, one thousand seven hundred and